HUNTERS AND GATHERERS 1

History, evolution and social change

EXPLORATIONS IN ANTHROPOLOGY
A University College London Series
Series Editors: Barbara Bender, John Gledhill   Bruce Kapferer

HUNTERS AND GATHERERS 1

History, evolution and social change

Edited by
Tim Ingold
David Riches
James Woodburn

BERG
New York / Oxford
**Distributed exclusively in the US and Canada by
St. Martin's Press, New York**

First published in 1988 by
Berg Publishers Limited
Editorial Offices:
165 Taber Avenue, Providence, R.I. 02906, USA
150 Cowley Road, Oxford OX4 1JJ, UK

Paperback edition 1991

British Library Cataloguing in Publication Data

Hunters and gatherers. — (Explorations in
   anthropology).
   1. History, evolution and social change
   1. Hunting and gathering societies
   I. Ingold, Tim   II.   Riches, David
   III. Woodburn, James   IV. Series
   307.7'72   GN388
ISBN 0–85496–153–4
ISBN 0–85496–734–6 (pbk)

Library of Congress Cataloging-in-Publication Data

Hunters and gatherers.
   (Explorations in anthropology)
   Papers from the Fourth International Conference on
Hunting and Gathering Societies, held at the London
School of Economics and Political Science, Sept. 8–13,
1986
   Bibliography; indexes.
   Contents: v. 1. History, evolution, and social change
   1. Hunting and gathering societies—Congresses.
I. Ingold, Tim, 1948– . II. Riches, David.
III. Woodburn, James. IV. International Conference on
Hunter-Gatherers (4th : 1986 : London School of
Economics and Political Science) V. Series.
GN388.H87   1987   306'.3   87–21216
ISBN 0–85496–153–4 (v. 1)
ISBN 0–85496–734–6 (pbk)

Printed in Great Britain by Billings of Worcester

Cover: Efe Pygmies, Ituri Forest, Zaire, 1983
Photo by Espen Wæhle

To the memory of
Glynn Isaac and Eleanor Leacock

Contents

Plates, Figures and Maps

Tables

Preface

The modern anthropological understanding of hunting and gathering societies effectively dates from 1966, when a conference was held in Chicago on the theme of *Man the hunter*, giving rise to a seminal volume with that title edited by Richard Lee and Irven DeVore (1968). Following this initial stimulus, a great deal of exciting and innovative research has been carried out among hunting and gathering peoples in many regions of the world. Twelve years later, in 1978, a major international conference was convened in Paris to review the fruits of this work. Such was the volume of interest, and the richness and quality of the work presented there, that it was resolved on that occasion to hold future conferences at regular intervals. The second international conference on hunting and gathering societies was held in Quebec in 1980, and the third in Bad Homburg, West Germany, in 1983. As at Paris, these conferences attracted contributions of outstanding quality, bringing to bear a great deal of new data and a number of revelatory theoretical insights.

At the Bad Homburg meeting, I presented a proposal for a future conference to be held, in 1986, in the United Kingdom. Following discussions with James Woodburn, an organizing committee was set up including almost all the leading specialists in hunter-gatherer studies in the country: besides Woodburn and myself, the members of the original committee were Alan Barnard, Barbara Bender, Nurit Bird-David, Signe Howell, Robert Layton, David McKnight, Brian Morris and David Riches. The committee first met in November 1983, and again on numerous occasions during the ensuing three years. There were some changes in composition: McKnight resigned at an early stage, and later on both Howell and Morris had to withdraw on account of their departure to the field. However we gained two new members: Harvey Feit, who was on sabbatical leave in London during 1985; and Howard Morphy, who arrived from Australia to take up a post at Oxford in January 1986. Representing the culmination of a lot of hard work put in by every member of the committee, the Fourth International Conference on Hunting and Gathering Societies took place, as planned, at the London School of Economics and Political Science, from Monday 8 to Saturday 13 September 1986.

1

Like its predecessors, the London conference was intended to provide a forum for the discussion of basic research on the social and economic organization and cultural life of hunters and gatherers in all regions of the world, as well as for the presentation of the results of new fieldwork. Significantly marking the twentieth anniversary of the original *Man the hunter* symposium, the conference brought together no fewer than 114 scholars from eighteen different countries, bearing testimony to the enormous growth in hunter-gatherer studies over the last two decades. Its major goals were to further the comparative understanding of hunting and gathering societies, to demonstrate the relevance of hunter-gatherer studies to the construction of anthropological theory, to draw attention to the current status of hunting and gathering peoples as citizens of the modern world, and to provide a medium for presenting the results of recent empirical research. In all these respects the conference fulfilled its purpose beyond our most optimistic expectations, and we hope it will stimulate much further work in what is surely a crucial area of contemporary research with major implications for all branches of the science of humanity, including human biology and prehistoric archaeology as well as social and cultural anthropology.

The articles published in this volume, and in its companion volume (*Hunters and gatherers II: Property, power and ideology*) represent only a selection of the seventy-four papers presented in the nine sessions of the conference. On account of their uniformly outstanding quality, the job of selection turned out to be an extremely difficult and painful one. In order to oversee the selection and preparation of papers for publication, the members of the original organizing committee have continued to work together, and both volumes are the result of a joint editorial effort. Each paper was carefully read and ranked by every member of the committee, and these rankings — together with a concern for balance and coherence within each volume — guided our ultimate choice of papers. However, on behalf of the committee, I should at this point acknowledge the important and valuable contributions made by all those whose papers we have felt unable to include. I hope that the present volumes will be seen to embody the spirit of their work, if not its substance. I also wish to pay tribute to the dedicated labour put in by David Riches, as co-ordinator of the editorial committee, in bringing both volumes to fruition.

There are a great many persons and organizations that we have to thank for helping to make the conference such a resounding success. First and foremost, of course, are those funding bodies without whose assistance the conference would not have been possible. These include the Economic and Social Research Council, the British Academy, the Esperanza Trust, the Centre National de la Recherche Scientifique, and the Maison des Sciences de l'Homme. For the funds from Esperanza we are grateful to the Council of the Royal Anthropological Institute, and to its Director, Jonathan Benthall. Maurice Godelier was instrumental in obtaining funds from CNRS. We should also like to acknowledge the support given to us by Sir Edmund Leach and by M. Clemens Heller.

One of the biggest jobs we had to cope with was the copying and precirculation of the majority of the conference papers. To save time and costs, sets of papers for Australian and North American participants were copied and circulated separately: for this we have to thank Nicolas Peterson, who undertook the Australian distribution; and Harvey Feit, who — assisted by a grant from McMaster University — produced a splendidly bound volume for distribution in Canada and the United States. However, the major distribution to remaining overseas and all UK participants was undertaken from the University of Durham by Lesley Bailey and Robert Layton. We are especially grateful to both of them for their efforts.

The conference was sponsored by the Association of Social Anthropologists of the Commonwealth, the Royal Anthropological Institute of Great Britain and Ireland, and the London School of Economics and Political Science. We are particularly grateful to the School for allowing us to use the comfortable facilities of the Shaw Library, which provided a most congenial setting for our deliberations, and to the LSE Department of Anthropology for putting up with a week-long invasion of its premises. We also express our thanks to the Museum of Mankind for the generous loan of Andaman Island artefacts. The Australian and Canadian High Commissions handsomely provided for a reception at the Australian Studies Centre. During the conference itself we were all sustained by the superb catering of Lisa Woodburn and by the secretarial skills of Joan Wells, as well as receiving invaluable support from our student helpers: B. Grzimek, J. Robertson, C. Zeiske and M. Stewart.

Professor Glynn L. Isaac, of Harvard University, was to have presented a paper to the session of the conference on 'comparative studies of hunter-gatherer societies'. His tragic death, on 5 October 1985, robbed the conference of a most distinguished contributor, and is a great loss to all of us who are concerned with the ways in which studies of hunting and gathering can contribute to our overall understanding of the evolution of humanity. It is entirely appropriate that this volume should be dedicated to his memory.

Just as we were going to press we heard the sad news that Professor Eleanor Leacock had died. Remembering her major contribution to the Paris conference in 1978, and her innovatory role over many years in the development of the study of Canadian hunter-gatherers, we also dedicate this volume to her memory.

TIM INGOLD
Manchester, May 1988

1. Twenty years of history, evolution and social change in gatherer-hunter studies

Barbara Bender and Brian Morris

Notions of history, of evolution and of social change, are themselves the products of history. The five volumes that have evolved from the International Hunter-Gatherer Conferences held over the last three decades chart the changing preoccupations and conceptions of those involved in gatherer-hunter studies. An appreciation of the different volumes would, at the very least, have to recognize the effect of the venue, organizational structure and specific national 'colouring' of each conference; the changing socio-political conditions within the First World bloc from which most of the participants were drawn; and the changing fortunes of contemporary gatherer-hunters within the larger context of the nation-state. This introduction offers a preliminary sketch.

The 1960s

The famous 1968 *Man the hunter* volume, edited by Richard Lee and Irven DeVore, emerged from the Chicago conference of 1966. The conference size and structure reflected not only the availability of considerable scientific funding, but also the relatively integrated nature of anthropological and archaeological studies in North America. American anthropologists and archaeologists had little difficulty in communicating with each other, and to a large extent shared the same paradigm. Indeed the conference served notice of a quite radical shift in American theorizing, in which Boasian cultural particularism, dominant for half a century, gave way to various forms of ecological functionalism. The shift was so extreme that historical analysis was rejected as being both ideographic and particularistic (Binford 1962; protest by Trigger 1968). The emphasis was on cross-cultural systemics hinging upon notions of rationality and ecological adaptiveness. In part this theoretical reorientation reflected (responded to) changing government priorities that increasingly funnelled funding towards 'scientific' and social manage-

4

ment projects. It was also a more direct response to changing socio-political conditions within the United States. This was the time of the Vietnam war when American military high-tech was seen to fail in the face of indigenous resistance; of 'flower power', which brought to the forefront issues of pollution and environmental degradation; and of ghetto riots, which concentrated attention on problems of overcrowding and alienation. This was the time, then, when the gatherer-hunter way of life was seen as an alternative, highly adaptive and ecologically sensitive system. And the focus was on how the system worked. This included, despite the title of the volume, radical reappraisals of the importance of gathering activities and thus of women (Lee 1968), and of the relative 'affluence' of gatherer-hunters in terms of time spent on subsistence activities (Sahlins 1968).

There was also a short section on the evolutionary process, which acted almost as an apologia for war. In contradistinction to Lee's emphasis on gathering activities, Washburn and Lancaster (1968), and Laughlin (1968), stressed the evolutionary significance of hunting and therefore — based on conventional wisdom — of *man* the hunter. Three million years of Man the hunter provides a strong legitimation of male dominance and aggression, as popular writers like Ardrey (1961) were quick to emphasize.

Although there was relatively little concern with processes of historical change in the volume, the archaeologists raised an important issue. They insisted that contemporary gatherer-hunters — geographically, politically and socially marginalized — could not be used to document a former way of life. The anthropologists had to work with the effects of contemporary socio-political conditions; and the archaeologists had to eschew the strait-jacket created by ethnographic analogy (L. Freeman 1968; cf. Wobst 1978). Archaeological data might be intractable, but its coverage of an enormous time-span and almost total geographical range provided essential evidence on the socio-economic variability of past gatherer-hunters, and thus held the key to an understanding of the dynamics of long-term change.

The 1970s

The venue of the 1978 conference was Paris; the organizer was the leading Structural Marxist, Maurice Godelier. The contradictions in organization, presentations and publication were interesting at many different levels (cf. Perry Anderson 1983, on the post-1960s divide between theoretical and political Marxism). The considerable political clout of the French left-wing intelligentsia was manifest in the high profile given to the meetings, which were held in the United Nations building. A degree of elitism was also apparent, and in contradistinction to Marx's insistence that the present can only be understood with reference to the past, the divide between anthropologists and archaeologists endemic to Western European academia was hardly breached — there was, at most, a handful of archaeologists. The agenda remained, by and large, wedded to the present, although by a quirk of publishing fate and, no doubt, the energy and theoretical proclivities of the two editors, the one book that finally emerged brought together and enlarged upon those sections most concerned with social change.

The publication, *Politics and history in band societies*, edited by Eleanor Leacock and Richard Lee (1982), made important contributions along two main axes. The first was to demolish the notion that contemporary gatherer-hunter societies were in any sense 'pristine'. Articles focused on the effect of contact with neighbouring farming communities — which often extended over many millennia (Bahuchet and Guillaume 1982); on different sorts of exchange and trade relations — that sometimes shaded into forms of coercion (Leacock 1982; Morris 1982b); and on government interventions. Rosaldo (1982) analysed changing forms of state and capital penetration in the Philippines, Chang (1982) the tribalization of Kenyan communities. In part these discussions relate to more general preoccupations, emerging in the 1970s, with world systems and First World/Third World interaction and underdevelopment — all undoubtedly directly connected to the increasing scale of neocolonial penetration in the Third World.

This focus on recent social change led on to the second issue in the volume: the question of political action on the part of both the gatherer-hunters and the anthropologists. The acceptance of the need for political involvement voiced by the contributors to the third section of the book marks an important development. The partisan paper by Lee and Hurlich (1982) on the militarization of the San as part of the South African offensive against SWAPO, implicitly throws into question assumptions about scientific neutrality, and serves as a reminder that all too often 'neutrality' has provided a legitimation of a status quo working to the detriment of minority groups and women (cf. also Asch 1982, on the Canadian Dene).

It was not only the lack of archaeologists or ethno-historians at the Paris Conference that militated against a discussion of longer-term historical developments, but also the materialist form of Marxism preferred by the editors of the volume. Both the introduction (Leacock and Lee 1982) and Leacock's article (1982) on 'Relations of production in band societies' remain wedded to the notion of a foraging mode. While insisting that a mode of subsistence is not the same as a mode of production, they conflate a 'foraging mode' with Marx's 'communistic mode' and assume that the former has quite specific socio-political attributes, including a lack of property rights, a dearth of leaders, and minimal gender inequality (see Ingold, this volume, for a critique). Political or social features within gatherer-hunter societies that contradict this pattern are viewed as post-contact phenomena linked, in particular, to commodity trading. This division is reminiscent of the early demarcation made by Service (1962), except that the substance of the typology has changed. The Cree, the San, the Inuit and the Mbuti thus become examples of 'pristine' foragers, and the Northwest Coast or Californian Indians post-contact phenomena. This is clearly illogical. The Cree, the San, etc., have not been preserved in amber; they are no more 'pristine' than any other gatherer-hunter society; indeed, their flexibility, tendency to fission and low-profile tactics may in part be a form of resistance to domination (cf. Blackburn 1982, on such strategies used by the Okiek in the face of Maasai aggression, and Gordon 1984, cited below). There can be no justification for assuming that one set of attributes is 'timeless', another the result of exogenous forces.

The insistence on the socio-political specificity of a foraging mode creates an evolutionary impasse. There is no place for change, except through external forces. Already in the Leacock and Lee volume, Morris (1982b) begins to query the 'foraging mode', and points up the strong underlying techno-ecological causality. He notes that Lee's model of flexible bilateral relations in gatherer-hunter societies assumes that residential patterns are a key feature, and that they constitute an adaptive response 'adjusting group size to resources and . . . resolving tensions and conflicts within the group' (ibid.: 172). Morris notes that 'kinship and sex groupings, marriage patterns, and ritual congregations are seen as essentially extraneous' (ibid.: 173). This focus on 'on the ground' band relations also colours Leacock's definition of egalitarian relations, in which she stresses the collective ownership of the means of production, general access to the forces of production and forms of generalized reciprocity (Leacock 1982). But access to subsistence resources and reciprocity form only a part — the most visible — of social relations. The potential for inequality resides at a different level: in the ability to manipulate marital alliances and other exchanges and to control ritual and initiation and thence labour. Such social controls are not dependent upon the specific mode of subsistence, or specific techno-environmental conditions (Bender 1978).

The 1980s

There have been three conferences this decade. The first, held in Quebec in 1980, with participants mainly from North America, Europe and Australia, did not lead to a published volume. The second was a smaller event, held in Bad Homburg in 1983. Though participants came from many countries the resulting publication, *Past and present in hunter-gatherer studies* (Schrire 1984), contained mainly American and South African contributions.

There remains, in this volume, a strong tendency to discuss change in terms of something inflicted from outside; the gatherer-hunter operates in nature, is adaptive, and is 'coerced' into change either through environmental or external political factors. So Griffin, for example, describes an interesting shift from gatherer-hunter to small-scale cultivator, and back again, among the Agta in the Philippines, and explains it as a response to changing environmental conditions (P. Griffin 1984). Denbow (1984) documents two millennia of contact between Kalahari gatherer-hunters and Bantu farmers and suggests that subsistence can slide between wild procurement and herding and cultivating. Again, change is assumed to be contingent upon a 'frontier' situation. Gordon, in another paper on the Kalahari, weaves skilfully between differing agencies of change during the last hundred years — commercial game hunters, pastoralists, mining operators and white ranchers. These different phases are inscribed within the world system and more local development (Gordon 1984: 220). He suggests that 'it is more than merely possible that the San are classless today precisely because they are the underclass in an inclusive class structure' (ibid., citing Wilmsen). Like Lee and Hurlich, Gordon stresses that research can never be a discrete 'scientific' undertaking: that it can and will be both used and abused by interested parties fighting their corner on contemporary issues. What is missing, however, is a sense of San identity. Gordon is anxious to grant them an active role in these situations; he describes them as 'hotshot traders in the mercantile world market' (1984: 196). But they are ahistorical; there is no sense of how their perceptions and actions relate to their specific social configuration. There is no sense of prior history or of alliances, exchange and change that operated over thousands of years; no sense of a history that is not dependent upon interaction with other, differently constituted, societies. Another important paper in this volume, by Hoffman (1984) on the Punan of Borneo, takes us through a history of commercial contacts between China and South-East Asia beginning as early as the first or third century BC. He too suggests that present-day forest gatherer-hunters may once have been farmers. Specialization and exchange between forest and coastal groups were perhaps responses to an intensifying external trade that provided the prestige items essential to a system of intricate marital and alliance relations. But once again, for Hoffman, farming and trade are the keynotes for change; before farming and commercial relations there was simply 'subsistence hunting and gathering'. This general insistence on a 'before-farming'/'after-farming' divide desocializes gatherer-hunters.

Two papers in the Schrire volume, by Conkey (1984) and Lewis-Williams (1984), begin to give gatherer-hunters their own history. Both focus on art (Upper Palaeolithic and San respectively) as a material expression of, and agent in, social relations. Both emphasize elements that move beyond the everyday residential and subsistence routine of the band. They stress the network of marital and kin relations, the cognitive and ideological systems that inform these relations, and the rituals and ceremonies that create and legitimate them. What perhaps is less clearly developed in these papers are the tensions inherent in these kin-based social relations: between what people think they should do and what they do; between social 'reality' and ideological justification; between the ethos of reciprocity and individual interests or cross-cutting group affiliations; between what is available in the environment and the social perceptions thereof; between social demands on production and the ability to meet them. Such tensions may be culturally defused but they hold the seeds of change.

The most recent hunter-gatherer conference was held in London in 1986, and the present volume, together with its companion, *Hunters and gatherers II: Property, power and ideology* (Ingold, Riches and Woodburn 1988), is the outcome. Owing to government stringency and politically and ideologically motivated cut-backs in social science funding, the constituency for this conference remained, perforce, primarily First World and Establishment. British academic boundaries were flouted by including both anthropologists and archaeologists but, interestingly, British institutional divisions tended to reproduce themselves in terms of theoretical orientation. Many of the British archaeologists work within a functionalist paradigm in which evolution and change tend to be explained in techno-environmental terms. This sat uneasily with the greater focus on social relations inherent in most of the explanations of change offered by the anthropologists.

Explanations of long-term change and of evolutionary processes focused on environmental and demographic causality. It is possible that we have to make a distinction between *long durée* processes, determined to a large extent by environmental factors, and the trajectories of historically constituted social formations which work on shorter, often cyclical, time-scales (Braudel 1980; G. Bailey 1981b). But it is not clear how or where the line should be drawn. Foley (this volume) discusses hominid evolution and, drawing upon morphological variability, suggests that early hominids were 'neither human nor hunter-gatherers'. He goes further and suggests that even in the Upper Palaeolithic, when *Homo sapiens sapiens* had emerged, morphological differences were such that it was unlikely that subsistence practices and mating strategies resembled those of present-day gatherer-hunters. He proposes that the differences are caused by adaptations to glacial conditions, but this is perhaps only part of the explanation, for the particular morphological forms noted by Foley extend far beyond the areas affected by glaciation. The question of time-scale, and of evolutionary process, must remain an important area of enquiry. It must be admitted that we have only begun to touch on the implications of these longer-term trends.

Foley's 'debunking' of anthropological or archaeological scenarios that attempt to push sexual divisions of labour, home-bases and even monogamy far back into the past, leads into another, very different, level of historical analysis: how and why we use the past (Bender, 1988). An innovation of this conference, reflecting, we suspect, the increasingly fragmented nature of contemporary theorizing in British and American anthropology, was a session devoted to Marxist analyses. This permitted a more self-conscious (heated) discussion of differing theoretical viewpoints, and a more 'reflexive' discussion of how we make and use history. Papers in earlier volumes broached this topic (Rosaldo 1982; Conkey 1984), but Keene (1986) and Handsman (1986) addressed it more directly. This self-consciousness seems particularly important *vis-à-vis* gatherer-hunters. The way in which perceptions of gatherer-hunters have swung — still swing — in the last hundred years, between 'not far above the anthropoid apes' (Worcester, cited in Rosaldo 1982) and (successful) 'primitive communism' (Lee, this volume), suggests that we use them as a foil to our own societies. The length of time it has taken for the notion of 'pristine' present-day gatherer-hunters to be abandoned suggests that being 'pristine' was somehow important to us: we did not want to know what they were like after we had decimated, demoralized and destabilized them; we wanted to know what they were like beforehand, because we wanted to know what *we* were like.

Then again, we have preconceptions of what 'pristine' societies *should* be like. Lee (this volume) discusses contemporary unease with the notion of 'primitive communism' and changing attitudes to the term since the time when Morgan — 'staunch member of the bourgeoisie' — proposed it in 1881. Lee concurs with the claims made by Morgan and Engels, and sees an acceptance of such a formation as a way of giving gatherer-hunters back 'their . . . history, their . . . inner logic, . . . stolen from them by colonialism'. It should, perhaps, be noted that the original nineteenth-century concept of 'primitive communism' was not limited to 'gatherer-hunters'. Iroquois shifting cultivators were Morgan's and Engels's prototype.

We construct history, we *use* history. Hall (this volume) notes how, in southern Africa, the past is wheeled in to justify the present; how the still-frequent assumption made by archaeologists, that variability in material culture reflects ethnic diversity, chimes well with the 'divide and rule' tribalization policies of southern African governments. The past can also be used more positively: the tools of oppression can be turned back on the oppressors. As D. Miller (1988) has recently pointed out, those in power are trammelled by their own ideologies and socio-political structures: Western juridical insistence on property rights can become a two-edged sword — can be used by aboriginal populations in laying prior claim to land (Leacock 1982; N. Peterson 1982).

The effect of political involvement by anthropologists requires further consideration. Feit (1986) unravels the spider's web of intellectual endeavour and political and ideological motivation that surrounds such involvement in processes of social change. In Canada, Speck's support of Indian land rights affected the collection and presentation of data. The need to find parallels for Western notions of property dampened a more rigorous analysis of how tribal and capitalist perceptions of property *differ* from each other (cf. Ingold, Riches and Woodburn 1988).

Feit, arguing that we have to focus on 'the obvious linkages between reflective analysis and socio-political action' (1986: 22), notes that the violent debate on whether Indians held property has always been characterized as an ideological debate (Marxist/non-Marxist) over the evolutionary status of primitive communism; its roots in practical action on behalf of the Indians have been obscured because Western academic discourse operates in 'a liberal democratic culture in which expertise must appear to be non-political to be legitimated' (ibid.: 22).

Lest we appear to be examining our navels too intently, the chapter in this volume by Ndagala, a Tanzanian researcher on the Hadza, forces us back to the desperate process of social change, with all its ideological, economic and political ramifications. Ndagala stresses the importance of anthropological 'knowledge' to gatherer-hunters in their fight to survive, and reiterates that it must not be allowed to 'lie in university libraries and [on the] shelves of individual scholars'.[1]

So we return to more specific studies that focus, on the one hand, on contemporary social change, on interaction and domination working at many levels, including neighbours, government and world economy; and, on the other hand, on the historical conditions that create both the present situation and whatever resolution is possible.

In the first section of this volume both Bird-David and Woodburn, along with Ndagala, explore the relationship of gatherer-hunters to outsiders. While Bird-David looks at the situation of the Naiken within the South Indian context and suggests that unequal and personalized

1. We would have liked to reproduce, verbatim, an exchange that took place during one of the discussions, when Naftali Zengu, a Hadza participant, got up and questioned the point of all this debate. 'What has it to do with my people, and their condition?', he asked. An 'elder statesman' thanked him, and attempted to proceed with the discussion. A furiously indignant student sprung up and demanded that, at the very least, we could be quiet for a short while and think about what had just been said.

economic relationships must be conceptualized as part of the Naiken social system, Woodburn offers a more comparative approach. Focusing on sub-Saharan Africa — and dealing specifically with the Hadza, Okiek and Mbuti — he explores the degree to which patterns of social organization, whether they exhibit an immediate- or a delayed-return system (Woodburn 1980; 1982a), can be understood in terms of their 'encapsulation'. Interestingly, his analysis assumes that the immediate-return system is a function of a social environment in which delayed-return systems have already historically emerged, and thus cannot be seen as 'pristine'. But Woodburn's tendency to identify the immediate-return pattern with *specific* bounded ethnic categories has limitations (cf. Wolf 1982).

Indeed, in the next section, which deals with sedentism and flux, Pedersen and Wæhle continue this line of discussion. Their analysis of the relationship between the Pygmies and their agricultural neighbours suggests that much of the flux and fission ascribed to these gatherer-hunters is dependent upon this interaction, and that, in part, the 'immediate-return' system is a strategy for evading domination. They therefore query the concept of 'immediate return', pointing out that the ability to fission is contingent upon a network of dependencies which of its nature invokes delay. In the same section Gardner and Sandbukt also underline the diversity of social patterns that can occur *within* the same community. Gardner proposes a long-term pattern of adaptation among the Paliyans of South India, oscillating between semi-sedentary contract labour on the Tamil frontier and a relatively isolated 'retreatism' pattern of self-sufficient nomadism. Sandbukt suggests that the subsistence pattern of the Kubu of southern Sumatra is based upon two distinct modes, cultivation and foraging, and that these indicate discrete alternating phases in peoples' lives.

Many of the chapters in the present volume begin to explore the historical trajectories of gatherer-hunters with a focus on internal dynamics. There is an acceptance that change need not depend upon interaction with differently constituted groups or, for that matter, on subjugation or environmental factors. The emphasis is on social reproduction, as distinct from the reproduction of biological populations: a reproduction which is not necessarily adaptive in the longer term. Thus, again in the second section, Ellen reconstructs the processes leading to subsistence intensification among the Nuaulu of central Seram. He shows how the development of sedentism, storage and sago collection is embedded within a system of ritual exchange, emphasizing that storage has more to do with facilitating ceremonies than with subsistence requirements. Delayed returns, he suggests, are 'triggered and then further stimulated through exchange . . . The pre-horticultural emergence of clans . . . arises from the construction of property relations based on the circulation of valuables, not as the consequence of a particular mode of subsistence'.

In the following section, which is more emphatically about historical and evolutionary transformations, Lourandos lays stress on the role of ritual, ceremony and intergroup activity in generating demands on the economy, and discusses how these are met by a variety of different aboriginal strategies in Australia. Three other chapters in this section also focus on internal dynamics. Hall discusses rock art and trances in southern Africa, and the role of medicine men in mediating tensions generated by labour demands inherent in the system of reciprocal exchanges. He suggests that the development of cultivation had little effect upon social relations, and that it was only the later, more systematic, animal husbandry that permitted increased self-sufficiency and underwrote a more hierarchical social order. Hence he questions whether there were any dramatic social changes associated with the original shift to farming. Marquardt documents an astonishingly elaborated social system among the Calusa hunter-gatherer-fishers of Florida, in which tribute was exacted from an enormous hinterland. He discusses how the contradictions and pressures within the system were played out in relation to the first Spanish colonisers. Finally, in a pertinent comparative chapter, Pálsson, affirming the strong correlation between fishing, sedentism and social complexity, gives priority to social rather than ecological causality, and suggests that the exploitation of coastal niches is 'just one avenue for intensification'.

The final section of the volume highlights some wider theoretical and comparative concerns. Besides the reflections of Foley and Lee, already touched upon, this section includes two important chapters. That of Smith draws on evolutionary ecology, and employs the concepts of risk and uncertainty to explain variations in gatherer-hunter social behaviour, exchange patterns and intergroup relations. Finally, Ingold carefully unpicks the difference between a foraging mode, which he sees as constituted by technical or ecological interaction, and a hunting and gathering mode which is one of social action.

Conclusions

History of, history by, history for: developments over the last two decades in the study of gatherer-hunters underline the relativity of notions of history and evolution, and of what constitutes social change. We have to move backwards and forwards between past and present, along a scale that moves from the individual and band to world geo-politics. There has to be a 'self-consciousness' about the socio-political and ideological filters through which we screen our understanding.

Above all, the message of this volume must be that gatherer-hunters have their own history. An understanding of the processes of encapsulation has to work in tandem with an understanding that gatherer-hunter variability, past or present, has an internal dynamic. Change in gatherer-hunter societies does not wait upon the arrival of land-hungry farmers, nor upon capitalist penetration.

Part 1

Hunters and gatherers and outsiders

2. Hunter-gatherers and other people: a re-examination

Nurit H. Bird-David

In this chapter I query the relevance of a question that recently has assumed central place in the study of hunter-gatherers: is the social organization of hunter-gatherers affected by their contact with cultivating and pastoral neighbours? Obversely, as has been the orthodox approach during the 1960s and the 1970s, is hunter-gatherer social organization internally generated (for example, by constraints placed by a foraging mode of subsistence), and thus an *influence* on patterns of contact? I suggest that this question is anachronistic, for it fails to take into account recent shifts of assumptions in the study-field which recognize that hunter-gatherers are not, and for a long time have not been, isolated. Through examining the social life of a South Indian group, the Naiken, I shall propose that internal relationships (between Naikens) and external relationships (between Naikens and others) are *both* integral to hunter-gatherer social life. I suggest that an analytical divide between internal relationships, separately conceptualized as social organization, and external relationships, considered as contact, is inappropriate and misleading. Looking for a causal link between social organization and contact is a straw man; it obscures the fundamental problem: how to conceptualize more accurately hunter-gatherers' social reality. I shall explore a possible framework for an answer to this basic question, drawing on the particular case of the Naiken, and by comparative reference, tentatively generalizing to well-known examples in the hunter-gatherer field, including the Hadza, the !Kung Bushmen, the Mbuti Pygmies and other South Indian groups. I propose that hunter-gatherer relations with non-hunter-gatherers should be understood in terms of role relationships within the hunter-gatherer social system.

The 'orthodox' view of hunter-gatherers has rested on three axioms: isolation, a pure foraging economy, and timelessness. People who were encountered in areas hardly accessible to Europeans, who were neither pastoralists nor cultivators, who were non-sedentary, and who hunted and gathered were classified (and still are) as hunter-gatherers because of a Victorian evolutionary schema which placed hunting and

17

gathering at the bottom, below pastoralism and cultivation. Through the evolutionary-tinted category 'hunter-gatherers' any deviations from the stereotype were seen as residual, or as by-products of recent acculturation. Having selected local groups for intensive study, ethnographers described them as subsisting on hunting and gathering *to a significant extent*, as having *minimal* contact with other peoples, and as having *hardly* changed since time immemorial. They focused on economic, social and cultural aspects of hunting and gathering, paying little attention to matters relating to contact with the outside or to other economic pursuits.

Recent work suggests a sufficient case for adopting an alternative working paradigm of modern hunter-gatherers; a paradigm that rests on the *assumptions* of contact and of economic diversity and flexibility. There has been a snowballing increase in acknowledging and examining the significance of contact with other people, which started with apparently idiosyncratic cases such as the 1950s study of the Mbuti Pgymies by Turnbull (1965a). This continued with the identification of a whole class of hunter-gatherers considered to be a special category, namely the South Indian groups, who were shown to have been in contact with adjacent societies for centuries and probably millennia (e.g. R. Fox 1969; Gardner 1972; Morris 1977). Then in the 1980s a similar claim was extended to many African groups (e.g. Blackburn 1982; Bahuchet and Guillaume 1982; cf. Woodburn, this volume).

In close association, the notion of hunter-gatherers as pure foragers has also been challenged. There have been increasing ethnographic descriptions of hunter-gatherers engaging in trade of minor forest produce, again probably from antiquity, first with reference to South Asian groups (Morris 1977; Gardner 1972; R. Fox 1969), then to African groups (Bahuchet and Guillaume 1982: 189, quoting S. Miller 1969; Phillipson 1976; cf. Woodburn, this volume), and finally with reference to the San and South-East Asian groups (Schrire 1984). The broadening of horizons in ethnographic description has revealed that even among hard-core hunter-gatherers a variety of still further economic strategies are pursued. These include work in cattle posts owned by neighbouring populations (for example, the !Kung, Lee 1979), guiding hunting expeditions (for example, the Hill Pandaram, Morris 1975), guiding pilgrims to forest shrines (for example, the Paliyans, Gardner 1982), labour in fields of neighbouring cultivators (for example, the Mbuti Pygmies, Turnbull 1965a) and, more recently, wage work (for example, the Naiken, Bird 1983b). People like the Agta of the Philippines have been described as 'generalists' who mix hunting and gathering with a variety of strategies according to ecological and social factors (P. Griffin 1984).

What are the ramifications of all this for understanding the hunter-gatherer social system?

Up to the 1960s, the dominant model, propagated in the work of Steward (1936; 1955) and Service (1962), depicted patrilocal, exogamous and territorial band organization, and related this to the importance of hunting and a scarcity of resources.[1] This model was later rejected in favour of one which depicted fluid, constantly changing groupings, the salient economic context being a world of affluence where gathering outranks hunting in its contribution to subsistence.[2] Either way the hunter-gatherer social system is described as geared towards, if not determined by, ecological constraints relating to a foraging economy. Before, a rigid patrilocal, territorial and exogamous organization was related to scarcity of resources and to the importance of hunting. Now, a flexible, fluid organization is related to abundance of resources and to the importance of gathering.

With the significance of contact between hunter-gatherers and adjacent societies becoming clearer, the currently popular question is whether and how the hunter-gatherer social system is geared towards, or influenced by, contact with adjacent societies. Before, the hunter-gatherer social system was seen as adapted to, if not caused by, a foraging economy; now, it is alleged to be adapted to, or even caused by, contact with adjacent societies, in particular because of trade. With reference to South Indian hunter-gatherers, Fox has thus argued that 'the social organization of these groups is transformed to meet the expectation of collection and exchange with the outside world' (1969: 142; cf. Morris 1977; Gardner 1966). He sees the nucleation of hunter-gatherer societies into individual, autonomous and migratory families as the result of the 'individually competitive system where each family tries to maximize the amount of forest goods collected for external transactions' (ibid.).

If to regard the hunter-gatherer social system as generated by a foraging economy can be described as too 'isolationist', then the full swing to presenting it as the outcome of trade-contact with adjacent societies can be seen as too 'integrationist'. Both explanations can be criticized as partial and simplistic — but that would miss a much more fundamental weakness. The key point is that both explanations are anachronistic, in the sense of still being framed within the paradigm of the isolated and self-sufficient hunting and gathering society. In the case of the 'isolationist' explanation, this is self-evident, since the premise is that hunter-gatherers pursue a foraging mode of subsis-

1. To give an example of how one variation of this argument runs: hunting is important; men, the hunters, need intimate knowledge of the territory in which they hunt, especially because resources are hard to come by; men, therefore, retain exclusive rights over their respective territories and stay there, joined by their wives. The upshot is a society with political, territorial and exogamous organization (B.J. Williams 1974).

2. To give one variation of such an explanation: there are constantly seasonal and local variations in the availability of wild resources; fluid organization is a mechanism facilitating adaptation to such ecological vicissitudes (Lee 1972).

tence. In the case of the 'integrationist' explanation, the reference to the paradigm is less clear but nevertheless there: against the context of the isolated and self-sufficient hunter-gatherer society the practice of trade is seen as a recent development, which has changed the hunter-gatherer social system.

Thus the question of whether, and to what extent, the hunter-gatherer social system is causally related to contact with adjacent societies, does not fully realize the implications of growing new data and an emergent paradigm. Of course, it is interesting to speculate on what, way back in the past, was the impact upon pure hunter-gatherers of contact with cultivators and pastoralists. However the data we have suggest that contemporary hunter-gatherers have maintained contact with adjacent societies for centuries, indeed, according to an increasing number of scholars, possibly millennia. Contact, in other words, is now generic to their social system and not an exogenous factor. What we should therefore ask is how the hunter-gatherer social system encompasses the contact with other people. How is it able to include, and provide a means to deal with, non-hunter-gatherers?

Within the conceptual framework dominant in the study of small-scale social systems it is difficult to pursue this question. Orthodox models of traditional social systems focus, in the main, on social relationships within self-contained political units, following Nadel's definition of society (1953: 187). Such social systems are commonly presented as closed. Analysis conventionally focuses on criteria of exclusion instrumental in the reproduction of constituent groups. Such orthodox models are clearly not readily applicable to hunter-gatherers, where there are no clear self-contained political units (cf. Woodburn 1979), and where relationships with outsiders — modes of inclusion — appear to be important.

Radcliffe-Brown's theoretical notions of society and social structure may present a suitable alternative framework in which the question of the structural relationship between hunter-gatherers and other people can be explored, though, to be sure, his specific study of Australian Aborigines gave impetus to the model of the closed hunter-gatherer society made up from patrilocal, exogamous bands. Radcliffe-Brown's unit of study — the society — is 'any convenient locality' (1940: 5), and not a self-contained political unit. His 'social structure' is an all-embracing notion that includes persistent social groups as well as all social relations of person to person and the differentiation of individuals and of classes by their social role (ibid.). The structure, then, to use Nadel's words, is 'a property of empirical data — of objects, events or series of events — something they exhibit, or prove to possess on observation or analysis' (1957: 7). Within such a conceptual framework undifferentiated attention can be given to relationships in a given locality, on the one hand among hunter-gatherers, and on the other hand between hunter-gatherers and their neighbours in that locality. I shall explore this with my Naiken material (see also Bird 1977).[3]

The Naiken are scattered in small local groups throughout the Nilgiri-Wynaad, which lies at the lower elevations of the Nilgiris in South India, where the Tamil-Nadu, Kerala and Karnataka regions meet. Each local group is situated discontinuously in a pocket surrounded by other populations. Naikens of one local group usually do not know where other Naiken groups are located, and if pressed simply refer elusively to the Wynaadu. A hundred years ealier, a similar observation was made with reference to the Kurumbas, of whom the Naiken are considered to be a subgroup: 'Their villages . . . are so dispersed over the slopes and base of the hills, that the inhabitants of one locality know nothing of those at a distance . . .' (Breeks 1873: 50).

I focus on one Naiken local group in its home territory to show that even within a given enclave contact with non-Naiken is far from residual. I draw on information collected from both Naikens and non-Naikens. There is a considerable range of variation among the individual Naikens concerned with respect to the extent of interaction with non-Naikens, which in the main directly relates to residential proximity. The bias in the present description, if any, is towards demonstrating contact, to balance the prejudice in the anthropological literature towards presenting isolation. I deliberately use the term 'non-Naikens', since I suggest that these people are not outsiders as such, and that the relationships with them are best understood in the context of the contrast with relationships between Naikens. Finally, for simplicity, I refer to this particular Naiken local group as if they were the Naiken in general.

The Naiken, then, inhabit a steep valley on the north-west slope of the Nilgiris, which is referred to as the Gir valley. This naturally demarcated area of about 5000 acres lies on the steep fall from the Nilgiri heights to sea level, about fifteen kilometres down from a small Indian village on the Nilgiri-Wynaad plateau. Part of the valley bed had been established as a marginal plantation, with rubber planted at the turn of the century and coffee added fifty years later. The valley constitutes a 'convenient locality'. The permanent population of the area is 206: sixty-nine Naikens and 137 non-Naikens, who are workers in the plantation. (I speak of the time of fieldwork, 1978, in the present tense.) The permanent non-Naiken population is not homogeneous, because their immigration, which started in the early 1950s, has been sporadic. It is about two-thirds Muslim (mainly Moppalas), with some

3. Fieldwork was carried out between September 1978 and September 1979, generously supported by Trinity College, Cambridge, and Anthony Wilkin Studentship, an H.M. Chadwick Studentship, the Smuts Memorial Fund, the Wyse Fund and the Radcliffe-Brown Fund. Place names and personal names are fictitious.

Hindus and Syrian Christians, the Muslims alone from at least nine known localities of origin. In addition, since the 1960s there have been groups of temporary workers, mainly from Tamil Nadu, who have stayed in the valley for several months at a time, felling trees. The Naiken trade with the non-Naiken inhabitants of the valley (for example, in firewood, grass for thatching, forest spices and honey), as well as providing occasional labour in clearing fields, constructing fences, and so on. In addition to gathering, fishing, collecting honey and a limited amount of hunting, a variable section of the Naiken local group (about two-thirds) is engaged in casual work in the plantation, an activity which started on a regular basis in the 1950s.

There are eight residential clusters in the Gir valley: five of Naiken huts, three of non-Naiken workers' dwellings, and two of shacks occupied by forest workers. Two Naiken hamlets, in which 48 per cent of the local Naiken group live, are on the bed of the valley, interspersed amidst the dwellings of the non-Naiken plantation workers. Indeed, in one case, non-Naikens moved to an area occupied previously by Naikens, and one non-Naiken family even moved into a hut abandoned by Naikens and renovated it. These hamlets are nearer to non-Naiken dwellings than to other Naiken huts, a distribution which reflects, in miniature, the way Naiken local groups themselves are mixed in among the various people of the Nilgiri. A third hamlet, bringing the proportion up to 66 per cent, is close by the forest-workers' shacks. Naiken men and women meet non-Naikens frequently, sometimes two to three times a day, in two local 'tea shops' (actually a shack and a veranda of a house, both situated on the bed of the valley), where they often chat about local affairs. They also meet regularly in the course of work in the plantation and in trade. Naikens not infrequently are engaged by non-Naikens to work near their houses or in their fields. The forest workers often draw water from the Naiken water points. The fusing of the Naiken and the non-Naiken spheres can at times be quite striking, as the following extreme example illustrates. A pedlar arrives at the Naiken hamlet and approaches Mathen for old metal pots. Mathen does not heed his request and the pedlar searches for himself. Finding an old rusty pot, he exchanges it with Mathen for a few cigarettes. Now, of course, at both the periphery and in the thick of the forest, the intrusion of non-Naikens is minimal. And Naikens have (and exercise) freedom to move between periphery and centre just as between the general areas of forest and plantation and trade.

In time, just as in space, there is no pronounced demarcation of an intra-Naiken sphere. Naikens are likely to come across non-Naikens sporadically throughout the day. Single persons meet non-Naikens most frequently, since they often eat meals in the tea shops, and occasionally go with non-Naikens to attend festivals in neighbouring Indian villages. Even those who do not work in the plantation are likely to meet non-Naikens each and every day, on their way to deep forest locations to engage in gathering, in the tea shops, or while trading commodities locally. The extent to which the non-Naikens are part of the universe within which the Naikens move can perhaps be gauged by the following two observations relating to traditional fishing expeditions. In the first example, traditional fishing is being carried out in full view of a gang of plantation workers clearing a hilly area for new plants. Naikens and non-Naikens alike are among the plantation workers. In the second example, non-Naiken children join in with a Naiken fishing party. It would not be stretching the point too far to suggest, merely on the basis of impression and extrapolation, that many Naikens spend, on average, at least one-third of their waking time with or next to non-Naikens.

Much of the contact between Naikens and non-Naikens revolves around economic transactions, involving transfer of goods or provision of labour. However, this is not to the exclusion of social contact; indeed, in some cases economic interactions take place because of pre-existing social ties. For example, a non-Naiken explicitly acknowledged that Cik Mathen would not have carried a bunch of bananas for him to the market village, nor would any other Naiken do it, were he not 'friendly' with him. The content of social contact with non-Naikens varies and, furthermore, not all Naikens maintain personal social ties with non-Naikens. To take one sample, from among eight resident males of one hamlet, only four had such personal social ties. But these features should not obscure the fact that personal social contact significantly exists, the range of which can be demonstrated by the following five examples. The first instance involves a Tamil forest worker who often visits Cik Mathen. They sit together outside Cik Mathen's hut, smoking, talking and joking, frequently joined by Cik Mathen's wife and daughter. The second example is that of Kungan, who offers shelter for a few nights to a non-Naiken acquaintance sought by the police for disruption of work in the plantation. The third instance involves a non-Naiken who visits his young Naiken 'friend', Chellan. Finding him very ill he immediately secures the required documents from the plantation office and on his behalf takes Mathen to see a doctor in one of the market villages. In the fourth example, another non-Naiken, friendly with young Chathen, accompanies him to a nearby market village to buy a cloth for his wedding. He also advises Chathen on how best to spend a relatively large sum of money that Chathen happens to obtain. Lastly, Naiken women usually keep company with a woman who gives birth for the first time, but when Mathi goes into labour, a non-Naiken 'friend' also joins the Naiken women. A few months later, Mathi's family attend the wedding of their friend's daughter. Non-Naikens are sometimes also directly called upon to intervene in intra-Naiken affairs. For example, when quite unusually

Banu mistreats his wife, her kin do not interfere, but approach the plantation superintendent to see if he would 'have a word with' him. In another interesting instance, in a certain play-act which is celebrated annually, Naiken spectators try to chase away *piccaico* (forest spirits) acted by two men. Failing to make them leave by providing them with food and money, they then threaten to call the police.

As groups, Naikens and non-Naikens often keep to themselves. For example, when sufficient numbers of Naikens and non-Naikens work together in the plantation, they tend to split into two subgroups according to the ethnic divide. The same happens in the tea shops. Yet there is a sufficient social contact across the divide. The contact is highly personalized, which may be contrasted with the more typical state of affairs, in which 'other people' are seen as a faceless, abstract category, even a 'non-people', or are cast in the role of sorcerers, witches or enemies.

I suggest that there is a complementary contrast between intra-Naiken relationships and relationships between Naikens and others. Among Naikens, autonomy, and independence from particular kin, are highly valued. Economic cooperation is limited. Kinship relations, to use Woodburn's words, 'do not carry a heavy burden of goods and services transmitted between the participants in recognition of claims or obligations' (1980: 105). To the extent that it exists, economic dependence is depersonalized. For example, the Naiken go to great lengths to ensure a strictly equal sharing of large game, thus minimizing moral and economic indebtedness between individual recipients and particular hunters. Material exchanges can be characterized as 'giving without the expectation of return' (Sahlins 1974) or sharing (see J. Price 1975), which also suppresses personalized obligations.

In contrast, individual ties between Naikens and non-Naikens are dominated by economic cooperation. This is personalized and of a contractual type (cf. Nisbet 1968: 385), which means that the persons concerned are economically interdependent for the duration of the cooperation. Material exchanges usually take the form characterized by Sahlins as 'balanced reciprocity', and occasionally even 'negative reciprocity'. Personal indebtedness is important in sustaining economic cooperation between Naikens and non-Naikens. On paying off previous debts with minor forest produce Naikens immediately take more commodities on credit. The cooperation ends with the withdrawal of Naikens leaving a debt unpaid.

The relationship between Naikens is that between equals. The relationship with non-Naikens is one between unequals. In the Naiken domain there is no institutionalized authority; the non-Naiken domain is drawn upon when intervention or institutionalized authority are sought.

Friendship among Naikens is a relationship that is mainly subsumed under the conjugal relationship, or, as Naikens put it, the conjugal partner is one's best and often only friend. In the main, leisure time is spent with the spouse, though of course in relative promixity to other couples sitting near their own respective fires. In general, apart from the conjugal relationship, social interaction with kin is restrained by *nachika*, which may be freely translated as 'reticence'. This is a notion which Naikens frequently invoke when referring to relations with kin, and by it they indicate, not a clearly defined set of behavioural conventions, but a certain emotional state — and a many-shaded state at that. *Nachika* imposes a variety of inhibitions, ranging from avoidance of physical contact to the minimization of leisure (non-purposeful) conversations. Loosely speaking, the degree of inhibition correlates with social proximity and degree of kinship relatedness. The closer the tie, the stronger the inhibition. Such inhibitions seem to counterbalance what I call elsewhere (Bird 1983a) 'involuntary intimacy', the state of affairs which prevails because of the particular material setting in which people are placed. Naikens, in brief, refrain not only from hierarchical relationships but from any other differential social attachments.

In contrast, it is possible to see contacts with outsiders, such as those reported above, as instances of social closeness or, to use the notion in a very vague way, as a sort of personal friendship. To take two of the examples mentioned already, it is a non-Naiken with whom Cik Mathen spends many an evening near his fireplace; and it is a non-Naiken who accompanies Chathen when buying a wedding cloth in the market village.

Lending support to such a contrast is the tendency, among Naikens, for help to be expected only from within the conjugal family, mainly from the spouse — and not from any other Naiken. To take an extreme example, an eighty-year-old man cares for his seventy-five-year-old blind wife, though they live next to their married daughter. Against this background such instances as the one reported earlier, where a non-Naiken helps Chellan when he is ill, stand out.

The final point of contrast seems trivial, but it is usefully illustrative. In everyday conversations adult Naikens usually address and refer to each other by kinship terms. The use of kinship terms in an everyday context emphasizes that all the Naikens in the local group descend from a 'common stock', and as such are equal. It tends to homogenize Naikens of the local group. In contrast, when talking with non-Naikens, Naikens use personal names of sorts to refer both to fellow-Naikens and to themselves. Within the intra-Naiken domain personal names, which distinguish between Naikens, are avoided — yet they are used in the external context.

Two 'bundles of features' seem to emerge: on the one hand, among Naikens, individual autonomy, independence, equality and the minimization of differential social attachments; on the other hand, in the contact with the outside, economic cooperation and dependence, in-equality and personalized social interaction. Logically, such features are opposites. But a functional complement may also be suggested. Social cohesion based on relations of equality and likeness calls for a minimization of economic interdependence, common authority and differential social attachments. But such institutional facilities can at times be vital for the well-being of individuals and for the smooth running of the social system. It seems as if the surrounding outside is drawn upon to compensate for the lack of such facilities within.

The 'bundle of features' suggested as being characteristic of intra-Naiken relationships is similar to the key features that Woodburn identifies for the 'assertively egalitarian' hunter-gatherer societies (1982a). These latter hunter-gatherer societies are all marked by a universal kinship system, where 'everyone — or at least everyone within the political community — is able to define a kinship or a quasi-kinship tie to everyone else' (Woodburn 1980: 105). As among the Naiken, people in such societies are not dependent on specific other people for access to basic requirements (Woodburn 1982a: 434), and relationships in general do not involve long-term binding commitments and dependencies (ibid.). A variety of means are employed to minimize social differentials. Again, as with the Naiken, this is clearly seen in the sharing of large game. Woodburn reports, for example, that the Hadza hunter who returns with large game is expected to sit down quietly with the other men, not mention the name of the species that was caught, nor any other detail, and allow the blood on his arrow shaft to speak for him (ibid.: 441). Finally, gambling appears to be popular in this sort of society, as indeed it is also among other hunter-gatherers such as the Inuit (Riches 1975) and the Australian Aborigines (McKnight n.d.). Gambling depersonalizes material transactions and minimizes the personal obligations which would have ensued from other forms of material exchanges (ibid.: 443).

It is not implausible that there is a reasonable affinity between the nature of contact between Naikens and non-Naikens and the sort of contact that obtains between other hunter-gatherers and their adjacent societies, though on this matter there are less comparative data to go by. As with the Naiken, generalized reciprocity among the hunter-gatherers contrasts with balanced reciprocity with the outside. In many cases contact with adjacent societies appears to be as frequent as among the Naiken — a matter of day-to-day living (see for example, Blackburn 1982, for the Okiek). Also widely reported, links between the hunter-gatherers and other people are personal, as for Pygmy groups (Turn-bull 1965a; Bahuchet and Guillaume 1982; Blackburn 1982; Schultz 1986), the !Kung San (Lee 1979) and the South Indian Kurumbas (Rivers 1906). In some cases such attachments involve mutual participation in life-cycle events, as for the Mbuti Pygmies. In others they take the form of a patron–client relationship, as for example between some !Kung and black owners of cattle posts (Lee 1979: 407). As in the Naiken case, there may be a variety of social ties between individuals among the hunter-gatherers and individuals of the adjacent societies. Lee, for example, reports three kinds of arrangements between !Kung and black owners of cattle posts (ibid.). Characteristically the relationship between the hunter-gatherer and his neighbour is one between unequals, which contrasts with the equality among the hunter-gatherers. Finally, it seems that, again as with the Naiken, any domination over fellow hunter-gatherers or interference in their lives is exerted with the backing of coercive powers derived from outside the hunter-gatherer society itself (see Woodburn 1982a: 436).

I make no claim that the complementary contrast between intra-Naiken relationships and relationships between Naikens and non-Naikens is found as such with all other hunter-gatherer societies. I only propose that the Naiken case seems to be a variant which points to a theme sufficiently apparent for other hunter-gatherers that the following question can be pressed: how may the structural importance of the contact between hunter-gatherers and adjacent societies be conceptualized? What theoretical formulation can explain how the hunter-gatherer social system includes and deals with people of the varied and changing surrounding societies?

I suggest, within the context of the Radcliffe-Brownian concept of social structure, that the relationship between hunter-gatherers and people of adjacent societies can be seen as a role relationship materializing in interactional settings and concerned with behaviour at the individual level. That is, the non-hunter-gatherers are viewed by the hunter-gatherers as within their social structure; and certain normative conventions guide the interaction between individual hunter-gatherers and individual neighbours.

As to the Naiken, they do not present their social system in terms of named categories, or bounded groups. Furthermore, they do not present their social system in an abstract way divorced from a concrete context. Instead, in a day-to-day context they use one term, *sonta*, for a variety of social aggregates. *Sonta* can be translated as 'family' in the classificatory, abstract sense of the word — as in 'species'. It emphasizes relations of 'likeness', rather than interrelationships between members. In varied contexts *sonta* is used to refer to ego's nuclear family, to his kindred, to the co-residents in his hamlet, to the co-descendants of given ancestors, and to the local group at large. But Naikens use the same term *sonta* to refer also to the local aggregate comprising both them and non-Naiken neighbours. Pressed to list ascendant levels of *sonta* the Naikens refer to the multi-ethnic local aggregate rather than to the totality of Naikens, the anthropologist's 'Naiken society'. If pressed they describe the latter by language or by manner of dressing and food habits — in other words by cultural rather than structural criteria. It can be suggested that, through the use of the notion of *sonta* in concrete contexts, a fleeting social map is constantly projected, depicting a growing concentric circuit around ego, much like the ripples created around a stone thrown into the water.

The term *nama sime*, which likewise is used only in a concrete context, correspondingly depicts, on the territorial plane, a second set of ego-centric ripples. It means 'our place'. According to context, *nama sime* refers to the abode of the nuclear family, to the hamlet, to the territorial tract associated with given ancestors or to the entire locality, namely the Gir valley. *Nama sime* is inhabited by non-Naikens as well as by Naikens. In everyday language its use projects a fluid demarcation, spreading outwards like ripples; the further the ripples, the weaker their resolution. Naiken social structure might indeed generally be captured by the metaphor of ripples. Such ripples potentially spread infinitely outwards and cover the entire experienced field of action. Part of this field is occupied by non-Naikens.

The extent to which the Naiken are idiosyncratic with respect to their view of their social system is difficult to ascertain. But it seems plausible that they are not unique. Since the myth of the neatly defined exogamous, patrilocal bands was dispelled by empirical findings, and fluidity and constant change in the composition of social groupings suggested instead, there has been a growing acknowledgement that hunter-gatherers, at least of a certain type, are characterized by that rather vaguely explicated notion, an open social system. Concluding his paper on egalitarian societies Woodburn states that: 'Hadza society is open. People . . . do not impose social boundaries between themselves and others'. A few sentences later he reiterates that 'the principle is that Hadza society is open and there is simply no basis for exclusion' (1982a: 448). Lee similarly emphasizes that 'the !Kung consciously strive to maintain a boundaryless universe' (1979: 335).[4] *Sonta* is a powerful emic concept suitable for a boundaryless, flexible social system that emphasizes inclusion.

Does the relationship with people of the varied and changing societies surrounding the hunter-gatherers conform in any way to a normative convention? Upon comparative examination a certain regularity appears to emerge, but it is not clear so long as attention is focused on the relationship between a given hunter-gatherer group and a given adjacent society at a given point of time. It seems that what guides hunter-

4. Compared with the Barasana use of expressions such as 'one people', 'one pile', and 'children of one man' (Hugh-Jones 1979: 24), notions like *sonta* are inclusive in essense. The folk model of many nomads similarly includes notions about society as an expanding family and the terminology nomads use to describe the corresponding segments is very undifferentiated (Khazanov 1982). Both Hugh-Jones and Khazanov seem to dismiss the possible analytical significance of such emic notions and in their analysis resort to etic models of exclusive groups and named categories.

gatherer interaction with non-hunter-gatherers is the convention best summarized as 'with Romans behave like a Roman'. For example, in the village the Mbuti Pygmy complies with Bantu norms, for instance in life-cycle celebrations, but complies with another set of conventions in the forest (Turnbull 1965a). To give another example, the South Indian Paliyan has a 'dual culture', for example using a Dravidian kinship system like that of his neighbours when a non-Paliyan is present, while using another system — his own — in the intra-Paliyan domain (cf. Gardner, this volume). Naikens, whose surrounding population is not homogeneous, behave similarly. In the context of work in the plantation Naikens are nominal trade union members. Another example: those who are in close contact with Malayalam-speaking people adopt certain Malayalam kinship terms, while those in more regular interaction with Tamils use some Tamil kinship terms.

When the 'Roman' requires hunter-gatherers to assimilate, as is the case with the Bantu who is afraid to deal with the Mbuti unless the latter is incorporated into the village culture, the hunter-gatherer complies in appearance with the relevant conventions. When the 'Roman' does not require long-term culturally-rooted cooperation, and simply expects a utilitarian economic transaction, the hunter-gatherer again conforms in appearance. For the hunter-gatherer lip-service to the conventions of others is a cultural digging stick, as it were, by which he extracts resources from his social environment.

'With Romans behave like a Roman' is a convention, then, which guides behaviour in a way appropriate to the interaction with other people. However, its exact content is changeable, depending on who the Romans are and their preferences as regards interaction with the hunter-gatherers. The hunter-gatherer convention is umbrella-like — a formula. Its substance depends upon context. It is an open-ended convention and it can also be characterized as inclusive. The formula enables 'other' people to be encompassed within the hunter-gatherer social system, presupposing nothing, not even an awareness — let alone acceptance — of the role assumed. Over and above these attributes, this normative convention prescribes behaviour, but in such a way as to accommodate social change, since how the Romans behave is never static.[5]

The inclusion of non-Naikens into the Naiken social world as occupants of roles articulated within the Naiken social structure, together with the sanctioned adoption of the non-Naiken code in the context of the interaction with them, may explain how hunter-gatherers have persisted in spite of the constant contact with people from varied and changing surrounding societies. The hunter-gatherer social system,

5. Such a formulation also provides a structural space for change within the Radcliffe-Brownian analytical framework, which has been criticized for its failure to accommodate change.

without being fundamentally changed, has been able to incorporate 'other people' as economic as well as social resources, to be used for maintaining the hunter-gatherer way of life.

3. African hunter-gatherer social organization: is it best understood as a product of encapsulation?

James Woodburn

Introduction

In a paper published in 1980, 'Hunters and gatherers today and reconstruction of the past', I made some preliminary comments about the relevance of political and economic relationships with neighbouring pastoral and agricultural societies for understanding hunter-gatherer social and economic organization and, in particular, for understanding why some hunter-gatherers have what I call 'immediate-return' organization while others have what I call 'delayed-return' organization. Stimulated by recent work (for example, Leacock and Lee 1982; Schrire 1984), my aim in the present chapter is to develop those preliminary comments.[1] As always, I regard the argument I am putting forward as tentative and I warmly welcome discussion and evidence, both in support of what I say and opposed to it, that will help me to improve or to discard aspects of the case presented here.

My distinction between immediate-return systems and delayed-return systems has been developed in a series of papers (Woodburn 1978; 1979; 1980; 1982a; 1982b). There are some changes, improvements I hope, in the formulation between the earlier and later papers in this series, and there will be other changes in future papers. But I am not concerned in the present chapter with further elaboration of the distinction, though I cannot escape summarizing it here, for my argument is unintelligible if the distinction is not understood. Here, then, are the characteristics of immediate-return and delayed-return systems:

1. This chapter has benefited greatly from my most recent visit to Kenya and Tanzania in 1985 and I would like to thank Grace and John Bennett for their hospitality, John Sutton and the British Institute in Eastern Africa for the loan of equipment and other help and the LSE Staff Research Fund and the University of London Central Research Fund for travel funds. I would also like to thank the many people who have commented helpfully on the paper — including Roderic Blackburn, Maurice Bloch, Corinne Kratz, Peter Loizos, David McKnight and Daniel Ndagala. Michael Schultz and Lisa Woodburn gave much valued help with word processing.

An *immediate-return system* is one in which activities oriented to the present (rather than to the past or the future) are stressed; in which people deploy their labour to obtain food and other resources which will be used on the day they are obtained or casually over the days that follow; in which people use simple, portable, utilitarian, easily acquired, replaceable tools and weapons made with real skill but not involving a great deal of labour; in which people do *not* hold valued assets which represent a yield, a return for labour applied over time, or valued assets which are held and managed in a way which resembles and has similar social implications to delayed yields on labour; in which people are systematically disengaged from assets, from the potential in assets for creating dependency.

A *delayed-return system* is one in which, in contrast, activities are oriented to the past and the future as well as to the present; in which people hold rights over valued assets of some sort, which either represent a yield, a return for labour applied over time or, if not, are held and managed in a way which resembles and has similar social implications to delayed yields on labour. In delayed-return hunting and gathering systems these assets are of four main types, which may occur separately but are more commonly found in combination with one another and are mutually reinforcing.

(1) Valuable technical facilities used in production: boats, nets, artificial weirs, stockades, pit-traps, beehives and other such artefacts which are a product of considerable labour and from which a food yield is obtained gradually over a period of months or years.
(2) Processed and stored food or materials usually in fixed dwellings.
(3) Wild products which have themselves been improved or increased by human labour: wild herds which are culled selectively, wild food-producing plants which have been tended, and so on.
(4) Assets in the form of rights held by men over their female kin who are then bestowed in marriage on other men.[2]

Some hunter-gatherers have immediate-return systems and some have delayed-return systems. All other societies (with a very small number of possible exceptions) have delayed-return systems.

I have argued that both immediate- and delayed-return systems are likely to have existed even in the pre-Neolithic period, though their relative frequency would probably have been quite different from today. I have also argued that in history there have been changes in

2. For some of the difficulties with this simple, indeed oversimplified, binary distinction between immediate-return and delayed-return systems, see Woodburn (1982a: 449, n. 3).

both directions — from delayed-return systems to systems of immediate return and vice versa — and have suggested in a preliminary way a range of factors that are likely, singly or in combination, to have promoted one type of system or the other or to have generated shifts from one to the other (Woodburn 1978; 1980). Contact with other societies is one such factor. I have claimed that

> the contact situation and the political and economic relationships with non-hunting outsiders are relevant. Turnbull (1965a) and Gardner (1966; 1969; 1972) both discuss societies with systems of immediate return, and attribute the systems directly to the relationships with outsiders. Turnbull, in his discussion of the Mbuti Pygmies, argues that their mobility and flexibility are a means by which they seek to avoid political domination by their agricultural neighbours. Gardner sees the situation more starkly and argues that the immediate-return system of the Paliyan groups which he studied is pathological and the result of breakdown caused by the dominance and exploitation of their predatory peasant neighbours. Both authors are, I think, wrong in treating immediate return as an unusual system which requires special explanation. As the examples I have listed earlier in this paper illustrate, the system is widespread and not all the societies in question suffer from exploitation by neighbours. At the same time I think the idea should be treated seriously and we should consider whether pressure from outsiders is one of the factors which tends, in combination with other factors, to push societies towards immediate-return systems. I think it is plausible to suggest that it is and that in a world consisting exclusively of hunters and gatherers, a higher proportion might have had delayed-return systems (Woodburn 1980: 112).

Taking these preliminary comments as my point of departure, my concern now is to consider more carefully how the *social organization* of hunter-gatherer societies may have been affected by pressure from outsiders.

I have argued that delayed-return systems depend for their operation on sets of ordered, differentiated, jurally-defined relationships through which crucial goods and services are transmitted. There are binding commitments and dependencies between people. For people to build up, secure, protect, manage and transmit the delayed yields on labour, or the other assets which are held in delayed-return systems, load-bearing relationships are necessary.

Social organization is *not*, however, merely an epiphenomenon of technology, the work process and the rules governing the control of assets. All I am saying, as I have indeed said before (Woodburn 1980: 111; 1982a: 434), is this: in a delayed-return system there must be organization having the very general characteristics outlined. The *particular* form the organization will take cannot be predicted, nor can one say that the organization exists in order to control and apportion these assets because, once in existence, the organization will be used in a variety of ways, which will include the control and apportionment of assets but which are not otherwise determined.

In small-scale, delayed-return pastoral, agricultural and hunter-gatherer societies the binding commitments and dependencies are most often those of kinship and affinity: we may find lineages, clans and other kinship groups; marriages in which women are bestowed by men on other men; marriage alliances between groups. We may also or alternatively find other sorts of formal contractual bonds to which people are committed. In contrast, the social organization of societies with immediate-return systems has the following basic characteristics: social groupings are flexible and constantly changing in composition; individuals have a choice of whom they associate with in residence, in the food quest, in trade and exchange and in ritual contexts; people are not dependent on *specific* other people for access to basic requirements; relationships between people, whether relationships of kinship or other relationships, stress sharing and mutuality but do not involve long-term binding commitments of the sort that characterize delayed-return systems; distinctions — other than those between the sexes — of wealth, power and status are systematically eliminated.

This chapter is intended to contribute to discussion of whether immediate-return systems and the forms of social organization associated with them are to be treated, at least in part, as a product of pressure from outsiders. Of course, members of all hunter-gatherer societies (and indeed of all human societies) have been subjected to pressure of one sort or another from outsiders. Such pressures may include:

— attempts to kill or injure them or to coerce them using violence;
— attempts to classify them as inferiors and to treat them as such;
— attempts to seize or entice them (especially their women and children) to work as slaves, servants or clients;
— attempts to dispossess them of their land or the natural resources of their land;
— attempts to seize their artefacts or the wild resources they have harvested;
— attempts to divert them from working to meet their own needs into working to obtain furs, ivory, honey, meat or other goods required by outsiders;
— attempts to dominate them politically, to define them as subject to the political authorities of some wider entity with powers to control their hunting, to sedentarize them or to otherwise organize their lives;
— attempts to proselytize them and to incorporate them, often in subsidiary roles, into outsider religious and ritual systems.

Pressures of these and other sorts are not new and indeed some of them will have been applied even in the pre-agricultural period. But with the expansion of agriculture and of pastoralism over the world during the past few thousand years, and the expansion of long-distance trade over the past few hundred years, such pressures have, in general, multiplied and become much more intense. The problem, then, is to discern what effects different types and different intensities of pressure have on hunter-gatherer social organization.

Let us start with a correlation: hunter-gatherer immediate-return systems appear to be commonly associated with encapsulation by small-scale agricultural and pastoral neighbours while hunter-gatherers with delayed-return systems are apparently not often thus encapsulated or were not thus encapsulated when they first entered the historical record. Groups such as the !Kung Bushmen of Botswana and Namibia (Marshall 1976; Lee 1979), the Mbuti of Zaire (Turnbull 1965a; 1965b; 1983), the Hadza of Tanzania (Woodburn 1968a; 1968b; 1972; 1982a), the Malapantaram (Hill Pandaram) of South India (Morris 1977; 1982a), the Naiken of South India (Bird 1982; 1983a; 1983b), the Paliyan of South India (Gardner 1966; 1969; 1972) and the Batek Negritos of Malaysia (K. Endicott 1979; 1983; 1984; K.L. Endicott 1981) can all be said to be thus encapsulated and to have immediate-return organization. The many different Inuit (Eskimo) groups, the peoples of the northwest coast of North America, the Australian Aborigines in general, all (or almost all) appear to have had delayed-return organization by my definition at the time of the first descriptions of their social organization and were not thus encapsulated. An important instance of a society to which the correlation does not apply is that of the Okiek or Highland Dorobo of Kenya (Blackburn 1970; 1971; 1974; 1982; Kratz 1981). They were encapsulated and yet had delayed-return organization; their case will be among those examined later in this chapter.

A correlation of this sort can be no more than suggestive. To be more than this it would have to be properly checked against a wide range of instances. And if it were then found to be statistically significant, we would still have to show that the key factor is indeed encapsulation/non-encapsulation. There are several other possible factors: one is that all seven of the immediate-return instances I have cited are either in the tropics or, like the !Kung, not very far away from the tropics, and, unlike hunter-gatherers in more extreme latitudes, not subject to a really harsh season each year during which food is particularly difficult to obtain and good shelter and warm clothing are highly desirable. It is conceivable that this is a more relevant factor for the generation and maintenance of these systems, with harsh seasonality tending to stimulate the development of and the endurance of delayed-return systems.

Another problem should be mentioned at this stage. It should not be assumed that the pressures from outsiders on encapsulated groups are, or have historically been, necessarily more intense than pressures from outsiders on groups that are not encapsulated.

Encapsulated African hunter-gatherers and what their farmer neighbours think of them

But let us look more closely at African hunter-gatherers, and especially at a few East African instances, to see whether or not encapsulation is a plausible candidate as a generator or part-generator of immediate return.

In most sub-Saharan African countries there are, or were until recently, small groups (or subgroups) of people who either obtained their food largely by hunting and gathering or regarded themselves as descendants of people who had until recently obtained their food in this way. Such groups exist (or existed) in Mauritania, the Central African Republic, Gabon, Cameroon, Equatorial Guinea, Congo, Zaire, Ruanda, Burundi, Uganda, Kenya, Ethiopia, Somalia, Tanzania, Angola, Zambia, Namibia, Botswana and South Africa and probably also in several of the other sub-Saharan African countries I have not mentioned. The majority of these groups are separated from each other by the much more numerous, and vastly more populous, groups of agricultural and pastoral peoples who are, and have long been, not just numerically, but also politically, dominant.

They include: the many different equatorial forest groups who are referred to in the literature as Pygmies (or if they are on average more than 150 centimetres high as Pygmoids!) and whom their neighbours call by such names as Mbuti, Mbute, Aka, Twa, Tuwa, Tswa or Chwa; the savannah groups rather further south, many of whom again are called by some variant of the term Twa; the many groups in Kenya and Tanzania whose neighbours call them by the Maasai term Ndorobo or Dorobo; the many groups in Botswana, Namibia and Angola who in the literature are usually called Bushmen or San; and again many other groups like the Hadza of Tanzania or the Kwegu of Ethiopia to whom no generalized term is usually applied.

Virtually all African hunter-gatherer groups are partly or totally surrounded by, and have rather frequent contacts with, the neighbouring pastoral and/or agricultural groups who divide them off from other hunter-gatherers (of whom they may have heard or of whom they may be totally unaware). I use 'encapsulation' to refer to this whole or partial enclosure or enclavement. The units thus encapsulated are very variable in size and their contacts with their neighbours are very variable in frequency: they range from one or two households separated from other similar groups by intervening farmers with whom they have daily contacts up to 'tribes' of a thousand or more people who may have an area of a thousand or more square miles more or less to themselves and who have only intermittent contacts with their farmer neighbours. In these latter cases, which are now extremely rare, perhaps even non-existent, but of which there were several in Africa only a few years ago, the term 'encapsulation' with its overtones of circumscription may seem inappropriate to us and would perhaps seem strange to the people involved if its meaning were to be explained to them. It might conflict with their sense of open horizons and freedom from constraint. The reality is that farmer neighbours are in most directions unlikely to be more than a long day's walk away and contact with them, for all its variation, is likely to be significant and to be seen by the people themselves as important.

The type and intensity of the pressures applied by the encapsulating groups were in some respects similar throughout Africa and in other respects rather variable. Reading through the literature, I have been particularly struck by a similarity. The encapsulating groups did not merely assert their political dominance over the hunter-gatherers and ex-hunter-gatherers they encapsulated; they also treated them as inferiors, as people apart, stigmatized them and discriminated against them.[3] But at the same time they regarded them as possessing certain powers often linked with the notion that they were the original inhabitants of the country. The stereotypes that are held by the encapsulating groups are politically potent and colour the whole range of interactions between them and the hunter-gatherers they encapsulate.

These points are best discussed by referring to specific instances and I shall look in turn at three different East African cases: the Hadza of northern Tanzania, the Okiek (Highland Dorobo) of central Kenya and the Mbuti of Zaire.

The Eastern Hadza live in an area of around 1000 square miles of bush to the east of Lake Eyasi in northern Tanzania. These days a proportion of them live in government settlements but the number of residents in the settlements varies depending mainly on the availability of food and other goods which the government provides at any particular time. Most of the remainder live by hunting and gathering in nomadic bush camps although a few have taken up residence in the settlements of neighbouring farmers.

What is unusual about the Hadza situation is the variety of different neighbours they can contact if they choose. To the south are the Isanzu, sedentary Bantu-speaking agriculturalists. To the east and north-east are the Iraqw or Mbulu, sedentary Cushitic-speaking mixed farmers.[4] Within Hadza country and to the east and south-east are the Barabaig,

---

3. Modern African governments have tried, not always successfully, to counter such discrimination.

4. To the west, Lake Eyasi, uninhabited for most of the length of its shore, constitutes a natural barrier and the forested slopes of Ngorongoro mountain, also largely uninhabited at their base, form a barrier to the north.

who are nomadic pastoralists. Also within Hadza country are two substantial tribally mixed villages, Yaida and Mangola, which contain members of these three and many other groups. Interestingly the views all these various groups hold about the Hadza are rather similar; the same stereotypes constantly recur.

The view that is most often put even when Hadza are present is that the Hadza are not a 'real' ethnic group but are an aggregation of people who, recently or in the past, fled from neighbouring societies into the bush for a variety of reasons — to avoid famine, to avoid punishment for some crime or because they had been ostracized, to avoid paying the head tax levied by the colonial authorities on all groups in the area apart from the Hadza. Nowadays the idea that they are victims of colonialism, people who were forced out into the bush by the actions of the colonial authorities, has some currency.

Their click language is, I was once told by a neighbouring tribesman, not a real language but a cacophonous creole bastardized from neighbouring languages and using animal-like sounds. Loan words in Hadza, heard in Hadza conversations, were triumphantly produced as evidence that Hadza is not a language in its own right.

The Hadza are, or were, also sometimes treated as being themselves almost animal-like, partly perhaps because they live in the bush, an unacceptable place associated with animals. The daughter of one of my elderly Hadza friends had married an Iraqw farmer. This farmer, annoyed about something, came with farmer friends and gave his Hadza father-in-law a serious beating. I persuaded the Hadza to seek damages for his injuries in an Iraqw tribal court (this was in 1958 or 1959). At the court one of the Iraqw court elders said, to my astonishment, that Hadza were like baboons but if you married one you had to treat your wife's father properly. Some other Iraqw elders seemed very doubtful about whether a Hadza had any right, even in these circumstances, to claim against an Iraqw. Damages were, in the end, awarded but I know of no other case in which a Hadza managed to secure damages in an Iraqw court.

The fact that some of the foods the Hadza eat are regarded as disgusting and unacceptable as food to some or all of the neighbouring farmers is sometimes mentioned. Hyrax, baboon, vulture (eaten by some Hadza) and tortoise (eaten by Hadza women) fall into this category. More emphasis is placed on the claim that Hadza eat meat raw and that they are impolite and greedy in the way that they eat. In these and other respects they are seen as violating acceptable behaviour.

They are much criticized for their begging and their supposedly child-like lack of attention to wealth and property. They are seen as poverty-stricken and their poverty is often said to be their own fault. However, nowadays they are sometimes treated by government officials as victims rather than as improvident poor and as appropriate recipients for government development aid.

Another theme that constantly recurs is the notion that the Hadza are mysterious, that they have special knowledge of secret medicines (especially anti-snakebite medicine) and that they have extraordinary supernatural powers (in particular the power of making themselves invisible). The Hadza are relatively few in number and only rarely venture outside their own country so that many people living within a few miles of them have never actually seen them. There is much speculative talk about them.

Like many other ethnic stereotypes, this composite one that I have outlined is almost wholly false. The Hadza have a rather clear and distinctive ethnic identity and speak a language which is unrelated to neighbouring languages and is in no sense a creole. The five hundred detailed genealogies that I have compiled and the genetic studies carried out by a physical anthropologist, Nigel Barnicot, with whom I worked in the 1960s, demonstrate conclusively that immigration during the past hundred years — and probably for much longer than that — has occurred on a very small scale except during a period of a few years early this century when harsh actions by the German colonial authorities and a series of famines did briefly cause a number of Isanzu farmers to come to live in the bush by hunting and gathering. Most are said to have lived apart from the Hadza and soon returned to Isanzu. Some lived with the Hadza and a number of these, almost all men, married Hadza spouses. Many young Hadza today have one of these immigrants among their ancestors. Erich Obst, who in 1911 was the first European to make contact with the Hadza, met several of these immigrants (Obst 1912) and I met one or two survivors when I started my research in 1957. The number of more recent immigrants is very small indeed. Usually they only stay if they are of part-Hadza ancestry, for example the children of women who have married out. There is nothing to suggest that the proportion of immigrants is any higher than it usually is in Africa between adjacent farming communities. Even the hungry are reluctant to live for longer than is necessary with a mysterious and stigmatized group.

Though there are foods which the Hadza eat which their neighbours reject, there are also foods — notably milk — eaten by neighbours which the Hadza traditionally rejected. The Hadza may eat liver raw — as some of their neighbours do — but they do not, in general, eat other meat raw. The claim that their food use is disgusting is just as ethnocentric as such claims usually are.

The Hadza are not impoverished. They obtain their food with relative ease and famine is unknown. Surveys in which I participated in the 1960s demonstrated that malnutrition almost never occurs. They are poor only in the sense that they do not accumulate property — domestic animals, stores of food, stores of artefacts — of the sort that their neighbours do.

They trade on their reputation as mysterious people in their dealings with outsiders, and especially in their sales of herbal medicines. But, for the most part, they do not place much faith themselves in the medicines which they sell. They certainly do not believe that other Hadza can make themselves invisible!

Why then are these false stereotypes held? They express, first, the power situation. The Hadza are manifestly politically weak in relation to their neighbours. They have neither the numbers nor the organization to be able to assert themselves politically. Their relative political impotence labels them as inferiors. At the same time nomadic hunting and gathering as a way of life does offer so many patterned contrasts to the cherished values of successful farmers that it is readily represented as alien and unintelligible: for farmers it simply cannot be a 'real' coherent way of life at all and must be a bastardized form.

Now who would live an inferior, bastardized way of life? Two categories of people offer themselves in the amazing world of ethnic stereotype construction. Either people who are themselves perceived as intrinsically inferior, or else outcasts from other groups who have no choice in the matter. Some of the neighbours of the Hadza undoubtedly do think of them as intrinsically inferior but the preferred explanation of these neighbours is perhaps the more generous one — that they are outcasts or outlaws who are living as they do because other choices have been denied them and who are at least potentially capable of redeeming themselves and living as these farmers believe human beings ought to live. On the other hand, this latter stereotype is ungenerous in denying them priority as the first inhabitants of the area.

Neighbours, even those who have dealings with the Hadza, are quite extraordinarily ignorant about them and this is certainly in part related to the barriers to communication that are imposed by the social distance they create between themselves and the Hadza. Outsiders, sometimes even long-standing immigrants into Hadza society, do not learn to speak or to understand Hadza. They expect the Hadza to learn their languages. Nor do they usually take much trouble to find out about Hadza custom — that would be treating the Hadza too seriously. It is wholly consistent that in this vacuum they attribute mysterious, unintelligible supernatural powers to the Hadza.

What, then, are the Hadza's stereotypes of their neighbours? Mainly because they learn to speak their neighbours' languages, they have far more genuine knowledge of their neighbours, than their neighbours do of the Hadza. Stereotypes exist, of course, but not on quite the same scale. For present purposes the stereotype that matters is the strong belief that their neighbours, and especially the Isanzu, are extremely dangerous witches who use their supposed powers to kill Hadza by witchcraft if they can, and especially any Hadza who settle near them.

And Hadza who do settle near the Isanzu and survive are often believed by other Hadza to have survived because they have acquired witchcraft from the Isanzu and become witches themselves. Such settled Hadza are then themselves likely to be treated, at least in some contexts, as dangerous outsiders.

Recent accounts of the Okiek, hunters and gatherers of the Mau forests of Kenya, show that they too are stigmatized as fundamentally inferior by many of their neighbours. They too are regarded as monkey-like and there is even a widespread belief that they have tails. They too are falsely accused of eating their meat raw (Blackburn 1970; 1971; 1974; 1982; Kratz 1981: 358). Their immediate neighbours include the pastoral Maasai. In a version of the Maasai origin myth cited by Blackburn (1982: 297), an Okiot man annoyed God by his profligate behaviour and as a result no more cattle were lowered from heaven. This denied Maasai more cattle. At the same time God condemned the Okiek to live from then onwards only from wild rather than domestic animals. Both the Okiek way of life and the Maasai shortage of cattle are thus represented as imposed by God as a punishment for Okiek misbehaviour. Even today the Maasai regard the Okiek as profligate and gluttonous because they often obtain cattle for slaughter and immediate consumption rather than to build up a herd. Their relative lack of cattle indicates, the Maasai believe, their poverty and their improvidence, their lack of ability to develop and care for possessions. Their consumption of game meat and of the meat of cattle that die of disease further condemns them. At the same time they are said to have no sense of respect or of honour and to lose their tempers and become violent among themselves in a shameful way. Like the Hadza in relation to their neighbours, the Okiek lack political power in their relations with the Maasai. Their perceived impotence is again translated into inferiority and in this case the inferiority is made additionally humiliating by being represented as a consequence of their own failings, their ancestral and present-day profligacy.

Blackburn labels as a gross misconception the notion put forward by unspecified outsiders that the Okiek are merely a conglomeration of criminals and runaways from other tribes (1971: 144), a similar stereotype to the one applied to the Hadza which I have discussed and sought to explain above. No doubt some similar explanation would be appropriate here.

The Maasai are not well informed about the Okiek. Blackburn tells us that Okiek life is a mystery to them and that they feel there is something mysterious and unknowable about the Okiek (ibid.: 141). Again there are obvious parallels with the stereotypes applied to the Hadza and similar explanations may be relevant.

These two East African instances should serve as a cautionary tale to suggest that we should be extremely careful before we believe outsiders' views about stigmatized groups. Much recent writing has, I believe, fallen into the trap of doing just that, with the result that misunderstandings have arisen about who East African encapsulated hunters and gatherers really are. What we need, of course, is more field research among the hunters and gatherers themselves to clarify the situation. It will in due course become clearer how typical these two instances are.

In the published literature on East African hunter-gatherers the term 'Dorobo' constantly appears. The term is used by the pastoral Maasai, and by writers who obtained their information from the Maasai and other people in the same area, for the very wide range of different hunters with whom they had contacts. It covers both those Maasai who have temporarily lost their cattle and who are forced to live by hunting until they can accumulate more, and hunting and gathering groups like the Okiek (and even occasionally the Hadza, though the Maasai today have scarcely any contact with them) who have distinctive cultures and languages, who have long occupied particular areas and who have apparently accepted relatively few in-marrying or other immigrants whether these immigrants are impoverished pastoralists or not. There has been a spate of recent articles suggesting that the Dorobo *in general* are best treated as impoverished pastoralists living only temporarily as hunter-gatherers until they can acquire stock (for example van Zwanenberg 1976). While undoubtedly there are some Dorobo of this sort (see, for example, P. Spencer 1973), we must beware of generalizing from these instances and taking the highly prejudiced ethnic stereotypes of the Maasai and other peoples at their face value when they deny cultural integrity to societies they despise and fail to understand. My own guess is that, in spite of their political weakness, indeed perhaps partly because of it and the stigmatization associated with it, most East African hunter-gatherer groups display at least as much stability and continuity of ethnic self-identification as do East African agricultural and pastoral societies. As Kratz (1981) points out, clear ethnic self-identification is for the Okiek combined with an ability to pass comfortably between cultures, to speak in the languages and interact in the cultures of their neighbours as well as in their own. The Hadza, too, have this skill and I would expect it to be widespread among low-status groups. This may be confusing for higher-status groups (and sometimes for anthropologists) but it must not be taken as an indication that such hunter-gatherers do not have a culture of their own.

The Mbuti, too, are stigmatized by their villager neighbours, as both Turnbull's material and some interesting new material presented by Wæhle at a conference I attended in Cologne in January 1985, reveal.[5]

<hr>

5. I am most grateful to Espen Wæhle for giving me permission to refer to this important material from an unpublished paper. A revised version of his paper is being published in

We are told that the Mbuti are labelled by villagers as savages, even sub-human (as being like chimpanzees or forest hogs), as associated with the uncivilised forest, as unreliable and as ignorant (Wæhle 1986). Here the emphasis appears to be on intrinsic inferiority rather than inferiority as outcasts — which is, I suppose, what one might expect given the striking physical differences between Mbuti and villager which the villagers' stereotype can hardly ignore. Yet at the same time their forest skills are recognized and they are said to have originally taught villagers how to live in the forest. Turnbull (1965b: 162) tells us that the Mbuti are recognized as the original inhabitants of the forest and are 'to a certain extent, feared and respected as such by the villager'.

Maquet (1961: 10) tells us that the Twa of Ruanda are said, half-jokingly, by most other Ruanda, to be more akin to monkeys than to human beings. The socially emphasized physical stereotype for a Twa is, he tells us, one that 'stressed all the features which could be interpreted as ape-like' — bulging forehead, flat face and nose, and so on (ibid.: 146). Only the Twa eat game meat, which is another reason why they are despised by the rest of the population (ibid.: 14). Twa are regarded as naturally gluttonous and lacking in restraint, but as loyal to their masters and courageous in hunting.

One could go on and on. Rather similar stereotypes are, or were in the past, applied by agricultural and pastoralist neighbours to San in southern Africa and, I think, more generally to hunter-gatherers all over sub-Saharan Africa.

Political relations between encapsulated hunter-gatherers and their farmer neighbours

The political context in which these stereotypes flourish is one in which numbers of people in hunter-gatherer groups are usually (but not always) so small that in spite of their formidable weapons they can be treated as politically impotent, as conquered or conquerable. Typically we find that they are, or were, treated as not having an entitlement to equal legal status with other people and as being either excluded as marriage partners or, at best, as only being acceptable when the husband is the farmer and the wife the hunter-gatherer. Hunter-gatherer women are often taken only as concubines or secondary wives or as the first wives of particularly low-status farmers.

As everywhere else in the world, the combination of stereotyped

the journal *Sprache und Geschichte in Afrika*, vol. 7, pt. 2, 1986. At the time of writing the journal has not yet reached libraries in England and I am therefore unable to adapt the page numbers to refer to the published version.

inferiority and of political impotence is potentially very dangerous, even lethal, for those so characterized, especially in times of political turmoil. The power exerted by the dominant groups has differed from place to place and from time to time but has always been a potential hazard. Schapera (1956: 128–9) described what happened when the Western Tswana tribes — pastoralists and agriculturalists — entered Bechuanaland from the Transvaal in the first half of the eighteenth century:

They found the country occupied by many small and scattered groups of Bushmen [hunter-gatherers], Kgalagadi, Tswapong, Yeei, and other peoples [mostly farmers], whom in some instances they fought and conquered, but who as a rule submitted to them without resistance. . . . The inhabitants of each district became the serfs (*malata*) of the local overseer. He made them herd his cattle and cultivate his fields, and usually also brought some of them into the capital to do the menial work in his home. In addition, he could appropriate whatever property they acquired. This referred especially to such hunting spoils as ivory, ostrich feathers, and the skins of wild animals, all of which he claimed for himself, leaving them only the meat. . . . Serfs remained permanently attached to the family of their master, and after his death were inherited by his children. They were apparently seldom, if ever, bought or sold, though their master could give or lend them to other men, and they often formed part of a daughter's dowry; but they themselves were not free to seek work with anybody else or to move away from their district. If oppressed, as they often were, they had no access to the tribal courts, and should they run away they might be followed up and brought back by force. They lacked many other civic rights, including participation in political assemblies, and were not admitted into membership of age-regiments, nor were they allowed to possess live-stock of their own . . . some, especially the Bushmen, are still considered inferior to other members of the tribe, who deem it degrading, for instance, to intermarry with them.

[Schapera then quotes the following passage from Mackenzie 1871: 132f.] 'The contest for the possession of certain villages of Bakalahari [Kgalagadi] or Bushmen, is a fruitful source of strife in Bechuana towns. The vassals with all their belongings are the subject of litigation and endless jealousies . . . . When rival chiefs fight for supremacy in the same tribe, the condition of the harmless vassals is wretched in the extreme. They are then scattered and peeled, driven hither and thither, and mercilessly killed, as the jealousy, caprice, or revenge of their masters may dictate. It is quite fair in such a struggle to kill all the vassals, as it would be to lift the cattle, of him who cannot be displaced from his chieftainship. And so with the varying fortunes of a "civil war", the vassals might be attacked by both parties in turn. Again, when one Bechuana tribe attacks another, the Bushmen and Bakalahari belonging to both are placed in the same category with cattle and sheep — they are to be "lifted" or killed as opportunity offers. In such cases, therefore, all Bakalahari and Bushmen flee into wastes and inaccessible forests, and hide themselves until the commotion is past.'

Schapera goes on to say that the Tswana discriminated against defeated peoples according to a scale of ethnic and cultural differences between themselves and the conquered. There was seldom any marked discrimination against conquered or immigrant peoples of the same stock as themselves. 'It is only if subject peoples differ obviously in language, culture or race from their new rulers that they tend to be exploited, and this applies even if they were not conquered but came as immigrants' (1956: 132).

Where, as in this instance, there is traditional state organization, seizure of whole communities and their land often occurs, and domination over and stigmatization of people defined as alien — of whom hunter-gatherers are almost the prototype — can be particularly severe. In Ruanda and Burundi, the Twa suffered many civil disabilities: in Burundi, even now when most Twa hunting lands have been cleared for farming by non-Twa farmers, they are apparently in practice not entitled to hold agricultural land. They are said not to be able to set foot in the houses of other people and commensality is said to be out of the question. In the past they did have special privileges and duties at the king's court. Schebesta (1936: 190) tells us that they had the sole right of acting as bearers of the king's sedan chair, that they served as constables at the court and as executioners (ibid.: 200). These privileges were seen as linked with the legend that in remote times the Batwa had helped the ancestors of the king to conquer the country and had stood by them in time of peril (ibid.: 191). Similarly, we find an apparent combination of discrimination and privilege in Kafa, one of the southern Ethiopian kingdoms where the Manjo, who were hunters living mainly by hunting monkeys taken in traps but who were said to eat any animal, had the privilege of guarding the royal enclosures and gates of the country (under Kafa commanders) and of fetching wood and water for the king. It was also their obligation to bury Kafa dead (Huntingford 1955: 136). No doubt their privileges can be explained in much the same way as the common use of slaves in other kingdoms with similar roles: belonging to an alien and politically impotent group, they were not competitors for political offices. Since their privileges depended on the king alone, their loyalty would be particularly great. But unlike slaves, their identification as first inhabitants of the country and their willingness to serve the king in this capacity helped to legitimize his right to rule.

Hunters and gatherers in the neighbourhood of traditionally acephalous societies or of petty chiefdoms are obviously unable to benefit from association with royalty but are perhaps less liable to be seized *en masse* with their lands. They are, however, very likely to be raided, and this was especially so in the struggle for ivory and slaves which spread all over Africa and which in East Africa became particularly acute in the nineteenth century. The Mbuti and the Hadza both suffered at this

time. Erich Obst, the German geographer who contacted the Eastern
Hadza in 1911, recorded what he then discovered of their history:

> They told me that as far back as can be remembered . . . they had had to
> wage constant bloody feuds with their neighbours, especially with the Wais-
> sansu [Isanzu] and the Wamburu [Mbulu, Iraqw]. Their strength was already
> shattered by this when the Massai [Maasai] broke in from the north east. . . . .
> Under their leaders, Boiyóge and Wassaráguaiu, they made repeated attempts
> to defend themselves against the tiresome intruders, but finally had to yield to
> their superior power. . . . [They] chose as a place of refuge the rocky heights
> between the Hohenlohe [Yaida] and Wembäre [Eyasi] valleys and now carried
> on a pitiful existence here in hordes of from one to three families. . . . Even
> after the flight from the Massai the Wakindiga [Hadza] were not fated to enjoy
> peace and quiet. So long as there were still herds of elephants in the Wembäre
> and Hohenlohe valleys the coming and going of the foreign peoples con-
> tinued. And while the Wassukuma [Sukuma] came only in small troupes, on
> account of the greater distance from their home, traded with the Wakindiga
> and obtained permission to hunt by handing over old iron hoes, knives, beads
> and by leaving meat to the Wakindiga, the Waissansu, on the other hand,
> always came prepared for war, feuded incessantly with the Wakindiga and
> seized women and children whenever they could lay hands on them. Only
> after the last decades, in which the elephants became rarer and rarer did the
> fights with the Waissansu cease. Silent trading[6] led to an exchange of the
> natural and cultural riches of the two peoples and to . . . peaceful invasion by
> the Waissansu[7] (Obst 1912: 17–18; I have inserted uninflected current spellings
> and names in square brackets).

In their accounts of the dramatic past, Hadza are, like most of us,
inclined to exaggerate and I have certain doubts about whether the
scale of raiding was necessarily as continuously severe as this report
suggests. Raids spread over much space and time may have been
coalesced. The high rocky area to which the Hadza are reported to have
fled is a central part of their country, rich in wild foods, and is likely to
have been so even then. Obst visited their country in the dry season
and may not have been aware that camps of from one to three families
are entirely normal in the wet season and even in the dry season would
not imply social collapse. Their country is large enough, and offers
enough good cover, for concealment to be practicable over long periods
from all apart from other Hadza. If trapped, Hadza proficiency with
their formidable bows and poisoned arrows (Woodburn 1970) — much
better weapons than the bows and arrows and spears of their neighbours, in most contexts better even against people than the muzzle-
loading rifles which may have been used by some outsiders to kill

6. In a paper that is currently in preparation I discuss at some length the question of silent
trading between hunter-gatherers and their agricultural neighbours.
7. The peaceful invasion by the Isanzu that Obst refers to here is the period of Isanzu
immigration mentioned earlier in this chapter.

elephants — means that they will have been able to kill as well as be killed. All the same, the evidence that I gathered in the late 1950s clearly supports the view that the Hadza were indeed under considerable military pressure from neighbours in the nineteenth century though there is no way of knowing how long this pressure lasted.

Their country was (and even today is) a frontier zone between a number of culturally and linguistically distinct peoples who have never in the known history of the past hundred years lived entirely at peace with one another. As I have described earlier (Woodburn 1979: 249), Hadza men always travelled armed with their powerful bows and arrows and outsider tribesmen hardly ever ventured into Hadza country unless they were armed with bow, spear or firearm. Occasional murders occurred, both of Hadza and of others, most commonly carried out by marauding groups of pastoral Barabaig, and these were generally not reported to the government authorities. The availability of game animals attracted outsider hunters of all types, some with legal rights to hunt and others without, some threatening to the Hadza and others not. The essential point is that the consequences of encounters with outsiders were unpredictable and potentially dangerous as they commonly are in frontier situations elsewhere where armed individuals and groups from quite different cultural backgrounds, and sometimes with no language in common, encounter each other from time to time.

Central Kenya, the area in which the Okiek live, has a long history of warfare and raiding. Blackburn tells how the Okiek survived the waves of pastoral invasions which decimated, scattered or assimilated other peoples in the area. The Okiek survived because they lived in the highland forests, areas of no interest for grazing and ideal as places in which to hide; because they kept no cattle or other stock to attract raids; and because they were useful as providers of valued honey. Nowadays, Maasai warriors sometimes act aggressively towards Okiek individuals or small groups whom they happen to meet when travelling. The Okiek, aware of their numerical weakness, tend not to retaliate for fear of attracting retribution (Blackburn 1982: 293–6).

From Wæhle's account (1986) it is clear that the Ituri forest was also wracked with warfare in the nineteenth century. Villages were surrounded by palisades and a woman fetching water would need two armed men to accompany her. Slave and ivory raiders were feared. Different groups of villagers were at war with each other and Efe Mbuti acted as guerrillas for their villagers. Strangers risked being shot at or killed. The Mbuti are depicted as having been particularly afraid and ready to fight. Fear of cannibal villagers (particularly the Mangbetu) is mentioned. Silent trade between the Mbuti and the Mangbetu may be explained by such fear and general suspicion. Stories also tell of strained relations between the Mbuti and villagers, and that villagers used commonly to beat their Mbuti. Turnbull, who mainly worked further south in the Ituri, tells of the years of warfare that accompanied the arrival of Arabs in search of ivory and slaves and the expeditions of Stanley through the area. But he says: 'Stanley's brutal expeditions had little impact on the Mbuti, except perhaps to warn them, as it warned others, what they might expect from other Europeans. Even slavery only touched them in so far as they were encouraged to kill elephants in order to provide the Arabs with ivory' (Turnbull 1983: 22). He also mentions the introduction of a new technique for elephant hunting — heel-slashing — which was introduced at this time, presumably stimulated by the demand for ivory.

Throughout Africa (and in much of the rest of the world) it seems to be the case that hunter-gatherers as a stigmatized minority are vulnerable to persecution, insecure in their holding of land and unable to prevent encroachment by their farmer neighbours, and, even when closely involved with their neighbours, unable by themselves to mobilize legal procedures to secure justice in their dealings with them. In this situation two alternative means of handling relationships between the hunter-gatherers and the farmer neighbours may arise (as well as intermediate forms). The hunter-gatherers may, voluntarily or involuntarily, enter into a form of alliance, based on individual patron–client ties, with their neighbours. If they do, the best that they can hope for politically is that the relationship will become a paternalistic one with the patron requiring some deference but accepting some fatherly responsibility for his client — to protect him and his assets, to represent him in legal contexts and more generally in his dealings with other outsiders. But this does reciprocally imply, if the relationship is to persist, an acceptance by the hunter-gatherer of domination, or at least of some control. There is an implication from the patron's point of view — though not necessarily from the client's — that the client's role is essentially a demeaning and servile one.

If, on the other hand, the hunter-gatherers avoid alliances (as the Hadza normally do) and seek to channel their dealings with outsiders largely through ephemeral relationships, then they do not have to do more than to play at deference and certainly do not have to accept the possibility of control over themselves and their labour. But without protectors in the outsider community they are very vulnerable if, for any reason, they lose their land or other assets and, in particular, if they lose their means of subsistence and are no longer able to provide for themselves. They are also very vulnerable to violence and to more general persecution.

From all this I think we can see that in sub-Saharan Africa there appears to be a widespread kind of ready-made discriminatory slot into which farmers seek to fit any hunter-gatherers who happen to be in the locality. But so long as they retain sufficient bush or forest in which to hunt and gather and, when necessary, in which to conceal themselves, hunter-gatherers commonly do not themselves accept subordinate status, and indeed often can be seen to succeed in partially negating the discrimination practised against them. Where they are in real difficulty is where they have lost their land, or the populations of wild plants and animals have become depleted, or where for some other reason they have become unable or unwilling to continue to live by nomadic hunting and gathering and have become sedentarized in situations in which they are controllable and exploitable (see de Carolis 1977; Wæhle 1986).[8] In such situations discrimination actually appears to increase.[9] For groups with an immediate-return system, it is particularly difficult to develop effective agriculture (Lee 1979: 409–14; Woodburn 1982a: 447) and their low status and relative propertylessness in the eyes of their neighbours mark them out, once they have become controlled, as suitable for menial labour and also prostitution in those cases in which their status is not so low that sexual contact is seen as polluting.

I have suggested that the stigmatization of hunter-gatherer groups is related in part to their political impotence and the ease with which they can be classed as alien. If this is correct, such stigmatization will not have existed to the extent that it does today during the period of pioneer agricultural and pastoral expansion into areas previously occupied by hunter-gatherers.

Language history may give us some clue to this: the Hadza language is today despised by speakers of neighbouring languages, and borrowings of Hadza vocabulary in the languages of their neighbours are virtually non-existent. Of course, linguistic history is full of cases of borrowings from groups that were in some way low status. But I would have thought that such borrowings would occur only if the gap in status is not too great, if the numbers of people in the low-status group are relatively high and if they have closer day-to-day associations with higher-status groups than the Hadza have had in their recent history. If the extensive Khoisan phonological and vocabulary borrowings in Southern Bantu languages came, in whole or in part, from languages which at the time of the borrowings were spoken by hunter-gatherers, and if Southern Bantu languages were then spoken by pastoral or agricultural peoples, this suggests to me that the then relationship

8. Helga Vierich gives a highly relevant illustration of this for the San or Basarwa of Botswana: 'On the whole, it seemed that the more dependent a family is on livestock and agricultural products, the less likely they are to actually own livestock or plant their own fields. It is a startling fact that among Basarwa of the remotest parts of the central Kalahari a greater proportion of families own livestock than do Basarwa who live on cattleposts, yet the latter are far more dependent on pastoralism for subsistence' (1982: 217).

9. There is an analogy here with the South Indian material. Discrimination appears to be much greater in relation to sedentarized ex-hunter-gatherers assimilated into the caste framework than it is to nomadic hunter-gatherers in the forest.

between hunter-gatherers and farmers might have been very different from the instances that we know in Africa today. Perhaps one could speculate wildly and suggest the possibility that pioneer farmers, bringing with them a variety of new technologies, some of which had important military implications, may have themselves been kept under control and excluded from political power by then dominant hunter-gatherers applying the type of discrimination that is today applied in the reverse direction. There is a possible analogy in the severe discrimination that is applied in so many parts of Africa by agricultural and pastoral peoples to blacksmiths who possess a crucial technology and yet are ostracized and excluded from all political power by members of many of the societies among whom they live.

Economic relations between encapsulated African hunter-gatherers and their farmer neighbours

I want now to examine some of the transactions of goods and services that take place between farmers and hunter-gatherers, at the relationships within which these transactions occur and at the yields for each party. Obviously we need to know whether the goods or labour transacted are substantial or relatively minor in comparison with goods and services transacted within each group. We also need to know whether they are indispensable to one or both parties. And are the transactions balanced in some way, with the parties able freely to negotiate yields, or are they controlled either ideologically, so that the goods and labour of the hunter-gatherers are devalued, or politically, so that the goods and labour provided by the hunter-gatherers are coerced rather than voluntarily delivered in exchange for things of equal value? It would seem likely that the stigmatization of hunter-gatherers would affect (and be affected by) the nature of exchanges with their farmer neighbours, and that these exchanges would be quantitatively and qualitatively different from the trading and bartering that typically occurs between members of adjacent farming societies, especially those occupying different ecological zones. We need to know whether a consistent pattern emerges which has implications for the system of social relationships and social groupings within the hunter-gatherer society.

Two aspects need particular attention. First, is a significant amount of people's time and energy devoted to production for exchange rather than production for use and, if so, does production for exchange operate within a framework of social relationships and social groups that is significantly different from the framework appropriate for production for use? Second, does the distribution of goods and services received from farmers affect the hunter-gatherers' social relatonships and social groupings?

It is now time to look at some more Hadza data. The Hadza obtain tobacco, hemp, metal for arrowheads, knives, axes, gourds, beads, pieces of cloth, old clothing, cooking pots, some flour and various other minor goods from their neighbours. This long list might suggest that they are heavily dependent on their neighbours and that they organize their productive activities so as to supply their neighbours with goods in exchange. It might even suggest that the neighbours are able to bind the Hadza to them by Hadza demand for these goods and that they are able to direct Hadza labour for profit. Nothing could be further from the truth. Apart from the occasional person who works as a herd boy or lends a hand with the harvest for some neighbouring farmer in return for food and for a few presents from time to time, the Hadza do not normally work for their neighbours nor are they normally commissioned to hunt meat or gather honey and other bush products for them. Hadza take trouble to avoid commitments to outsiders or to other Hadza.

How then do they obtain their wants? The methods they use depend heavily on the very large number of neighbours and the very small number of Hadza. Most of the objects they seek are of relatively little value. A handful of tobacco or a piece of broken hoe to make arrowheads can easily be obtained by begging. Some of the other items — particularly cloth or an axe — may be more difficult to come by. What the Hadza do is to seek out such objects opportunistically, searching for them among their numerous neighbours much as they search for game or honey in the bush. They trade on their exoticism much as Gypsies do in begging for scrap iron or selling lace in Europe, though they spend far less time in dealings with outsiders than Gypsies do. They may make extravagant offers of reciprocal gifts of meat and honey which are rarely delivered. They at times make such a nuisance of themselves that the neighbour in the end gives way and hands over whatever it is that is being sought without recompense. The Hadza, recognizing that they are stigmatized and realizing that nothing that they do is likely to gain them much respect, are not much interested in maintaining face and respectability. Items received are treated casually and are usually not husbanded or stored. The Hadza spend some time begging from each other for trade goods as well as begging from outsiders.

Some bush products are bartered or sold to outsiders — honey, zebra tails (used for making ornaments), zebra fat (used as a medicine), hartebeest and wildebeest hides, herbal medicines and a small amount of game meat. They make no craft goods for trade nor do they devote significant amounts of labour to processing the goods they trade. Most meat obtained is consumed by Hadza rather than traded. Honey is more valuable as a trade good than meat but even in this case probably more is eaten than is traded. It is particularly important as a food for small children. Usually honey is sold for cash or bartered directly for cloth but no great trouble is taken to get a good price. Hadza often boast about how much money they are going to get and then settle for a mere fraction of the sum they have specified.

The 'unseemly' way that the Hadza beg, break their promises and usually barter their goods for an immediate yield rather than giving them as gifts, confirms their low status in the eyes of their neighbours but it avoids the claims, debts, binding commitments and orientation to the future (rather than the present) which the Hadza find unacceptable both in their dealings with other Hadza and with neighbouring farmers. I think it is misleading to describe the relationship with neighbours as one of interdependence or dependence. The Hadza do depend on obtaining certain goods from neighbours from time to time though not with any great regularity but neither individuals nor groups enter into specific relationships on which they depend.

There is nothing to suggest that Hadza enter or ever entered into patron–client relations with their neighbours though some individual Hadza do establish friendly ties with individual outsiders. The evidence strongly suggests that there is and was in the known past no significant pressure on them to exploit the area for the benefit of outsiders or, if there ever was such pressure, that they resisted it. The most striking aspect of this is the fact that Hadza do not hunt elephant which were until the 1970s abundant in their country[10] and which they eat with enthusiasm if one is found dead or is killed by someone else. Hadza hunt individually, and what they say is that they do not hunt elephant because their arrow poison is insufficiently strong to kill elephant. But it is strong enough to kill rhinoceros or buffalo and there can be little doubt that three or four arrows or one poisoned spear, if they were to use poisoned spears, would kill an elephant. My view is that there was no substantial obstacle of technology or skill to the development of elephant hunting. The demand for ivory has for at least the past 150 years, and probably much longer, always been strong in this and other parts of East Africa. It would be possible to argue that the Hadza do not and did not hunt elephant because such hunting has been illegal for bow-and-arrow hunters since the imposition of colonial rule or soon afterwards. But this is, I think, implausible. There were always Hadza willing to break colonial game laws and it is unlikely that the Hadza would have even heard of colonial game laws until after their first encounter with a European, Erich Obst, in 1911, a period well within the memory of many of my informants when I started my research. The true reason for the failure to trade in ivory is, I think, quite simply that the Hadza were not sufficiently interested in devel-

10. Apparently elephants became rare for a while at the end of the last century (Obst 1912: 17–18, quoted earlier).

oping their trade ties with their neighbours. To hunt elephant would have required a degree of coordination and of planning that would have been difficult in an immediate-return economy and the yield in meat for consumption and in ivory for trade was not a sufficient inducement. The Hadza seem to have been content with the role of acting as guides and trackers for occasional outsiders with firearms who have come to hunt elephant in Hadza country; their main reward has been the meat of any elephant killed.

There are innumerable other instances of trading possibilities which are not exploited. In recent years itinerant outsiders have often come to Hadza country to catch Fischer's lovebirds and other birds for the European market. The birds are taken by the simplest of techniques, the use of birdlime near water. Other outsiders have come to make charcoal for sale, again using techniques which are entirely straightforward. But Hadza do not seem interested in participating in such trade in their own right: all they do is occasionally act as casual helpers.

When I described this situation at a recent symposium, one critic suggested that the Hadza were in an even worse position than many other African hunter-gatherers: their neighbours would not even let them enter into stable relationships but forced them to go from place to place casually begging. My response to this is that all the indications are that the reluctance to enter into and to fulfil the commitments of stable relationships comes largely from the Hadza side and is entirely consistent with other aspects of their system. Stable relationships spell out domination and dependence to the Hadza and they avoid them. It seems to me thoroughly ethnocentric to presume that the Hadza should see stable relationships as desirable.

It is also important to be aware that the Hadza do not apparently covet the cattle of their neighbours. I know of no Hadza individual living in the bush, even in areas which are relatively free of tsetse, who has ever sought to acquire cattle. A few were given to Hadza in one of the government settlements but were not properly looked after. The Hadza usually reject milk and blood as foods and until the past few years the majority would not drink beer. They thus dissociate themselves from certain foods that are central for their pastoral and agricultural neighbours and, as with Jews and Gypsies in Europe in the past, their food usages limit the scale of commensality with potentially hostile outsiders and stress the sharing of food with members of their own group.

In the case of the Okiek, more goods are exchanged and more organization and time are devoted to obtaining goods which are to be traded. The Okiek trade large amounts of honey which is produced in beehives which they make and maintain. Hadza honey, in contrast, is all wild honey, obtained from the nests of wild bees in hollow trees and holes in the rocks, and the total harvest is very small in comparison.

Okiek honey is used by the Maasai as food and for making into wine which is necessary for ritual (just as it is among the Okiek). The honey is bartered directly with the Maasai, or is sold to shops which resell it to Maasai or others. Alternatively it may be given as a gift by an individual Okiot to an individual Maasai with whom he has established a freely-negotiated formal relationship of friendship. The Maasai may then give occasional gifts of meat in exchange. Friends linked in this way give each other other forms of assistance as well. They are acknowledged to have a commitment to each other and are usually additionally linked as members of the same age-set and often also as members of the same clan.

Many other items are or were given by the Okiek in trade including buffalo hide shields, ivory and buffalo horn tobacco containers, giraffe and wildebeest tail-hair fly-whisks, lion manes, ostrich feathers for head-dresses, colobus monkey skins for leg bands, kudu horn for a trumpet, rhino horn and ivory for a chief's club, eland hide for leather thongs, eland meat for food (in extreme necessity), ivory, animal hides, bows and arrows, sword sheaths and decorative skin necklaces (these latter two are made and traded in considerable numbers). The most important item received in exchange by Okiek is domestic stock which is not normally kept — it would be liable to be stolen by other Maasai — but is needed for ceremonies and is used as food for visitors. Milk is also obtained and so are cow hides for making sword sheaths and sleeping mats (Blackburn 1982: 298–300).

The Okiek also perform various services for the Maasai. They circumcise Maasai boys (and are given a heifer in payment) and sometimes help in slaughtering and cooking oxen in the bush or in herding cattle. These services are less important than the exchange of goods. Blackburn comments that in the Mau area the Maasai are more dependent on the Okiek than the Okiek are on the Maasai. The Maasai need honey but the Okiek do not need any Maasai product to the same extent. There are, however, other Maasai areas where there are no Okiek and the Maasai meet their needs in other ways. Blackburn tells us that it is totally unsatisfactory to talk of Okiek servitude and Maasai overlordship though the Maasai might see the relationship in these terms (1982: 299–302). The political domination by the Maasai does not give them control over the goods and services of the Okiek, who appear to be free to dispose of their goods and services as they choose either to Maasai or to other outsiders who do not seek to dominate them. Indeed the relative equality of the exchanges appears to stand in contrast to the political domination of the Maasai.

Interestingly the economic links of the Okiek with the Maasai are closely connected, in the Okiek communities which Blackburn studied, with Okiek commitment to Maasai culture and Maasai values. The Okiek dress like Maasai and indeed most people other than Okiek and

Maasai find it impossible to distinguish Okiek from Maasai as their appearance, ornamentation and dress are so similar. The Okiek age-set system is patterned on the Maasai one and domestic stock have to be obtained from the Maasai to carry out age-set and other ceremonies. The Okiek now share Maasai views about the desirability of accumulating stock and are apparently beginning to build up herds of their own (Blackburn 1982: 294).

Before we consider the Mbuti case let us examine very briefly some aspects of the social organization of the Hadza and the Okiek. There is a clear contrast in social organization between these two societies: the Hadza have an immediate-return system while the Okiek system is one of delayed return. The Hadza, both in their system of production and in the transactions which they carry out among themselves, seek to avoid investments, commitments and dependencies. This is directly matched in the transactions which they carry out with outsiders: unlike the Okiek they tend to avoid entering into formal friendship contracts with outsiders; they seek to beg the trade goods they want and to avoid any liability to reciprocation; they trade away their own goods casually on the spur of the moment without making any great effort to maximize the yield. They see many of the formalities and deferences associated with property transfers as ridiculous.

The Okiek, with their system of honey territories, of clans and lineages, of formal commitments between father and son and other pairs of kinsmen, have an organization which centres on the control and management of their honey assets but which can be and is used for other purposes. The elaborateness of the transactions between the Okiek and the Maasai — the range of items exchanged and the fact that some of them involve a substantial input of co-ordinated labour — all fit well with their delayed-return system. So also does the system of contractual friendship bonds in which the Okiek and the Maasai partners give gifts to each other of honey and of meat.

Earlier I discussed how stigmatized groups may respond to their vulnerability to domination and to persecution in one of two ways — either by dealing with outsiders only through ephemeral relations and thereby retaining control of themselves and their own labour or, alternatively, by entering into a relation of clientship with some outsider patron, to whom they will have to defer, but who may offer paternalist protection against other outsiders. From what I have said it will be clear that the Hadza exercise the first option. The Okiek do neither; they seem to be less politically vulnerable and manage to establish ties of alliance which are reasonably balanced, in which they and their outsider exchange partners exchange goods with each other which are important for both and without the Okiek having to take on the status of client. The Mbuti, however, are involved as clients in relationships with agricultural villager patrons. In the Efe Mbuti area where Wæhle worked, every Mbuti has a patron. But he can change from one patron to another (Wæhle 1986).

Basically the Mbuti provide meat, mushrooms, fish, honey, wild yams, nuts, building materials, plant fibres for mats, poisoned arrows and medicinal plants together with much agricultural labour. Villagers provide cultivated food, arrow-heads, knives, machetes, spears, cooking pots, tobacco, marijuana and salt — these last three items being particularly desired (ibid.). Both parties obviously value the transactions and derive real benefits from them. The labour provided by Mbuti clearly, however, puts them into a menial role *vis-à-vis* the villagers. Here much work and effort are devoted to production for exchange rather than production for use in the case of both Mbuti and villagers, but far more in the case of the Mbuti than the villagers. As the Mbuti are marked out as political inferiors, one would expect that this scale of exchange would provide leverage for economic exploitation and political domination.

But, in reality, such exploitation and domination do not seem to occur. Wæhle explains that the Mbuti have considerable room for manoeuvre over whom they exchange with and whom they work for. They are not tied to their patron alone. They often exchange with and work for a wide range of other people including small-scale growers of cash crops who have recently moved into the area (ibid.). The patron–client relationship is manifestly viewed differently by patrons and by clients. The patrons talk of 'their' Mbuti; they see the relationship as essentially a committed one and Wæhle comments that they never get rid of clients by asking them to leave (ibid.). The Mbuti, however, do not treat relationships with patrons as involving real commitment (ibid.): the labour and the forest products they provide are given spontaneously and casually rather than reliably or predictably. In the immediate pre-colonial period, Wæhle tells us, the villagers had more authority; the fighting in the area meant that the Mbuti needed the security of an enduring relationship, were therefore unable easily to change patrons and were willing to accept rather greater authority (ibid.).

Oversimplifying matters, I think one can argue that both the Mbuti and the villagers get enough out of the relationship for it to be possible for the villagers to accept a measure of Mbuti immediate-return unpredictability and for the Mbuti to accept a measure of villager delayed-return formal authority.

There are, I believe, grounds for arguing that in these three instances, unlike the nineteenth-century Bushman cases described by Schapera (1956) and Mackenzie (1871) (see above), serious exploitation of the politically dominated and stigmatized group does not occur. There is no evidence in these three instances for politically coerced extraction of goods and labour or for ideological devaluation of goods and labour. In both the Okiek and the Mbuti cases, production for exchange does take up a significant proportion of people's time but the social context in which this production occurs is, for the most part, not significantly different from the context of production for use.

Turnbull argues that, for the Mbuti he studied, so-called dependence 'is voluntary and temporary, the forest world remaining an ever-present, ever-accessible sanctuary of independence' (1965a: 37–8). This gives an important additional clue to the way not just the Mbuti, but also the Hadza and the Okiek, manage to transact without being manifestly exploited. They cannot be controlled. In all three cases, they can and do retreat into the forest or bush and live there incommunicado for long periods without having to obtain new supplies of trade goods.

Conclusions

Let us now return to the key issue. Are the interactions with neighbouring pastoralists and agriculturalists that I have described — the political domination, the discrimination, the violence, the range of economic transactions — likely to have affected the incidence of delayed-return and immediate-return systems among African hunter-gatherers?

I think there is a whole range of possible relevant factors but the historical evidence is far too fragmentary for us to be able to do more than speculate about their relative importance.

(1) Delayed-return hunter-gatherer systems are, in a sense, pre-adapted for the development of agriculture and pastoralism. They have the organization (the binding ties and the social groups) which should make the development of an economy based on agriculture or pastoralism easy when the techniques become available. Blackburn reports that the Okiek have in recent years taken up agriculture and the keeping of stock. I have myself seen, on a short visit with Corinne Kratz in 1985 to the area where she carried out field research, that their agriculture is now quite well developed.

People with immediate-return systems do not seem to have any difficulty with the technical aspects of agriculture and pastoralism but their ability to grow enough crops and keep enough animals to feed themselves effectively is seriously inhibited by their social organization and values — by their lack of binding ties needed for agricultural and pastoral cooperation, by their ownership rules and by their rules of sharing and other powerful levelling mechanisms (Lee 1979: 409–14; Woodburn 1982a: 447). This being so, people with immediate-return systems will tend to remain hunter-gatherers as long as they retain access to sufficient land and wild foods.[11]

Hunter-gatherers with delayed-return systems will tend to become farmers. Political pressures may well have given additional impetus to the transformation of delayed-return hunter-gatherers into farmers. If this is correct, it may help us to understand why the incidence of immediate-return systems is relatively high.

(2) In a world of hunter-gatherers, the interaction of adjacent societies with each other, particularly in ritual and ceremonial exchange, might tend to reinforce the ideological basis for delayed return. This would be particularly significant for systems like those of the Australian Aborigines in which the delayed-return element is based largely in men's ritual labour and the control of ritual assets and of assets in the form of rights held by men over women rather than in the mundane subsistence economy. Such systems might not easily survive long-term encapsulation and could become transformed into immediate-return systems. Sahlins has drawn attention to the fact that few hunter-gatherers apart from Australian Aborigines are now involved in elaborate ceremonial exchange cycles. Such systems may, he suggests, have disappeared elsewhere in the earliest stages of colonialism. I would add that they may have disappeared in some instances when hunter-gatherers became cut off from other similar societies and encapsulated by farmers. 'It is', Sahlins writes, 'as if the superstructure of these societies had been eroded, leaving only the bare subsistence rock, and since production itself is readily accomplished, the people have plenty of time to perch there and talk about it' (1974: 39). The argument here must not be exaggerated: the Hadza, !Kung and Mbuti all have quite an elaborate ritual life but they have immediate-return systems. But it seems possible that more elaborate ritual systems of the Australian type, on their own or in combination with ceremonial exchange, if they ever did exist in Africa, might not have survived long-term encapsulation. The effect of this would again be to reduce the proportion of delayed-return systems.

(3) Delayed-return systems could be threatened directly by loss of assets, or loss of control over assets, on which the delayed-return

11. In the modern world severe land loss is in some places making immediate-return hunting and gathering no longer viable as a means of meeting people's needs. As John Marshall and Claire Ritchie have so ably shown, some !Kung are now struggling to acquire cattle and to build kraals for them and in the process to 'overcome obstacles created by the culture of their hunting and gathering past, that are deep and real' (1984: 77). The transition from immediate return to delayed return is not easily accomplished.

system is based. At the beginning of this chapter I specified four sorts of assets which singly or in combination underlie delayed-return systems:

(a) *Valuable technical facilities used in production: boats, nets, artificial weirs, stockades, pit-traps, beehives and other such artefacts which are a product of considerable labour and from which a food yield is obtained gradually over a period of months or years.*

The Okiek, though militarily weak, have been successful over time in maintaining rights over their beehives but they have been helped by the difficulties of their forest terrain for outsiders. It does seem plausible to suggest that the military weakness of hunter-gatherers might have led to the occasional loss of technical facilities used in production in some other instances. The delayed-return system linked with the control and use of such facilities would only be threatened if the facilities could not be replaced.

We should also consider the possibility that contact with farmers might lead to the direct transfer from the farmers of skills that could be employed in the production of facilities, or alternatively contact with farmers — and, say, the possibilities of trade — might stimulate hunter-gatherers to themselves develop facilities and the delayed-return organization that would allow such facilities to be used effectively.

The hunting nets used by some Mbuti are not substantial enough assets in terms of the amount of labour needed to produce them to provide the basis for a delayed-return system, but it is interesting that these (or rather the skills to make them) are said to be borrowings from local farmers. If the skills for making nets can be transferred, so too could other skills that might be used to produce more valuable assets. This would obviously be particularly likely to happen in patron–client relationships. On the other hand, the sharing and the levelling mechanisms that are a fundamental part of immediate-return systems would tend to inhibit such a development.

It might be argued that the use of large numbers of beehives in honey production by the Okiek — and the binding ties, the lineages and the land rights associated with such use — are a product of relationships between the Okiek and the Maasai. Leacock and Lee (1982: 15) seem to be making such a case. I think it is based on a misunderstanding. Okiek honey is not, as they believe, to be treated as 'a "commodity" produced for exchange rather than use'. Blackburn (1971) tells us that its use *within* Okiek society is of central importance. Kratz (1981: 361) tells us that most honey is eaten as food or brewed into honey wine for home consumption or ceremonies but that many Okiek sell or trade a third of their honey crop. Both in quantitative terms and (apparently) in Okiek evaluation, the internal use of honey overrides its importance in exchange with outsiders. In this situation it seems reasonable in principle to argue that the social organization linked with honey production is more a product of internal use than of external exchange, though it is of course a product of both. Comparative research on the social organization of the many different Okiek groups scattered over the highland forests of Kenya and who have very different economies would be valuable in relation to this issue. It is, I think, plausible to argue that both honey production and trade on the scale which Blackburn and Kratz report, from the honey-rich highland forests down to the arid plains below, could well have occurred even when the plains were occupied by hunter-gatherers rather than pastoralists. It would be very difficult to mount a convincing argument that Okiek delayed return is a historical development deriving from their encapsulation.

(b) *Processed and stored food or materials usually in fixed dwellings.*
Loss of such assets would usually be far less serious than loss of productive assets because they could be more readily replaced.

(c) *Wild products which have themselves been improved or increased by human labour: wild herds which are culled selectively, wild food-producing plants which have been tended and so on.*
Loss of such assets could be serious. Obviously they would be lost if political pressure displaced people from the area over which they habitually hunted and gathered.

(d) *Assets in the form of rights held by men over their female kin who are then bestowed in marriage on other men.*
I have argued that the acquisition of such rights is particularly important for understanding the development of delayed-return systems ('The routes in the difficult transition from immediate to delayed return are likely to be many and varied but one broad highway among them lies, I think, in the intensification of control by men of rights over women who are to be given in marriage' [Woodburn 1980: 111]). Equally, I think there is a strong case for arguing that the loss of such rights is likely to be important in the transformation of delayed return into immediate return.

Encapsulation can affect this process directly if the encapsulating farmers themselves take control — or a measure of control, through providing or helping to provide bridewealth — of the marriages of the women of the hunter-gatherer group. This is, or was, the case among the Batua of Zaire (Michael Schultz: personal communication).

(4) Another possibility is that delayed-return systems might be threatened not by the loss of control over the assets on which they are focused but instead by breakdown of the committed relationships and the group structure of the delayed-return organization. Fragmentation caused by constant raiding or other political violence might over time have this effect. So might a system of exchange with outsiders in which vertical ties with outsiders displace horizontal ties with insiders.

(5) Yet another possibility is that a delayed-return system might be destroyed if the assets on which it is focused lose their value for the participants in the system. A system focused on the production of fish might be destroyed if people ceased for some reason to make much use of fish. Stigmatized hunters and gatherers run the risk that products that they value may be scorned by their politically dominant neighbours. Over time this may affect their patterns of production and consumption.

The historical data available to us, and indeed the historical data ever likely to be available, are insufficient to allow us to be able to tell how often in history these various processes have occurred. Nor can we tell why it is that the Mbuti and the Hadza and other specific groups now have immediate-return systems while the Okiek have a delayed-return system. But it does seem reasonable to maintain for sub-Saharan Africa my claim (Woodburn 1980: 112, and see above) that in a world consisting exclusively of hunters and gatherers, a higher proportion may have had delayed-return systems. Through history the number of hunter-gatherer groups in sub-Saharan Africa has been drastically reduced to a tiny fraction of their former number. The overwhelming majority of the hunter-gatherer groups of the past have adopted farming or have been assimilated in whole or in part by farming groups or have been exterminated. The various processes that I have discussed above are likely, singly or in combination, to have biased the rate of survival of immediate-return as compared with delayed-return systems; it is probable that a higher proportion of societies with immediate-return systems remain among surviving hunter-gatherer groups.

All this depends on two crucial propositions. The first is that African hunter-gatherers of today, or peoples who were until recently hunter-gatherers, are, for the most part, descendants of groups that have a long history of hunting and gathering. Their own claims, their own oral histories, strongly support such an assumption, and must be treated with more respect than the stigmatizing histories allocated to them by their farmer neighbours. Again, the fact that so many of them are genetically or linguistically distinctive and different from their farmer neighbours certainly renders implausible the suggestion that in general they are impoverished drop-outs forced by their poverty to hunt and gather. The data I have provided on their economic ties with their neighbours certainly do not favour the proposition that they are groups directed into hunting to provide the game meat or other bush requirements of neighbouring farmers, that their specialized hunting and gathering skills and way of life are a product of an intercultural division of labour. Only in the case of some forest groups is there evidence that substantial amounts of meat are transferred to farmer neighbours.

The second crucial proposition is that immediate-return systems have long existed and that they make sense in societies that are autonomous or near-autonomous. A counter-argument to this would be that autonomous hunter-gatherers have delayed-return systems, that encapsulation destroys most of them and that immediate-return systems are a historically recent product of such destruction. This argument is based on a serious misapprehension: immediate-return systems would not operate as they do if they were destroyed systems. They are not just former delayed-return systems without assets and without the committed relationships and social groups which are linked with such assets. All immediate-return systems have particularly demanding and elaborately sanctioned rules and values which are strongly focused on sharing, especially the sharing of the meat of large animals throughout the camp unit, and on morally valued egalitarian levelling mechanisms which actively restrict the development of property rights and of internal inequalities of wealth, rank and power (Woodburn 1982a). To treat such institutions as a product of breakdown simply does not make sense.

A more plausible alternative explanation for immediate-return systems might be that they are a combined product of breakdown of delayed-return systems and of opposition to outsiders, in other words destroyed systems of delayed return that have developed a new form of organization to oppose outsiders. Have their sharing and their egalitarian levelling mechanisms developed in opposition to domination by outsiders? Have we here a form of egalitarian oppositional solidarity of low-status groups, akin to the egalitarian solidarity manifest in some working-class or millenarian movements?[12] Is it egalitarian solidarity born of a fear that any hunter-gatherer with more power, wealth or status than another might be tempted to increase it and to exploit his fellows by allying himself with outsiders and that outsiders might be tempted to use such power holders to impose some form of

---

12. Egalitarianism as a moral ideology in hierarchical systems is, of course, not confined to low-status groups. Members of high-status groups may display egalitarianism within their groups and such egalitarianism, far from being a reaction to or a rejection of hierarchy in the wider system, may well provide a means by which the wider hierarchical system is maintained.

control, some form of indirect rule?[13]

Such an approach has obvious attractions. Oppositional solidarity may well have played some part in the perpetuation of immediate-return systems at particular points in their history when they were under great pressure. But I am sceptical about the idea that it constitutes an adequate general theory for their emergence or for their perpetuation through time when pressures from outsiders are not so severe. If delayed return is fundamental why does it not re-emerge when pressures ease? From the known history of immediate-return systems, I see little indication of such re-emergence. And again, if immediate return is a form of oppositional solidarity, why has it apparently not emerged in its characteristic form in Canada and Australia in response to the discriminatory and, at times, ruthless pressures on hunter-gatherers from outsiders in those countries?

The fundamental reason why I am sceptical about the idea of oppositional solidarity as a *general* explanation for the emergence and persistence of immediate-return systems is that a simpler theory in which explanatory priority is given to people's day-to-day dealings with fellow-members of their own society makes better sense to me than one which makes the structure of such dealings dependent on the less frequent and, for the people concerned, less important dealings with outsiders. Much of my own and other people's work in recent years in societies with immediate-return systems has demonstrated that their systems are internally coherent and viable, that they make sense politically and economically for their members and allow them to live reasonably rewarding and satisfying lives. These highly flexible systems, which lack the social groupings and binding social relationships familiar to earlier generations of anthropologists, can offer, as I have repeatedly witnessed, reasonable security, good health and nutrition and a greater amount of leisure than is available in most societies (Woodburn 1980: 106). It seems strange to suggest that people would wait to invent such systems until outsiders imposed pressures on them. I would expect that where economic circumstances are appropriate such systems would be repeatedly invented and reinvented historically in autonomous and near-autonomous hunter-gatherer societies as well as in hunter-gatherer societies with extensive dealings with politically dominant outsiders.

The reason why a theory of oppositional solidarity is attractive to us lies, I think, partly in an ethnocentrism to which we, as anthropologists, are not immune. The farmer neighbours — all delayed-return property-holders — of the Hadza, the Mbuti and the San feel uneasy

---

13. That such fears are not implausible is, I think, confirmed by some dramatic incidents I have described in which Hadza have made use of contacts with outsiders in their dealings with their fellow Hadza (Woodburn 1979: 261–4).

about the apparent propertylessness of the hunter-gatherers and see it as bizarre, as an indication that something is wrong with their system and that it requires special explanation. We may imagine that we, as trained anthropologists, are effectively inoculated against such ethnocentrism but, of course, deep cultural prejudice is not easily shed. There is a widespread and dangerous tendency among us anthropologists, property-holders all, to deny to low-status groups with little property the relative autonomy and integrity that we are more willing to concede to high-status groups with their, to us, more familiar and intelligible hierarchies and wealth.

The ethnocentric temptation is to treat the apparent propertylessness of people like the Hadza as comparable to the propertylessness of low-class groups in our own society — as a product of impoverishment. Certainly this must be considered as a possibility, but the issue must be judged on the evidence, and alternatives must be given adequate consideration. The valuable but much-misunderstood work of Sahlins on the so-called original affluent society (Sahlins 1974), and the work of the substantivists more generally, should surely have alerted us to the fact that it is not bizarre or even remarkable that people in some societies are not seeking to maximize their acquisition and control of property. Obst, writing more than seventy years ago, realized that the Hadza were not to be treated as impoverished: 'To be free from all the fettering luxury of sedentary peoples, to be able to wander around without having to take any homestead into consideration, that is the ideal of the Wakindiga [Hadza]' (Obst 1912: 5).

4. Free or doomed? Images of the Hadzabe hunters and gatherers of Tanzania

D. K. Ndagala

Introduction

The Hadzabe hunters and gatherers live in northern Tanzania around Lake Eyasi. Their territory is part of three administrative districts, each belonging to a different region. The districts are Mbulu in Arusha Region, Iramba in Singida Region and Maswa in Shinyanga Region. Until a few decades ago this area was regarded by many people as an 'inhospitable wilderness' (Bagshawe 1925). Though full of game it is heavily infested with tsetse fly and, generally, very short of drinkable water. Rainfall is very low and unpredictable, thus making the area marginal to agriculture. Roads are almost non-existent and the few car tracks available are impassable at some times of the year. For many years these features of Hadzabe territory have limited the influx of people from other societies, thereby keeping the hunters and gatherers in relative isolation from the rest of the nation.

Although fairly well known in academic circles, the Hadzabe are known to few Tanzanians apart from their agricultural neighbours, with whom they have had exchange relations for a long time. With a population of less than 3,000 in a country with about 20 million people the Hadzabe constitute an indigenous minority in Tanzania. The fact that they are still living by humankind's oldest subsistence strategy, hunting and gathering, makes some people, especially planners and policy-makers, regard them as archaic or primitive and as disgusting to the nation. Consequent policy measures have been discussed at length elsewhere (Ndagala 1985b). The purpose of this chapter is to examine the place and fate of these hunters and gatherers in Tanzania's nation state. I am of the opinion that this very much depends on how they are seen by the state institutions and other nationals. There are two images which tend to haunt any serious discussion on Hadzabe development. The first image presents the hunters and gatherers as a *free* self-sufficient people who need not be disturbed by the state. This image has mainly resulted from, and is supported by, anthropologists, who have 'invaded' Hadzabe territory following the pioneering anthropological work of the late 1950s. Comparing the size of the society and the number of researchers, the Hadzabe may be said to be over-researched relative to other societies in Tanzania (Ndagala and Waane 1982); the findings of most of these researches reproduce the image of a free and self-reliant people. The second image presents the Hadzabe as a *doomed* people, who should either be left to die out or be quickly saved from 'primitivity'. Let us look at these images individually and determine their weaknesses and strengths.

A free people

The Hadzabe remained relatively ungoverned throughout the colonial period because they were the only people who paid no taxes and had no 'chief' appointed to administer them. They still obtain their subsistence from the wild resources of their territory, through what Woodburn (1982a) calls the immediate-return system. Under this system people

> obtain a direct and immediate return from their labour. They go out hunting or gathering and eat the food obtained the same day or casually over the days that follow. Food is neither elaborately processed nor stored. They use relatively simple, portable, utilitarian, easily acquired, replaceable tools and weapons made with real skill but not involving a great deal of labour (ibid.: 432).

Moreover, their social organization allows them a high degree of mobility and flexibility. Anyone may live and gather wherever he or she likes without restriction. Individual freedom is not limited and is usually seen as something healthy and desirable in itself. In this way, individuals are able to avoid constraint by freely detaching themselves from others at a moment's notice without economic or other penalty (ibid.: 435).

The Hadzabe, due to their subsistence strategy and social organization, have been able to live free from famine and command a relatively higher nutritional status than many other East African societies (Jellife 1962; Woodburn 1979; Ndagala 1982). McDowell (1981a: 11) found that on the average the Hadzabe consumed 174.7 grams of meat protein per person per day, which is four times the minimum daily protein requirement. Remarkably, they are able to get all this and still enjoy three-quarters of their waking time in leisure activities (McDowell 1981a: 8). A good number of Hadzabe are known to work as labourers in a number of enterprises which are increasingly springing up. They are paid in cash or in kind. They work as labourers when the wild foods are relatively scarce or when the respective tasks for which they are employed are relatively easy to perform. For example, when the sweet potatoes are ripening in the fields of their agricultural neighbours they may come looking for casual employment — and be paid in potatoes. I would argue, then, that the Hadzabe's non-performance of various other activities is not necessarily out of ignorance, but because these activities have, to them, a relatively higher opportunity cost. The Hadzabe are not remnants of a past era struggling to survive in modern times (cf. Were and Wilson 1972: 6). They are a dynamic and happy people who are looking to the future with hope. All things being equal, it is correct to view them as a free self-sufficient people who are capable of adopting various innovations selectively. The question which has been asked by most researchers, albeit implicitly, is why should the state not leave these people alone?

A doomed people

By its very nature the state regards an individual useful if he or she contributes to its coffers, especially through the payment of tax. Individuals who produce no taxable surplus are regarded as useless unless they contribute wealth in other forms, such as manual labour. The colonial government, in order to make the Hadzabe (who produced no taxable surplus) 'useful citizens', attempted to put them in permanent settlements, in 1927 and 1937 (Woodburn 1962, Ndagala 1982; 1985b). The idea was to have them supply manual labour while they learnt to produce cash crops. After both attempts failed the Hadzabe were left alone to avoid further moneys being expended on a minority group that 'produced nothing' (Ndagala 1982: 27). It was not until 1964, after Tanganyika gained independence, that fresh moves to resettle the Hadzabe were started. The Hadzabe were collected on pre-selected sites in the respective districts and required to start a new way of life as agriculturists and livestock keepers. Houses were built for them, while schools and dispensaries were established in every settlement. To introduce the new 'settlers' to agriculture and animal husbandry the state provided the settlements with cattle and goats, cleared the land and planted it with crops; all the 'settlers' had to do was weed the fields and harvest the crops for their own use. Food was to be provided to the 'settlers' until they were able to produce enough for themselves by agriculture and the keeping of livestock. A relatively large number of extension officials were posted to these settlements, in most of which piped water was installed, while in others recreation centres were constructed. If numbers are anything to go by, then the government of the new nation state had a quick success in resettling the hunters and gatherers. By 1967 only about 200 Hadzabe were still in the bush (Woodburn 1968a). The district authorities were so satisfied that in one of the official correspondences it is recorded that: 'The Hadzabe are already used to a sedentary way of life and are no longer interested in going back to the bush' (Ndagala 1982: 28). Evidence shows, however, that the Hadzabe had *not* adopted sedentary living. Their stay in the settlements at that time can be explained by basic utilitarian factors.

During their stay in the settlement the Hadzabe were able to satisfy their subsistence needs more easily than was possible through traditional means. In order to get food all they had to do was to stay in the settlement. As a government measure to give the Hadzabe no cause for returning to the bush, wild meat was regularly supplied by game scouts. The free food seems to have been the peg which held the hunters and gatherers to the settlements. We found in Mbulu district, for instance, that two-thirds of all official correspondence on Hadzabe settlements was about food. And all the letters from the Yaeda Chini settlement emphasized the point that unless food was supplied promptly the Hadzabe would return to the bush (Ndagala 1982: 29). Later, following the Decentralization Programme in 1972, which abolished District Councils, there was nobody immediately responsible for the supply of food to the settlements. When no more handouts were forthcoming most of the hunters and gatherers went back to the bush where it was now relatively easier to obtain their subsistence needs. Like the colonial attempt, the post-independence attempt to sedentarize the Hadzabe failed. What motivated this second attempt?

The main motive for resettling the Hadzabe after independence was to help a doomed people. The Hadzabe were seen as an underprivileged 'primitive' portion of the new nation, who had to be 'saved'. Sedentarization was part of the 'civilizing mission' through which the Hadzabe, like other citizens, could get access to education, health care and other services offered by the state. It was a concern for all nationals to be able to fend for themselves. Hunting and gathering was regarded as a precarious way of life which an independent nation could not allow its people. The collapse of the settlements in 1972 not only frustrated the policy-makers, but also strengthened the belief of administrators and planners that the Hadzabe were an impossible people who had to be left alone. Some of the administrators, however, came to believe that the Hadzabe were a lazy, irresponsible people on whom a harness had to be put. They had to be controlled, and utilized in the building of the nation by producing a taxable surplus. These beliefs gave further weight to the contradictory images of Hadzabe society.

Effects of resettlement

As I have indicated elsewhere (Ndagala 1985b), the effects of the attempts to resettle the Hadzabe were many and varied. The settlements were looked upon with envy by neighbouring societies. Some members of these societies complained openly against the government's provision of food and social services to 'these bush dwellers who did nothing productive'. In spite of these complaints the government continued to provide the services and food exclusively to the Hadzabe. The availability of water and other services suddenly made Hadzabe territory attractive to members of other societies. In order to gain access to these settlements many members of these societies pretended they were Hadzabe, and those who could speak the language were even able to get the food handouts. Consequently, there were increasingly more 'Hadzabe' than actually existed. When the true Hadzabe finally went to the bush the 'opportunistic Hadzabe' remained behind and continued to enjoy the social services. Today, in all the settlements, almost all the houses built for the hunters and gatherers are occupied by members of other societies. Where Hadzabe children are still attending school they constitute a minority in schools originally built for them. Therefore the services which were meant for the minority Hadzabe ended up in the hands of the larger societies, which further opened up Hadzabe territory to other uses.

As the cultivators moved into Hadzabe territory so did their slash and burn method of agriculture. This, together with charcoal burning (McDowell 1981b), has destroyed the traditional subsistence resources of the hunters and gatherers. Alienation of this territory has, of course, been going on for a long time. In the past thirty-five years very many people have moved into this area to undertake agriculture, due to population pressure and land shortage in the surrounding areas (cf. Ndagala 1985b: 23). What started as small isolated agricultural enclaves have recently expanded so much that they are a threat to the territory's wild resources. In addition tsetse clearance in the 1950s opened up the territory to the pastoral Tatoga of the south-west. The fact that the Hadzabe's 'extensive' land utilization leaves no indelible marks makes even the parts of their territory which they most utilize appear as if they were free or unused land.

Contacts between the Hadzabe and government authorities, and time spent in the settlements along with members of other societies, brought the Hadzabe closer to the national society. They learnt to speak KiSwahili, Tanzania's national language, and could perform several other tasks hitherto unknown to them. Many Hadzabe children completed primary school and a number of them went to secondary schools and teacher training colleges. Some of these young people have subsequently gone back to their territory, where they work as teachers, dispensary attendants and administrative assistants. In the absence of recognised leaders in Hadzabe society these young people serve as links between their people and government. In spite of all this, the Hadzabe still regard the settlements as a bitter experience. Yet they are conscious of the fact that the government may want to resettle them at any time. So whenever they are talked into the subject of being resettled they claim that they are willing to return to the settlements as long as food is readily supplied. They make this claim with full awareness that the government is not very keen on giving them handouts indefinitely. It is thus a tactic calculated by the Hadzabe to enable them to be left alone.

The government, on its part, was not very keen on spending more money on the Hadzabe unless sure the respective programmes would succeed. Even the running and maintenance of the facilities established in Hadzabe territory were no longer given the necessary attention. For example, most of the teachers posted to the schools in the settlements were those considered stubborn by their education officers. These postings were a kind of punishment and the respective teachers felt very bitter about it. The original spirit of sending the best personnel in the area to 'save' the otherwise 'doomed' Hadzabe had long disappeared.

Possible mediation

Due to the opposed images of 'freedom' and 'doom' the Hadzabe have been subjected to various measures without ever being consulted. The government always 'knew' what was good for them and therefore told them without ever having time to listen to them. Before the place and fate of the hunters and gatherers as a minority in the nation state could be understood, these images had to be mediated, by grounding them to reality. The Rift Valley Project was started in 1978 under the Ministry of National Culture and Youth with such an aim (Utamaduni 1982; Ndagala and Waane 1982). It was confirmed in the course of the Project that the subsistence strategy which gives the Hadzabe both relative freedom and a relatively higher nutritional status was possible only when and where there was extensive territory with abundant wild resources to crop. Moreover, it became clear that due to the increasing number of people in Hadzabe territory it would not be long before the Hadzabe found it difficult to obtain their subsistence or move freely. The hunters and gatherers were aware of this flow of people into their territory but did not seem to realize the rate at which this process was closing in on them. Even if they realized the looming danger to their subsistence strategy they were personally unlikely to halt the ongoing alienation of their territory. As pointed out elsewhere (Ndagala 1985b), the land tenure system in Tanzania tended to favour people with more visible evidence of use or occupancy, such as agricultural fields, houses and cattle kraals. In any dispute over land in Hadzabe territory the Hadzabe would tend to lose because of their lack of those things which are nationally regarded as evidence of use.

It was also realized that by being spatially closer to other societies, the Hadzabe were losing marriageable girls. The movement of brides was from Hadzabe to other societies and not the other way round. There were two reasons for this. First, the Hadzabe could not raise the necessary bride wealth payable in these societies. Secondly, the Hadzabe commanded a low social status among the other societies so that no girl from the latter was 'willing' to have a Hadzabe husband. This outward movement of Hadzabe girls worried the Hadzabe, particularly the men, and is said to be one of the reasons why they do not want to go back to the settlements or stay very close to other societies. As a minority they seemed afraid that they would lose their cultural identity and become socially and culturally extinct.

Evidence suggests that the Hadzabe, though free and relatively self-sufficient in food, are doomed unless fitting action is taken to save them from physical or social extinction, or both. As their territory becomes smaller and smaller and the wild resources get destroyed they will no longer be able to support themselves by the immediate-return system. They will have to adopt other means of supplementing their subsistence needs, including agriculture and livestock keeping. Yet it may not be possible for them to undertake agriculture or livestock keeping when zero hour strikes. All suitable land may already have been taken by the other societies. Steps have to be taken now to help the Hadzabe help themselves. Nyerere (1967) stated correctly that development is brought about by the people themselves. However, the Hadzabe, as a minority unrepresented in any of the decision-making bodies, are likely to be squeezed out of their rightful place unless special safeguards are provided. Of necessity, the hunters and gatherers need education and the skills with which to demand and protect their rights. Moreover, as a minority in a democratic state, they need articulate legislation to protect their rights and interests, given the fact that sometimes the number of votes may overrule reason.

The political history of the Hadzabe indicates that policy mistakes will continue to be made, thus making their life more vulnerable, unless there is dialogue between the parties concerned — the Hadzabe themselves, the government and the researchers. While so much knowledge has been accumulated on various matters relating to the hunters and gatherers, most of it still lies in university libraries and on the shelves of individual scholars. This knowledge could be effectively utilized in making the hunters and gatherers aware of the alternative possibilities open to them. It could be used to enlighten the government functionaries who often lack the necessary information. Hunters and gatherers, like other nomadic peoples, are capable of participating in the making of decisions about their future (Salzman 1985: 2). Nevertheless, for effective participation they should have access to existing information. It is for this reason that we proposed that anthropologists should make an effort to disseminate their research findings to the researched people and their respective governments (Ndagala 1985a: 5). This was tried under the Rift Valley Project by organizing research workshops which brought researchers, government administrators and planners together with the researched people. All parties were able to learn from each other during these workshops. The Hadzabe are now listened to through some kind of representation. They are allowed subsistence hunting using their traditional tools when nobody else in Tanzania is allowed to hunt except with special licence during certain times of the year. Time will tell how the Hadzabe will fare in Tanzania's nation state because it is one thing to recognize the special needs of a given people and another to fulfil them.

Conclusion

When arguing that the Hadzabe are doomed I do not want to give the impression that the days of hunting and gathering are coming to an end. I am proposing only that hunting and gathering societies have to undergo qualitative changes if they are to survive in nation states where they are minorities. The direction these changes will take will vary from one nation to another. The policy moves that have been proposed in order to affect such qualitative changes among the Hadzabe amount to discrimination in their favour. Such discrimination is positive because it aims at protecting the minorities from being squeezed out by the larger groups. Experience shows, however, that positive discrimination is not easy to implement. For example, the services which were provided exclusively for the Hadzabe were soon dominated by members of other societies, most of whom claimed to be Hadzabe. It would not be easy to keep these 'invaders' out without antagonizing them and their respective groups. This brings us to the second problem. What should be the definitive category when looking at hunting and gathering societies as minorities? Should it be their subsistence strategy or their ethnicity? Should we, for example, deal with 'hunters and gatherers' or with 'the Hadzabe'? These are important questions in Tanzania, and possibly other places, because both categories are rather too fluid to be definitive. As with the Hadzabe, 'membership' in these categories is subject to variations depending on the conditions prevailing at the particular time. Given the mounting competition for resources, the fluidity of the categories is likely to complicate any work dealing with the minorities in question. I believe, however, that communication between the respective peoples, the governments and the researchers would go a long way in evolving viable approaches.

Part 2

Flux, sedentism and change

5. The complexities of residential organization among the Efe (Mbuti) and the Bamgombi (Baka): a critical view of the notion of flux in hunter-gatherer societies

Jon Pedersen and Espen Wæhle

Introduction

Following Turnbull's work on the Ik and the Mbuti (1965a; 1965c; 1968), anthropologists are by now accustomed to describe hunter-gatherer residential arrangements as being characterized by 'flux'. Thus, local bands are seen as constantly changing and as having no fixed memberships, even though the existence of the bands themselves may be more or less permanent. According to Turnbull, flux is made possible by a permissive environment, but cannot be explained as an ecological adaptation. Instead, it is to be related to political processes: by fission and fusion of local bands conflicts are moderated because the contestants remove themselves physically from one another. The fissions and fusions are facilitated by the seasonal division of the bands in smaller groups, which may assemble in new configurations the next season. Since, in Turnbull's view, political authority among the Ik or the Mbuti is not mediated by kinship, he also states that the flux is not structured along kinship lines. As Turnbull sees it, 'the composition of each camp is *ad hoc*, responding to the needs of the moment rather than to any preconceived plan, or any notion derived from tradition' (1965a: 107).

We find this difficult to believe. Instead, we would suggest that Pygmy residential arrangements are as determined by social organization as residential arrangements in other societies. It is not so that the reasons for changes in camp composition are 'nearly always personal' (Turnbull 1965a: 107); they are structured by regularities in Pygmy social organization and, as we will show, by relations with the neighboring agriculturalists. This is not to imply that the composition of local groups is immutable or inflexible, but that the mutability and flexibility vary according to local circumstances. Therefore, in order to understand flux and mobility, one has to take as the point of departure the social organization, values and conceptions relating to flux and mobility.

To substantiate our claim we will discuss the composition of camps and local groups among two groups of Pygmies: the Bamgombi of the Central African Republic and Cameroon and the Efe of the Ituri forest in north-eastern Zaïre.[1] But before entering the discussion, we will briefly consider some of the literature on residence groups among hunter-gatherers in East and Central Africa.

Even though Turnbull's work is influential, a number of alternative interpretations of hunter-gatherer residential mobility exist. Some authors accept Turnbull's description and use it as a building block in more general theories of hunter-gatherers (Godelier 1977; Meillassoux 1972; 1973). Woodburn (1982a) portrays flux as distinctive of societies characterized by immediate-return systems, that is, economic systems where people receive return from their labor without having to wait. In contrast, delayed-return systems are those where people do not obtain a direct return from their efforts. Hunting and gathering are arch-examples of economic activities in immediate-return systems, just as is agriculture in delayed-return systems. Nevertheless, hunter-gatherer societies do not all have immediate-return systems because the social distribution of resources and products also determines the type of 'return' system. According to Woodburn, immediate-return systems are characterized by flux because people in such systems are only to a very small extent dependent upon specific others. Thus, movement from one place to another presents few inconveniences.

In our view Woodburn's position represents an advance on that of Turnbull because the scope of the description is reduced: only some hunter-gatherer societies are characterized by flux. However, we do not believe that whole societies, ethnic groups or 'tribes' may be

1. The Bamgombi also call themselves Baka and are sometimes known as Bangombé, Bampenga (which their Mpimu neighbors call them) or Babinga (a general name for Pygmies used in the Central African Republic). Jon Pedersen carried out fieldwork among the Bamgombi from February through May 1985. We are grateful for assistance from officials of the government of the Central African Republic, in particular the Haut Commissaire à la Présidence du Comité Militaire de Redressement National, chargé de la Recherche Scientifique et Technologique, M. J.C. Kazagui, and the local administration in Nola and Bilolo. Sylvie Grand'Eury made the collection of the Mano data possible and Mwonlou Lambert made everything much easier. The Efe are the Mbuti archers in the north-eastern, eastern and south-eastern parts of the Ituri forest. Espen Wæhle carried out fieldwork in Ituri from November 1982 through November 1983. We would like to thank the 'Harvard Ituri Project' and the Centre National de Planification du Nutrition Humaine under its director, Dr Kabamba Nkamany, for affiliation and help, and also the administration of the Zone de Mambasa and Collectivité Walese Dese. Both fieldworks were financed by the Norwegian Council for Science and Humanities, and Espen Wæhle also received support from the Nansen Fund and the Institute for Comparative Cultural Research. We are most grateful, however, to the individual Bamgombi, Efe, Mpimu and Lese Dese who through their hospitality made our research possible.

depicted as having the one or the other return system. Consequently, whole societies cannot be described as having fluid local groups or as not having them. Large differences in the degree and kind of mobility of local groups may be traced back to local variation with regard to resources, as well as to political affiliations with outside groups. This variation in how local groups are constituted is well brought out by Terashima (1985), who demonstrates the futility of a discussion about whether Mbuti form patrilocal bands or whether they live in territorial units with a high degree of flux. The Mbuti do both, but in different circumstances. Terashima concludes that there really is no specific rule for Mbuti residence choice. This he relates to the hunter-gatherer group's need for flexibility in their economic and ecological adaptation.

While both Turnbull and Woodburn state that there is no specific ecological reason for flux, Terashima relates flux to subsistence strategies. Arguments based on ecological considerations are indeed the most common alternative view of hunter-gatherer mobility. With respect to the Mbuti, Arbruzzi (1980) offers the most explicit example of this line of reasoning. He maintains, contrary to Turnbull, that the Ituri forest is neither uniform as regards resources nor a 'permissive environment'. Flux emerges in situations where there is a high return on labor, because then people do not need to cooperate. Although Arbruzzi is undoubtedly correct in pointing out the deficiencies in Turnbull's description of the ecological conditions in Ituri (Bailey and Peacock 1988; Hart and Hart 1986), he shares with Turnbull and Woodburn the general idea that people will not stay together unless forced to do so.

The Bamgombi

The Bamgombi referred to here live in the rain forest near Bilolo, about thirty kilometers south-west of Nola in the Sangha Economic Prefecture of the Central African Republic. Our data are mainly collected from three local groups: Asegi, Bikoula and Mano. Being neither net-hunters nor archers, Bamgombi men usually hunt with spear and dog, but sometimes they also use the crossbow. Women gather, and one kind of tuber is predominately collected even though the Bamgombi know of many other edible plants. With the Mpimu agriculturalists the Bamgombi trade forest products for 'village' and external products. They also work on Mpimu fields and hunt for the Mpimu. Some Bamgombi also farm a little. In the 1970s many Bamgombi men in the area worked for lumber companies, but now very few do so because the companies have shifted their operations elsewhere. For most of the year, the Bamgombi live in their own villages close to those of the Mpimu. In February, they leave the villages for the forest and live in small camps for two to three months. There they hunt, gather and, to them perhaps most important, collect honey.

The Efe

Our data on the Efe were collected in the Efe settlements, Apomasa, Apugbe, Batodo and Malembi, in the Collectivité Walese Dese in the Zone de Mambasa, Haute Zaïre, approximately twenty-two kilometers north of Nduye. Efe men hunt mainly with bow and arrow, and the Efe are therefore usually described as archers as opposed to net-hunters (the variety of hunting techniques is presented in Terashima 1983). Many wild plants and wild foods are gathered, predominantly by women. Both men and women exchange forest products with neighboring agriculturalists and work for them in their gardens and in their households, these activities constituting a major source of Efe subsistence (R. Bailey 1985; R. Bailey and Peacock 1988). Immigrant cash croppers and a few plantations also offer opportunity for trade and work. For parts of the year the Efe live in settlements close to the villages of Lese Dese agriculturalists, while from December through March the Efe may stay for weeks or months in hunting and fishing camps deeper into the forest. From July through October they stay in forest camps gathering honey and termites. Some Efe groups combine the hunting and fishing season with trading expeditions to the west where the Budu agriculturalists are settled. Efe experience with agriculture is limited, but some households clear small gardens (which are left untended during stays in the forest).

The identity and composition of local groups

Both the Bamgombi and the Efe recognize several kinds of local groups. Also, since the Pygmies share the region with the agriculturalists, it is useful to compare how all these various societies identify the different forms of community. This is most easily done in the case of Bamgombi and Mpimu, peoples who do not speak the same language.

There are several forms of settlement in the Bilolo area. We may distinguish between:

villages — permanent settlements of the Mpimu;

homesteads — Mpimu households outside the village proper;

Bamgombi villages — more or less permanent Bamgombi settlements, usually located in the close vicinity of a Mpimu village;

forest camps — camps in the forests used as a temporary residence when hunting, fishing, etc. As a physical site, the camp may be permanent. Both Mpimu and Bamgombi have forest camps.

Table 5.1: Mpimu and Bamgombi classification of settlement types

	Mpimu	Alternative Mpimu	Bamgombi
Mpimu village	*Dali*	*Dali*	*Gba (kaka-o)*
Mpimu homestead	*Mbo*	*Mbo*	*Gba (kaka-o)*
Bamgombi village	*Bajega Bampenga*	*Mbanda*	*Gba (baka-o)*
Forest camp	*Mpala*	*Mbanda*	*Bagala*

As Table 5.1 shows, the Mpimu and the Bamgombi classify settlements differently. Most noticeable is the fact that the Bamgombi use the same word for both Mpimu and Bamgombi villages, while the Mpimu distinguish the two. As indicated in brackets, the Bamgombi may specify the ethnic group pertaining to a village, but they do not usually do so (*kaka* means 'villager', and *baka* is an alternative name for Bamgombi; the *-o* suffix is possessive). Both the Mpimu and the Bamgombi may specify the ethnic affiliation of a forest camp but, again, they seldom do so. The Table also indicates that there is an alternative Mpimu usage, which employs the same word for both forest camps and Bamgombi villages. This may be taken as showing that the Mpimu set a distinction between village and forest, the border between the two coinciding with the boundaries of their own villages. However, one should not carry the village/forest opposition too far because the Mpimu emphatically describe themselves as 'forest people'. In any case, the two groups' terminologies indicate that while Mpimu see their own villages as different in kind from the Bamgombi villages, the Bamgombi do not follow suit. In the Bamgombi view, both peoples live in villages and have camps in the forest. Following this usage we will, in the discussion on the Pygmies, designate villages or settlements as 'local groups', and reserve the word 'camp' for forest camps.

A question linked to the way in which both the Bamgombi and the Efe conceptualize local groups is how the settlements are given social identity. The Bamgombi, the Mpimu, the Efe and the Lese Dese all identify Pygmy local groups as units basic to Pygmy identity, but in rather different ways. The Mpimu identify a Bamgombi village as the unit with which a Mpimu village has relations. Although the Mpimu feel themselves greatly superior to the Bamgombi, they do not think of the Bamgombi local groups as their 'property'. The Bamgombi, for their part, identify their local groups in relation to a name and to a number of rituals particular to each local group. Most important among these rituals are those associated with the forest spirit, Edjengi. Edjengi is a guardian spirit for all Bamgombi, often conceived of as a nuclear family living, like Bamgombi families, in the forest; each local group has its own unique names for the Edjengi father, mother and son. In addition, each Bamgombi local group has its own set of dances. Both the Mpimu and the Bamgombi also identify the Pygmy local group with reference to territorial rights *vis-à-vis* other Pygmy groups. The Lese Dese identify an Efe local group not only as a unit with which they have relations: they also conceive of the group as their property. As with the Mpimu, they see the Pygmies as less developed and civilized than themselves. Also, both Efe and Lese Dese define the Pygmy local group territorially against other local groups.

All Bamgombi belong to a named *mobila*. Men and women with the same father are members of their father's *mobila*. Thus the *mobila* are based on patrifiliation — though the Bamgombi show a singular lack of interest in genealogies. When women marry they retain membership in their *mobila* of birth; the Bamgombi say that a hut (that is, a nuclear family) has members of two *mobila*, namely that of the husband and that of the wife. Among the Bamgombi there are only a few distinct *mobila*; we registered fifteen, while Vallois and Marquer (1976: 119–21) report twenty-seven from the same ethnic group across the border in Cameroon.

All Bamgombi local groups thus consist of *mobila*; but the *mobila* are not local groups. The *mobila* may act as corporate groups within a local group, and conflicts within a camp are often organized along *mobila* lines. Members of the same *mobila* living in different camps do not act together as a group. In the settlements, whether in the forest or close to the Mpimu villages, the huts are set up so that male members of the same *mobila* reside close to each other. However, participation in communal activities, such as elephant hunting, is not organized along *mobila* lines.

In a given Bamgombi local group one may distinguish between two kinds of *mobila*, namely the core and the periphery. The core *mobila* are ranked by the order in which the *mobila* arrived there. In practice this is not always so clear-cut, because the several members of a given *mobila* do not always arrive at the same time. As to periphery *mobila*, the members of these are all persons who are married into the village or who are present carrying out bride-service. The presence of seniors (*kobu*) is important for deciding whether or not a *mobila* is counted in the ranking list of *mobila* in a local group. When asked about the *mobila* of a local group, Bamgombi often reply with the name of the most important person in the *mobila* concerned. Usually the most important person of a *mobila* will be a man, but there is no stated principle ruling out women. There is, however, little chance that a woman would be counted as the most important member, for a middle-aged or old woman will usually live with her husband in his local group.

Bamgombi *mobila* are exogamous. Moreover, Bamgombi men, at least, prefer that brothers and sisters marry into the same *mobila*, formulating this preference in more or less these terms, and not as a rule of 'sister exchange'. Bamgombi men carry out bride-service and do not, as a rule, place much emphasis on brideprice, although it is sometimes paid, especially when a Mpimu man marries a Bamgombi woman.

All Efe belong to an *àdì*, of which there are a large number.[2] In KiSwahili this is translated as *fungu kidogo* (the correct lexical spelling being *ufungu*), where *fungu* means kinsmen or relations and *-dogo* small or little. As with the Bamgombi *mobila*, an *àdì* is based on patrifiliation and women also retain their *àdì* membership upon marriage. The *àdì* are exogamous and each has a unique name. One *àdì* may be present in several localities, but not necessarily in all Efe local groups. The *àdì* are not ranked, but the Efe identify core *àdì* of a local group.

The core *àdì* of a local group (and smaller local groups may have only one) share the same animal totem and the same local group name, and the members regard themselves as patrilaterally related. They call each other *acu*, which means 'brother', a term that may be extended to male and female classificatory siblings and parallel cousins. In KiSwahili, people who call each other *acu* are termed *fungu*.

Among both Bamgombi and Efe, the village is thus conceptualized as a unit, but is divided into kin groups based on patrifiliation. Nevertheless, there are institutions which tie the local group together: in the case of the Bamgombi the shared dances and, especially, the rituals associated with the forest spirit, Edjengi; in the case of the Efe, the common totem and ideology of being related by *acu*-kinship. Therefore, not only is the village a territorial unit; it also has a socially recognized set of members.

Rights of residence

Although, among both the Bamgombi and the Efe, local group organization is heavily influenced by the presence of kin groups, such groups form only a framework for the rights of residence in a local group. As Terashima (1985) has noted, Efe rights to membership of, and residence in, a local group may rest on patrilateral, matrilateral and affinal relations between individuals. This is also true of the Bamgombi, but one should note that they, at least, seem to distinguish between 'proper' members of the local group (those who are members of a core *mobila*) and people who merely have a right to live in the village. For the Bamgombi, we have already discussed some of the implications of patrifilial relations for rights of residence. But while these are perhaps primary, there is no doubt that the affinal and matrilateral relations are

2. The Efe language, often called Kimbuti, is related to Kilese, yet not identical. Generally we have not attempted to make a correct tonal and phonological notation: éfé for *efe*, bɔ́dé for *bode*, etc. (cf. Vorbichler 1966), but an exception was required for *àdì* and *ádi*.

also important in choice of residence.

Bamgombi men carry out bride-service, *mekokope*. The newly-wed couple lives in conjunction with the woman's parents' household, but in a separate hut. After a few years, the couple moves to the husband's local group. Yet there is no definite time limit to bride-service; men regard it as a life-long obligation. During residence in the in-laws' local group a man has to carry out many services: any game he procures he shares with his wife's parents; it is he who has to cut trees that have honey; and so forth. Although the relatives of a man carrying out bride-service may exercise a right to move into the local group where he resides, they rarely do so. Here it may be mentioned that a local group's matrilateral relatives have a similar right but, again, this right is not often exercised, with the exception of children: Bamgombi households sometimes 'guard' children from other local groups, and these children may be either matrilaterally or patrilaterally related to the members of the household in question.

The Efe provide quite a contrast. The Efe term *bode* means 'brother-in-law', but it is also extended to include a wife's male siblings in particular and all her *acu* in general. A man has the right and, in some circumstances, the duty to stay with his *bode*. Efe men see an exchange of women as the preferred way of establishing marriage, creating an intimate and friendly relationship between *bode*, often leading to one of them living uxorilocally. As this right is mutual, the men tend to alternate residence, switching local group after a period of months or years (at least, this happens in the first years after marriage; the majority of men seem to end up in virilocal residence). Efe men do not see this as a burden, or regard it as bride-service.

The next Efe category to examine is *àdi*, meaning matrilateral relatives, or 'mother's brothers' in a more narrow sense. Efe marriages are fragile. In the case of divorce or the death of one of the spouses, the way that the union was established determines the rights to the children. If the marriage was based on an exchange of women, a divorce or the death of the husband leaves the husband's *àdi* with rights to the children — provided that the woman who was exchanged for the mother of the children stays with her husband. In the case of brideprice the husband's *àdi* has rights to the children; but only if all the brideprice has been paid. According to the Efe, brideprice is normally contributed in three 'instalments': before marriage, upon marriage and after all the children have been weaned. If these requirements relating to marriage ('exchange' type or 'brideprice' type) have not been met, the children's maternal relatives will take care of them. Normally such children retain their father's *àdi* name, but in a few cases they receive the *àdi* name of their maternal relatives. Thus Efe have both the right to stay with their matrilateral relatives and the matrilateral relatives have, in some circumstances, rights to raise their sisters' children.

Actual residence

Neither the Bamgombi nor the Efe live exactly according to designated local group memberships. In the Bamgombi local group, Asegi, the inhabitants counted seventy-seven persons as 'members' of the village, while only fifty-six of those were actually present (in February 1985). However, during February, March and April there were changes: notably, one family of five returned to Asegi and one woman returned after leaving her Mpimu husband. Meanwhile, between December 1982 and October 1983, the Apomosa Efe settlement retained an average of 91 percent of its residents from one month to the next, and at any one time an average of 18 percent of the population had not been present the previous month. Similar to the Bamgombi in Asegi, the changes mostly involved persons defined as members of Apomosa. Of a total of 128 movements from and into Apomosa, 23 percent involved visitors. Only two of the changes constituted a recognized transfer in village membership.

The degree of mobility in the two local groups for which we have data is therefore considerably less than the mere 40 percent continuity from one month to the next which Turnbull describes in his researches among the Mbuti (1972a: 300). But the discrepancies do not necessarily imply that either Turnbull's or our data are wrong; it may simply be that different groups enjoy different mobility. Thus all the residents in the Bamgombi Asegi and the Efe Apomosa groups have either patrilateral, matrilateral or affinal relatives present, yet though this seems to be a common pattern it is not true of every Bamgombi and Efe local group. In each society at least one local group stands out, having a composition that seems more arbitrary.

Among the Mbuti, the Epulu settlement, which furnished the main data for Turnbull's analyses, is special (Ichikawa 1978; Tanno 1976; Terashima 1983; 1985). From 1928 through 1954 Patrick Putnam, an American student of anthropology, lived for long periods in Epulu. Rather than doing research, Putnam devoted his energy to putting up a small dispensary for the local population, and later a road station for motor-travelers and a small zoological garden. Putnam had an intimate knowledge of, and close relations with, local Mbuti. They supplied him with meat for his road station and some danced for the visiting tourists, guided them on forest excursions and sold them curios. This Pygmy band was even called the Putnam Pygmies, and they are still known as the *Mbuti ya Amerikani*. With numbers up to 250, the Epulu Pygmy settlement was larger than most Mbuti settlements and consisted of Mbuti from various parts of the Ituri; Putnam himself fetched a number of them from as far south as Beni. The agriculturalists in Epulu were also an ethnically heterogeneous community: the area housed members of both the Ndaka tribe and their neighbors, the Mbo. The Bira, the Lese Dese and the Ngwana also lived there, in enclaves in the Ndaka territory. Indeed, the Efe group, Apomasa, from an area several days' walk north of Epulu, came there with their Lese Dese villagers and remained for years. Some Apomasa *àdì* still live around Epulu, whilst others now live north of Nduye (in the location where we carried out research; see Wæhle 1986). Further, Epulu had a white community and for some time a hotel (Turnbull 1965a; 1983). And in some periods, the colonial authorities made heavy demands on the labour of both agriculturalists and the Mbuti (in road construction, cash-cropping, and so on). Interestingly enough, non-scientific accounts from Epulu put more stress than did Turnbull on the Mbuti's involvement in a world outside the deep forest (Falk-Rønne 1972; Eisner Putnam 1954; Mohn 1960).

The Bamgombi village, Mano, is an interesting parallel to Epulu. Like Epulu, Mano is quite large compared to other local groups, with 160 inhabitants. Likewise, it is the result of outside intervention: a Frenchman, Charles Pernot, has initiated a 'rural development center' there (Centre Rural Mano), and tries to get Bamgombi to adopt agriculture, educates Mpimu agricultural extension workers, operates a small dispensary and organizes a consumer cooperative. Like Putnam, M. Pernot has recruited Pygmies from different local groups and, as was the case in Epulu, this has resulted in a social organization different from that in other localities. These differences include a higher frequency of polygynous unions, less marked spatial organization along *mobila* lines and changes in the use of the forest resources.

Both Epulu and Mano are thus unique in their areas. Of particular importance, perhaps, is the fact that both settlements are larger than other local groups. This may mean that the usual methods of conflict resolution are hard put to cope with disagreements within the local group. Among the Bamgombi, an important way of resolving conflicts and deciding on matters common to all the local group is for nightly speeches to be made as everybody rests in their huts. In a village as large as Mano this is simply not possible, since everybody would not be able to hear the speech or comment upon it. Also, a large settlement invites conflicts, for instance because the resources close by soon get exhausted. And as to Epulu, one wonders if the conflicts and quarrels that Turnbull describes and which he sees as an explanation for constant fission and fusion, may similarly stem from the sheer size of the settlement. Certainly, only a few of the moves we observed in Apomosa and Asegi were related to quarrels. More often, people left on visits to affines, paternal or maternal kin; attended dances in other settlements; or, in the case of men, went in search of partners. And, as we will show in the next section, movements were also to a large extent influenced by relations with the agriculturalists.

Local group composition and relations to the agriculturalists

We have demonstrated that relations with Europeans profoundly affect Bamgombi and Efe social organization. But, in fact, relations with agriculturalists are much more important, if only because they are much more common.

The members of a Bamgombi village may be linked to the Mpimu in one of two main ways: each *mobila* may be linked to one Mpimu clan, or the whole Bamgombi local group may be linked to the whole of the Mpimu village via the village headman. In both cases the parties carry out the Mpimu ritual *mponi*, which establishes ritual kinship between the two groups. This is the ritual which Mpimu use to link two Mpimu clans. In addition to formalized relations the various members of the two villages engage in many *ad hoc* transactions involving hunting, agricultural work, barter, and so on.

The character of the link between the Mpimu and the Bamgombi has implications for Bamgombi mobility. For instance, Bikoula, the Bamgombi village which is connected as a whole to the Mpimu village of the same name, seems to be acting more as a group in relation to the Mpimu than are the Bamgombi of Asegi who are connected *mobila*-wise to Mpimu clans in Bilolo. Thus the Mpimu in Bikoula arrange communal work in which the Bamgombi group participates more or less as a whole. Such is not the case in Asegi/Bilolo where the Bamgombi only work for the Mpimu individually or in groups consisting of a single *mobila*. Following from these differences, all the Bikoula Bamgombi leave for hunting and gathering trips in the forest simultaneously, while Asegi Bamgombi more often take to the forest in single households or in *mobila*.

The relation with the agriculturalists also indirectly influences Bamgombi residential organization through its effect on resources. Unlike what prevails in Ituri, the Mpimu agriculturalists use the forest a lot. They collect plants and hunt and fish there — among the Mpimu there are even specialized hunters who do not farm at all. This means that there is competition between Mpimu and Bamgombi for forest resources, especially resources close to the Mpimu villages. The Asegi Bamgombi, connected to the very large Mpimu village, Bilolo, have thus found it necessary to move their settlement a few kilometers away from Bilolo, both in order to avoid competition for resources, and as a means to reduce constant Mpimu demand for work and services.

The Mpimu and Bamgombi control strategic resources and goods in different proportions in various settings. In the area around Bilolo iron, classically an exchange item under the control of the agriculturalists, is not significant, for lumber companies have abandoned so much damaged equipment in the forest that the Bamgombi are self-sufficient in metals. However, the Mpimu still control strategic commodities: one such is modern guns, which are much sought after by the Bamgombi and which no Bamgombi owns. Yet guns and iron, even though in some ways they fulfill similar roles in the Bamgombi economy, have very different effects on Bamgombi social organization. All Bamgombi households need iron, but only some, namely those with hunters who can shoot, are lent guns by the Mpimu. The result is that Bamgombi households with access to guns hunt differently from those without. The former will more likely stay close to the Mpimu village. This is because Bamgombi can rarely borrow a gun for more than a day at a time, and also because the gun makes for easier hunting of, for instance, medium-sized monkeys — animals which are inefficiently secured with crossbows and traps, and which are therefore still found close to the Mpimu villages. In Asegi, households hunting by traditional means ranged over much larger areas than those using guns.

Economic activities which are, at the outset, Mpimu concerns also influence the Bamgombi, because such activities influence Mpimu demands for Bamgombi labor. Of particular importance here is the degree to which Mpimu women farm independently. Nearly all Mpimu women farm, and are responsible for meeting their households' needs for the staple foods. To do this, they get 'help' from their husbands, and, more importantly, from their sons and daughters; these persons' right to the crop is indeed partly seen in relation to this help. Such a notion becomes particularly important when a Mpimu woman decides to produce more than is needed by her household and sells the surplus. Then she will have the option of getting help from her sons and daughters (thus having to share), or enlisting Bamgombi. The latter strategy is much more profitable because the Bamgombi need not be given nearly so much as the woman's household members. A woman's need for Bamgombi labor is also determined by the stage in the developmental cycle of the Mpimu households: both old women and young ones with few children in the household will have more need of this labor than those with many children who can work. Accordingly, the relation between an Mpimu village and a Bamgombi village may be expected to vary with the age distribution of the Mpimu village. Should there be few children of working age, the Mpimu will have greater need for Bamgombi. An interesting footnote on this is that Mpimu women have more friendly relations toward Bamgombi than do Mpimu men. It may be that Mpimu women more carefully cultivate their relationship with Bamgombi, because they are more dependent upon it than are men.

According to the Efe, the traditional system for linkage with the Lese villagers was a one-to-one system. An Efe adult male was hereditarily attached to one specific agriculturalist, with members of one àdì linked to members of the same village lineage. This is not the case today. The explanation given by the Efe is that agriculturalist families have died away and that some have left the area in any case; adult male Efe clearly outnumber adult male agriculturalists in the area in which we worked. Several Efe men may now be attached to a single agriculturalist or to a group of brothers, but these Efe are not necessarily of the same *àdì*. The present system appears more open than the former in terms of negotiation, flexibility and the possibility of switching alliances: the relationships certainly have permanence but they are not immutable and shifts and breaks between partners do occasionally take place. Although the agriculturalist regards himself as the owner of the Efe, the Efe do not trade with and work for one partner exclusively, but with other agriculturalists in the area as well, such as Budu agriculturalists to the west, immigrant cash-croppers and plantation personnel. Yet it is not only the type of relationship as such, but also the quality and dynamics of the relationship, which influence the composition of Efe local groups.

The traditional partner has a special significance to the Efe. Compared to exchanges with other partners, the reciprocity is generalized rather than balanced. Nevertheless, the character of the link is not only defined in terms of type of relation. Wealthy agriculturalists tend to have more Efe attached than those not so well off. 'The Efe go after their nose', agriculturalists used to say, indicating that when wealth diminishes the Efe are likely to search for other partners. Thus over the years and as household development cycles progress, Efe households and local groups drift over to other agriculturalists or move to more distant localities. On the receiving end of this was an agriculturalist in Takuna, who had lost most of his Efe over the last ten to fifteen years. And the few Efe remaining were constantly discussing if they should join the ones who had left, or if they should stay. So they travelled a lot to seek out and test other agriculturalists.

For an agriculturalist, wealth is not a sufficient qualification to hold on to a group of Efe; relations have to be managed cleverly. The local group, Apomasa, was attached to two paternally-related agriculturalists. One of these men was young and had only recently established his own household, so the older of the two was effectively this Efe group's main agriculturalist partner. He was by no means as wealthy as surrounding Lese Dese or the cash-croppers to the south and north of Takuna, but the Efe judged him by his patience, clever conduct and the fact that he showed them respect. His Efe worked regularly for other Lese Dese in the area; some stayed for weeks with cash-croppers to the south; and almost every year they embarked on month-long trading expeditions to the Budu in the west. Still, he felt secure that the Efe were loyal to him and would return one day. Had he been more authoritarian, as Lese commonly are (by complaining, shouting, ordering, sometimes threatening and even beating or sending for the tribal police), individual Efe, Efe households and maybe the whole local group would have searched out other partners. In such a situation Efe could have joined relatives in the Epulu area, or set themselves up in attachments to other Lese Dese, or tried to work with cash-croppers or on plantations — either as a group or split up into segments. The relationship could have had another character if there were cash-croppers and plantations in the immediate neighbourhood: in such localities relations tend to be more commercialized and fluid, not building on the traditional system of mutual rights and obligations.

Both among the Bamgombi and the Efe, then, relations with agriculturalists influence the foragers' residential arrangements and mobility in many ways. The actual influence depends on the demographic situation (the relative and absolute sizes of the Pygmy groups and the villages), resource utilization patterns (especially the degree of competition for resources) and the relative wealth of the parties and their control over strategic goods and resources, as well as their relative skill in manipulation and negotiation.

In Woodburn's terms (1982a; this volume), we would argue that the relations with agriculturalists provide the basis of *both* immediate- and delayed-return tendencies among the Bamgombi and Efe. As Woodburn points out, moving must be seen partly as a strategy for evading domination. But moving presupposes someone to move to. Therefore the Pygmies continually have to maintain and affirm their relationships with other groups; this creates networks of dependency and thereby the basis of delayed return. Also, given that the resources which the sedentary villagers control may represent a major contribution to the foragers' economy (see Bailey and Peacock 1988; Hart and Hart 1986), we find it difficult to describe, as does Turnbull (1965a), the Pygmies' exchanges with the agriculturalists as just another kind of hunting expedition.

With our cases we have focused mainly on contemporary variations between different local groups. But as Vansina (1986) convincingly shows, there are strong indications that the variations in equatorial Africa have been just as great in the past. For the Efe, one of us has documented changes in relations to agriculturalists in recent history (Wæhle 1986). For the Bamgombi the little work relating to this topic (see, for example, Althabe 1965) indicates similar trends. Also, the changes in the external relations of the Bamgombi's western neighbors, the Aka, particularly in respect of commercial elephant hunting and rubber extraction (Bahuchet and Guillaume 1982), may very well be valid also for the Bamgombi.

Do only hunters and gatherers move?

One matter which is often overlooked in the discussion of hunter-gatherer residential mobility is comparison with other kinds of society. Will data such as those presented both here and elsewhere in the literature (see Terashima 1985) indicate that flux is a specific characteristic of hunter-gatherers? We believe not. One may easily find examples of pastoralists and agriculturalists whose social organization can be characterized as especially fluid. One very explicit discussion of residential mobility among agriculturalists is that of Burnham (1980), who characterizes the residential units of the Gbaya of Cameroon in terms of a 'structural fluidity' determined, to a large extent, by political processes and a permissive environment. Similarly, Colson (1962: 172) observes for Plateau Tonga society that while the village is an important social unit, villages move and have ever-changing memberships. Like Turnbull with the Mbuti, Colson traces the immediate cause of the flux to quarrels, but goes further and states that the quarrels stem from Tongan social organization, particularly the structural position of fathers and sons in the context of matrilineal kinship (Colson 1962: 204). Finally, speaking of riverine communities of Central Africa, other authors consider movement based on seasonal and environmental variations, exchange between the riverains and agriculturalists, and long-distance trade, as the most enduring feature of social life (Harms 1981, Kuper and Van Leynseele 1978).

Conclusion

Two main points have been established. First, the organization of local groups among two groups of African Pygmies is not arbitrary or based on purely personal preferences and whims. Patrifiliation, though not accompanied by a well-defined ideology of patrilineal descent, forms an important framework for residence choice. This does not imply that the Bamgombi or the Efe should be described as 'patrilocal bands' in a strict sense; matrilateral and affinal relations are also used for legitimizing residence choices. Still, our view does imply that a general picture of residential mobility as characterized by extreme flux cannot be maintained. Nevertheless, we believe that Turnbull's treatment of political processes as being indispensable for an explanation of mobility among hunter-gatherers is more fruitful than explanations based solely on ecological considerations. However, by considering only quarrels and personal conflicts as important political processes, Turnbull unduly restricts his analysis.

Our second point is that the actual organization of Pygmy local groups is to a large extent dependent upon relations with agriculturalists and other outsiders. Both by influencing the resource base of the hunter-gatherers, and by presenting opportunities and constraints for their activities, these relations are among the main variables underpinning Bamgombi and Efe residence choice. One should therefore expect fairly large variations in the composition of Pygmy local groups as relations with agriculturalists vary.

6. Pressures for Tamil propriety in Paliyan social organization

Peter M. Gardner

Introduction

Enclaved foraging peoples who have had lengthy exposure to sedentary, more powerful neighbors are recognized widely as being culturally distinct from other foragers (Kroeber 1919; 1945; Leacock 1954; Bose 1956; Murphy and Steward 1956; Steward 1961; James 1961; Service 1962; Turnbull 1965a; Gardner 1966; Deetz 1968; R. Fox 1969; B.J. Williams 1974; Morris 1977; 1982a; J.T. Peterson 1978; Woodburn 1980; Testart 1981; 1985). But explanations for their distinctiveness are diverse: Leacock, Fox and Morris say external market involvement shapes them in basic ways; James and Gardner emphasize psychological effects of their harassment; Service and Williams claim that geographic displacement and depopulation restructure them socially; Orans (1965) contends that the enclaved emulate, then concede rank to, their neighbors; and so on. Possibly several situational factors, together, overdetermine the most notable characteristics of enclaved foragers. In order to assess the various explanations we need more detailed case studies of long-term contact; the present chapter is offered toward that end.[1]

Paliyan foragers interact sporadically but systematically with their Tamil, South Indian neighbors in a frontier zone near the forest's edge. As is true of other foraging peoples in India, they have long figured in the extraction of forest produce. Some are also moving out beyond the frontier to take up agricultural labor. Paliyans speak a dialect of Tamil

1. The research for this paper was supported, during 1962–4, by a Foreign Area Fellowship granted by the Ford Foundation and administered by the Joint Committee of SSRC–ACLS and, during 1978, by a grant from the American Institute of Indian Studies and a Faculty Summer Fellowship from the Research Council of the University of Missouri-Columbia. Development of some of the ideas was made possible during 1983 by a further sabbatical grant from the Research Council. Responsibility for statements made in the text rests solely with the author. The name *Paliyan* is given in a form which serves in Tamil as both a singular noun and an adjective; an Anglicized plural is used here in place of Tamil *Paliyar*.

91

and they have sufficient competence in aspects of Tamil culture that one may characterize them as being partially bicultural. In some realms they know the Tamil practices and formulae, but are uncertain as to their meaning; in others they are acquainted with Tamil ideals and explanations, too. It is the nature of intergroup relations in the region that they hear frequent critiques of their own practices.

Possessing at least some knowledge of two social structures, Paliyans in the frontier zone (and beyond) organize their social life contextually, in versatile ways, reflecting not only practical pressures and opportunities but also principles. By examining their knowledge, circumstances and variable social organization in six related realms and in more than one community, I seek here to identify specific ways in which new social organizational forms are being generated. These realms are: postmarital residence; household types; dimensions of husband–wife roles and gender relations; kin terminology; marriage preferences; and remarriage.

This chapter follows upon a number of other papers. In describing Paliyan culture, I have generally centered on the importance of culture contact. Because my approach to Paliyan–Tamil relations has been changing, a prefatory word is needed. Initially, I portrayed Paliyans as having a culture shaped in essential ways by their contact situation; this extended even to their staunch individualism and cultural simplicity. I also dwelt on their use of protective orthopraxy in contact settings (Gardner 1965; 1966; 1969; 1972). Four more recent articles were based upon two things: the results of totally reexamining contact data; and the findings of a brief revisit in 1978. I discovered reason to propose a long-term pattern of Paliyan oscillation between semi-sedentary contract labor in their Tamil frontier and retreat into isolated, relatively self-sufficient nomadism (see Gardner 1978; 1982; 1983; and, especially, 1985, where this pattern is most fully described). This did not void or supplant the earlier portrait; it elaborated and helped to explain it.

Given my perennial emphasis on cultural contact, it should be mentioned that Paliyan economic data do not corroborate Richard Fox's long untested theory — that enclaved, South Asian 'professional primitives' collect 'primarily' for specialized market goods and are unable to subsist on foraging alone (R. Fox 1969: 141–2; cf. Gardner 1985). Fox offers a bold theory, worthy of thorough testing. What is the Paliyan evidence? In the 1960s most Paliyan gathering (even in the frontier zone) and virtually all their hunting and fishing were observed to be for subsistence items, which were never traded; their resource base was broad; and they lacked human competition for their main foods. It was in the area of tools alone that a customary reliance on Indian society was manifest — yet a brief period of trade or contract labor each year or two would more than meet that need.

The study

The present chapter offers a wholly new perspective on Paliyan culture contact. It draws upon a previously unanalyzed body of data from five months' ethnographic study of a long-established Paliyan community of sedentary agricultural laborers, here labelled H (Paliyan bands are named for their customary locales; thus H stands for the Paliyan group and for its main settlement). Paliyan bands vary culturally. While I cannot perforce maintain that this community before settling (some one-and-a-half to two centuries ago) was culturally similar in all ways to other bands and communities studied, H Paliyans share much culturally with forest-oriented bands: they keep up contact and inter-marriage with forest groups and cannot originally have differed greatly from them. The type and magnitude of some of the apparent recent changes in H are instructive. These tell us about probable pressures felt by other Paliyans and reveal what may underlie certain observed trends in the region.

Twenty-four Paliyan households, six non-Paliyan households (of differing castes, one household identifying itself as Nāyakkar, two as Sāmban Idaiyar, and three as Harijan), and a tiny shop made up the settlement. In 1963, it was a compact hamlet, some thirty-two by forty-seven meters, overhung by giant tamarind trees, on the flat holdings of a large agricultural landowner. Importantly to the Paliyan residents, it was less than 100 meters from the forested foot of a steep mountain range that rose 2000 meters above them. The nearest Tamil community was a few kilometers away, on the plain. All non-Paliyan homes and just half of the Paliyan dwellings had puddled mud walls, and the remainder had walls of grass or sticks. Ridge-pole roofs were usually thatched with palmyra leaves, overlain with a cutting grass. Some houses abutted one another; those which stood free were in short rows, clustered so as to leave five public areas. A usual-sized puddled mud hut, measuring 2.4 by three meters, was built for me, overlooking two of the public areas. H Paliyans worked seasonally under foremen for the big landowner, ploughing rice fields, transplanting rice seed-lings, weeding, driving off wild pigs at night, and harvesting. Other landowners competed for their labor at peak times, to work with crops such as turmeric, peanuts and cotton. This was all sporadic labor, paid by the day or month. The Paliyan 'headman' of the community was permitted to cultivate about half a hectare for himself and to use the landowner's draft animals and equipment for that purpose.

I will take up social organization one realm at a time, first sketching Paliyan institutions as usually seen in the forest (including the frontier), then describing Tamil institutions and contact circumstances and, finally, examining the practices in H. Changes will be discussed as they are made apparent.

Postmarital residence

Forest Paliyans neither voice a postmarital residence rule nor think quite along those lines. At marriage or otherwise, their choice of a community or band is constrained by two simple, explicit considerations: a principle and a preference. The principle is that a couple, or a lone individual after the age of discretion, should exercise independent choice over such matters as movement and residence, opening the possibility of neolocality. In actuality, they see few choices as being attractive. Their preference is to live in a group containing primary relatives. They speak especially of being near mothers and siblings (and, late in life, near children). If a husband and wife come from different groups they may move back and forth irregularly; commonly, one of them takes the initiative and the other follows. A different path to the same end is for grown siblings, married or not, to move to a new group together. This is a common form of migration. Sets of siblings are prominent in every band studied and sibling exchange marriages are frequent (eight out of sixty-seven unions in one sample were with sibling's spouse's sibling). The general outcome of all this is sufficiently balanced to be called bilocal.

Adapting a formula developed by June Helm (1969), for each of five Paliyan bands I have weighed all possible male–male, female–female and cross-sex primary bonds between conjugal pairs (or formerly-married persons) co-resident within the group (Gardner 1969). For the five-band aggregate, virilocal and uxorilocal tendencies are 53 percent and 47 percent, respectively. Although two small, closely related bands were 75 percent virilocal and 38 percent virilocal, the others were all within a few points of the mean. These actual figures correspond well with what I have just portrayed as the dynamics of residence choice.

Many generations of sedentary life in H, new work patterns, and increased exposure to Tamil concepts of virilocality and patrilineal property inheritance stand to have had an impact on residence choice. Paliyans of H even talked about virilocality. The unusual size of the community might also have had some impact, for there were eighty-one Paliyans as contrasted with the usual band size of eighteen to thirty. What was found, however, was continued concern in H with both individual rights of choice and residence near primary kin. Nothing had interfered with these. Increase in community size had actually facilitated co-residence with kin: in eighteen of twenty-six recent marriages both parties had primary relatives in the community, an unusual frequency. Though choices were made as before, it must be reported as change (with implications for the future) that endogamy was on the increase and that less movement was needed to meet both spouses' needs. One goes a long way toward describing H by saying that it was built around fourteen living sets of siblings.

Notably, they had relationships of affection, and not corporate economic relationships such as Pehrson has reported for Könkämä Lapps (1964: 36, 41, 47–72, 107). Ten of the fourteen were brother-sister sets of two to five individuals, two were sets of brothers and two were sets of sisters — proportions indicating no sex bias. Male and female bonds between primary-related conjugal pairs (according to my adaptation of Helm's formula) were skewed not towards Tamil virilocality, but away from it — virilocal bonds having a frequency of 38 percent. Small sample size and the disproportionate number of elderly women in H account better for this shift than does culture change. Removing only two of the elderly women from the sample, for instance, brings the figures back to a more familiar 43 percent virilocal and 57 percent uxorilocal.

What accounts for the lack of change in residence rule? There are reasons for thinking that it is the lack of basic change in property relations or patterns of cooperation. Be that as it may, change in residence rule, which George Murdock holds to be a cornerstone of the evolution of social organization, is not to be part of the restructuring.

Household types

Household composition is also undergoing no obvious change. Briefly put, a third of all forest Paliyan households are slightly extended. They are what Kolenda calls 'supplemented nuclear families' (1967: 147). Such households are formed when: (a) people of advanced age live with their children's families; (b) youths (married or not) join married siblings, especially when orphaned; or (c) recently married young people stay on temporarily with the parents of one of them. Bonds that extend households are ones of affection. There may be considerable coordination of the members' work and play activities, yet a survey of their work and of the disposal of the fruit of their labors shows that their efforts are usually parallel rather than cooperative. The code is one of self-reliance and only those who are truly unable to attend to their own needs are permitted to be dependents. When that time comes the help is, ordinarily, forthcoming and gracious.

Among Hindus the factors behind extended family formation appear to be quite different from those of Paliyans. An ideal is involved, but large Hindu families are artefacts of corporate interests and the lack of bargaining power of the wife, not of fondness and disability (Gough 1956; Cohn 1961; Sarma 1964; Kolenda 1967). Thus there should be little or no pressure on the poor, landless Paliyans of H to comply with the Tamil ideal and no salience to them of the models. Eight of the twenty-four Paliyan households in H were slightly extended — the types of extension, as well as their overall frequency, being precisely those seen in the forest. A reasonable conclusion to draw is that, in this realm, Paliyan criteria for decision-making were unchanged and still operative.

Dimensions of husband–wife roles and gender relations

It is difficult to discuss husband and wife roles independently of the wider subject of gender relations. Accordingly, they will be treated together. In both areas there are major differences between Paliyan and Tamil social structures and the pressures for Paliyan change are extraordinary.

Although I have reported that it is 'acceptable' (Gardner 1972: 416) and 'fairly common' for forest Paliyan couples to 'live together with little or no economic cooperation' (Gardner 1965: 19–20), except perhaps in feeding children, I have also made clear that 'most' marriages involve economic sharing and cooperation (ibid.: 21). Both statements are correct because the division of labor is slight and we are looking at the exercise of options. Up to this point I have described only the economics. Watching various couples digging the staple yams or fishing, one finds that their sharing is more often playful or companionly than a matter of efficient, need-based, patterned complementarity. One sees them passing a digging stick back and forth at work with light verbal parries, for instance. When a long-married husband and wife break with custom and dance as a couple, instead of with circles of uniform sex, others gather to encourage them, stirred, displaying open appreciation. The group's recognition of their play as a couple resembles the response when, say, an elderly husband and wife (both in their fifties) emerge from their hut in the morning to go off for the whole day working in each other's clothes. Couples are privileged in their possibilities for play. Life with another is not a simple function of survival, it can be savored. We must avoid overstating these matters. The play is not something universal and incessant; and nor is the occasional absence of cooperation something stark and ominous — despite what some colleagues understand me to have meant. Morale and sociability in noncooperative unions may be good: the self-reliance is positive and principled, not an unwelcome imposition, and the results of that self-reliance are totally unlike the abandonment which occurs among the Ik (Turnbull 1972b).

There is another way of approaching this. Adult Paliyans owe each other respect as persons, which they talk of as owing each other freedom from the indignity of dependence. While, without question, marriage entails a flirtation with interdependence, neither spouse may take the other for granted. Mutual respect remains obligatory, a formal expression being the ban against either spouse using the other's name. Neither partner has authority over the other in any regard; neither has greater property rights, greater rights to divorce, greater freedom in sexual matters, and so on. Male and female may do some things with a different style, but it is symmetry that really matters in the field of rights and privileges.

South Indian social structure is just the opposite of this. With exceptions, such as the one discussed below, the usual rule is for males to have authority over females and seniors over juniors, for wives to owe deference to their husbands as shown by such means as not using their names, for males to possess greater property rights, and for females to have domestic as against public roles (summarized in Mandelbaum 1970: 34–41). I mentioned exceptions. Tamil laboring women number among those outsiders with whom Paliyans interact at the frontier, and heavily so in H. Such women enjoy more freedom of action than just outlined, their labor outside the home is necessary, they are economically independent, they participate in decision-making, and they retain close ties with their natal families (see Gough 1956; Gough Aberle 1978; Kolenda 1967). But if their behavior illustrates the acceptability of practical compromises in regard to Tamil social structural norms, these laboring women do at least know how to be circumspect. There is little compromise when it comes to social propriety and, like other Tamil women, they are subject to external controls. In keeping with this, Paliyan men are ridiculed for the independence 'permitted' their wives and daughters in matters which the men think of as solely the women's own business. They are ridiculed by people who deem it logical to equate unchecked independence of women with sexual indiscretion. Forest contractors' agents and foremen tell loud, derisive or teasing stories about the innocence and foolishness of particular Paliyans, doing so by name and within earshot of those very individuals. Although Hindu values are relativistic and group-specific, this does not protect Paliyans. Hindu groups jockey for rank in terms of the purity of their practices; moreover, as most Tamils in the frontier region see it, the Hindu paradigm is quite unable to accommodate an ethic as divergent as that of Paliyans — unless, in a religious context, they are likened to ascetics (Gardner 1982). Their principles are just not seen *as* principles.

I noted inconsistent trends. First, for many Paliyans, when familiarity with people results in trust, this leads to the adoption of an open, direct manner toward them. It takes time for Paliyans to get to know others, strange Paliyans included. One hears it said that it will be the children in immigrating families who will really belong to their new band. Shyness is an opening response yet, over time, a striking boldness can develop, even toward Tamil co-workers and employers. Notably, in the forest and frontier most women are slower than men to acquire the requisite familiarity. However, in H, a familiarity with outsiders was difficult to avoid. For the Tamils, shy restraint is proper wifely behavior, and openness only made the already-independent Paliyan wives seem further beyond their husbands' control. What is more, open women were likely to defend forcefully their rights to independence of action when feeling that these were challenged — a brazen, impudent response in Tamil eyes.

The contrary trend in situations of intensified contact was a height-ened orthopraxy — an accentuation, by Paliyans, of claimed and actual practices that accord with Tamil expectations. Five examples from H illustrate the trend. The first example has to do with public versus domestic gender roles, the next three with male responsibility and authority, and the final one with deference of women and children to adult males. (1) A young father who was relatively conservative about Paliyan values answered a question about possible differences in be-havior of boys and girls thus: 'Boys work outside and girls work in the houses'. When checked against behavior abstract Paliyan statements tend to be hesitant, low-level empirical generalization. My observations indicate that this one was, rather, a Tamil formalism about gender roles. (2) Paliyans occasionally referred to other Paliyans' houses by means of the husbands' names. In the forest this would be a tactless cause for offense; it hints of male ownership or male responsibility as household head. (3) Two women, insulted and harassed by a foreman at work, announced in tears that they would tell their husbands. They spoke as if dependent on their husbands, as if their husbands took responsibility for them. (4) Two young men watched the behavior of their unmarried teenage sisters and followed them on several occa-sions, checking suspiciously on their movements and activities. Al-though one had spoken to me of his intended sister-exchange marriage, by acting as if he was in charge of his sister's behavior he directly violated her right to autonomy. (5) Great difference was noted in the organization of communal feasts by H Paliyans in 1963 compared with 1978. In 1963, we sat in a rough circle, with men's, women's and children's sections, eating simultaneously. In 1978, by contrast, even when I cited the earlier feast as precedent, invoked Paliyan egalitarian values, and even objected outright, this was inadequate to prevent a two-stage feast — men and visitors first, women and children after-wards. There was no wavering over the need to show deference to the adult males. What had happened? In 1972, due to a government construction project, H Paliyans had been displaced more than a kilometer and coalesced with a larger, new community of Tamils. The level of verbal harassment had risen sharply. By 1978 most Paliyans (about two-thirds of H's population) had already migrated to quieter communities, whilst those who remained spoke of intense social pres-sures. As examples of orthopraxy, all these instances, except the last, betrayed little actual organizational change. However, they were different from most other Paliyan attempts to appear proper to Tamils in that central Paliyan social structural principles were contradicted. More than this, all these statements and acts went unchallenged. Looked at in this way, and taken together, they foretold possible general acceptance in H of something radically new — social asymmetry.

Kin terminology

Paliyans in the forest and frontier have a shadowy generational kin terminology which lurks behind the Tamil (Dravidian) terminology that they exhibit before outsiders (Gardner 1972: 426–9). Despite the systematic character of their generational terminology and notwithstanding its fit with their bilocal residence, they are hesitant (perhaps due to protective orthopraxy) to acknowledge it as a terminological system in its own right. It shows up largely through heavy 'interference', in the linguistic sense.[2] The terms themselves are Tamil ones; it is their referents which are at variance from those usual to the region. Paliyans make distinctions according to sex, generation and affinity.

Tamil kinship terminology is patterned in terms of sex, generation, relative age, and bifurcate-merging distinctions. Paliyans take the striking feature of it to be the classing of cross-kin with affines rather than with parallel-kin; Paliyans would differentiate only kin from affines. Because all Paliyan terms are found in the Tamil system, Tamils have to learn the Paliyans' intended referents to understand that Paliyans employ the terms differently. Once they do understand this, the revelation is startling. From a Tamil viewpoint Paliyan generational usage obscures a crucial distinction between wife-givers and wife-takers, between members of one's own line and marriageable people. No more consequential 'error' would be possible for Tamils and, on discovering it, their shocked responses have surely ranged from derision to helpful lessons. Meanwhile, in keeping with their relatively successful attempts to use kin terms 'acceptably' at the frontier, Paliyans also claim, uniformly but inaccurately, to practice cross-cousin and cross-niece marriage in the Tamil fashion. It all goes together for, as Louis Dumont (1953) aptly expressed it in the title of his early paper, 'The Dravidian kinship terminology [is] an expression of marriage'.

Even though residence in H has remained bilocal, which is consistent with generational terminology, in that community the Paliyans' own kin term system has dropped from use. For bicultural Paliyans of the

2. Fifteen percent of all terms elicited were intrusions from the Paliyan system (Gardner 1972: 427). Because over half one's immediate relatives are given the same term in both kin-term systems, the rate of interference in terms for one's remaining close relatives was well over 30 percent.

forest, Tamil kinship serves a protective function, even when employed very superficially. In the case of H it has become the only kinship system and appears to have become so quickly. It is reasonable to ask how difficult that change might have been. The two kinship systems do not have many points of difference. Two of the main changes needed to transform the Paliyan system to a Tamil one were recognizing cross-kin and learning to class them with affines. Sedentary Paliyans are an exception to Murdock's finding that kin terminology is usually the last aspect of a changing social system to come into line with the new structure (1949). Among H Paliyans it led the way.

Marriage preferences

Paliyans, among themselves, are heard to give preference to marriage with *sondakārar*, members of a fuzzy set of their closest consanguines and affines. About 35 percent of their marriages in the forest are indeed with secondary, tertiary, or quaternary relatives. As just mentioned, forest Paliyans, when talking before outsiders, offer formulaic prescriptions that men marry '*atte mahalum akka mahalum*' or '*māma mahalum maccān mahalum*', either phrase describing cross-cousins and cross-nieces (the nieces being older sister's or brother-in-law's daughters), but in practice their marriages belie their claims. While 25 percent are with actual or classificatory 'prescribed' partners, 18 percent are with actual or classificatory parallel-cousins, parallel nieces, and other 'proscribed' relatives (these are slight corrections of previously published figures of 22 percent and 19 percent, respectively; they are based on better sampling. Gardner 1965: 42, 46; 1969: 156; 1972: 428).

There are two things to be said about the Paliyan preferred age difference of spouses. First, relative age *per se* is not of great moment. Out of twenty-nine forest couples for whom I have careful age estimates, there is only one couple in which the partners are the same age; in twenty couples the husband is two to thirty-six years older ($\bar{x} = 14$ years difference, $\sigma = 11$ years) and in eight couples the wife is two to forty-one years older ($\bar{x} = 15$ years difference, $\sigma = 13$ years). Affairs show a similar pattern. Second, five of the same twenty-nine unions were once pedogamous — marriages which grew out of stepparent–stepchild relations. This is considered by some a durable, desirable type of marriage and my data do attest to its durability. In a wider sample of four forest bands, at least sixteen out of 153 past and present marriages were of this type (to use their idiom, eleven involved 'bringing up' girls, five involved 'bringing up' boys). It is not everybody's preference, but some who have options make deliberate plans for it.

Tamil marriage prescriptions are more restricted in some *jāti* (castes) than others, the full range of prescribed partners for a man being matrilateral and patrilateral cross-cousins, older sister's daughters, and their classificatory equivalents. Other relatives are categorically excluded. It is also important to South Indians that husband be older than wife.[3] As already outlined, the Tamil marriage rules are integral to their kinship systems. These latter are so tightly structured that improper marriage is almost inconceivable.

With forest Paliyans claiming to follow some Tamil marriage rules and preferences, we might anticipate that in H there would be actual compliance. And indeed: (1) Only 10 percent of thirty marriages in H were with close relatives (cf. 35 percent in the forest). (2) Whether close or classificatory, 'irregular' parallel unions had a much diminished frequency of 7 percent; 'proper' cross unions continued at 20 percent. (3) Spouses' age differences were usually less than five years and were never more than eight or ten years, with husbands always being senior. Finally, (4) pedogamy was not in evidence. Except for the fact that some parallel marriage continued (and one case entailed a very distant relationship), compliance with Tamil social structure appeared to be taken very seriously.

Remarriage

Because of their overriding concern with retreat from antagonists, forest Paliyans have fragile marriages. This I have described elsewhere (Gardner 1966; 1972). Not only is social harmony more important than continuation of relationships, but divorce and remarriage are free of legal and economic obstacles and are viewed as the principal parties' own business. Actual figures on Paliyan remarriage are given below.

In Hindu India, although one or both sexes of a given *jāti* may traditionally have had legal rights to divorce, marriage is accorded sanctity. It also entails complex exchanges between families and severing a union involves one or both of the natal families in financial and social complications. For all but low-ranking Hindus there are also impediments to the remarriage of widows, which has come to be treated as an index of group laxity and impropriety; there has been a trend toward upwardly mobile *jāti* enacting and enforcing bans against it for the group's sake.

Whether it was simply people acting in terms of Hindu marital beliefs and practices, or whether other factors were involved (such as changing styles of conflict resolution and demographic imbalances), the Paliyans of H had considerably less frequent remarriage than other

3. One rare and relatively unknown alleged exception is marriage of boys to mature women in a *jāti* occupying the upper slopes of the range behind H.

Table 6.1: Frequency of remarriage of Paliyans in different settings

| | No. of marriages/no. and percentage of adult population | | | | | | | | | |
| | 0 | | 1 union | | 2 unions | | Over 2 unions | | Total | |
Setting	no.	%	no.	%	no.	%	no.	%	no.	%
Forest	2	5	17	44	9	23	11	28	39	100
H	10	19	33	62	4	8	6	11	53	100

Paliyans studied. Table 6.1 summarizes the marital histories of ninety-two Paliyans. It shows the number and percentage of adults who had never married and those who had contracted one, two and three or more marriages; it shows these figures for H and for forest Paliyans on whom there is roughly comparable genealogical information. What really underlies the difference? I will take up three major possibilities.

First, there was less use of mobility to solve problems of social stress in H than in the forest. If change toward use of forbearance and conciliation (and away from separation) had been the main thing to alter the frequency of remarriage in H, then that frequency ought to show a similar drop for both sexes. Also, remarriages after the death of spouses ought to constitute an increased share of the remarriages that still occured. Whether these expectations are borne out can be ascertained empirically.

Second, H had a surplus of adult females and the forest Paliyans had the opposite problem. If sex ratio were the main factor affecting the remarriage rate, we would expect unmarried women and widowed or divorced men in H to have exploited each other's availability, pushing up the rate of remarriage of H men relative to that of women. There should also be few unmarried men in H. We would expect a corresponding elevation of the rate of remarriage of women in the forest and a dearth of unmarried women there.

Finally, people of H were known to be hearing about correct forms of marriage from Tamils. While Hindu obstacles to divorce and remarriage pertain much more to women than men, unavailability of women for remarriage would have direct implications for men too. If the situation in H was merely one result of Paliyans acting in terms of Tamil social structural propriety, we would expect to see men remarrying as able to do so and widowed women remaining unmarried.

What *is* the frequency of remarriage for the two sexes? Table 6.2 presents the same information as Table 6.1, with a breakdown by sex, and Table 6.3 summarizes information on never-married and unremarried people in the two settings. Although the groups studied are too small for reliable conclusions to be drawn, the samples are total sam-

Table 6.2: Frequency of remarriage of Paliyan males and females in different settings

| | No. of marriages/no. and percentage of adults, by gender | | | | | | | | | |
| | 0 | | 1 union | | 2 unions | | Over 2 unions | | Total | |
Setting/gender	no.	%	no.	%	no.	%	no.	%	no.	%
Forest female	0	0	4	25	6	38	6	38	16	100
H female	6	20	21	70	2	7	1	3	30	100
Forest male	2	9	13	57	3	13	5	22	23	100
H male	4	17	12	52	2	9	5	22	23	100

Table 6.3: Never-married and unremarried Paliyan males and females in different settings

| | Marital status/no. and percentage of total adults, by gender | | | | | | | |
| | Never wed | | Widowed | | Divorced | | Total single | |
Setting and gender	no.	%	no.	%	no.	%	no.	%
Forest female	0	0	0	0	0	0	0	0
Forest male	2	9	0	0	0	0	2	9
H female	6	20	5	17	2	7	13	43
H male	4	17	2	9	0	0	6	26

ples and the patterns are striking.

The extraordinarily similar statistical profiles of remarriage of men in the two communities (seen in the lower half of Table 6.2) bears mentioning. There may be diverse factors behind the similar patterns, but it is difficult to look at just the male figures and speak of circumstances in H in terms of patience or conciliation replacing marital separation. The proportion of all remarriages which follow upon divorce, rather than death of a spouse, is virtually identical in the two settings (forest 77 percent, H 75 percent), lending further support to the idea that new ways of handling marital stress are not what is responsible for changing frequencies of remarriage.

The possible effects, in H, of sex ratio imbalances and Tamil pressure against remarriage are difficult to separate from each other, because the expected remarriage patterns for women would be very similar in the two instances. We can read Table 6.2 as meeting both expectations: first, women have higher frequencies of remarriage than do men in the forest and lower ones in H, which is what sex ratios led us to predict; second, the frequency of female remarriage is markedly lower in H, as Tamil pressure regarding Hindu values led us to predict. Indeed, if both these factors were involved, the opposing pressures for and against H males remarrying could account for constancy of male remarriage frequencies. Other data need to be examined.

One of the most telling sets of figures is the number and proportion of men and women in H who were single at the time of the study (Table 6.3). The shortage of adult males ought not to have permitted 26 percent of them to be single, especially with 43 percent of the adult females in the community single and with people preferring village-endogamous marriage. These figures are mute concerning the importance of other factors, but they give us, at last, a basis for speaking of restraint in remarriage among H Paliyans, probably under the influence of Tamil Hindu social structure. Other reasons for the restraint were not obvious.

In keeping with the apparent Tamilization in H with respect to preferences for marriage and remarriage, there was a change in wedding ceremonies. One sees modest Tamil ritual orthopraxy among frontier Paliyans (Gardner 1972: 436); at the edge of the forest, some skip wedding ceremonies, but others respond to their neighbors' advice and expectations, and spend up to half a month's income on new clothing, ornaments, wedding paraphernalia and food. Meanwhile, in H, the still more proper weddings were costing three to ten times as much. Yet marriage remained essentially a personal matter. The Paliyan code of self-sufficiency was applied to the business of preparing for the new wedding expenses, with interesting implications. While they would not have to bear the entire expense themselves, young people of H worked assiduously to put aside money for their own weddings. In the process, marriage was being delayed well past puberty. I got the sense that marriage was becoming a more serious matter, that a stricter line was being drawn between play and accepted marriage. Certainly the casual, often fragile marriage between adolescents was disappearing. The phenomenon deserves further study.

Conclusions: pressures for Tamil propriety in Paliyan social organization

Although it gives us an initial framework, it is also oversimplifying to say that Paliyans know two social structures and organize their social life variably in terms of them. Paliyan knowledge of different realms of Tamil social life varies. Circumstances vary, too, and so does Tamil pressure for Paliyan change. We need to look at all this to grasp the Paliyan organizational changes which may result from their interaction with Tamil neighbors.

We have seen that in H remarriage may be a function of more than one factor. In other realms it is Tamil ridicule, censure, and advice — all in the name of propriety — which loom as the main things influencing which aspects of social organization are changing and what rates of change occur. Looking at two kinds of community (forest-frontier and sedentary) has helped to facilitate the analysis, because what were merely possible frontier trends have been seen in more certain forms. We must not lose sight, though, of the assumption which this approach entails, as to the nature of the culture of H Paliyans before they became sedentary.

There were reasons for the order in which the six selected realms of Paliyan social organization were described in this chapter. But much can be learned from scaling the changes found in these realms, as is done in Table 6.4. We see in this tabular summary that it is in kinship and marriage, the heart of the elegant Tamil social system, that Paliyans appear to pay the greatest heed to Tamil social structure. Tamils are vocal and explicit about that structure, they press for related changes, and the outcome is systematic.

Special attention needs to be paid, too, to what is occurring in the realm of gender and relations between spouses. The two social structures are mutually contradictory in that realm. Although organizational changes in gender relations are not advanced in any of the communities studied, such changes *are* under way and they stand to have considerable impact on the Paliyan way of life. They promise to undercut key Paliyan egalitarian principles. If the trend continues, from a Paliyan viewpoint it will surely be the most consequential aspect of the changing order.

We must remember, none the less, that two-thirds of the 'original' population of H elected to leave during the 1970s, moving away from intensifying pressures. This is the time-honored Paliyan solution to intercultural stress and unbearable compromise. If the H Paliyans who departed were true to their tradition, that move meant not only a chance for peace but also an opportunity to restore what they regard as principled living.

Table 6.4: Changing Paliyan social organization as revealed by a comparison of forest-frontier communities and sedentary Paliyans of H

The two social structures	Realms of Paliyan social organization, scaled for extent of change					
	household types	residence rule	remarriage	Hu-Wi roles, gender	preferred marriage	kin terms
Paliyan social structure; Tamil patterns not voiced	forest, H	forest				
Paliyan social structure; knowledge of Tamil patterns		(H)	forest	forest		
Paliyan social structure; claims to Tamil patterns		(H)			forest	
Paliyan social structure; some Tamil behavior				H		forest
Paliyan social structure; considerable Tamil behavior			H		H	
Paliyan patterns not voiced; Tamil social structure						H

7. Tributary tradition and relations of affinity and gender among the Sumatran Kubu

Øyvind Sandbukt

My aim in this chapter is to demonstrate an instance of uncommon historical continuity in the external relations of tropical forest foragers, and to show how the nature of these relations crucially affects aspects of internal organization.[1]

Unlike the tropical foragers identified by Woodburn (1980) as having 'immediate-return' type socio-economic systems, the Sumatran Kubu are strongly characterized by social asymmetries and binding ties between specific others. Most notably, they differ in this respect from the Malaysian and South Indian forest foragers, in spite of the fact that, in ways comparable to these groups, the Kubu have a long history of enclavement by populations of cultivators and by trade-oriented kingdoms, of engagements in the collection of forest produce for external exchange, and of exposure to considerable intensities of exploitative pressure. Thus, the theses propounded with respect to the situation of the South Indian foragers, that competitive procurement of forest products for external trade (Fox 1969) and pressures exerted by powerful neighbours (Gardner 1966) will generate fragmented or individualistic interpersonal relations, appear to be invalidated in the Kubu case.

Assuming that basic configurations of social structure may need considerable time, possibly generations, to crystallize or attain institutional integration, it would be a great advantage, to say the least, to be able to assess their determinants in a historical perspective. The basic

1. The fieldwork on which this chapter is based was carried out in 1979–80 and 1985–6 under the auspices of Lembaga Ilmu Pengetahuan Indonesia and the local sponsorship in Sumatra of Fakultas Hukum, Universitas Jambi. Financial support has been received from the Norwegian Research Council for Science and the Humanities, the Institute for Comparative Research in Culture, Oslo, the Fridtjof Nansen's and Affiliated Funds for Advancement of Science and the Humanities, Per Rygh's Fund, and Carl Lumholtz's Fund. Writing up has, additionally, been supported by a Wigeland Fellowship awarded by the American-Scandinavian Foundation. The maps were drawn by Lene Østergaard, at the University of Michigan, Ann Arbor. She has, furthermore, contributed greatly by constructively criticizing the paper, which has also been helpfully read and commented upon by Jeff Kingston and, in an earlier version, by Aram Yengoyan.

quandary, certainly for the area in question here, is that reasonably detailed data are generally unavailable for the period prior to colonial rule while that very same rule fundamentally changed the basis for political and economic power, especially on the supralocal or intersocietal level. In my own research experience, this kind of discontinuity has been particularly sharp in the case of the coastal populations of eastern Sumatra and the south-western Malay Peninsula,[2] but it is also very prominent with respect to the forest-dwelling populations of the Sumatran interior.[3] While there are some institutional continuities at the supralocal level, their interactive content and significance have, by and large, undergone fundamental change. However, for reasons of topography and historical circumstance, the Kubu[4] in one particular enclave exhibit an extraordinary degree of institutional and interactive continuity which makes for a particularly instructive case study.

Those Kubu who possess a tradition of nomadic foraging have a distinctive geographical distribution that corresponds roughly to the piedmont zone (about 50–150 metres above sea level) in south-central Sumatra. This coincides with those upstream parts of the Batang Hari and, to some extent, the Musi drainages where numerous small and medium-sized interfluves (typically between 500 and 2000 square kilometres) are formed by fans of navigable tributaries (see Map 1).[5] Being inhabitants of these interfluves, which are covered by rainforest, the Kubu are surrounded by sedentary riparian populations who, although known traditionally as Orang Batin (*batin* being the generic name for their headmen), are in effect Muslim Malays. Until they

2. My main fieldwork there has been among the so-called Orang Kuala or Duano on the Indragiri/Jambi coast and among the migrants from this area on the south-west coast of Johor (cf. Sandbukt n.d.). Surveys have also been carried out among the Orang Utan and the Orang Akit who inhabit the littoral to the north of the Orang Kuala.

3. In addition to the Kubu, these are the Orang Talang Mamak between the Batang Hari and the Indragiri rivers, the Orang Talang between the Indragiri and the Kampar and between the Kampar and the Siak rivers, as well as the Orang Sakai between the Siak and the Rokan rivers. These populations were surveyed in the course of 1985 in connection with my return to the Kubu.

4. 'Kubu' or 'Orang Kubu' is the name applied to the non-Muslim forest dwellers by the Malays of the Batang Hari and Musi river basins of southern Sumatra. The basic meaning of the word *kubu* is 'fortification' or 'defensive refuge', the implication being that the forest is used as such by its inhabitants to remain independent from outside society.

5. The best known Kubu are the inhabitants of the huge interfluve on the downstream peneplains *between* the Batang Hari and the Musi rivers. It was within this area, referred to by the Dutch as Koeboestreken, that both Bernard Hagen, the author of a monograph (1908), and Paul Schebesta, his later critic (1926), visited the Kubu. Except for his initial glimpse of the Ridan Kubu (1906), it was also on the basis of experience in this area that the Dutch colonial civil servant, van Dongen, wrote his account of the Kubu (1910). However, it appears that this population, like those of the other peneplain interfluves of eastern Sumatra (namely, the Talang Mamak, the Talang and the Sakai), does not possess a nomadic foraging tradition as much as one of swiddening combined with collection of forest produce for external exchange. As Schebesta (1926) has argued, it may well be that they have at times been driven to evasive mobility because of Malay depredations, thus giving the impression of being nomadic forest foragers. At present this population has become substantially assimilated to the Muslim Malay identity.

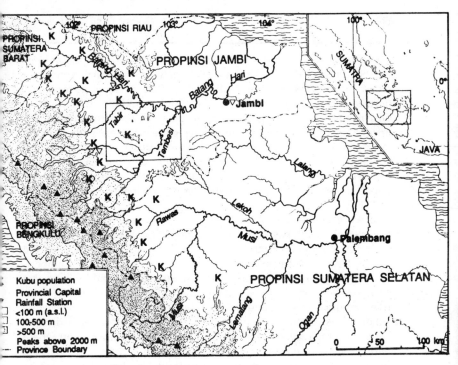

Map 7.1. Distribution of Kubu population associated with foraging.

adopted rubber cultivation in the present century these Malays, in addition to subsisting by horticulture, were strongly oriented towards the forest for the collection of valuable trade products. In the pre-colonial era, the Batang Hari and Musi river systems were controlled, respectively, by the kingdoms of Jambi and Palembang. Being the most durable of the Sumatran state formations, these trading polities have been linked with the identity of the seventh-century empire known as Srivijaya and its antecedent kingdoms (Wolters 1967). While the Palembang kingdom was occupied and abrogated by the Dutch as early as the 1820s, Jambi remained formally intact until the opening years of the 1900s. Only the people living along the Batang Hari mainstream were direct, corvée-yielding subjects of the kingdom. The riparian population on the branchings of the Batang Hari (the Orang Batin) was constituted in a large number of nominally autonomous communities that were subject to payment of tribute. That tribute was collected by functionaries, known as *jenang,* who were elected by — and ideally from amongst — groupings or 'federations' of local communities, their choices being subject to confirmation by the ruler. Backed by the authority of the Sultan, the jenang also acted as arbiters in disputes that could not otherwise be settled within or between communities in their respective tribute areas. Historical sources also indicate that the interfluvial Kubu maintained very similar relations to *jenang* (Tideman 1938).

Replacing the Jambi sultanate with a 'residency' comprising a number of territorial subdivisions (*onderafdeelingen*), the Dutch sought to retain or to refashion the traditional entities of local government (termed *marga*) to facilitate a measure of indirect administration based on customary law (*adat*). Among the physical infrastructures developed, a major north–south road following the piedmont with connecting upstream–downstream roads was particularly important. These roads opened the upstream interfluves inhabited by the Kubu, bringing about a very considerable diversification of their external exchange opportunities and an increasingly direct participation in the market economy.

However, the largest of the interfluves within the Batang Hari drainage system was bypassed by such infrastructural developments. This 'island', of roughly 2500 square kilometres, is surrounded by the Batang Hari mainstream and its two largest tributaries, the Tembesi-Merangin and the Tabir, while the upstream gap is filled by extensive swamps. Furthermore, constituting the geographical heart of Jambi, this interfluve was divided between no less than four administrative subdivisions. In the present Indonesian scheme, it remains divided between three regencies (*kabupaten*) which, in fact, disagree on where within the interfluve their boundaries should be. Accordingly, this area has remained very much an administrative no man's land where certain archaic political institutions hold remarkable sway.

Totalling about 800 individuals (up from an estimated 400 some seventy-five years ago; cf. Waterschoot van der Gracht 1915), the Kubu within this interfluve are distributed between 'home ranges' which correspond to the upper reaches of major drainages. The main distinctions are thus between the people of the Mengkekal, the Kejasungs (Besar and Kecil — 'major' and 'minor'), the Air Hitam and the Serenggam (see Map 2). The subsistence regime of these forest dwellers comprises two distinct modes, foraging (*remayow*) and cultivation (*behuma*), which are conceptualized and generally experienced as alternating phases in people's lives. In either subsistence mode, forest produce is also collected for the purpose of obtaining certain essentials or valuables through external exchange.[6] At the time of my fieldwork, the Kubu were not direct participants in the money economy but practised exchange in kind to obtain such commodities as salt, tobacco, metal tools and cloth. Though used as loincloths, sheets of cloth are mainly accumulated as a store of wealth or as a medium of internal exchange and debt payment.

Although the surrounding Malay world is thus a source of desired goods, the Kubu strongly perceive it as a domain characterized by

---

6. A fairly detailed account of the resource use of the Kubu and how it relates to their socio-political organization can be found in Sandbukt (1988).

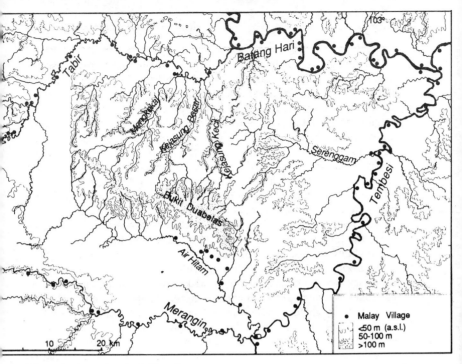

Map 7.2. Area of main fieldwork.

danger (*bahayo*), a perception that is very much sustained and symbolically elaborated in their cosmology and ritual practices (Sandbukt 1984). The threat of slave capture — which was real only a few generations ago (Winter 1901) — is of course a thing of the past, as is debt-bondage. However, the idiom and some of the implications of bondage in connection with indebtedness to external authorities remain real. The Kubu are very conscious of the fact that their way of life is perceived in extremely negative terms by the external world and that the present Indonesian government, like the Dutch one before it, would prefer to have them brought out of the forest and concentrated in settlements. To the Kubu, this would be tantamount to bringing about the end of the world as they know it. Also, the outside is greatly feared for its devastating epidemics of which there are traumatic memories. Outsider hostility and extreme contempt remain for the Kubu a stock experience as do efforts to exploit them in various ways.

Avoidance constitutes a basic strategic ingredient in the way these Kubu have adapted to the reality and perceptions of external dangers. It is dramatically evidenced in the response of seemingly panic-stricken flight on the part of Kubu women and children to the approach of outsiders. More importantly, however, there is a pervasive stress on mobility in Kubu culture and, especially, on the capacity for sustained residential mobility, or nomadism, based on foraging.

The primary rainforest contains a diverse and stable resource base for foragers. However, the carrying capacity of the tuberous vines, which constitute the most important staple food, appears to be very low. The Kubu themselves certainly consider the unremitting effort involved in digging deep-rooting tubers to be very onerous as well as relatively unrewarding. Foragers are thus propelled towards the extensive eco-tones created by Malay cultivators on the fringes of the forest. Fallows contain residual quantities of domesticated tubers that can be harvested with less effort than wild ones and, concomitantly, pig hunting can here be better than in the primary forest. Moreover, food may be begged or stolen from owners of cultivated fields or obtained in ex-change for transient work or forest produce.[7] This situation implies a potential for mutualism, but also for conflicts with outsiders and vulnerability to hostile attentions.

By making swiddens of their own within the forest, the Kubu solve some of these problems, but at the risk of becoming less adaptive to variable economic opportunities and more vulnerable to political coercion. Accordingly, swiddens tend to be treated as basecamp sites which are frequently returned to rather than continuously lived in. Indeed, small plots may be maintained with kin in widely-dispersed fields in order to increase residential flexibility. The fundamental ambivalence attendant on sedentarizing tendencies comes to the fore whenever a swidden group member dies. The state of mourning (*belangun*) then brought about entails the abandonment of the field and a nomadic foray away from the locality.[8] Although there is considerable variation in the duration of *belangun* observance, the important point remains that this institution affords an unimpeachable excuse for breaking up and escaping an ambivalent or disadvantageous situation.

While nomadic mobility has apparently constituted a basic element of a strategy of coping in a situation of hostile enclavement, an equally basic element has been the maintenance of a formal politico-jural tie to an external authority accompanied by the payment of tribute. This authority is vested in a Malay personage, who holds the traditional title *jenang* discussed above. He resides in a village on the Air Hitam, the largest river draining the interfluve and the only one along which permanent Malay village communities are found. Enshrined in custom-ary law, his overt function is a mediating one between the forest dwellers and the external govenment. The *jenang* is thus perceived by the government as someone who has the special trust of the Kubu, who

7. The availability of resource-enhanced ecotones may constitute a necessary condition and thus an ecological explanation for the nomadic foraging adaptation of the Kubu in the piedmont.
8. This period should be long enough for the remains of the unburied corpse to vanish, or even for any direct signs of the activity of the deceased — epitomized as machete chop-marks on tree stumps — to disappear.

is able to communicate with them and, ultimately, to bring influence to bear on them. The Kubu, in contrast, perceive him as a personal guarantor of their autonomy and consider their continued adherence to the customary law, which defines them in relation to the *jenang*, as constituting a basic legitimization of their traditional way of life.

Although succession to the *jenang*-ship is heavily weighted in favour of sons or sons-in-law, the Kubu themselves are the ones to select and formally install incumbents. The present one succeeded his father in the 1930s. How his father apparently usurped the title from the previous holder, who was not a close relative, is not entirely clear, but some Kubu informants credit him with having secured the release of forest dwellers who had been captured by the Dutch. This was probably in connection with the Jambinese rebellions in the early part of the century to which the forest people, willingly or pressed, allegedly lent support. The implication seems to be that, after the sultanate was abrogated, the new *jenang* was somehow able to establish himself as an effective protector of the Kubu with reference to his apparent influence with the new source of power.

According to *adat* precepts, the *jenang* is entitled to tribute (*jajah jenang*). Precisely in the manner of the tribute collectors under the sultanate, he advances goods (mainly cloth and metal tools) as 'obliging gifts' (*serah*) that must be reciprocated in the form of forest produce, especially dragon's blood resin, within a number of months. The *jenang*'s profit on these 'gift exchanges' amounts to several hundred — even thousand — per cent. To facilitate his dealings, the *jenang* makes use of a hierarchy of Kubu headmen who act as his intermediaries and receive goods on special terms or even as outright gifts. These headmen are also empowered to impose fines (assessed in sheets of cloth) in accordance with their formal title and rank,[9] the *jenang* remaining the ultimate judicial authority. Though appointed or confirmed by the *jenang*, the headmen acquire legitimacy through internal competition between incumbents and candidates in which they demonstrate mastery of *adat* law and formal oratorical display of its sayings.

The political situation is considerably more complex than this brief sketch allows for. In particular, there are other authorities that have, to an increasing degree, been able to usurp the *jenang*'s position. However, the basic point remains that external relations have given rise to a sphere of politico-jural interactions that constitute a wellspring of formal *adat* laws which the Kubu have adopted and adapted to suit conditions of life in the forest. Moreover, these external relations are almost exclusively a male domain. It is considered inappropriate, even dangerous, for females (and children) to be exposed to outside contact.

---

9. The main titles are, in descending order of importance, *temeggong*, *dipati* (each with a *wakil* or deputy), *mangku*, *anak dalam* and *menti*.

While there may well have been very good grounds for such avoidance in times past, strategic benefits remain in selectively or situationally limiting outsiders' access. Perhaps more importantly, the image of an essentially evil and threatening external world is actively nurtured by males and especially by headmen who, because they are generally also influential shamans, are able to elaborate and manipulate collective socio-cosmic conceptions (cf. Sandbukt 1984). In any case, the implication is that females not only need protection from perceived external dangers, but necessarily depend on males for access to certain essential or highly valued goods derived from external relations. Concomitantly, in the phraseology of the *adat* law, females are referred to as dependants or minors, such as in the stock expression, *anak bini, anak gediy, jendo rando orang* ('someone's child and wife, unmarried daughter, divorced/widowed female relative').

The application of *adat* law within Kubu society is, in fact, extensively concerned with the control of females or, more accurately, control of male access to female sexuality and reproductive capacity. Whereas women are regarded as minors, hardly accountable for their actions in point of law, men are not only legally responsible but, being perceived as the more active agents, are also considered inherently more culpable than women. While large fines are prescribed for committing adultery, indemnities are also provided for a range of transgressions that either carry an implicit threat of adultery or constitute undue intimacy.[10] The implication, then, is that marital unions are probably more stable than would be the case if such sanctions were unavailable.

The *adat* law, furthermore, provides males with a definite basis for claiming authority over daughters, in contrast to sons who, even as adolescents, are themselves jurally responsible and autonomous agents rather than dependants. Unmarried daughters are hedged with legally sanctioned prohibitions similar to the ones applicable to wives, the main import of which is that a high price can be exacted from suitors. This price entails, first of all, what in effect is bride-service for an unspecified period that may last several years. During this period the suitor should show his worth by avidly performing all the provisioning tasks encumbent on a male — providing meat, honey and exchange goods and, in the cultivation mode, helping to clear swiddens.

While a marriage may be negotiated and formally arranged by the families involved, such an arrangement is, in fact, a rarity. The Kubu say they do not wish to 'give away' daughters and a suitor is eventually forced to precipitate a crisis by running away with one of the girl's belongings. This leads to a formal gathering (*perkaro*) of the parties to resolve the matter, which requires payment by the male's family to that

10. For example, entering the inappropriate part of a dwelling, stepping on a woman's mat, winking, talking improperly.

of the female of a fine or, literally, 'debt' (*hutang*) of thirty pieces of cloth. Moreover, it is part of the proceedings that female and pre-adult male relatives of the bride respond to the requisite admission of (usually unspecified) guilt by the groom with a more or less frenzied physical punishment of him. This can involve quite severe beatings and is said to deter at least some males from precipitating marriage before their in-laws have been softened up by avid service.[11]

The advantages to the bride's family in avoiding a negotiated marriage are significant. A properly arranged marriage entails the payment of a brideprice of ten sheets of cloth which, apart from being considerably less than the fine, may actually carry an implication of entitlement to the bride which the payment of a fine does not. Payment of a portion of the fine may be deferred and then possibly never made, resulting in a condition of implicit debt-bondage and, therefore, accentuated subordination to the in-laws. In any case, it is specified by *adat* that sons-in-law should continue to follow their fathers-in-law, providing them with succour and support. Indeed, this can be enforced since parents and, by filiative extension, brothers, are jurally entitled to divorce daughters/sisters if sons-/brothers-in-law are deemed not to fulfil their affinal obligations. In such a case a man may be forced, as the *adat* phrase goes, to depart with only his loin-cloth, although property bestowed as marital endowment by a husband's family should revert to its source.

While sons are dispersed in uxorilocal marriage, daughters remain in greater proximity not only to their parents, but also to permanent parental property such as stands of fruit-trees (*nuaron*), which are generated as a consequence of swiddening, or honey-yielding bees'-nest trees (*sialong*). According to one of the *adat* law sayings, daughters should inherit the 'heavy' (*nang berat*) and sons the 'light' (*nang rehat*). While this is sometimes said to refer to 'immovables' versus 'movables', the more general implication is that daughters are the recipients and users of the material aspect of the inheritance and sons its jural custodians. In other words, it is incumbent upon brothers to protect their sisters' property rights against usurpation. This duty entitles brothers to a share in the produce from inherited trees and to contributions from mobile wealth (especially cloth) to pay debts or fines. While women are thus the effective recipients of property passed on from one generation to the next, they are, more generally, the formal owners of what men procure, such as exchange goods and meat. These goods, in contrast to the pleated utensils for personal use (such as sleeping mats, food satchels, tobacco pouches) and the starchy foods that men have a reciprocal right to receive from women, are extremely valuable and

---

11. The overt justification for the punishment, which is called *bunoh* (literally, 'kill'), is to extirpate the *malu* or sense of shame of the bride's kin.

socially salient. Women, then, not only have the right to satisfy their appetite for meat in precedence to men, but also preside over the distribution of meat within and between camps. Moreover, they determine the disposal of accumulated cloth. Finally, women are able collectively to demand that husbands' efforts to provide meat and exchange goods be intensified on the grounds that such provisioning, while basically an aspect of the gender division of labour, also constitutes a sanctioned affinal obligation.

The external tributary relations of the Kubu constitute a politico-jural sphere, which has been shown to be a wellspring of formal *adat* law and internal social differentiation. An almost exclusively male domain characterized by competition and hierarchy, it provides the interactive grounds and the conceptual means for defining females as jural minors and dependants. However, this does not so much imply control of women, who can hardly be held legally responsible for their actions, as heavily sanctioned access to them on the part of men, who are culpable jural majors. Suitors and sons-in-law can thus be made to do brideservice and even to remain permanently supportive in an uxorilocal mode of postmarital residence. In consequence, adult men are dispersed and marginalized, their interests being divided between natal and marital associations, between their roles as brothers/mothers' brothers and husbands/fathers. Moreover, as in-marrying affines and as actors in the formal political domain, exposed to constant scrutiny and competition, they are subject to severe behavioural constraints.

In contrast, closely-related women tend to remain together, forming cohesive groups, and are able to exert very considerable collective influence. Freely emotional and, as jural minors, unrestrained by punitive sanctions, women are apt to vent dissatisfactions with husbands — even to the point of beating them. Entitled to treat the gender-based procurement tasks of husbands as affinal obligations, women are able to extract intensified efforts, their goadings enhanced further by the status ambivalence and competitiveness of men. And, ultimately, women can count on their brothers and other close kin, whose prestige and privileges are at stake, to provide them with jural and physical support.

The abject female inferiority prescribed by the *adat* law, then, is highly deceptive. In sum, it almost amounts to a legal fiction, whose primary consequence is that men can be made subject to control by male affines, a control of which women are in fact both the immediate agents and the prime beneficiaries.[12]

---

12. Some of the wider implications of the general analytical perspective presented here have been discussed elsewhere (Sandbukt 1986).

8. Foraging, starch extraction and the sedentary lifestyle in the lowland rainforest of central Seram

Roy Ellen

Introduction[1]

An outwardly curious feature of Nuaulu subsistence is the high level of extraction of what I will begin by describing as non-domesticated and non-cultivated resources. While gardening and related activities are energy-intensive, visually prominent and occupy a crucial determining role in patterns of settlement and the management of man–environment relations, their yield in return for effort and relative dietary contribution is low. Any attempt to explain this apparent paradox must consider that it is possibly illusory (the product of applying inappropriate categories), or at least an artefact of recent changes in settlement patterns, the division of labour and participation in a wider sphere of exchange. I shall argue, however, that Nuaulu culture and society continue to reflect, in a number of significant respects, a mode of subsistence geared to hunting, forest foraging and sago extraction, despite the sometimes ambiguous distinction between 'gathering' and 'cultivation'. I will conclude by suggesting that a sustainable high level of extraction of certain kinds of non-domesticated terrestrial resources is consistent with sedentism and the forms of social organization which we associate with it, though insufficient to explain the basic structure of Nuaulu society, the dynamic of which must be sought in the articulation of the material possibilities inherent in a particular mode of subsistence and a historically specific pattern of regional exchange.

1. This paper is based on twenty-four months' research conducted on various occasions between 1970 and 1986, and sponsored by the Indonesian Academy of Sciences. Most of the ethnography discussed here has appeared in other publications listed in the bibliography at the back of this volume, and it is in these that full acknowledgement has been made to the funding bodies concerned. Unless otherwise indicated, data refer to the period 1970–1.

Subsistence effort and the ecological significance of non-domesticated resources

Narrowly defined, the Nuaulu are a small population, numbering some 600 individuals in 1971, located on or near the south coast of central Seram in eastern Indonesia. In several earlier publications (Ellen 1975; 1977b; 1978a; 1978b; 1982) I have presented data which document the significance of non-domesticated resources in Nuaulu ecological relations, in terms of their overall economy and pattern of settlement. I discuss some of the difficulties inherent in the concepts of 'domestication' and 'cultivation' in a separate section, but the basic ethnographic details which support this position can be summarized as follows:

(1) Most Nuaulu calories are obtained from *Metroxylon* palm sago, which provides some 1958 Cal per adult day, 63 per cent of the entire energy intake. Fifty-four per cent of all sago is obtained from vast reserves of palms which, for the most part, regenerate naturally, providing a mean gram weight of 300.04 moist flour per day compared with 256.2 for palms in tended groves, or 1056 Cal per person per day, being 76 per cent of the total weight of non-domesticated plant resources converted into available food energy. Since these figures were obtained during the wet season, when the conditions are least favourable for the collection of wild sago, the real figures are quite probably higher (Ellen 1977a: 107; 1978a: 61–80, 167–9).

(2) Virtually all Nuaulu animal protein, and 64 per cent of all protein, is obtained from non-domesticated sources. Hunting effort is intensive, but productivity is low, with an overall energy loss (Ellen 1978a: 78; cf. Dwyer 1974).

(3) Gardens and groves combined provide most greens and fruits and a substantial supplement of carbohydrate, but are not overridingly critical in nutritional terms.

(4) An extensive and diverse range of utilized wild resources, with some 120 species of animal and forty-eight species of plant (excluding fungi) are consumed as food at one time or another. The number of plant species with non-food uses is vast. (For trees alone see Ellen 1985: Table 1, 565–7.).

(5) 1813 Cal, more than 40 per cent of the total daily calorific intake, is from non-domesticated sources. If we add to this calories obtained from 'cultivated' sago, which in view of its minimal management and the fuzzy boundary between cultivated and non-cultivated palms (discussed further below) it might seem reasonable to do, this rises to 2174 Cal, or more than 70 per cent.

(6) Fifty-six per cent of all adult male energy expended in subsistence activities relates to the procurement of non-domesticated resources. If we include subsistence effort connected with the 'cultivation' of sago, then the percentage increases to a staggering 72 per cent. However, by

adding female food-getting effort, which is primarily in the domesti-cated sector, the percentage total of adult effort expended in procuring (though not processing) non-domesticated resources falls below 50 per cent.[2]

(7) Most non-domesticated resources have year-round rather than seasonal availability and are less subject to pathogens and other en-vironmental hazards affecting productivity and survival. There is greater continuity, stability and reliability in supply than with domesticated crops (cf. Ohtsuka 1978: 347), while at present levels of consumption both sago and meat are being extracted at rates which broadly sustain the existing populations of wild species which provide them.

My own methods of calculation may, of course, be suspect. The work-schedules on which the figures are based extended over a four-month period only, while the translation of raw diet sheets into calories and protein and of time-and-motion studies into calories expended is far from perfect. Indeed, there are differences between the estimates given in my doctoral dissertation and my published monograph, which arise from revisions to tables of food values (Ellen 1973; 1978a). But the crucial information is contained not in absolute figures but in basic ratios and, whatever the method employed, the significance of non-domesticated resources holds up, as do data relating to the time spent in extracting and processing them.

Cultivated plots, because they are constantly visible, and because gardening is an accessible activity, give the impression of being more important than they actually are. Hunting and gathering not only supply most calories and all animal protein, but appear to be more productive than activities focused on gardens, which take up most Nuaulu subsistence time, both of males and females. Indeed, it would be possible for the Nuaulu to subsist entirely on non-domesticated resources without too much difficulty, and there appears to be a structural incentive not to expand or elaborate gardening practices. All this has resulted in the underdevelopment of agriculture. For Seram more generally, this tendency has long been recognised. For example, Thomas Forrest (1969: 42), reporting on the situation in the second half of the eighteenth century, remarks: 'No wonder then, if agriculture be neglected in a country, where the labour of five men, in felling sago trees, beating the flour, and instantly baking the bread, will maintain a hundred'. This view was shared by Wallace (1962: 292) writing almost one hundred years later, and is echoed in various Dutch colonial sources and official publications (NSID 1918: 213, 367; Sachse 1907: 14).

---

2. Figures for subsistence effort in the non-domesticated sector include an element of food-processing, mainly washing sago and butchering meat. The distinction between procurement and processing is not easy to make.

Relations of appropriation in the non-domesticated sphere

If hunting and gathering, and particularly sago extraction, are so important in Nuaulu economy, one might reasonably expect that this might have some connection with, and impact on, the structure of relations of appropriation, both technical and social. What in fact we find would be not altogether surprising for students of aboriginal Australian societies, namely that social cooperation is limited, with relatively few implications for understanding relations of production and exchange more broadly defined.

Sago extraction is sometimes undertaken by single individuals, usually working planted palms near a village (Plates 8.1, 8.2). Because such palms are easily accessible they tend to be felled before their starch reserves have reached a maximum level. However, most mature sago palms are located in swamp forest at distances in excess of thirty kilometres from the village. Whereas cutting sago stands near settlements is a fairly leisurely activity spread over a period of days, trips to more distant localities require a degree of organization and more intensive effort. Teams usually consist of five or six individuals (and minimally a single pair) who may stay several days at a work site. Occasionally they may be larger and include women and children (*matueu*), as when large quantities of sago are needed for festivals. The technical constraints of sago extraction require that no more than three individuals can effectively work a single palm, though it is most usual for individuals to work in pairs. Teams of two or three commence by felling the palm, splitting the trunk and clearing away trash. One person (or two) can then begin extracting the pith with a bamboo adze, releasing the remaining partner to construct, and then operate, the apparatus used for filtering and separating out the starch. Thus, teams of two and three work effectively as extractor–processor units, and larger parties inevitably split up along the same lines. Once filtered flour has settled out in suspension (a process which normally takes place overnight), one member of a team can concentrate on packing up flour into palm-leaf containers.

Hunting and trapping are also primarily undertaken by individuals or pairs (*yakahohu*). Occasionally large collective hunts (*kasari*) are organized involving upwards of twenty individuals, and these may range over many square kilometres. Hunting parties are generally recruited from among immediate consanguines, although they sometimes include individuals who are only indirectly related. In my experience, large hunting parties lack mobility and flexibility and are not very productive. Like collective sago trips, they are primarily social and ritual occasions, seldom lasting more than a day and, for the most part, restricted to the zone demarcated by the most distant gardens. The fact that most game are captured from this inner zone leads to certain

Plate 8.1 (left): Young Nuaulu man extracting sago pith from felled and split palm using green bamboo adze.

Plate 8.2 (below): Young Nuaulu man pressing wet sago pith against a semi-permeable membrane of coconut leaf sheath, which separates starch granules from the fibrous residue.

Both photographs were taken by the author near Rohua, south Seram, Indonesia, in 1973.

problems in conceptualizing subsistence which I discuss below.

Freshwater fishing, with bow and arrow or by trapping or stunning, are mainly individual male activities. The same is true of marine fishing from canoes, although this was rare until relatively recently. Women undertake collective expeditions to obtain freshwater shellfish and crustacea, and with children scavenge in rock pools exposed at low tide. There are no technical reasons why beach foraging should be a collective undertaking and there is no division of labour within the team.

What is striking about the organization of these various subsistence activities is that none demand more than two individuals for their effective performance. When more individuals are involved in forest extractive activities, this is primarily for the purpose of obtaining certain kinds of timber (Ellen 1985). Cooking and food preparation are essentially individual and household-oriented. So, since most Nuaulu hunting and gathering activities do not require cooperation for their technical accomplishment there can be nothing *intrinsic* to the techniques which requires (rather than permits) the particular kinds of social arrangement which characterize Nuaulu society. Only with the construction of dwellings and ritual houses does collective effort become really crucial, but here it is directed not towards the reproduction of biological populations, but rather social formations.

Historical changes in patterns of resource utilization

Nuaulu patterns of resource extraction have never been static, and have probably been multifocal for many centuries. I have elsewhere (Ellen 1979: 50–2) suggested that we might hypothesize an Elementary Moluccan Subsistence Unit (EMSU) focused primarily on sago-extraction, hunting and gathering, with which to model protohistoric and early historic Moluccan societies.

The shift from foraging to cultivation was gradual, and we must assume that the process might have begun at least as early as the dates currently being cited for the emergence of agriculture in the New Guinea highlands (Golson 1985: 308). Yam, taro and banana gardening have no doubt been among Nuaulu techniques for many centuries on a small scale, but in the Seramese context there is ample circumstantial evidence for the early systematic husbanding of fruit trees and palms (especially *Metroxylon*), rather than roots. Such evidence, which is consistent with that drawn from eastern Indonesia and the Pacific more generally (Glover 1977; Yen 1974; 1985), suggests that Harris, though right to challenge the importance of swiddening in explaining South-East Asian agricultural origins, was wrong to relocate the emphasis entirely with fixed-plot cultivation (D. Harris 1973: 405).

Systematic agriculture has always been more important along the coast, where larger settlements, sedentariness and spatial constraints have combined to make extraction of non-domesticated terrestrial resources a more risky and high-cost strategy. This echoes Sauer's fishing model for the origins of agriculture (Bronson 1977: 35). However, it must also be taken into account that coastal places are generally better connected to trading networks (Ellen 1987: 173–4), bringing new ideas and people and placing a greater pressure on production for exchange. As forest products were located outside the effective control of coastal centres, such places had to enter into exchange relations with foragers and swiddeners of the interior (cf. Hutterer 1977: 180).

Nuaulu contact with the global system, especially from the seventeenth century onwards, led to the introduction of new and more productive cultigens: manioc, tania, sweet potato and maize (Ellen 1987). The availability of more reliable crop production, combined with clove cultivation, encouraged gardening at the expense of foraging. Increasing production for exchange meant that producers had to work harder to obtain the same amount of calories (cf. Elder 1978) and to satisfy their wants. So rather than attribute the spread and intensification of agriculture on Seram to 'stress' induced by population pressure or other factors (D. Harris 1973; 1977b), it appears to have been a means of marginally reducing the costs of forest collecting and sago extraction, consistent with an increased sedentism associated with clove cultivation and, later, other cash crops. I suspect that in most parts of Seram expansion in the planting of manioc, tania and sweet potato has been, for the most part, a nineteenth-century development.

The spread of clove cultivation to Seram during the sixteenth century led to coastal populations becoming increasingly reliant on domesticated resources and on an exchange economy (Ellen 1979: 53–60; but see Knaap 1985). The ensuing Dutch extirpations of clove groves and attempts to maintain the monopoly curtailed a process which, had it been allowed to continue, would have led to even more extensive clove cultivation on Seram during the seventeenth century. Though never completely or effectively enforced, the Dutch monopoly was not finally lifted until 1850, by which time there was a slump in the demand for Moluccan spices. As the clove trade picked up again during the twentieth century, and with the spread of new cash crops, such as coconut and (to a lesser extent) coffee, so increasingly the balance again shifted from reliance on non-domesticated to domesticated resources. And the pressure to plant cash crops brought with it a tendency to plant more subsistence crops, a process accompanied in the present century by the introduction of new ideas of land tenure (Ellen 1977b). Although this process was most advanced along the coast, it must also have been taking place in some mountain settlements (Ellen 1979).

It is reasonable to predict that the greater land and labour requirements of increased expansion into cash cropping (which continues apace) will lead to a further decline in hunting and gathering, albeit mitigated by slumps in market prices and occasional crop failure. The contemporary imbalances between cost and benefit in both the domesticated and non-domesticated spheres are therefore partly due to recent acceleration of effort in the domesticated sector, which is increasingly directed towards the exchange economy at the expense of the food-getting subsistence sector. The extraction of non-domesticated resources, in fact, subsidizes activities in the domesticated and exchange sectors.

In addition to the economic pressures for a shift from a collecting to an agricultural economy, there were also political ones. Although the mountain settlements of Seram have been historically remarkably permanent, Dutch 'pacification' in the second half of the nineteenth and the first quarter of the twentieth centuries brought with it attempts to control the physical character of settlements, by insisting on fixed locations, nucleation and in many cases the removal of peoples to the coast. The fixing and concentrating of villages within the highlands increased pressure on resources by making movement more difficult, and by increasing the population of particular selected hamlets. Relocation on the coast led both to population increase and to the loss of flexible response by moving and shifting subsistence strategy. Coastal locations often reduced by 50 per cent that extractive area environmentally suitable, and because of the existence of prior human habitation, restricted land available for cultivation (Ellen 1978a: 108–30). This left the Nuaulu and other populations with the less desirable land, and (ironically) may have acted as a brake on the transition from a forest-extractive to an agricultural economy which might otherwise have proceeded more rapidly.

If we accept that the data I collected for the village of Rohua are typical of all contemporary Nuaulu, then the present population den-sity as expressed in terms of the total extractive area is 0.8 persons per square kilometre.[3] There is no reason to assume that the total Nuaulu population has changed much in the last few hundred years, and recently it has in fact increased. Reconstructing extractive zones from historical data on the location of mountain hamlets (Ellen 1978a: 14, Map 3), we can estimate a total extractive area for all Nuaulu of 2496 square kilometres. This gives a population density of 0.17 persons per square kilometre. Although it represents an increase by a factor of five, the figure is still sufficiently low not to have had a significant impact on subsistence returns, and is well within the range for contemporary hunter-gatherers (Lee and DeVore 1968: 10–11). More significant, how-

---

3. The extractive area of Rohua (anyway extensive) is 214.75 square kilometres and the 1971 population 180, representing five clans.

ever, is demographic concentration, funnelling the populations of twelve optimally dispersed highland hamlets into five coastal settlements all within three kilometres of each other, and four within a radius of less than one kilometre and adjacent to a large existing coastal village. This has accentuated the already sharp asymmetry between foraging patterns in the immediate vicinity of settlements and those more distant.

Problems in conceptualizing the Nuaulu mode of subsistence[4]

Now all of this is fine except that it presupposes that the description of subsistence types is uncomplicated. We now know that the conceptual boundaries between anthropological and archaeological definitions of different subsistence techniques are often arbitrary and may obscure important ecological and sociological features (e.g. G. Bailey 1981a; Ellen 1982: 129; Ingold 1983: 553). The position with regard to the category 'hunter-gatherer' has recently been the subject of much critical discussion (see, for example, Barnard 1983: 208–9; Testart 1982: 523). These problems arise partly because definitions of subsistence involve (and sometimes conflate) three separate axes of variation: (1) degree of morphogenetic manipulation; (2) degree of human protection of other species; and (3) social control of subsistence. The terms we use to describe these processes, or various aspects of them, have been much discussed in the literature and it would entail too extensive a diversion to provide even a summary account of the contesting possibilities. Nevertheless, it is necessary to be quite clear about the way in which I use the terms in the ensuing analysis. Manipulative or incidental genetic modification of other plant and animal species by humans is what I understand by the term 'domestication', and the results of this activity are populations which we refer to as 'cultigens' or 'cultivars'. 'Cultivation' is the process by which plant and animal species are moved, protected, harvested and stimulated to grow in ways which increase their usefulness to humans. Protection can be afforded to either domesticated or non-domesticated species and may be a prelude to domestication. Though such techniques may not be aimed at morphogenetic manipulation this may sometimes be an unintended consequence. The social control of subsistence, which must be kept rigorously distinct conceptually from the first two processes, indicates the degree to which resources are accessible to particular individuals and groups, whether they be domesticated or non-domesticated, cultivated or non-cultivated.

4. Some of the conceptual issues raised by my use of the term 'mode of subsistence', particularly as they relate to Tim Ingold's contribution to this volume, are discussed briefly in a postscript to this chapter.

When we apply these distinctions to a description of Nuaulu subsistence, certain difficulties are immediately apparent.

The procurement of animal protein is relatively unproblematic, since Nuaulu do not, as a rule, tame or domesticate animals other than chickens and dogs. In the New Guinea highlands, for example, the situation is different. Here the boundary between domesticated and wild pigs may be very fuzzy, with intermixing of feral and domesticated stock and varying degrees of taming, feeding, breeding, attention and confinement (Morren 1977). Although this is not the case on Seram, it must be noted that pigs and deer are attracted to gardens, which in some cases supply the bulk of their food. They have, therefore, to some extent become commensal to *Homo sapiens*, with 'garden hunting' a substitute for animal domestication (Linares 1976: 331). This facilitates human predation on animals logistically, in terms of energetic efficiency and of scheduling, but tends to blur the distinction between wild and husbanded resources.

In the case of plant resources the conceptual and descriptive problems are more acute. In particular, the differences between cultivation, incipient cultivation (proto-cultivation) and non-cultivation are quite indistinct (D. Harris 1973). Consider, for example, the following grey areas:

1. Retention of certain useful trees in swiddens during felling and burning. This is a technically difficult operation, but is known.
2. The planting of individual useful trees outside swiddens and groves, usually in secondary forest.
3. The protection of useful trees, herbs and root tubers which have grown up naturally in the forest.
4. The replacement of the crown of tubers at sites from which wild yams have been removed. (cf. Bellwood 1976: 158; Fernandez and Lynch 1972: 304; Yen 1976: 160–1).
5. The harvesting of useful trees from apparently wild settings, but which may represent former village sites or groves, and of introduced or domesticated plants or trees which now occur in completely uncultivated settings (Ellen 1985: 563).
6. Many of the plants grown in gardens either also grow wild or have suitable wild substitutes (Ellen 1973: 450–64).

However, the greatest difficulties lie with sago. When planted in village areas, in gardens or in owned groveland, sago is grown from transplanted basal suckers, rather than from seed. Nevertheless, planting is generally haphazard, with stands being left to vegetatively propagate themselves. Young suckers will sometimes be brought back from wild forest palms and planted in swiddens so that wild and cultivated stands coexist in the same groves. In wild sago swamp forest, most of the palms cut have been naturally propagated, either by seed or by sucker. However, occasionally young wild palms will be protected, or basal suckers planted in areas of otherwise wild forest. Though hardly purposeful activity, the delay in cutting preferred stands until they have fruited acts as a selective pressure which encourages a form of proto-domestication. Thus, while sexual reproduction is relatively rare, especially in cultivated groves near the village where constant harvesting of trees prior to flowering reduces its occurrence and therefore the possibilities for genetic variation, the various practices outlined ensure that where sexual reproduction does take place there is a high probability that the genes of wild and planted palms will intermix. This must be part of the reason why distinct varieties of sago palm, and particularly distinct cultivated and wild varieties, are so difficult to distinguish (cf. Barrau 1959; Ohtsuka 1978: 345–6; Yen 1985: 316).

Similar practices are found in relation to other trees and plants used by the Nuaulu, such as species of *Agave, Aleurites, Amaranthus, Areca, Arenga, Artocarpus, Canarium, Celosia, Codiaeum, Dioscorea, Durio, Eugenia, Gnetum, Languas, Lansium, Musa, Myristica, Pandanus, Portulaca* and *Zingiber* (cf. Yen 1974).

The palm starch extraction nexus as a subsistence base

Although I am inclined to avoid polarizing categories which tend to obfuscate the analysis of subsistence, Nuaulu *Metroxylon* palms can best be described as being managed minimally though not obviously domesticated, with technical practices which are more comfortably described as 'well-husbanded collecting' rather than 'agriculture'. After all, the kind of interference involved is no more than that which is quite common among populations for whom the description 'hunter-gatherer' is less controversial.

However, I am intuitively repelled by the kind of simplistic solution which places societies along a scale depending on their degree of 'hunter-gathererness', or the degree to which they 'husband' resources.[5] It would be grossly misleading, while avoiding the crucial issues, to include the proto-Nuaulu in a category of 'sedentary hunter-gatherers' along with, say, the hygrophytic forest peoples of the American north-west Pacific coast. It would be equally dangerous to think of them (or any other similar group) as if they occupied some classificatory (and by implication evolutionary) space, let us say between the Tasaday and other South-east Asian swiddening peoples, transitional between foraging and agriculture. The Nuaulu hunt, gather and extract

5. See, for example, the scale devised by Watters (1960: 63), on which the Nuaulu would be placed between types 1 and 2, being almost equally dependent on hunter-gathering and gardening.

wild vegetable products and small animals, as well as tending gardens and groves, but that does not make them 'half-way' hunter-gatherers. Such labels as 'gathering' and 'cultivation' are inadequate and often conceal important and distinctively different subsistence strategies and resource bases.

It may be far more useful to typologize at a lower level of generalization and group subsistence systems which share certain key ecological, technical and social characteristics and which focus on particular non-human species, or groups of related species. Although it runs the risk of establishing yet another inflexible category, I think it is instructive to consider palm-starch extraction as such a type. There are many palms which are used in this way, principally from the genera *Arecastrum*, *Arenga*, *Caryota*, *Corypha*, *Eugeissona*, *Mauritia*, *Metroxylon*, *Roystonia* and *Nypa* (see Ruddle *et al.* 1978: 3–5). Closely related, and justifying comparison, are those economies focused on the tapping of palms such as *Borassus* (J. Fox 1977), or involving starch extraction from cycads (D. Harris 1977a: 426–9). The precise social impact of palm starch extraction will vary compared with other strategies employed, but in the Nuaulu case it is clearly dominant. Palm starch extraction also represents an additional pathway to agriculture to those listed by Harris (D. Harris 1977b), and in places its cultivation is obvious, extensive and systematic. Although informal indigenous arboriculture in general, and the proto-cultivation of sago in particular, almost certainly preceded systematic agriculture on Seram, it is most unlikely that had its progress not been averted by the introduction of clove groves and the cultivation of new root tubers it would have developed into a fully-fledged form of agriculture, as Yen (1974: 247, 282) has suggested for elsewhere in the Pacific basin. As we have seen, the natural productivity of *Metroxylon* is as likely to discourage the development of agriculture as encourage it. Where systematic cultivation does develop in palm starch extractive systems it is as likely to involve other species and result from the sedentariness which the technique permits rather than being a direct outcome.

The characteristics of sago subsistence which, in the Nuaulu context, make it so important are that it is abundant, can be stored for long periods, is consistently reliable (the harvest can never fail), is available in a concentrated form and suppresses the necessity of residential mobility. Put concisely, it allows for both storage and sedentism, possibilities which are inextricably wedded in their implications. This is so because the accumulation of substantial food reserves (and other material goods) inhibits movement while permanent settlements are a prerequisite for effective storage. But, having said this, there is no alternative but to consider each separately.

Sago can be stored over extremely long time periods. The effective life of a cut palm, or of extracted but unprocessed pith, is about one month. Nuaulu will protect felled but unexcavated palms from oxidation and insect infestation, by placing fronds over the exposed trunk or by replacing pieces of removed bark to form a lid. However, the protection this affords is slight, and the pith is rapidly colonized by adult sago weevils, which lay their eggs in it.[6] Once the pith has been transformed into flour, if stored slightly wet, to encourage fermentation, it will keep for up to one month without appreciable deterioration (Ellen 1977a: 107). The edible life of the hard biscuits is even longer, extending to many years if kept quite dry.

In addition to sago, the Nuaulu also store large quantities of *Canarium vulgare* nuts and dried and smoked meat. *Canarium* nuts are simply extracted from their hard outer casings and stored in covered baskets, their oil preventing deterioration if kept dry. Meat is smoked over house fires for several weeks and stored in rat-proof containers hung from rafters.

It is undeniable that in general evolutionary terms, storage represents a crucial development: levelling-out resource fluctuations, fostering larger permanent concentrations, easing residential flux and facilitating delayed consumption foraging systems (Ingold 1983: 554; Woodburn 1980). However, in the Nuaulu case seasonality is not a critical factor, while resource failure and shortage are rare. Though storage does permit a degree of flexibility in the scheduling of different subsistence activities and patterns of pragmatic consumption, the advantages of storage must be explained in social rather than technical terms. Storage is less a matter of practical staggering of production and consumption schedules than a necessity to meet the prerequisites for staging ceremonies (Ingold 1983: 555). It is significant that (apart from seeds and tubers set aside for planting) all stored food comes from non-domesticated sources.

Nuaulu society is characterized by a high degree of sedentariness. Although there is historical evidence, both documentary and oral, for clan movement, Nuaulu populations in their routine subsistence requirements have been and remain remarkably sedentary. Although sedentariness certainly incurs high energetic costs in transporting and locating non-domesticated produce, compared with populations which are more dependent on foraging, the maximum and optimal Nuaulu ranges from base camp in food-getting trips are low, probably well within the range radii of many tropical forest hunter-gatherers. An economy focused on extraction of wild products, hunting and gathering can, in fact, cope with a high degree of sedentarization and population

6. In April 1986 I discovered a large sago trunk which had been washed up on the small island of Kidang between Seram Laut and Gorom, and which had been secured in readiness for extraction. Kidang has no sago of its own but acquires it through trade. Though the trunk had been penetrated by salt water, and the sago obtained from it would definitely be regarded as inferior, the salinity would have afforded some degree of protection against oxidation and infestation.

concentration, given the right kind of non-domesticated resources. In this case, it is starch extraction which makes this a viable lifestyle.

Social organization, subsistence and economic circulation

How, then, do Nuaulu patterns of non-domesticated resource utilization relate to the principal institutions of their society? I would argue that the possibilities offered by storage and sedentism are crucial though not determinant. As we have seen, there is nothing in the techniques used in appropriating non-domesticated resources which requires more than very low-key organization. Therefore, there can be no easy causal relationship between Nuaulu clan and political organization and the technical needs of a hunting and gathering economy. It is true that clans may, in the past, have provided the corporate groups necessary for the drawing of territorial boundaries, but this is no longer a practical consideration. We can only understand the coexistence of a non-domesticated infrastructure with a clan superstructure as the outcome of a dynamic interaction between a characteristic delayed-consumption system made possible through storage and permanent residential sites (Woodburn 1982a: 432–3, 482), and patterned exchange relations, both between clans and between Nuaulu and non-Nuaulu.

I wish to suggest tentatively that the Nuaulu clan system, in its present form, has developed partly as a structural consequence of pre-existing exogamous local groups, and partly as a consequence of economic exchange and circulation between groups facilitated by delayed consumption and the existence of permanent occupation sites. Original Nuaulu mountain settlements were hamlets, and formal groups emerged as a result of exogamous patri-virilocal groups being focused on 'houses' (*numa*), which were at the same time both physical and social entities. These 'houses' paired to form exogamous clans (*ipan*) and were consequently transformed into clan-sections. Out-marriage sustained this local descent group structure and an ideology of patrilineality. The matrimonial alliances created by systematic and repeated out-marriage with particular groups reinforced exchanges of material objects and provided the social framework for the flow of goods and services over wide areas (Valeri 1976).

For many centuries the highland people of Seram have been linked to the global economy through the extraction and exchange of small quantities of certain high-value forest resources. These have altered from time to time, but have included dammar resin, bird plumes, wild nutmegs, and so on (Ellen 1984: 184; 1985; cf. Dunn 1975; J.T. Peterson 1978). Moreover, 'traditional' Nuaulu social structure was dependent on (and partly arose from) long-distance trade (Ellen 1984), in shell bangles from Gorom, Oriental and European porcelain, different kinds of textiles and metal anklets (Ellen 1987: 184–5). These were, and continue to be, required for exchanges linked to rites of passage and other major ceremonials connected with housebuilding and the life cycle of the ritual house, and with dispute settlement. They are also part of the input to a system of matrimonial exchanges, where they serve to reify clan and clan section structure. The maintenance of the social order in a particular form has depended on such items being available in predictable and constant quantities. Any change in the availability of an item has structural consequences, making social exchanges more difficult or devaluing them. Thus, the ready availability of a certain kind of red cloth required for Nuaulu ceremonies has led to its increased circulation in recent years, and inflation which has undermined the clans as property-owning units. On the other hand, the non-availability of *patola* cloth of Indian origin and certain kinds of porcelain is making rituals and exchanges difficult or impossible to conduct, having much the same effect. Thus, the pre-horticultural emergence of clans (as in the American north-west) arises from the construction of property relations based on the circulation of valuables, not as a consequence of a particular mode of subsistence.

Now, all of the objects involved in these exchanges are relatively durable exotic items rather than foodstuffs (Ingold 1983: 562), and it is their durability which enhances the possibilities for delay in transactions while their lack of bulk facilitates easy storage and transport. This sphere of exchange in exotic items has relatively few repercussions in the subsistence sector, and therefore provides some of the economic benefits which elsewhere can only be obtained through subsistence intensification (Peterson and Peterson 1977: 559). Thus the capacity to store foodstuffs has only an indirect and marginal bearing on external trade and the integration of Nuaulu into wider Moluccan networks (contra Ingold 1983: 554).

On the other hand, economic exchange does not of itself provide sufficient conditions for the emergence of corporate groups. Many populations of foraging peoples, especially in south and south-east Asia (see for example, Dunn 1975; Morris 1982a; J.T. Peterson 1978), are involved in extensive production for exchange, and yet maintain flexible non-corporate structures. Such exchange is individual, and for the most part arises from appropriation at the household level. It is usually found where storage or sedentism are prevented or where the possibilities have not been fully realised. As I have intimated, in the Nuaulu case it is the combination of residential permanence, delayed consumption and exchange that is crucial.

The supra-clan aspects of Nuaulu social organization can be explained in terms of regional political considerations. We know that periodically Nuaulu clans came together in response to wider political considerations (Ellen 1988), from as early as the seventeenth century. Thus, in explaining Nuaulu social history it is important to understand the regional, political and economic context in which they operated as hunters, gatherers and sago-extractors. They were hardly 'professional primitives', in the sense used by R. Fox (1969) — that is, economic specialists caught up in a wider division of labour — even though their indirect contribution to the wider economy cannot have been entirely negligible. On the other hand, their involvement in exchange networks of valuables and women meant that they were dependent upon the outside world less for the biological reproduction of populations than for the ritual reproduction of clans.

The development of notions of property linked to the circulation of valuables has had a feedback effect on the representation and organiza-tion of activities in the non-domesticated sector. Where large-scale co-ordinated effort is involved in food-getting it is for social rather than technical reasons, as in collective sago and hunting trips. Moreover, the development of notions of property has affected attitudes towards non-processed as well as processed resources. Not only do planted sago groves become the property of particular clans and individuals, but these rights are also extended to areas of wild resources (Ellen 1977a: 107). Other wild fruit trees are owned, though these are some-times fruit trees at old village sites. Sago and meat become important not only as daily food but are also conceptualized as ritual foods whose consumption in a specified manner is periodically necessary in order to redefine the relationships between groups. Nuaulu hunting is impor-tant in terms of social rather than biological reproduction, and would probably be less frequent were it not a prerequisite for the performance of key ceremonies. But meat (and other foods) are of significance only until they are consumed, and it is clear that this temporary character is a distinct drawback in treating food as property akin to valuables. Such a disadvantage can be overcome if inedible residues can stand for what has been consumed and the social relations which underpin consump-tion. Thus, hunted animals provide Nuaulu with permanent property in the form of *penesite*, the mandibles of pigs and deer and the breast-bones of cassowaries. These are accumulated in ritual houses where they arrive as gifts to clan chiefs and *kapitane* from hunters belonging to the same clan section and clan. Thus, the accumulation of *penesite* serves to define the clan symbolically with respect to others.

It is difficult now to envisage the Nuaulu clan system not related to agriculture. After all, clans are also defined very much in terms of the way land is distributed and circulates between them, while the in-creased collective effort which gardening and arboriculture involve finds a convenient organizational framework in a clan structure which de-fines labour obligations in more formal terms. Moreover, as elders and clan and village heads increasingly take on managerial decisions con-cerning labour recruitment, land selection and production (with or

without government pressure) so the Nuaulu clan system may continue to change. The rigidification of rules relating to land tenure, as
garden land becomes more important, and as Nuaulu are brought
within a wider political and legal orbit, is also affecting clan structure,
paradoxically making clans more conscious of their legal title while at
the same time encouraging the individualization of property holding,
and therefore the ultimate breakdown of the clan system. But Nuaulu
relations of production, as they are realized in ideas concerning land
tenure, lack of sophistication in swiddening techniques, variable amne-
sia concerning land owned and boundaries, and flexibility in the
attribution of rights of ownership, can only be understood in relation to
the role of non-domesticated resources and the activities connected to
them (Ellen 1977b: 65–7).

To summarize, the extraction of non-domesticated resources plays a
key role in Nuaulu economy and society, while their mode of subsistence can only awkwardly be fitted into conventional typologies. The
nexus of activities associated with the extraction of sago from the
Metroxylon palm in particular, and the appropriation of non-
domesticated resources in general, provide the historical context in
which all other subsistence activities and social structures must be
viewed. Although the sago extraction/hunting nexus is a necessary
condition for the emergence of the clan system, through permitting
storage (and therefore delayed consumption) and permanent residential sites, Nuaulu social organization can only be understood as an
articulation of these features with a sophisticated exchange economy.
This discussion may go some way towards explaining the unlikely
disjunction between Nuaulu subsistence and social structure.

Postscript: on the concept of 'mode of subsistence'

The concept of 'mode of subsistence' has become a matter of controversy (see Ingold, this volume). I shall try here to clarify what I mean
by the concept and why I am convinced that it must not be confused or
conflated with 'mode of production', a theoretical notion of a quite
separate order. Put simply, a mode of subsistence is *the aggregate of
extractive processes characterizing a particular population.* These involve
technical practices, long-term genotypic changes, cultural information
and interspecific relations. It would be absurd to reduce this to just
'equipment' or 'technology'.

All modes of subsistence are necessarily encapsulated in a particular
web of social and ecological relations, no less than are separate technical practices or tool-using behaviours. This web may be conceptualized
in terms of a specific 'mode of production' situated in historical and
evolutionary space. Thus, a mode of subsistence can be understood

only as part of such a socially-determined structure (it cannot be approached analytically except in this context), as inevitably a consequence of social action which is in part purposive, and as having its origins in particular social practices. In a very real sense, people *do* produce their own subsistence, social consciousness *is* integral to production, while the labour process is *much more* than 'a mere aggregate of behavioural executions'.

But the concept 'mode of subsistence', as an aggregate of extractive processes, can in itself say nothing of the means by which its particular manifestations are socially integrated. Any designated mode will be composed of a number of more specific techniques or elements, though it is hardly to be expected that these will always be discrete entities. Because the kinds of activity referred to by the conventional labels merge into each other (hunting, trapping, collecting . . .), and because the particular combinations of techniques are so varied, simple typologies are dangerous and best avoided. Nevertheless, there are at least two reasons why a concept of this kind is inescapable:

(1) There is no fixed relationship between particular subsistence practices (or combinations of such) and relations of economic production. Social relations themselves can hardly 'characterize the practical activity' if social relations vary while the practical activity is held constant. A conceptually independent concept of mode of subsistence permits us to distinguish one from the other and avoid any implication of technicist reduction.

(2) The second reason is one of practical academic discipline. If we reject the kind of concept which I have argued for, then where do we begin our analyses, how do we speak to each other at conferences of the kind which are reported in this book? It seems to me that if we do not distinguish between 'mode of production' and 'mode of subsistence', as between the social and the technical, people will anyway continue to do so implicitly. Mode of subsistence is — if you like — a device which permits some degree of description and comparison without making assumptions regarding the generalizability of particular definitions or typologies of more abstract constructs. Ingold's argument is a clever one, though it is theoretically austere (even, perhaps, mystifying) and less than helpful if we wish to go beyond the analysis of a particular local system.

Part 3

Historical and evolutionary transformations

9. At the frontier: some arguments against hunter-gathering and farming modes of production in southern Africa

Martin Hall

Introduction

The pre-colonial history of southern Africa, in common with many other parts of the world, has been cast in a typological/environmental mould. Earlier archaeologists, bringing their knowledge of the European sequence to the subcontinent, established first a 'Stone Age' and then, in the middle years of the present century, a succeeding 'Iron Age' (no case was found for an intermediate 'Bronze Age'). These general categories, as well as their internal subdivisions, were characterized by typical artefacts: microlithic stone assemblages for the later Stone Age and diagnostic families of decorated ceramic assemblages for the early and late Iron Ages. In more recent years archaeologists, again following general trends in the field, began to emphasize the importance of other sorts of evidence — the faunal and floral data, together with data on settlement location — which allowed the study of adaptive responses to environments. But these new interpretations were still placed *within* the older typological frame, allowing, for instance, comparison of adaptive behaviour between the Early and the Late Iron Age (Hall 1984; 1987).

This conventional approach to the past has, in southern Africa, been highly successful. Until radiocarbon dates began to be more available in the region from the early 1960s, the typological scheme provided a means of ordering and interpreting data. Although the new radiometric dates demanded that earlier projections of the past be stretched and adjusted (for recent summaries of radiocarbon dates from the subcontinent, see Maggs 1976a; Hall and Vogel 1980; Parkington and Hall 1987), and in some cases that the sequence be rearranged (for instance, Maggs 1973), many of the typological categories have been retained with only incremental modifications and continue to be an important source of relative dating within the carbon 14 framework. Adaptive interpretations have fitted in well with the concerns of other,

137

ecologically oriented disciplines, allowing an enhanced understanding
of interactive relationships between human communities and their
environments. In the light of these achievements, it is hardly surprising
that most archaeological work in southern Africa continues to be
informed by these traditional perspectives.

Nevertheless, it can be shown that both the typological and the
environmental traditions of interpretation rest on assumptions that
may be prejudicial to further theoretical advances. Behind most archaeologists' use of the typological framework is a Childean (or its
American equivalent) assumption of the archaeological culture (Binford
and Sabloff 1982). For Gordon Childe, of course, the interpretation of a
group of related artefactual assemblages as the equivalent of a 'people'
was just a working hypothesis and one, moreover, that in his later
writing he himself began to doubt. But many archaeologists have
ignored these qualifications and have taken the equation as axiomatic. I
have argued (although my interpretation has been contested) that, in
southern Africa, this culture/people model has been strongly reinforced
by an ideological system in which ethnicity is constantly emphasized as
a natural and absolute order, thus reinforcing the political and economic power of the modern state. As a result, an untested and usually
subliminal *social* assumption lies at the very heart of the typological
model (Hall 1983; 1984). This may have been valuable when the concern was with technological and adaptive interpretations, but for a
social archaeology it is likely to prove disastrous: if the system of
categorization and analysis assumes the interpretation from the start,
only circularity can result. In other words, to try and find the nature of
a late Stone Age or early Iron Age social formation would be mis-
guided, since the very concept of the late Stone Age and the Iron Age
rests on the assumption that the nature of the social formation
is known.

The limitations of the environmental approach to understanding the
southern African past have been more fully explored. Thus it is already
clear that important aspects of the pre-colonial record cannot be explained as environmental responses alone — paintings on the walls of
rock shelters, for instance, are much more than passive reflections of
the environmental milieu, although the symbols employed may often
be drawn from the natural world (Lewis-Williams 1980; 1981; 1982),
while village architecture and layout cannot merely be seen in terms of
the need for shelter and the raw materials available to the builders
(Huffman 1982). Many would accept that social interpretations are
essential to avoid the reductionism of purely environmental interpretations.

In this chapter I argue that, for such social interpretations to succeed,
the typological distinction between Stone Age and Iron Age must be
abandoned and that, by implication, the conventional divide between

hunter-gatherer and farming economies must be reworked. Materialist theory, and in particular the concept of the mode of production, provides a starting point for this process, but also contains its own problems — in particular the problem of establishing relations of production from the archaeological record without recourse to interpretation solely by analogy. Therefore material culture must be integrated into a new theoretical frame. I suggest that, on first examination, there are more similarities than differences in the relations of production within social formations conventionally distinguished as Late Stone Age hunter-gatherers and Early Iron Age farmers.

Were there distinct later Stone Age and early Iron Age modes of production in southern Africa?

Of course if, on re-examination, there *did* turn out to be distinct hunter-gatherer and farming modes of production that coincided with the conventional typological distinction between the later Stone Age and the early Iron Age, then part of the problem that I have set would be pedantic, for the external skin of the old model could be exchanged for a new set of terminology and the basic structure left unchanged. The first task, then, is to look again at the evidence and see whether this was or was not the case.

Although the issue has been much debated, I have taken the mode of production to be a structured relationship between the forces of production and the relations of production, in which the relations of production are dominant (Hindess and Hirst 1975). This definition avoids the danger of reducing the mode of production to a mere list of technical attributes, and places the emphasis firmly on the importance of the distribution of the product, and therefore on the social relations which provide the character of any given social formation.

Obviously, the very distinction between hunter-gathering and farming assumes differences between the forces of production. But in examining what is known of the social formations in southern Africa which are placed in these two categories, there are also clear overlaps.

Although the evidence on settlement location (Hall 1981), as well as occasional floral remains (for example, Davies 1975, Klapwijk 1973), from villages dated early in the first millennium AD, indicate that crop plants such as sorghum and millet were grown, wild plant foods must also have been extensively collected. It is probable that the first 'Iron Age' communities of the subtropical south-east African littoral did not have domestic animals, instead relying heavily for protein on shellfish collected in the rocky intertidal zone (Hall 1981). By the sixth century AD villages were well established on the fertile soils of river valleys away from the coastlands, and cattle and caprines were kept (Maggs

1984). But herds and flocks of domestic stock were small in size and faunal collections from sites such as Broederstroom (beneath the Magalies mountains) show that hunting was still a very important activity (Mason 1981).

'Stone Age' economies seem to show little evidence for the narrow specializations that are typical of the European Mesolithic and have been interpreted as part of the process of animal domestication. Nevertheless, it has been argued that hunter-gatherers were careful to burn vegetation in order to encourage grazing for prey species, and to propagate geophytes that were intensively gathered at the appropriate time of the year (Deacon 1976). This suggests a degree of the 'forward planning' that is also a vital behavioural component in the management of domestic species.

Similarly, 'Iron Age' and 'Stone Age' technological sets are not as discrete as is often assumed. Although hunter-gatherers do not seem to have manufactured iron implements themselves it has been argued that, once the new technology was available, metal implements were used by hunter-gatherers, perhaps over considerable periods of time (Maggs 1980; Mazel 1984). The reciprocal of this was the use, and probably the manufacture, of stone tools by farmers, for many 'Early Iron Age' sites have extensive scatters of lithic implements with distributional patterns that suggest that this is not a post-depositional coincidence (Maggs 1980). Ceramics — the hallmark of the southern African 'Iron Age' — have also been recovered from dated 'Stone Age' contexts (Walker 1983), and despite attempts to pass these off as the result of trade with farming villages, the dating and character of wares such as Bambata indicate that they were a distinct hunter-gatherer technology.

Thus, as far as the forces of production are concerned, the terms 'hunter-gatherer' and 'farmer' describe in southern Africa two economic positions within a spectrum of complex variation. Over a period of about a thousand years communities provided for themselves by obtaining a variety of resources with different technological combinations. There would seem certainly to be a case for arguing that to categorize such patterns of behaviour in terms of Stone and Iron Ages oversimplifies the situation and directs attention away from the complexities of the pre-colonial past.

Establishing the relations of production in archaeological situations where there are no direct historical sources — documentary or oral — to indicate the manner in which commodities were distributed within and between communities presents particular methodological problems. Ethnographic analogies may be instructive but also misleading, for to read the present back into an imperfect and malleable artefactual record may be to impose a reading on the past and deny the possibility of identifying change. It would seem preferable to set up models of the possible relations that could have served to define the modes concerned and then test the applicability of these against the archaeological evidence. But interpreting artefactual evidence as indicative of relations of production is difficult, for whereas techniques for identifying the forces of production in floral assemblages, faunal remains and settlement patterns have been developed, there seems to be little satisfactory theory that can be used to read social relations from material culture.

Elsewhere, I have suggested that a way into this black box of southern African prehistory may be through combining ethno-archaeological studies of material culture as 'active symbols' with Anthony Giddens's concept of structuration (Hall 1985; 1986). Briefly, Giddens (1981; 1984) argues that social formations may be analysed as power relations, in which actors cause intentional and unintentional effects on others, and have such effects caused against them. But to become tangible, power, in Giddens's sense, must be *signified* by identifiable behaviour patterns or material objects. This fits in well with the contention of Ian Hodder (1982) and others (Miller and Tilley 1984) that material culture contains a set of active symbols which may mark or transgress social and economic boundaries — in other words the social relations of production. This perspective allows the outline of the relations of production in early southern African social formations to be discerned, although it must be stressed that the exercise is still preliminary.

Insights into the relations of production within social formations conventionally categorized as Stone Age have come through the study of rock art. David Lewis-Williams (1982) has shown convincingly that these paintings, rather than being naturalistic representations, or art for art's sake, are part of a complex set of social behaviour in which people in a state of trance represent and reinforce the connections between camps. Thus medicine men, in a state of 'out of body travel', present interdependencies between communities which may have only periodic contact, establishing the rights of people to move from camp to camp and share resources, and the obligations of people to share the resources that they have. Painting is a product of this ideological realization of relations of production, and not in itself central to the ideology that is being developed; thus San communities in the Kalahari use the trance experience in the same way, but without graphic representation.

Phrased within the theory of structuration, rock art may therefore be seen as the signification of a set of power relations, for, by using a complex set of metaphors, medicine men 'make real' the complex ideology that they reproduce in trance (Hall 1985). Ethnographic work has shown that the major elements in the relations of production that structure social formations — mutual reciprocity and sanctions against accumulation — may be signified in other ways as well. Thus Wiessner's (1982) study of gift exchanges within and between Kalahari camps demonstrates how items of material culture are exchanged between individuals as tokens of mutually acknowledged relationships that may remain formal for long periods, to be used when one or other partner needs support. Again, the relations of production are signified in the real world of objects and images.

This identification of the signification of hunter-gatherer relations of production immediately suggests an interpretation of an aspect of early farmers' material culture that has so far eluded satisfactory explanation (Hall 1986). The ceramics that define the early Iron Age in the subcontinent show a marked conformity within a specific time bracket over a distance of a thousand or so kilometres (Hall 1987; Maggs 1984). Most archaeologists have avoided the implications of the culture–people assumption within which they work (that this must indicate a common society, which is hardly consistent with the apparent lack of centralized political and economic organization at this time), or have sought to explain the typological conformity as indicative of population movements or of 'ethnicity' (neither of which has much grounding in theoretically consistent models of human behaviour). It would seem more reasonable to see such ceramic decoration as part of a common set of symbols which signify power relations in the same way as rock art or the exchange networks of the Kalahari. In other words, just as the ideological work of the medicine man depended on members of camps widely separated from one another recognizing common symbols — which has resulted in structurally equivalent depictions in Zimbabwe (Huffman 1983), the Natal Drakensberg (Lewis-Williams 1977) and the south-western Cape (Yates, Golson and Hall 1985) — so there was reason for early farmers in southern Africa to decorate pottery with motifs also recognized and used by members of different chiefdoms.

But there must have been good reason for such conformity by both rock artists and early potters, for ethno-archaeological work suggests that such 'active symbols' will tend to have specific meanings for the immediate actors involved in social interactions, leading more towards local innovation in style rather than widespread conservatism (Hodder 1982). Here it must be remembered that the forces and relations of production are not separate compartments within a mode of production but are, rather, closely intertwined, defining the specific nature of each mode (Hindess and Hirst 1975). Thus it is in the economies of hunter-gathering and early farming that an explanation may be expected to lie.

Ethnographic work in the Kalahari has shown that reciprocity and sanctions against accumulation serve to counter the risks inherent in dependency on hunting and the collection of wild food resources (Wiessner 1982). Thus it is not scarcity that is the central factor (although scarcity may obviously occur) but rather the need for flexibility in order to cope with variations in abundancy and the difficulties of predicting the location and abundance of crucial resources from one year to the next. Thus the symbolic labour of the medicine man serves to concretize a pattern of social behaviour which is closely tuned to the constraints and possibilities of key resources.

At first sight, it would seem that farming would imply different relations of production, with cultivation removing many of the risks and uncertainties of hunter-gathering, allowing accumulation and thus making structured reciprocity far from desirable. But as I pointed out earlier in this chapter, early farmers in southern Africa still made extensive use of hunted and gathered resources and probably had few domestic animals. In addition, cultivation of small stands of crop plants was probably fraught with difficulties in the early first millennium: soils, particularly in the south-eastern coastal areas, were often inherently low in fertility, the climate variable and crops at risk from disease, insect damage, wild fauna and a host of other factors (Hall 1981; 1987). Thus I would suggest that, after crop plants were introduced into southern Africa some two thousand years ago, the modified forces of production demanded relations of production in which reciprocity and sanctions against accumulation were, if anything, more greatly stressed than they had been earlier (Hall 1986). Ceramic decoration, with its widely distributed set of commonly recognized motifs, was, I would argue, part of a set of active symbols which served to signify these relations of production in precisely the same way that rock art and gift exchanges signified relations of production within and between hunter-gatherer camps.

Returning now to the problem presented earlier in this chapter, it would seem that there is a case for suggesting that, although Stone Age and early Iron Age communities can be distinguished from one another in their forces of production, including the technological sets that they employed, the relations of production were more similar than different. Thus there can be no theoretical justification for distinguishing between a hunter-gatherer mode of production and a farming mode of production, or between a Stone Age mode of production and an Iron Age mode of production. On the contrary: it is likely to prove more instructive to consider all the social formations that existed in the subcontinent between 1000 BC and AD 1000 (during which time domestic crops and animals were introduced into southern Africa from the north) as structured by a single mode and its variants which, for convenience — and following Lee (this volume) — can be called a 'primitive communist mode of production'.

The primitive communist mode of production in precolonial southern Africa

Once the distinction between hunter-gatherer and early farmer in southern Africa is broken down it becomes possible to reassess the implications of the origins of agriculture in the subcontinent. In this consideration, it is taken as given that cereal crops, cattle and sheep were not brought independently into domestication in this region, for there is no evidence for the appropriate wild progenitors in southern African floras and faunas (Hall 1987: Maggs 1984). It is also accepted that iron working was probably first developed in the Sahel (Grebenart 1983), and that metal tools were part of a technological set that was closely linked with cereal cultivation (Stemler 1984). This in turn implies diffusion, and probably a movement southwards of the practitioners of the new economy. But recognition of these patterns in the evidence does not constitute explanation, for the crucial question remains: why did some communities within social formations structured by the primitive communist mode of production adapt their forces of production while others did not?

The key to answering this question is again in the theory of the mode of production. Obviously, modes cannot be seen as static systems with self-regulating properties for otherwise change could not have taken place in the past. Instead, each mode must contain *contradictions* which may eventually lead to its dissolution and replacement by another mode (Hindess and Hirst 1975). I would suggest, as regards southern Africa, that the primitive communist mode of production contained a fundamental contradiction, that an important part of the ideological work of the medicine man was to disguise this contradiction, that cultivation of domestic crops was incorporated into the forces of production in an attempt to solve this contradiction, but that the contradiction could not be resolved until about AD 1000, when social formations structured by new modes of production came into existence.

The contradiction within the primitive communist mode of production lay in the tension between day-by-day distribution of the product within the camp and the recurrent obligation to fulfil reciprocal obligations with other camps. For although a given camp facing a call on its resources by outsiders may at the time have had abundant food, this food still had to be realized by labour, and new people had to be incorporated in the social relations of the camp. Of course, if this camp's members were themselves experiencing difficulty in obtaining resources, the new demands would reduce available food and introduce the possibility that they, in turn, would have to take up reciprocal claims against other groups elsewhere. I would suggest that the ritual of the shared trance experience, and the signification of power relations through rock art, worked to mystify this contradiction by stressing the unity of the wider group: the lines of intimate connection between people widely separate in space who may, at any time, have had to be incorporated into daily real world experience. In other words, trance and its symbolism was not a passive celebration of the orderliness of society and the general acceptance of mutual reciprocity, but was quite the opposite: it was precisely because of the tensions between 'insiders' and 'outsiders' that the ideology presented and signified by the medicine men was of such central importance.

Clearly, the solution to this contradiction lay in accumulation, thus making camps more self-sufficient and curtailing the need for wide-ranging networks of mutual obligation. Such accumulation was not possible within the southern African indigenous resource set. Also, it could only be *partly* resolved by adopting northern strains of domestic cereals, which could be stored only in limited amounts in sub-tropical environments (Sansom 1974) and which were themselves subject to many risks and uncertainties. But by adopting domestic crops *and* domestic livestock — which could be successfully accumulated — the primitive communist mode of production could be transformed.

But why did almost 1000 years pass between the initial availability of domestic plants and animals in southern Africa and the transformation of the primitive communist mode of production into successor modes? I have suggested that the answer to this lies in the ecology of those areas in southern Africa where domestic plants and animals were first brought into use. For although the woodlands and forests of the subtropical lowlands were suited to swidden cultivation, keeping livestock would have been at first difficult, and in some areas impossible. Thus, for example, the coastlands which are today Mozambique and northern Natal would have supported a closed forest infested with tsetse, carrying trypanasomiasis damaging to domestic animals. It was only much later, when these woodlands had been largely removed by successive generations of swidden cultivation, that cattle could be kept on any substantial scale (Hall 1986; 1987). In the interior valleys, the situation was more favourable and, as already mentioned, small numbers of domesticates form part of the faunal assemblages from those sites that have been excavated. In these locations faunal assemblages reveal a recurrent pattern: initial villages have faunal assemblages in which caprines outnumber cattle, and this ratio steadily changes with later settlement until, towards the end of the first millennium AD, cattle are the dominant domesticated species. This probably mirrors the progressive opening of the landscape, as woodlands were cleared by cultivation and more grazing became available (Hall 1987).

Thus I am suggesting that the contradiction within the primitive communist mode of production could not *immediately* be resolved by the availability of domestic crops and animals. Some limited accumulation was possible in the first millennium, but a sustained 'dialectic with nature' (Slater 1976) was necessary before cattle could be kept in any substantial numbers and a transformation of the relations of production was possible. In this situation, mutual reciprocity — signified in this case by a shared and highly conservative set of ceramic motifs — was still essential.

When the transformation of the primitive communist mode of production in some parts of southern Africa *did* finally occur, the effect was marked. Although still controversial (Hammond-Tooke 1984; Kuper 1982), this new structure has been termed the lineage mode of production by a number of writers (Bonner 1981; Hedges 1978), and was characterized by forces of production in which cattle keeping was far more heavily emphasized, and by relations of production in which resources, and particularly domestic livestock, were accumulated at the village level or among sets of villages: clearly a contrast with social formations structured by the primitive communist mode of production, whether these were 'Stone Age' or 'Early Iron Age'. Both the demands of cattle-keeping and the possibilities presented by accumulation (and in particular the opportunity to initiate trading relationships for scarce commodities) led to extensive settlement by farmers of the higher grassland regions (Maggs 1976b), with villages built in stone with elaborate architectural styles, often suggesting control over labour on a fairly extensive scale. Within a few centuries, this lineage mode of production was itself replaced in some areas by a tributary mode of production (Wolf 1982), on which were based the first southern African states of Mapungubwe and Zimbabwe (Hall 1987).

In conventional historiography, the change from the primitive communist mode of production to the lineage mode of production is distinguished as the divide between the early Iron Age and the late Iron Age and is evidenced by a marked change in settlement style (Maggs 1984). Again, this has been 'explained' by postulated population movements, the models of which have become more and more tortuous with the emerging complexity of the data (Huffman 1978; Oliver and Fagan 1975; Phillipson 1977; 1985). But it seems more likely that late Iron Age pottery, with far more localized distributions of characteristic motifs, had a different social role from earlier ceramics. With the lineage mode of production, mutual reciprocity was replaced by localized accumulation and there would be no place for the widespread signification of connections. Therefore pottery decoration would have taken on a more specific, regional role in the signification of the relations of production, perhaps following models of the sort described by Ian Hodder (1982) as a result of his ethnographic research elsewhere in Africa.

Conclusion

Obviously, much of what I have suggested in this chapter is speculative and preliminary, and will remain so until a better theoretical understanding of pre-capitalist social formations has been achieved, and until more methodological work has been completed, thus allowing in particular the unambiguous identification of relations of production in the archaeological record. However, I do feel that there is a case for arguing that the concept of a hunter-gatherer mode of production as defined by Leacock and Lee (1982), and its implied parallel of a farming mode of production, is flawed. Such definitions fix attention on the forces of production and in so doing simply recreate the older typological/ economic categories of conventional archaeology. If a case is made for seeing the relations of production as dominant within the mode, as I have done in this chapter, then the nature of pre-capitalist society begins to look rather different and a number of anomalies that have defied earlier explanation begin to fall into place.

There are, of course, wider implications of this argument which I have not considered here. Central to these is the question of what happens to social formations not structured by the lineage mode of production after about AD 1000 in southern Africa. Presumably in some areas the primitive communist mode of production may have remained intact, but how general was this and, more importantly, to what extent was this the case with the Kalahari San, whose economy, ecology and society have been so central to analysis of hunter-gatherers for many years? Some recent studies suggest that the San may for many years have been marginal to the widespread trade and exchange networks that often form part of the relations and forces of production within the lineage and tributary modes (Denbow and Wilmsen 1983). If this is the case, has there really been a 'pure' primitive communist mode of production in southern Africa during the present millennium, and are hunter-gatherers, as has been argued for pastoralists, not rather integral parts of wider economic systems? These are questions for future research.

10. Palaeopolitics: resource intensification in Aboriginal Australia and Papua New Guinea

Harry Lourandos

> . . . . the ethnography of hunters and gatherers is largely a record
> of incomplete cultures. Fragile cycles of ritual and exchange may
> have disappeared without trace, lost in the earliest stages of
> colonialism, when the intergroup relations they mediated were
> attacked and confounded. If so, the 'original' affluent society
> will have to be rethought again for its originality, and the
> evolutionary schemes once more revised (Sahlins 1974: 38–9).

Introduction

The problem of change within hunter-gatherer societies has traditionally received far less attention than the shift from hunting-gathering to
agriculture. However, more recent studies among non-farming peoples
are beginning to provide clues as to how transformations to more
complex social and economic levels (not necessarily definable as farming) may have occurred (Price and Brown 1985). Recent studies of
Australian Aboriginal hunter-gatherers can be placed in such a category (Lourandos 1985).

Australian Aboriginal societies have long served as universal analogues for hunter-gatherers, including those of the Pleistocene. This is
so even though for large sectors of the continent, such as the fertile east
and south-east, little information exists on traditional societies, since
these had been extinguished in the early days of colonial occupation.
The Australian examples were drawn mainly from more marginal arid
or semi-arid, as well as tropical, environments, where traditional
Aboriginal populations still resided. Thus the anthropological accounts
were 'generations too late', when Aboriginal society had already been
considerably altered by European contact.

In contrast to this situation, current ethno-historical and archaeological studies are producing a broader picture of Australian Aboriginal
cultural variation. Archaeological evidence has also shown that Aus-

148

tralia has a lengthy prehistory of some 40,000 years or more. As no agriculture appears to have been employed on the Australian mainland, interpretations of this prehistory have dwelt predominantly upon long-term stability — which has unfortunately tended to represent Australian Aborigines as rather static peoples when compared with their more dynamic Melanesian neighbours. Socio-economic and demographic changes in Australia have not been regarded as significant. This viewpoint of long-term stability has reinforced the classical dichotomy between the passive hunter-gatherer, on the one hand, and the resourceful farmer, on the other. Such a viewpoint is common to many studies on hunter-gatherers generally.

Recent ethnohistorical and archaeological studies are beginning to challenge these models of long-term stability. Cultural (including economic) transformations of the last 4000 years or so (and especially of the last 2000 years) are being seen as more significant than was previously thought. There is also a change in emphasis from seeing hunter-gatherers, including Australians, mainly in an environmental and ecological framework, to considering social and economic factors as agents of change (Lourandos 1985).

In this chapter I will specifically discuss aspects of the organization of production in Australian societies, demonstrating that intensification of resource use and its manipulation is connected largely with intergroup occasions (festivities, ceremonies, exchanges, and so on). I argue that competitive relations between groups may have led to increases in production (including surpluses), and also to increases in environmental productivity. In this way, a dynamic may have been generated which led to still further changes. Finally, I draw parallels with Highland New Guinea and suggest that processes qualitatively similar to the Australian ones may have led there to the intensification of agriculture.

Change

Hunter-gatherer societies are mostly viewed as rather stable entities which undergo change only once external stress factors have come into play: 'A system will remain stable until acted upon by forces external to its organisation as a system' (Binford 1983: 221). External pressures are generally characterized as being either environmental or demographic. If internal, or social, factors are invoked, these are more often ascribed, in a functional sense, to stress brought about by, for example, information overload (for example, scalar stress: Johnson 1982; Ames 1985). The internal dynamics of society itself, the processes characterized by tensions within and between 'systems', or parts of these, are less often discussed. Social relations are viewed as 'solutions to problems' brought about by other factors (such as environment, demography);

that is, as epiphenomena rather than as determining forces in their own right.

These viewpoints often fail adequately to consider social theory itself — in this case the operation of hunter-gatherer societies within the broader socio-political network of alliance systems (Bender 1978; 1981; Lourandos 1983; 1985). In such a context concepts such as 'system' are not easy to apply (Salmon 1978), for individual societies are composites of a large number of interrelated, overlapping and conflicting parts; these include linguistic and political, as well as social networks, all at varying hierarchical levels. The concept of 'tribe', as for example applied to Aboriginal Australia, has always been problematic for just this reason. In short, it becomes very difficult to determine just what entity is, say, 'adapting' — the ill-defined 'system' itself, or parts of it, or, in the strict Darwinian sense, individual organisms.

Given these problems, my approach is to examine the processes operating between 'systems' or parts of systems, namely the social dynamics, or social relations. The objective is to demonstrate how social relations can themselves establish the context for change and generate a dynamic which fuels further changes. While social relations are influenced by other variables (such as environment, demography) they have their own internal dynamic and because it is here that decisions are made they may be viewed to a large degree as primary (see also Meillassoux 1973; 1981; Godelier 1975; 1977; Bender 1978; 1981, Friedman 1979; Gilman 1984).

I argue that the arena of intergroup relations (for example, feasting, ritual and exchange) provides the context for change, rather than the domestic level of production (cf. Sahlins 1974). Such institutions and occasions mediate the relations among autonomous societies, lacking as these do centralized political controls. Between these societies, and their representatives and leaders, competition takes place for resources, spouses, exchange partners, information and the like. Thus the status of individual groups is validated, and the underlying political tussle masked by ritual. Incentives therefore exist for increasing production beyond normal subsistence levels, to produce a 'surplus' and/or control local resource productivity in order to meet or exceed social obligations. This is so for all subsistence-based societies, whether hunter-gatherer, horticulturalist or otherwise. That is, technological means (the forces of production) are less important than the overall organizational aspects, or, relations of production.

Social relations of production

Recently, a change in the perception of Australian Aboriginal society has taken place. Traditional approaches, emphasizing the egalitarian and 'anarchic' side of Aboriginal social organization (Meggitt 1966; Maddock 1972), may now be contrasted with recent studies discussing the ethno-politics of acquisition, control and inheritance of land and resources (Sutton and Rigsby 1982), and the role of leaders in these events (von Sturmer 1978). Thus Bern (1979) has argued that the ideology of economic relations lies in the rich Australian religious life (cults, ceremonies, and so on). Ethno-historical studies have also altered the perception of Aboriginal economy, from a notion of its being passive and 'parasitic' (Meggitt 1964) to the recognition that there exists land and resource management of varying levels and intensity (D. Harris 1977a; Hynes and Chase 1972; Lourandos 1980a; 1980b; Williams and Hunn 1982). However, the connection between the complexity of Australian social and ritualistic relations and the level of economic production still remains to be drawn. Put another way, what is the relationship between complex kinship systems and rituals, and the organization of the hunter-gatherer economy?

Earlier ethnographic accounts hinted at a close association between the level of production and the demands of social relations. For example, Hart and Pilling's classic studies of the Tiwi of Bathurst and Melville Islands of northern Australia (1960) indicate that production of resources was increased, and surpluses provided, by the development of relatively efficient domestic labour units in the form of large polygynous households. Because of their larger retinue, such households were also relatively sedentary. Thus, increased female labour was employed to host lengthy feasts associated with status funerals. In this way, a polygynous, gerontocratic system (with one individual male recorded as having twenty-nine wives) controlled both production and reproduction. The distribution of wives, goods, services, feasts and rituals and the like, was governed, and competed for, by a minority of 'big men' (the ethnographers' term).

Parallels with Melanesian horticultural societies are obvious. The monopolization of social and economic forces, and competition between 'big men', are reminiscent of many New Guinea societies, such as those of the Highlands. The latter societies range from small-scale, low-population-density hunter-horticulturalists to dense, predominantly agricultural communities. The distinction between hunting-gathering and horticulture is by no means clear in the New Guinea Highland societies (P. Brown 1978), and it could be argued that they overlap in many ways with the hunter-gatherer economies of Australia (Lourandos 1980a). I could also suggest that Australian societies, such as the Tiwi, were operating along broadly similar lines to many societies in New Guinea, but *without* recognizable horticulture. In distinguishing between Australia and New Guinea too much emphasis has been placed on the material aspects of technology, thus contrasting hunter and farmer. In fact, the organizational elements, or relations of production, of hunting and farming societies bear strong similarities.

While not necessarily 'typical', the Tiwi display many similarities with other Australian societies. For example, Thomson (1949) detailed the elaborate exchange systems of Arnhem Land and their close association with ritual leaders and the production of items of exchange; and Keen (1982) has recently pointed to the ways in which varying kinship systems allow for differential levels of polygyny. Both examples are indications of ways in which social relations may affect the level of production. In the first case, specialist craftsmen emerged, together with production being stimulated for purposes of exchange; in the second, the potential size of the labour force of the polygynous household was to a large degree controlled by the form of the particular kinship system. Thus the Murngin system allowed certain individuals to acquire up to ten wives. Polygyny, and the related existence of prominent leaders who also maintained their rank through ritual, exchange, feast giving, and so on, has been recorded for other Australian societies (for example, in south-eastern Australia), as have complex economic practices and increased levels of sedentism (Lourandos 1985).

The overall implication is that many Australian hunter-gatherers differ mainly in terms of degree, and not kind, from New Guinean hunter-horticulturalists. Effectively in support, Woodburn (1980) distinguishes between the varying organizational levels of hunter-gatherer societies, and places the Australians closer to agriculturalists than to such hunting peoples as Bushmen and Hadza. Thus his 'delayed-return' system, claimed to characterize both agriculturalists and Australians, refers to such features as polygyny and elaborate kinship, ritual and exchange, as well as to more complex economic strategies and facilities.

How, then, does this somewhat close relationship between the social relations and the economic base affect the intensification of resources in hunter-gatherer Australia? And what parallels can be drawn with horticultural New Guinea?

Examples of intensification

In this section I present Australian examples of relatively intensive harvesting and land-management practices which in all cases are associated with intergroup relations, including ceremonial occasions and extensive exchange networks. A case study from south-eastern Australia, which illustrates many of these features, is discussed first of all.

South-western Victoria

Recent research in this region, and indeed the wider Victorian area of south-eastern Australia, has revealed societies more complex, populous, sedentary and culturally varied than previously believed to exist. The characteristics of these societies include specialized, and in some cases intensive, use of resources, and a complex web of social interaction involving ceremonial and exchange systems (Lourandos 1977; 1980a; 1980b; 1983; 1985).

The fertile humid coastal plain of south-western Victoria is located at a latitude of thirty-eight degrees south of the equator. Population densities appear to have been among the highest in Aboriginal Australia — comparable in some ways to those of the northern tropical coastline (Lourandos 1977; Butlin 1983). Settlement seems to have been semi-sedentary throughout the district, including the inner hinterland. The pattern included complexes of 'villages' composed of durable huts and also domestic earth mounds in waterlogged areas. A broad-based specialized hunter-gathering economy was practised, with an emphasis on relatively intensive fishing and the harvesting of indigenous plant species (daisy yam, *Microseris scapigera*; bracken fern, *Pteridium esculentum*). Migratory fish (for example, eels, *Anguilla australis*) provided the main catch and specialized technology included sizeable weirs, traps and drainage systems. The most elaborate examples of eeling involved large-scale labour-intensive earthworks. The ethnographic examples at Mount William, described in 1841, consisted of fifteen acres (six hectares) of complex artificial drainage, and the archaeological example at Toolondo stretches some two to three kilometres in length (Lourandos 1980a; 1980b). Ethno-historical information indicates that these complexes operated to harvest large quantities of migrating eels, and were associated with intergroup occasions which possibly involved ceremonies and exchange. A broad network of linguistic groups attended these gatherings, and between 800 and 1000 people were recorded. Construction of the drain involved the manipulation (regulation) of local swamps and their resources, including eels, and can be argued to have increased the production of eels and their numbers.

The considerable labour thus invested in these durable facilities, plus the increased production of eels, can be directly related to the large number of consumers (that is, large groups of people) — for consumption was immediate, with no long-term storage methods employed. In contrast, eeling for domestic purposes took place on a much smaller scale, with the use of weirs, traps and small drains. At the domestic level of consumption elaborate devices such as those described above would have been unprofitable, and thus unnecessary. Intensification and manipulation of eeling therefore operated mainly at the intergroup level (Lourandos 1985: 408). While both environmental and demographic factors may have been involved in the emergence of these devices (Lourandos 1980a) we have an example here of complex

technology developed to meet the needs of intergroup politics —
beyond immediate domestic concerns.

Intensive resource procurement also took place within the context of
intricate social relations. A complex of social networks cross-cut the
district, and appears to have dominated the entire area of Victoria. The
two examples of elaborate eeling devices (above) were associated with
the inland *Kulin* network, which embraced between five and six 'tribal
languages', or dialects. The neighbouring coastal *Mara* network was of
similar composition, and included at least 2000 to 3000 members. The
extensive *Kulin* was even larger. Such social networks were intersected
by a web of competitive intergroup festivities, ceremonies and exchanges, somewhat in line with those described above, which were
sustained by the harvesting and/or manipulation of local resources
(eels, land mammals and birds, whales, fruit).

Extensive and complex exchange systems criss-crossed Victoria and
wider south-eastern Australia, based upon prestigious greenstone
edge-ground axes and other raw materials. McBryde's (1978) archaeological studies have demonstrated the complexity of these exchange
systems and support ethno-historical evidence detailing the lack of
interaction between the heartlands of the *Kulin* and a third network,
Kurnai, in contrast to the complexity of interaction along the border
region between *Kulin* and *Mara*. These alliance systems, composed of
complex kinship, polygyny, exchange, ceremony and feasting, were
dominated by prominent and powerful individuals whose status was,
in addition, defined by their position in the religious hierarchy. Overall, therefore, the evidence from south-western Victoria adds considerably to the impression of complex Aboriginal socio-economic relations
to which I alluded earlier in this discussion.

Comparative Australian examples

A series of ethno-historical examples, broadly comparable to the Victorian information, of intensified resource use and/or manipulation in
association with intergroup meetings, ceremonies and exchanges, can
be drawn from a wide range of Australian environments. A short
description of some of the main examples follows.

Fish. Comparable in some ways to the eel fisheries of south-western
Victoria, were extensive stone-walled complexes of fish traps at Brewarrina on the Darling river in western New South Wales. Feasting,
ceremony and exchange were enacted by a broad-based social network
(Mathews 1903). Elsewhere, as in south-eastern Queensland, the function of coastal, stone fish traps has been described in similar terms — as
being associated with communal social and ceremonial purposes (Walters 1985).

Cereals (including Panicum decompositum, Portulaca*).* The laborious harvesting, processing and, in some cases, storage of grass seeds of a wide range of plants dominated the economies of arid and semi-arid Australia in the ethnographic period. Fire, dams, the broadcasting of seed and the introduction of seed into new areas were devices employed to manage plant yields. Staggered harvest practices were also employed and considerably extended the season of plant availability. More than this, in central Australia, the use and storage of cereals were also increased to sustain large intergroup festivities and ceremonial occasions (Spencer and Gillen 1912: 259; Allen 1974; Tindale 1977; W. Jones 1979; Hamilton 1980; Kimber 1984; M. Smith 1986).

*Cycads (*Macrozamia, Cycas*).* The fruit of these toxic tropical plants, requiring laborious purifying techniques, was prepared and stored in quantity for ceremonial occasions.

> The fact that it is abundant gives *ngätu* (*Cycas media*) a special value in native economy, for it enables the women to maintain an adequate food supply on ceremonial occasions when hundreds of people are gathered in one camp for weeks or months at a time, who could not otherwise be supported for such periods on local resources. *Ngätu* is also the principal food eaten in Arnhem Land on ritual occasions (Thomson 1949: 22–3).

Fire was also employed to increase yields (D. Harris 1977a; Beaton 1982).

*Bunya pine nuts (*Araucaria bidwillii*).* In south-eastern Queensland nut harvests (with some storage of nuts involved) were accompanied by large-scale, competitive and often antagonistic social gatherings, ceremonies, and so on which drew disparate populations from a wide geographical area (Petrie 1902; Sullivan 1977).

Tropical yams (including Dioscorea*).* In Cape York, northern Queensland, yams in large quantities were laboriously detoxified and stored in bulk, especially to support elaborate ceremonial occasions.

> A certain amount of food, especially however *Dioscorea sativa* var., the tubers of water lilies (*Nymphaea spp.*) and *Parinarium nonda*, is stored during the height of the vegetable harvest earlier in the year. The storage of food is practised only to a limited extent, and most often in connection with ceremonial activities, either for initiation, or for the ceremonial presentation of food required during mourning, and other such occasions (Thomson 1939: 216).

Yam heads were planted in a quasi-horticultural fashion (D. Harris 1977a). Recent studies in tropical Arnhem Land by Meehan and Jones (R. Jones 1975: 32) indicate that surplus labour was employed to support people for lengthy periods as they prepared to participate in major ceremonies. Ten men are cited as being supported for forty weeks.

Moths (Agrotis infusa*)*. In the highlands of south-eastern Australia the intensive collection of seasonally available moths formed the economic basis for competitive social gatherings and rituals, together with some exchange, attended by people from far-flung regions. While there is no indication of resource management, most reports indicate that moths were exclusively eaten by men in connection with rituals. Prearranged battles between competing populations took place on the lower slopes, with the victors ascending to the higher ritual areas, where there were supplies of moths, while the vanquished returned home empty-handed (Flood 1980). Moths, however, were also available in the home territories of most participants, so they were obviously not the main purpose of the gatherings.

In many of these examples (for example, Bunya, south-western Victoria, south-eastern highlands) competition between groups took the form of skirmishes or organized combat, and exchanges, feasting and the like accompanied the ceremonies. In many cases (those involving cereals, cycads, yams), although not all, the women's labour was employed to provide increases in production to meet the economic demands produced by this social interaction. Given the above information and the obvious gaps in our knowledge of Aboriginal levels of production, the possibility must be raised that even higher productive levels may have operated in recent times (also Hamilton 1982). This would go some way towards explaining Gould's apparent 'paradox' of 'a storable staple that is not stored' (1980: 102).

Organization of production

The above examples suggest that Australian Aborigines not only took advantage of gluts of local seasonal resources for maintaining relationships with their neighbours, but actively managed or manipulated these key resources. It should also be mentioned that the resources concerned were seasonally abundant with high levels of regeneration (that is, of the *r*-selected variety). The productivity of these resources would, in this way, have been stabilized or regularized and, in some cases, increased. Productivity was, therefore, under control.

Production was also increased by, for example, efficient harvesting methods, although these were not necessarily dependent on the availability of large numbers of people. One could argue that a 'surplus' was often produced exceeding domestic needs. Technology, including storage methods, was also developed and in some cases (for example, with cereals in south-western Victoria) attuned to local conditions. In this way the process could be viewed as one of econiche expansion.

Other examples of environmental manipulation are available (D. Harris 1977a; Lourandos 1980a; 1980b; Hynes and Chase 1982) which overlap with what traditionally is considered as 'farming' practice. The Australian Aboriginal examples, however, have often been brushed aside as not 'true' farming. Definitions are thus ambiguous and straddle the divide between ecology and economy, 'manager' and farmer. Are we merely viewing differential levels of resource manipulation and intensification?

My point is that for Aboriginal Australia we have enough evidence to suggest that resource manipulation and surplus production are closely associated with 'wider' (i.e. extra-domestic) social relationships, specifically those linked to ritual and exchange. We may infer that there was generally a fairly close tie between the operation of social relations and the economy itself. In this connection, there is an evident parallel with agricultural societies such as those of New Guinea.

Such an analogy can be taken a step further. Highland New Guinea society is also characterized by elaborate festivals, ceremonial occasions, exchange systems and antagonistic displays and battles operating between neighbouring groups (P. Brown 1978). Surpluses (pigs, yams, and so on) are produced to meet the demands of such social occasions. Rappaport's (1967) classic ecological study of the Tsembaga-Maring demonstrates that up to a 30 per cent surplus of yams would be produced to support pig herds. Domestic pork, however, was not a daily item of diet ('everyday' pork was obtained in small quantities from hunting). Pigs were slaughtered, usually at intervals of up to ten years, during festive occasions. The substantial agricultural investment in garden produce to maintain large pig herds is, therefore, not directly associated with subsistence needs. The large surplus produced supported ceremonial occasions which mediated the relationships between autonomous societies, that is, societies lacking centralized political controls.

Australian examples of foods connected with social occasions (eels, cereals, cycads, yams and the like) might be viewed similarly, that is, in connection with the regulation of social relations. Thus the communal foods of Australia were in some ways the functional equivalent of the pig (and other such foods linked to social occasions) in Highland New Guinea.

These examples raise the possibility of change through time leading to further intensification of resources as well as social relations. To explore this question a review is required of archaeological evidence for past resource use in south-western Victoria and wider Australia.

Archaeology: recent changes

Mainland Australia witnessed a broad series of cultural changes over the last 3000 to 4000 years (Lourandos 1985). Cultural introductions and/or innovations include: stone artefact types; aspects of fishing technology; a domesticated animal (dog); art styles. Cereals appear to have been first employed in central Australia during the last 2000 years (M. Smith 1986), and cycads in highland Queensland since about 4000 BP (Beaton 1982). Moths, in the southern highlands, appear to have been intensively harvested only in the late Holocene (Flood 1980), and the same could be said of eels in south-western Victoria (Lourandos 1980a; 1983). Therefore, resources associated with communal foods and ceremonies appear to have been intensified or introduced only during the last few thousand years or so. Throughout Australia, archaeological evidence reveals increasing numbers of new habitation sites and more intensive use of established sites. Overall, changes in settlement patterns and use of resources appear to have occurred.

In south-western Victoria the latter trend, of increasing establishment and use of archaeological sites, is evident especially during the last 2000 years, when marginal environments (wetlands, rainforests) are more intensively occupied, and new site forms (earth mounds as habitation sites) begin to appear in quantity in association with wetlands (Lourandos 1980a; 1983; 1985; E. Williams 1987). Intensive fishing practices (as above) are also involved. The extensive exchange systems of the wider Victorian region also appear to be of recent age.

Arguments have been advanced to suggest that here we have recent evidence for: (a) economic changes (broad-based economies and use of communal foods such as cereals, cycads); (b) trends towards semi-sedentism; (c) more complex social relations (exchange, art, and so on). Such aspects are not evident in earlier stages of Australian prehistory. In broad terms, it may be hypothesized that these early and recent patterns indicate a shift towards more logistically organized subsistence strategies, and delayed-return systems (Lourandos 1987).

These broad changes cannot solely be attributed to accompanying environmental changes, as they do not fit any one climatic trend (for example, stabilization of sea levels, climatic amelioration) (Lourandos 1985). Nor can they be explained by demographic shifts, although these may have been connected in some way (Ross 1981; Lourandos 1985). Explanations, therefore, must also take into consideration the influence of social dynamics.

Social dynamics

I have argued that the dynamics of competitive social interaction, which involved resources and their manipulation, provide the context for change. To some extent, an expandable, self-amplifying system may have been fuelled, which included the following factors (Figure 10.1): mediation of competitive political relations between local populations taking the form of intergroup festivals, rituals, feasts and exchange, together with a certain amount of combat; the size and duration of these communal events being sustained to a large degree by the production of surpluses, that is, communal foods; successful participation of this kind increasing social connections (for example, via marriage, multiple marriage, exchange and ritual partners), in turn possibly further expanding alliance networks. Therefore, incentives existed for further intensifying social relations and their economic correlates. A dynamic spiral is thus produced which is self-amplifying.

Figure 10.1 A schematic representation showing how competitive social relations can produce a self-amplifying system which generates an increase in surplus and alliance

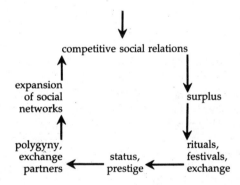

In a similar vein, Modjeska (1982) has argued that the intensification of pig husbandry in Highland New Guinea for purposes of ritual exchange led to the expansion of horticulture in these areas. We have seen that pigs were generally sustained by agricultural surplus and employed largely for ritualistic purposes. Archaeological evidence indicates an intensification both of agriculture and of pig husbandry in recent times — that is, within the last 1000 to 2000 years or so (White and O'Connell 1982: 174–89). Alternative explanations place emphasis on dietary and ecological factors: food shortages; demographic and subsequent agricultural expansion; protein supplementation by increased pig husbandry (Watson 1977; Morren 1977). While it may be conceded that it is difficult to disentangle demographic processes from these general events, it has also been shown that domestic pigs are not raised for subsistence purposes — which considerably strengthens Modjeska's point of view.

I likewise argue that many of the socio-economic changes of the recent period on mainland Australia (for example, south-western Victoria), and especially those connected with communal foods (eels, cereals, cycads) are explained to a large extent by the above model. The connection has already been drawn, in the case of the Tiwi, between the development of more economically efficient households via polygyny, and the generation of surplus, increased sedentism, together with a centralization of control in both social and ritual realms. When viewed from an evolutionary or dynamic perspective the development of these features is well accommodated by the above model. The overall socio-economic context, it has been argued (Lourandos 1983; 1985), would be that of expanding alliance systems.

These social processes would be influenced by both environmental and demographic factors but, I maintain, they also have their own independent dynamic. Demography too is interwoven with social factors and so both influences, and is influenced by, other changes (Cowgill 1975).

Conclusions

Change in social relations should be viewed not merely as a solution to problems caused by environmental or demographic conditions. Competitive political relations can generate a dynamic which may lead to economic intensification in both hunter-gatherer and farming societies, among others. This process tends to be amplified at the intergroup level. Broadly similar explanations could be employed for economic intensification, including the development of plant and animal domestication and agriculture, in other parts of the world (Friedman and Rowlands 1978; Bender 1978).

Australian interpretations are to some extent premature and more archaeological investigation is required, as well as theory developed at the middle range to accommodate these issues. For example, while the more recent processes of socio-economic intensification are becoming increasingly evident, their genesis, presumably in the mid-Holocene and earlier, is less clear. Overall, however, the explanations offered here answer a wider range of questions concerning the operation of hunter-gatherer societies than alternative environmental and stability-oriented approaches.

11. Politics and production among the Calusa of south Florida

William H. Marquardt

Introduction

The Calusa of south Florida are unusual, if not unique, by virtue of their status as a sedentary, politically powerful, centralized, stratified, tributary fishing-gathering-hunting society. Information on native south Florida is limited to a few documents, whose principal authors are: Fontaneda (1945), who learned four native dialects while the Calusa's captive from *c.* 1550 to 1567; Solís de Merás (1923), whose account focuses on the career of Menéndez, a Spanish governor of Florida; and Laudonnière (1975), the French founder of Fort Caroline. In addition, the publications of Vargas Ugarte (1935) and Zubillaga (1946) bring together a number of letters and documents of the sixteenth and early seventeenth centuries. Also relevant are certain letters, reports and testimony on file in Spanish archives (see Carlos II 1698; Conner 1925; García 1902; López de Velasco 1894; Olivera 1612; Sturtevant 1978; Wenhold 1936). Useful summaries of early Florida and Caribbean history are found in the works of Lyon (1976), Parks (1985) and Weddle (1985).

Although the ethno-historic accounts are valuable and suggestive, present-day readers must realize that the documents are not ethnographies, but accounts, communiqués and justifications, often having been written in the hope of influencing the opinions of others. Furthermore, the sixteenth- and seventeenth-century observers were not trained anthropologists; thus their perceptions were undoubtedly heavily conditioned by their own Western European concepts. At their best, even ethnologists and archaeologists never completely escape biases determined by their own experiences and training.

Although archaeologists first took notice of the area well over a century ago, only limited excavations have been undertaken.[1] Research

1. Brief histories of archaeological work in south-west Florida are provided by Marquardt (1984: 1–5; 1986: 63–4). A more detailed history is given by Widmer (1988: 37–54).

is now under way that will provide reliable chronological and paleo-environmental data and guidance for more extensive excavations in the Calusa heartland (Marquardt 1987), but as of this writing, little information is available on the developmental history of the Calusa domain.

Nor are any reliable data available on prehistoric contacts between the Calusa and people of other regions, such as the Caribbean and what is now the south-eastern United States. Some superficial similarities to Weeden Island (*c.* AD 200–900) and Mississippian (*c.* AD 700–1500) manifestations of the greater south-east can be observed in south Florida (e.g. in ceramics, the presence of burial mounds and certain cultural practices such as Black Drink consumption), but the mechanisms of exchange, trade and migration are poorly understood. On the continental scale south-west Florida lies at a climatic boundary between tropical and temperate regimes, a boundary that itself fluctuates from time to time. South Florida is hard to characterize both culturally and environmentally because it seems to include aspects of both center and edge. On the one hand it forms a cultural and economic center unto itself (an apparently nonhorticultural base of subsistence located between growers of corn to the north, manioc to the south) and, on the other hand, one finds evidence of contacts with other regions through time. Ultimately the dynamics of cultural and environmental centrality and peripherality must be fathomed before an understanding of the region will be complete, and their investigation is only now beginning in earnest.

In this chapter I characterize the Calusa social formation in terms of productive and reproductive relations, including a consideration of the role of ideology in the legitimation of authority. Contradictions inherent in the tributary mode of production practised in sixteenth-century south Florida are explicated as a background to a consideration of changes in response to the European presence. Finally, I briefly consider the question of the timing of the development of Calusa complexity, and suggest areas for fruitful investigation by archaeologists.

The Calusa social formation in sixteenth-century south Florida

The Calusa, and indeed all the natives of south Florida (see Map 11.1), are thought to have been nonhorticulturists. Spanish records explicitly say that they did not grow crops, and archaeobotanical remains from prehistoric sites are not those of domestic species (Marquardt n.d.; Scarry 1985: 246; Widmer 1988: 229), except in the case of the small gourds and gourd-like squashes found at Key Marco (Cutler 1975) which are thought to have been used as net floats. The documentary evidence, as well as all zooarchaeological identifications to date (see Wing 1965; Cumbaa 1971; Fradkin 1976; Milanich *et al.* 1984: 278–87;

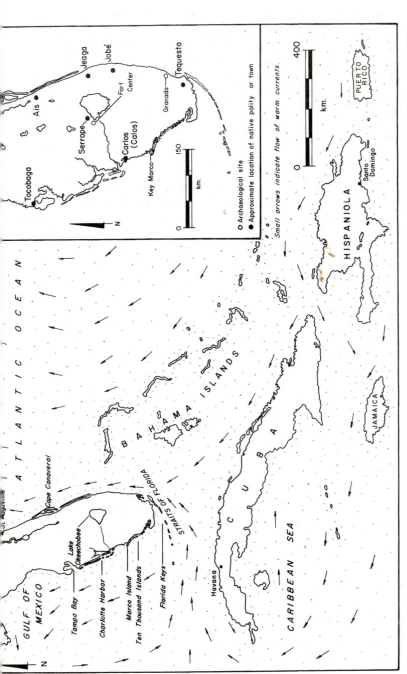

Map 11.1: South Florida and environs, with inset showing locations of certain archaeological sites and approximate locations of Indian towns, c. 1568.

Widmer 1986a), indicate that fish provided the main dietary staple, supplemented by shellfish, turtles, wild plant foods and game animals (birds, deer, raccoon, and so on). Most of the fish were obtained near the shore and could have been caught in tidal traps or nets. Some species, a minority in the faunal record so far, favor deeper water and would have required a hook-and-line or harpoon technology (Widmer 1986b).

Few attempts have been made to recover plant and animal remains systematically. Analyses using fine-screen techniques are of very small samples representing relatively brief time intervals at quite extensive sites. Also, because most mainland interior sites have been destroyed by the construction of modern buildings, floral and faunal analyses have been confined to island and coastal localities, where one would expect saltwater fish and shellfish to be more frequently encountered than land mammal or freshwater fish remains. Only with more extensive excavations and analyses will one be able to confirm or refute the importance of horticulture among south Florida's natives in the sixteenth century (see Dobyns 1983: 126–30; Goggin and Sturtevant 1964: 183–6; Marquardt 1986; Milanich 1987; and Widmer 1988: 229–34 for varying points of view). For the moment it must be assumed that the scant historical documentation and archaeological/paleobiological data in hand are correct and that horticulture played little or no role in Calusa subsistence production. Before discussing the social aspects of production, I first summarize what is known about subsistence and technology among the Calusa and their neighbors.

Subsistence in south Florida

Fish and other aquatic resources

Fishing must be considered the foundation of Calusa subsistence. Broad, flat, shallow estuaries surrounded by dense stands of mangroves are rich in nutrients favoring the production of fish and shellfish (Odum *et al.* 1982). More than thirty species of fish, sharks and rays, and more than fifty species of mollusc and crustacean have been identified in recent analyses of sediments from prehistoric sites in the Calusa area. Also frequently identified are several kinds of turtles, birds, and mammals, but these categories invariably account for a minuscule percentage of the estimated meat weight. Fish and, to a much smaller extent, shellfish account for the bulk of the meat represented (Marquardt n.d.).

When Pedro Menéndez was received with much formality by paramount chief Carlos in 1566, the latter provided 'many kinds of very good fish, roasted and boiled; and oysters, raw, boiled, and roasted, without anything else' (Solís de Merás 1923: 148). Some coastal Florida natives were witnessed eating whale (Vargas Ugarte 1935: 76), and in the Keys seals were eaten[2] along with a wide variety of fish, crustaceans, sea turtles and other animals (Fontaneda 1945: 26). Manatee and porpoise were hunted in the Keys as well (Goggin 1940: 282, citing Swanton). In south-central Florida the people were said to subsist on fish, eels, deer, birds, alligators, snakes and other reptiles, opossums, and turtles, as well as several kinds of roots (Fontaneda 1945: 27).

Unfortunately the ethno-historic record is nearly mute concerning the division of labor. Quite probably hunting and fishing were men's activities, but it cannot be assumed that women and children took no part in fishing or in the collection of other aquatic resources. Nor does any information on ownership of fishing or collecting localities come to us from documentary sources. We do know that in sixteenth-century Cuba hundreds of mullets and turtles were stored alive in enclosures made of reeds (Weddle 1985: 28), and it can be assumed that this storage technology was known to the natives of south Florida, only 150 kilometers distant. It seems reasonable to suggest that the chief and perhaps some members of the nobility had private storage corrals, perhaps maintained by servants. The degree to which commoners could fish, gather, or hunt at their own discretion is unknown. Fish could have been preserved, at least for a time, by smoking, and there is documentary evidence from south-east Florida of the drying of whale meat (San Miguel, cited from Goggin and Sturtevant 1964: 184–5).

The sheer bulk of some of the south-west Florida coastal shell middens is remarkable. Many occupy over a hectare (2.47 acres), and there are still several extant over three hectares (Useppa Island, more than four hectares; Big Mound Key, more than fifteen; Josslyn Island, more than three; Buck Key, also more than three). Battey's Landing at Pineland, heavily mined in the early twentieth century for road fill, was in the 1890s reported to have covered about thirty-two hectares (Cushing 1897: 342). Most of the middens are three to seven meters high. By comparison, the largest of the famous Ertebølle shell middens in Denmark range from 1.8 to twelve hectares, but none is over two meters high (Rowley-Conwy 1983: 122, Table 10.3). The great bulk of these south-west Florida shell middens gives a false impression of the relative dietary contribution of the shellfish, however, which in all cases thus far examined is much less than the meat contributed by fish (Marquardt n.d.). The nutritional content of shellfish is low compared with that of fish, although shellfish are high in protein (Waselkov 1987: 122). None the less, given seasonal and other variation in the availability of various fish, crustaceans and turtles, the quantities of available shellfish form an important, readily harvestable and plentiful source of food. Shellfish also lend themselves well to 'embedded'

2. Monk seal (*Monachus tropicalis*) bones have been identified from the Granada site in south-east Florida and from the Wightman site on Sanibel Island in south-west Florida (Wing and Loucks 1985: 267).

procurement strategies, that is, they can be easily collected on the way to and from the deployment of tidal nets, or on the way back from a canoe trip taken for some other purpose. The archaeological record clearly shows that a single species was sometimes collected in great numbers. A thick deposit of surf clams (*Spisula solidissima*) at the Buck Key site and several dense layers of scallops (*Argopecten irradians*) and whelks (*Busycon contrarium*) at the Josslyn Island site, for example, show that certain localities could, at least on occasion, produce particular species in abundance, and that this feature was exploited by the natives (Marquardt n.d.).

Mammals, reptiles and birds

Remains of deer, raccoon, land turtles, ducks and the occasional snake, skink, small bird or mouse are present, if never abundant, in faunal samples from prehistoric sites (Fradkin 1976; Marquardt n.d.; Widmer 1986a; Wing and Loucks 1985). In addition, the written record shows that alligators, opossums, rabbits and squirrels were also consumed. Observers noted abundant deer in south Florida (Dobyns 1983: 81–4), and near Lake Okeechobee it is said that the natives preferred to eat deer and fowl when they were available, although bread made from roots was their main food 'the greater part of the time' (Fontaneda 1945: 27). Deerskins were part of the tribute brought to Carlos from the interior in the sixteenth century (Zubillaga 1946: 278). The natives may have periodically set fires in order to promote grasslands favored by game animals (Dobyns 1983: 83–4). Most of the exploited animals are those captured or killed with relative ease, at least during certain seasons of the year. The south Floridians were known as excellent archers, and were equally skilful with spears and harpoons.

The extraordinarily well-preserved carvings and paintings from the Key Marco site (Cushing 1897; Gilliland 1975) offer some additional hints as to animals the natives thought noteworthy. A carved turtle plastron shows circling porpoises; a bone pin represents a pelican. Medallions in gold and silver are engraved with an abstract design that some have interpreted as a spider or were-jaguar (J. Griffin 1946: 298; Sears 1982: 60). Additional animal images include zoomorphic masks, a carved and painted alligator (or crocodile) head, a feline figurine, a deer effigy and a painting of a woodpecker (or possibly a kingfisher). The woodpecker seems to be speaking, or perhaps giving its characteristic call (Figure 11.1); it may have been valued for its red plumage or have been associated with spirits of the dead.

At the prehistoric site of Fort Center near Lake Okeechobee a platform built over a lake had been used for depositing bundled human skeletal remains, *c.* AD 200–800. Realistically carved images of animals, some fashioned from the tops of supporting pilings, surround the

Plate 11.1   Wooden artefacts discovered in the 1890s at the Key Marco site, Collier Country, Florida, attributed to the prehistoric Calusa.

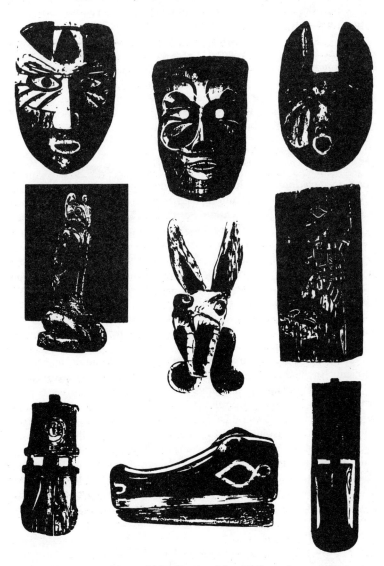

All photographs except the seated feline figurine (left, center) are of water colors by Wells M. Sawyer, housed in the National Anthropological Archives, Smithsonian Institution. The figurine, about 15 centimeters high, is in the collection of the National Museum of Natural History, Smithsonian Institution, number 240915. Reproduced by permission of the Smithsonian Institution. See Gilliland (1975) for detailed descriptions of the artefacts from Key Marco.

platform, and appear as though they are guarding or overseeing the
human dead. Among the represented animals are bear, cat, panther,
fox, otter, dog, bear, also many kinds of birds (woodpecker, owl,
osprey, eagle, hawk, ibis, spoonbill, heron) (Sears 1982: 42–58).

Unfortunately, one can only speculate about which animals held
ritual significance, which were totems or clan emblems, which were
commonly eaten and which were reserved for the elite. Archaeologists
have had some notable success at recognizing high-status foods, as in
the work at Moundville (Peebles and Schoeninger 1981), but extensive
excavations and analyses of several village sites will be necessary if
such information is to be inferred for south Florida.

The gathering of plant foods and other wild foods

The extremely limited archaeobotanical research done in south Florida
to date has shown that numerous wild plants were used, but there is as
yet no evidence for domestication. South-west Florida (Marquardt n.d.)
and south-east Florida (Scarry 1985) archaeobotanical analyses have
yielded the remains of numerous wild plants — for example, cocoplum
(*Chrysobalanus icaco*), sea grape (*Cocoloba*), false mastic (*Mastichodendrom
foetidissimum*), cabbage palm (*Sabal palmetto*), saw palmetto (*Serenoa
repens*), hog plum (*Ximenia americana*), acorns (*Quercus*), red mangrove
(*Rhizophora mangle*), black mangrove (*Avicennia germaninans*), pine
(*Pinus*), red cedar (*Juniperus*), dogwood (*Cornus*), goosefoot (*Chenopo-
dium*), sea purslane (*Trianthemia*), mallows (Malvaceae) and grasses
(Poaceae).

Numerous wild plants in the area are edible and some are mentioned
explicitly in historical documents, for example, prickly pear cactus
(*Opuntia*), grapes (*Vitis*), sea grapes (*Cocoloba*), palmetto berries (*Serenoa
repens*), heart of palm (*Sabal palmetto*), wild potato (*Apios tuberosa?*) and
other roots (summarized by Dobyns 1983: 53–77). Undoubtedly berries
and nuts were consumed, and may have been seasonally quite abundant (ibid.: 61–2). Some floating water plants are edible (ibid.: 68) and
wild rice is available in the wetlands of south Florida (ibid.: 63).

The question of root foods is intriguing because roots are mentioned
by Spanish commentators. For example, not only did the south-central
Florida natives 'make bread of roots, which is their common food the
greater part of the time', but they brought roots to Carlos as tribute
(Fontaneda 1945: 27–8). When the lakes were flooded, the root was
inaccessible, suggesting the 'mud potato' (*Apios tuberosa*), later used by
the Seminole, as the most likely candidate for this staple food. It was
said that 'there is no better bread to eat anywhere' (Laudonnière 1975:
111).

Roots, nuts, berries, palm fruits, grapes and cactus fruits could have
been gathered with little effort by anyone, including children and the

aged. Snares and traps were probably set for small animals and land tortoises could be collected when found. Like certain aquatic turtles, terrestrial turtles, such as the box turtle (*Terrepene carolina*) and gopher tortoise (*Gopherus polyphemus*), are easily kept in captivity until needed for food. Bird eggs, insects and other such foods were probably collected, but these could easily escape archaeological detection or notice by European commentators.

Procurement of nonfood raw materials

A final consideration in characterizing production is the great variety of raw materials on which daily life depended. Firewood was needed for cooking, heating, insect control and pottery firing. Clay and sand were needed for making the utilitarian pottery used for cooking and serving food. Wood and thatch were needed for constructing dwellings and temples, as well as for domestic facilities, such as roasting or smoking racks. Palm and yucca were used to make mats for a variety of purposes. Wood and fiber were also needed to fabricate corrals for fish and turtles as well as fish traps. Trees were needed for canoes. Wood was also used for making canoe paddles, shafts for arrows, harpoons, spears and handles. Fibers from yucca and palm leaves were used to make strong twine for nets, fishing lines, ropes and cords. Clothing was made from hides and fibers. Wood was necessary for carving a variety of utilitarian items (boxes, mortars, pestles, seats) and sacred ones (such as masks). Robust whelk shells were fashioned ingeniously into a variety of picks, hammers and woodworking tools (Luer *et al.* 1986: 95). Resins were used as adhesives for securing handles to tools, and so on. Bones from deer, birds and other animals were shaped into hairpins, net shuttles, weaving needles, awls and projectile points. Shark teeth were used for cutting a variety of materials. Natural dyes were needed to make body paint,[3] worn daily by the men, as well as pigments for paints used on boxes, carvings, masks and deer skins. Feathers were worn by some individuals, and were brought from the interior to Carlos as tribute (Zubillaga 1946: 278). Palm oil was used on the hair (Vargas Ugarte 1935: 86). Finally, we must assume that numerous wild plants and other materials were gathered for medicinal purposes, although no knowledge of such uses has come to us either from archaeological or historical sources.

3. The Spanish often commented on the body paint habitually worn by the natives. European captives, male and female, were also made to dress in the native way, wearing only paint and the briefest of loincloths (Solís de Merás 1923: 140, 142).

Class relations and tributary relations

Subsistence for the south Florida natives consisted of intensive fishing, gathering and hunting. An elaborate technology was needed to produce tools, containers, canoes, weapons, dwellings, temples and ritual paraphernalia. At the regional scale, but *not* at the local village scale, all these materials were readily available in the natural surroundings. If necessities could not be obtained locally, then they had to be acquired by means of trade or tribute.

People lived in sedentary villages composed of several dozen to several hundred individuals, and were stratified into nobles, commoners and captives, who were servants (Solís de Merás 1923: 226). Among the nobility, special statuses were recognized, and these were likely associated with privileged access to subsistence and wealth. Specialized skills, such as wood carving, painting, engraving, navigation and curing were surely rewarded with special recognition or compensation. Village-wide ceremonies involving scores of dancers and singers were held at times of transition.

The Calusa paramount chief was thought responsible for the productivity of the environment (Laudonnière 1975: 110), and he regularly retired with his close associates to a temple, where special rites were performed (see also Estevan 1698). The paramount chief was assisted by an individual whom the Spanish called the 'captain general'. In 1567 a captain general succeeded to the position of paramount chief under unusual circumstances (Zubillaga 1946: 309–11; see discussion below). Also important was a high priest who was responsible for maintaining the temple and its idols (ibid.: 309). Such priests had the power to summon the winds (Sturtevant 1978: 147), probably coordinated preparations for treatment of the dead and carried on communications with their spirits. The natives were said to obtain guidance from the dead (Zubillaga 1946: 279), although they greatly feared them, and they made daily offerings to them in the form of food and herbs placed on mats on top of graves (Parks 1985: 59; Sturtevant 1978: 148). The Calusa believed that each person has three essences, or 'souls' (*alma*), one in one's shadow, one in one's reflection and the third in the pupil of the eye. At death, two of the souls die, but the one in the eye lives on; it was probably to this soul that the Calusa spoke in their cemeteries (Zubillaga 1946: 279). One's soul could also become separated from one's body during the course of life, and a curer had to be summoned to find it and physically drag it back; once this had been accomplished a fire would be set outside the door to force the errant soul to stay within its human vehicle (ibid.: 279). According to another belief the human soul, at death, enters a smaller animal; when the latter dies, the soul passes to a still smaller one, eventually disappearing altogether (ibid.: 279).

Clearly the chief was the head of state for it was he who received important guests, such as Governor Menéndez. The chief's house was large enough to accommodate 2000 people (Solís de Merás 1923: 145). The Spanish accounts refer frequently to 'principal Indians' who accompanied a chief when he traveled, and with whom he consulted on important matters (ibid.: 227). One can deduce that these 'principals' were males as well as nobles because reference is sometimes made to the 'principal Indians and their wives and children' or 'Indians and their women'. Nobles probably took no part in food-procurement activities (Parks 1985: 63), ate special foods denied to commoners (Fontaneda 1945: 26) and participated in religious rituals restricted to those of their station (Dickinson 1985: 24–5).

The military formed another special group, and one gets the impression that this was a standing army rather than a citizen's militia. Even if not a standing army of specialists, then certainly the warrior group could be mobilized quickly and efficiently, and were well disciplined, expert archers and courageous fighters. When necessary, the paramount could call to his assistance warriors from all the towns under his control (Solís de Merás 1923: 228) and could command that people in all villages produce bows and arrows and other weapons (Zubillaga 1946: 307). One account says that the Indian warriors were not expected to work (Parks 1985: 63).

Few Spanish accounts accord any prominence to women. We know that they, like the men, wore only the briefest of hide or mat coverings and that they otherwise went naked. Several sources refer to the men wearing body paint, but body paint for females is not mentioned (Parks 1985: 59; Sturtevant 1978: 148; Dickinson 1985: 26). Chief Carlos's principal wife wore a collar of pearls and stones and a necklace of gold beads (Solís de Merás 1923: 147), but it can be safely assumed that such finery was reserved for the very highest nobility. During the formal meeting between Carlos and Menéndez, Carlos's wife was seated next to Carlos, although at a slightly lower level; Carlos and his wife ate from the same plate (ibid.: 148). Nobles, both men and women, were seated within the same room as Carlos and Menéndez, while hundreds of girls outside the house sang in a highly organized fashion (ibid.: 146). Women are also reported to have sung during a (presumably male) procession of masked priests (Zubillaga 1946: 607). From these observations, it can be suggested that women provided a necessary complement to male ritual activities. Probably women sang or danced at other rituals of transition, as well, such as initiations and funerals. Women do not seem to have functioned as diplomats or spokespersons, but noblewomen apparently felt free to speak their minds. Carlos's older 'sister' (strictly, parallel cousin) and also erstwhile wife, whom the Spanish called Antonia, openly expressed her disapproval to Governor Menéndez when he refused to help the Calusa attack

Tocobaga (Solís de Merás 1923: 229). From north of the Calusa area there is a reference to the mother of a chief Mocoso coming to the Spanish camp to demand an account of the whereabouts of her son (Varner and Varner, cited from Dobyns 1983: 161).

Children were apparently highly regarded by the south Florida natives (Parks 1985: 57); women must have been valued as the producers of children, as well as for their roles as gatherers of food and fuel and as processors and preparers of food (Fontaneda 1945: 28). We do not know whether women made pottery, wove mats or maintained the domestic quarters, but the likelihood is high that this was the case among commoners, given their other known domestic tasks. The degree to which noblewomen were expected to perform domestic labor is unknown.

Little is known about male rituals. The masked processions have already been mentioned. In Dickinson's account (1985: 37–8) six principal men dance, wail and shake rattles around an eight foot (2.5 meter) high upright pole with a broad arrow for a head. The pole is painted red and black, as are the dancers. An aged man leads the ritual and bows repeatedly to the pole. Then all the males, who are also painted, girdled with rope and armed with weapons, dance in a frenzied fashion many times until exhausted. They drink quantities of cassina (black drink), but otherwise consume only berries. After two days of this, they are joined by men from other towns, and then no woman may look upon the proceedings (Dickinson 1985: 38–9). Another account (quoted by Parks 1985: 58) describes exhortations of a sacred erect log, and 'races' run for three days to exhaustion, the point of which is said to be an experience of death and rebirth. Such exhaustion and ingestion of stimulants would quite likely cause hallucinations and 'out of body' experiences.

Perhaps the most serious gap in knowledge of class relations among the Calusa is our ignorance of rules that determined ownership of the means of production. We can be certain that the nobility fared better than the commoners, and that specialists, such as curers, were compensated for their services. On one occasion among the Tequesta in 1568, the Jesuit missionary Vallarreal baptized a sick child who then regained his health. The grateful parents, the chief and his wife, 'gave me many tortoises, which I refused' (Vargas Ugarte 1935: 76), apparently to pay for his services.[4]

There is mention that chief Carlos had a sizeable private store of treasure from Spanish wrecks, brought to him as tribute (Laudonnière 1975: 109–10). Whether such a hoard was perceived as a legacy of the

---

4. The Jesuit missionaries took a dim view of native curing practices, which consisted of the curer shouting and dancing around and squeezing the body of the afflicted person (Vargas Ugarte 1935: 77). Spanish remedies for illnesses at that same period (repeated bloodletting and purging; ibid.: 118) seem no more comprehensible to today's readers.

chiefly leader (a 'crown jewels' concept) or the personal wealth of the chief alone will probably never be known. Neither are there data on the extent to which members of the elite estate could accumulate wealth, or on the degree of economic independence of commoners. Perhaps some fishing grounds were considered the domain of all, while others were reserved for the chief and his 'principals'. What seems more likely is that the choicest fish and game animals were reserved for the nobility, who did not procure their own food, while the commoners subsisted on smaller and less desirable fish that could be had with ease by simple shallow-water net or trap technologies (see Vargas Ugarte 1935: 127–8) and on shellfish, which could be easily gathered while setting and monitoring the nets and traps.

Finally, there exists only fragmentary information on methods of redistribution within communities and on the ranking system used to apportion food to various segments of society. Some redistribution may have occurred in ritual contexts, which we know were attended by hundreds. The paramount redistributed some of the spoils from Spanish wrecks among chiefs of client polities (Fontaneda 1945: 34–5). In the mid-sixteenth century about twenty-five 'towns' were directly governed by chief Carlos, and another twenty-five paid him tribute (ibid.: 30–1). Each town was apparently under the control of a chief (*cacique*). The town chiefs were probably responsible for extraction of surplus, regulation of production, dispute resolution and coordination of ritual activity in their own communities, while maintaining their tributary responsibilities to the paramount chief.

Inter-village exchanges outside of the tributary system are unknown, although surely some must have existed. There is one tantalizing statement that on an island situated in a great lake there grew

> many sorts of fruit, especially dates from the palms . . . the Indians made a good trading business from these [dates], but . . . it was not so great as the business from a sort of root from which they make a flour for bread . . . for fifteen leagues around there the whole countryside is fed with this root, which is the reason why the inhabitants of the island make a great profit from their neighbors, because they will not part with this root without being well paid for it. Moreover, these Indians are held to be the most belligerent of all men . . . (Laudonnière 1975: 111).

Such a combination of economic and military strength could pose a challenge to the authority of the paramount, and in fact it was the chief of this territory (Serrope) who defied Carlos by seizing Oathchaqua's daughter (Oathchaqua was chief of the polity near Cape Canaveral) on her way to be wed to Carlos (Laudonnière 1975: 111) — a marriage that would have sealed a relation of clientship between the two chiefs.

Although certain foods available in periodic abundance can be stored (drying or smoking fish, storing turtles or fish in corrals, drying palm fruits), it also makes sense to distribute surplus foods to kinsfolk or neighbors, with the assumption that they will reciprocate at some future time (for North-west Coast examples of this practice, see Suttles 1960: 302, 1968: 67). Such 'banking' may have been done between south Florida towns.

To summarize: it is reasonably certain that a hierarchical system of tribute-taking characterized the sixteenth-century Calusa domain. A rigid estate structure dictated unequal access to the means of production and to surpluses, which were common. This mode of production was legitimated by a conflated political/religious ideology that equated the prosperity of the paramount chief with productivity of the environment. A highly mobile and well-armed military served to maintain the boundaries of the Calusa domain, to enforce the extraction of tribute if necessary and to protect the chief from his enemies.

However, inherent in the sixteenth-century south Florida social formation were two contradictions. First, historically-based conflicts within the Calusa ruling family had led to the formation of factions among the principal Calusa nobility. Second, local surplus takers (town chiefs), especially those far from the coastal heartland, sought new opportunities in clientelistic relations with Carlos's rivals. Neither of these contradictions in itself held the potential for radical social transformation, but in combination with the European presence, which began to affect south Florida in the earliest years of the sixteenth century and which also began to provoke uncertainty and to offer opportunities to change the balance of power, these contradictory relations effectively denied all possibility of Calusa expansion northward into (coastal) Tocobaga or into the southernmost Timucuan polities. Before relating some of the historical events of protohistoric south Florida, a brief discussion of power relations and ideology is necessary.

Ideology and authority

The supernatural and the rational, easily dissociated by contemporary Western thinkers, must have been one inseparable system for the protohistoric south Florida natives. In the minds of the commoners the absolute power of the paramount chief was a function of — and ample proof of — his direct identification with both the material and the spiritual features of their everyday natural world. As he prospered, so did the land and the waters bring forth their abundance. His struggles against the forces of disorder, his dealings with the spirits of the dead and his wars with rival paramounts were in the interests of all, and whatever he required of them had to be given without question. It follows that spiritual authority and political authority, also easily discussed separately in our culture, were for the Calusa one and the same.

To separate the chief from the spiritual world was to destroy him as an authority figure and deny him his reason for existence.[5] In June 1567 the Jesuit Juan Rogel observed the following about chief Carlos: 'I learned concerning the king that he was so close to his idols that on being told falsely that we were to destroy his idols, he wrapped himself up and was determined, if the idols were burned, to throw himself into the flames with his wife and sons to be burned with them' (Zubillaga 1946: 276, trans. Alfred Wong).

With his authority the chief exerted control far beyond those villages which could be reached in a half-day's walk or canoe trip. To gather together the resources of the more distant lands the chief required the assistance of town chiefs, whose relationship to him was established through affinity: each of the chiefs provided him with a daughter or sister to be his wife. From the moment of this union, the enemies of one were the enemies of the other, and the resources of the hinterlands could be called upon by the paramount at will.

Thus, relations of affinal kinship at the level of the chiefly families functioned as relations of production and distribution at the regional scale, and an ideology that equated the health and prosperity of the chief with the productivity of the natural world legitimated relations of inequality between nobles and commoners. The inequality was so pronounced that commoners were expected to provide food for the chief, the nobles, the military and certain other specialists, as well as certain raw materials and manufactured goods upon request.[6]

5. One description (López 1698) refers to *mahoma*, a long, tall temple structure with one door. There was matting on the altar, which was surrounded by several firepits. The walls and altar were covered with masks. The remains of such a structure may have been excavated in the muck of Marco Island in the 1890s (Cushing 1897: 362–94). There, numerous painted and carved objects, such as boxes, insignia and masks, were unearthed, as well as a variety of wooden, bone and shell implements, and also netting and cordage. Carving, painting and engraving were done in both abstract and realistic styles. Some animal and human forms are strikingly realistic, and at least one object, a wooden feline figurine about fifteen centimeters high, is a combined human/animal form (Figure 11.1). Dating of the site is controversial, with estimates ranging from the eighth to the fifteenth centuries AD. However, all authorities believe the site to be prehistoric (see Gilliland 1975: 257; Milanich 1978b; Van Beck and Van Beck 1965; Widmer 1988: 89–93).

6. Certain gaps in archaeological and ethnohistoric data and the complete absence of any ethnographic study lead one to search for parallels in the anthropological record. The natives of the North American north-west coast are an obvious starting point. Although they moved to separate villages in the winter, they lived for the most part in permanent coastal towns. They cultivated no crops, with the exception of small plots of tobacco, and their only domesticated animal was the dog. In common with the Calusa are a specialized fishing economy, sedentary villages, a complex technological inventory, social stratification, elaborate ceremonies and an extensive symbolic/artistic tradition. Other comparisons are not so clear-cut. North-west Coast natives had estate, but not tributary relations. They developed the kin-ordered mode of production to perhaps its most complex level, with redistribution being effected through a complicated system of honor and obligation within autonomous clan and lineage-based residential groupings (Drucker 1963; 1965; Suttles 1960; 1968). They did conduct warfare and feud with other groups, encroaching on the resources and properties of others and taking captives, but unlike the Calusa they did not extract tribute from their neighbors. There is diversity among North-west Coast natives in terms of

Structure and transformation in the Calusa domain

Having now discussed the mode of subsistence, ranking, tributary relations and the legitimation of authority by means of ideology, I now turn to an analysis of concrete historical processes in the protohistoric period in south Florida. To understand these events, one must consider processes not just at the local and regional scales discussed above, but also at the supraregional scale of the expansion of European mercantilists into the Caribbean and Florida. These activities are in turn related to other world-scale processes (Wolf 1982: 101–57), which will not be discussed here.

Christopher Columbus's ships, which made landfall in the Bahamas on 12 October 1492, reached the island of Cuba fifteen days later. On Christmas Day the flagship *Santa Maria* was lost on the north-western coast of an island that would come to be known as Hispaniola. By 1496 the colony of Santo Domingo had been established on the south-eastern coast of that island, today the oldest European city in the Western Hemisphere. By 1502 the Spanish were bringing African slaves to work in Santo Domingo and were exploring other islands in the vicinity. Cuba, which Columbus believed to his death in 1506 to be a peninsula, appears as an island on La Cosa's map that some commentators date to 1500. There is no doubt that Cuba had been circumnavi-

---

social relations. In general, the basic kin unit, whether clan- or lineage-based, was territorial and politically autonomous. Social status derived from a combination of heredity and wealth. Among the Haida the two great moieties were divided into local lineages, each in its own village of forty to several hundred individuals. This lineage had its own chief, owned its own means of production (for example, salmon streams, fishing grounds, plant collecting and hunting tracts), made independent political decisions and maintained an intralineage (intravillage) ranking system that depended for its logic upon the degree of kin affinity. The Tlingit moieties were divided into clans, which in turn were divided into localized lineage groups. The Coast Tsimshian were divided into four clans, each represented by a single local segment. The Gitksan, or Upriver Tsimshian, had three large clans, also associated with specific localities. Farther south, in the Vancouver Island/Washington State area, descent was not matrilineal but bilateral, and moieties, clans and lineages did not exist. However, extended families held land and privileges in a way similar to their more northern counterparts. All North-west Coast societies graded individuals into a series of relative statuses, with the exception of slaves, who had no status. However, a warrior or craftsperson could move up in rank by achieving recognition for special skills or accomplishments, and be rewarded with symbolic or material privileges (Drucker 1963: 107–27). Redistribution of food was handled by village chiefs, who favored the higher-ranking individuals (Ray, cited from Suttles 1968: 59). The chief's authority was unquestionable, due to his primary position in the social ranking system. The Manus of the Admiralty Islands, north of Papua New Guinea, provide another example of a sedentary coastal fishing society. Like the coastal Calusa, they needed certain plant foods and other materials from their inland neighbors, but among the Manus the exchange of coastal for inland products was handled through barter. The Manus loathed their bush counterparts, on whom they depended for vital resources, especially when the latter began moving down to the coast to live. Because the bush people (the Usiai) still cultivated their gardens but also had access to the coast, the Manus stood to lose their only trade advantage (Romanucci-Ross 1985: 14). The Calusa apparently solved the problem of acquiring needed interior resources by requiring tributary payments from inland groups.

gated by 1509, by which time wholesale slave raids were being conducted regularly to the Bahamas. Natives of Hispaniola who had fled to
Cuba to escape enslavement or execution soon found that if offered no
safer haven. Spaniards such as Narváez and Esquivel massacred many
hundreds in Cuba, and by 1514 its conquest was complete. Puerto Rico
and the Lesser Antilles followed soon thereafter (Weddle 1985: 15–33).

In the spring of 1513 Juan Ponce de León's ships landed on the east
coast of Florida. By May they had reached the Florida Keys, and by
June Charlotte Harbor. There they encountered a native who spoke to
them in Spanish. They received a report that a king 'Carlos' had a
hoard of gold, but hostile natives drove them back with a hail of
arrows. The next day warriors in eighty canoes came to shoot arrows at
the Spanish (Weddle 1985: 42–5). Ponce de León and his associates did
not return to Florida immediately, busy as they were in Trinidad (1515)
enslaving natives and massacring those who resisted. The ships of
Cordoba stopped briefly on the south-west Florida coast in 1517, and
were attacked; the Spanish are said to have killed twenty-three natives.
In 1521 Ponce de León again reached south-west Florida, intending
to build a settlement. His settlers were attacked and many were
wounded, including Ponce de León himself, whose wound eventually
proved fatal.

In 1528 the Narváez expedition landed well north of the Charlotte
Harbor area, encountering many native groups during a long series of
misadventures. In 1539 Hernando de Soto's complement of soldiers,
horses and pigs landed on the Florida west coast, probably at Tampa
Bay, and made their way to present-day north Florida at the considerable expense of native groups along the way. Ten years later a group of
Dominican missionaries reached Charlotte Harbor by mistake, where
they encountered natives who spoke Spanish and recognized the
crucifix. Juan Muñoz, lost from the Soto expedition a decade earlier,
appeared and warned them that the natives at Charlotte Harbor were
unfriendly. Fray Luís, who persevered, was killed by the natives, true
to Muñoz's prediction (Weddle 1985: 56–63, 208–50).

It is clear that sixteenth-century Europeans exploring Florida were
greeted with hostility in most encounters with the natives. Indians who
cooperated with the Spaniards were usually interested in obtaining
European food, clothing and other commodities, a generalization that
holds true in relation to all of the known missionary efforts. The
Spanish also enjoyed the cooperation of the natives when the latter
wished to enlist Spanish aid against their enemies, an example of
which is the allegiance of first Carlos, then Felipe, among the Calusa in
the late 1560s (discussed below). Ponce de León is usually given credit
for 'discovering' Florida in 1513, but in that year he was met by hostile
natives, some of whom spoke Spanish and who already possessed
gold. I argue that the hostility toward the Spanish was a result of both

direct and indirect contacts with Europeans in the very early years of the sixteenth century.

One must bear in mind that the tributary relations that characterized south Florida would have facilitated the rapid spread of information from polity to polity. Well-known paths connecting the various aboriginal domains were easily traveled by messengers, diplomats and bearers of tributary or other goods. Canoe travel along inland rivers and into the Gulf of Mexico at least as far as Cuba and through the Florida Straits at least as far as the Bahamas was commonplace. Any unusual event, such as a shipwreck on the Florida east coast or in the keys, would be communicated promptly to town chiefs and to the paramount. Similarly, native fishermen, traders or diplomats traveling in the Gulf of Mexico or the Florida Straits would report back to their chiefs what they had heard about activities in the Bahamas and Cuba.

It would be surprising indeed if tales of Columbus's landings in the Bahamas, Hispaniola and Cuba were not reported to chiefs in south Florida. Spanish slave ships were arriving in Hispaniola by 1502, and were exploring the Caribbean by 1508. Florida is shown on the 1502 Cantino map (Lowery 1901: 123). A number of Spanish ships were wrecked in Cuba, four of them in 1510 alone, leading to grave consequences for the Cuban natives in terms of atrocities from the Spanish survivors (Weddle 1985: 22–33). Furthermore, the voyages recorded in various archival records undoubtedly represent only a fraction of the actual shipping traffic, much of it unofficial (ibid.: 19). For example, the exile, Sebastián de Ocampo, circumnavigated Cuba in 1508 and conducted extensive trading missions around the Caribbean, but his activities could not be reported officially because of his exile status (ibid.: 21).

I suggest that freelance mariners conducted slaving forays into Florida and the Bahamas well before Ponce de León's 1513 landing.[7] The crews of those vessels would have made a dramatic and unquestionably negative impression on Florida natives, and probably a number of ships were lost in the Florida Straits and on the eastern coast, where Gulf Stream currents are quite strong. Finally, there are the statements that Senquene, father of Carlos, allowed refugees to settle in southwest Florida (Fontaneda 1945: 29) and that by 1513 a chief known as 'Carlos' already possessed gold and had among his villagers a Spanish speaker.

7. Here the comments of historian David True are relevant: '[Fontaneda's statement] suggests what is known to be true but has not yet been proven, that early slavers from Santo Domingo visited Florida on raiding expeditions previous to Ponce's expedition. Lowery . . . concerning 1520, wrote: "Pedro de Quexos, in search of Caribs to sell as slaves, in virtue of the general license of October 30, 1503. . .". In a letter Miss Irene Wright stated "that it was my distinct impression that the Spaniards, especially the slave traders of Cuba and La Española, knew the Florida coast very well before it was officially chartered or occupied. I think evidence could be found that slaving expeditions had visited its ports before 1512" (Fontaneda 1945: 62).'

This evidence, although circumstantial, suggests that both direct experience (with slavers and shipwrecks) and indirect experience (from hearsay and communication with refugees) had conditioned Florida natives to be wary of and hostile toward Europeans long before Ponce de León's first landing. The later *entradas* of Narváez and Soto did nothing to improve the European image, as the Spanish carved their way through Florida, seizing food and taking captives.

The Florida coast continued to claim Spanish ships long after Soto's time. Some were wrecked in storms, but a number of them were victims of the strong Gulf Stream currents, especially at Cape Canaveral and near the Florida Keys. Natives often made prisoners of any survivors, eventually offering them, along with their ships' cargoes, as tribute to the paramount chief for distribution at his will. Prisoners were taken from wrecks in 1545, 1547, 1550–1, and probably many others. A thirteen-year-old boy bound for Spain and lost in the 1550 wreck was destined to spend seventeen years of his life among the natives of south Florida. Escalante Fontaneda, whose memoir provides one of the few eyewitness accounts of daily life among the natives (Fontaneda 1945), was to play a pivotal role when Pedro Menéndez de Avilés, governor of Spanish Florida, arrived in Charlotte Harbor in 1566.

In the fall of 1565 the governor had driven the French from their fort at the mouth of the St John's river, massacring hundreds of Frenchmen who had surrendered. This victory ensured the security of the town of St Augustine, the first permanent European settlement in the present-day United States. He then turned his attention to the remainder of the Florida peninsula, wishing to search for a water route across Florida and to find his son, whose fleet had been lost in the Gulf of Mexico in 1563. I now describe the events of 1566 to 1570 because they provide insight into the political structure of native south Florida.

In February, 1566, Menéndez's ships reached Charlotte Harbor, there to be met by a 'naked and painted' man who was almost certainly Fontaneda (Lyon 1976: 148). Menéndez was received formally by the paramount chief whom the Spanish referred to as 'Carlos', probably a Latinization of the name of the chiefdom (in Laudonnière's account the name is spelled 'Calos'). Carlos indicated that he wished to take Menéndez as his 'elder brother', and offered his 'sister' (also his former wife) to become Menéndez's wife; by doing so, he was offering his allegiance to Menéndez (Solís de Merás 1923: 144). Not wishing to offend Carlos, Menéndez pretended to accept the woman, who was christened Antonia and treated with great respect (ibid.: 150). Menéndez was much aided in the formal interactions by Fontaneda, who provided a script for Menéndez to read to the natives in their language. Fontaneda probably also coached the Calusa chief on what to expect from the Spanish.

Menéndez sent Antonia and several other natives and some former captives to Havana, and then went to St Augustine, only to hear that over a hundred of his soldiers had deserted their posts and sailed south to Tequesta (near present-day Miami), where twenty men had been stranded on shore. Interestingly, instead of killing or capturing the Spanish mutineers, the chief Tequesta had treated them well because he was aware of Menéndez's 'marriage' to Antonia, who was kin to Tequesta. Tequesta had gone so far as to protect the mutineers from Calusa soldiers who had been sent to kill them (Barcia, cited from Parks 1985: 22–3).

In March 1567, Menéndez arranged a peace between Carlos and Tequesta, but could not convince Carlos to make peace with Tocobaga, who held captive a dozen of Carlos's countrymen, including one of his and Antonia's 'sisters'. Antonia, who had returned from Havana, was visibly angry with Menéndez for not helping Carlos make war on Tocobaga (Solís de Merás 1923: 229). Carlos had been disgraced by Menéndez's refusal to attack Tocobaga, and seemingly could regain his authority only by destroying the Spanish. Carlos's plans to overthrow the Spanish were ended when the Spanish executed him and called on his captain general (christened Felipe) to assume the chieftaincy (Zubillaga 1946: 306–9).

At the death of Carlos, Tocobaga quickly gained control of several of the Calusa towns, enraging Felipe (ibid.: 295). Taking a lesson from the demise of Carlos, Felipe professed friendliness to the Spanish (ibid.: 281–2), but this cost him favor among a faction of town chiefs and principals, who sought to undermine his authority. Felipe used Spanish support to his advantage, however, and put to death fifteen town chiefs whom he suspected of treachery; when the Jesuit Juan Rogel's party arrived at the Calusa capital on 2 October 1568, Felipe and some supporters were seen 'dancing about with the heads of four chiefs whom he had been informed intended to rebel and go over to his enemies with their people. For this he had them slain' (Vargas Ugarte 1935: 91).

The Spanish repeatedly pressed Felipe to 'burn his idols' and become a good Christian (ibid.: 163), but he made excuses. By February 1569 Menéndez had promised to come and help Felipe in his war against Tocobaga, who had clearly signaled his antagonism to Felipe and his Spanish allies by killing the Christians left under his control by Menéndez and by taking towns from Felipe (ibid.: 103–4). Felipe, having eliminated the anti-Spanish faction among his town chiefs *and* so far avoided becoming a Christian, mobilized for war against Tocobaga. Still he was pressed by Father Rogel to renounce his beliefs, and specifically to repudiate his marriage to his 'sister'. Again Felipe stalled, saying that upon becoming a Christian he would abandon her and that he would become a Christian when the governor returned to assist him. At last a representative of the governor arrived, and Felipe was finally faced with having to renounce his 'sister'/wife (and any hope of producing an heir) and to destroy his temple with its 'idols'; he gathered together his supporters and did so 'in fear and trembling', believing that in so doing he risked bringing his world to an end. In a sense his fears were well founded because the Spanish then massacred Felipe and 'some other 14 or 15 Indians, most of them important ones, and wounded some others, and brought the queens to Havana . . . ' (Zubillaga 1946: 416). Felipe was replaced by a man called Pedro, about whom no further information exists except that he was the son of a man whom the Spanish called Sebastián. The Spanish withdrew their missions from south Florida in 1570. Menéndez became convinced that the only solution to the problem posed by the presence of native Floridians was forcibly to remove and enslave them (Menéndez, cited from Parks 1985: 41–2).

This sequence of events reveals contradictions within Calusa political relations. *If Carlos was the most powerful chief in south Florida in 1566, why did he decide to become subservient to Menéndez?* I suggest that the answer is that Carlos was fighting for his political survival because of a recent escalation of a long-term conflict with Tocobaga, which had rekindled in the minds of the nobility doubts about his authority and efficacy. Widespread sickness and an unusually high death-rate due to respiratory diseases (Dobyns 1983: 269) may have exacerbated the situation by interrupting shipments of needed raw materials and commodities from subject towns. Carlos reasoned that if he became a client of the Spanish governor, then the latter would be obliged to help him defeat his enemies, and Tocobaga would be no match for the Spanish. With Tocobaga's resources at his disposal, Carlos could easily afford to reciprocate by providing tribute to Menéndez. He would give to Menéndez his thirty-five-year-old 'sister'; they had been married when Carlos was only six and he had recently put her aside as principal wife in favor of a young beauty, now twenty years old.

When Menéndez accepted Antonia, but then wanted Carlos to make peace with Tocobaga, Carlos was inconsolable. Antonia, too, expressed anger to Menéndez, telling him that he 'had two hearts, one for himself and one for Tocobaga, and that for herself and her brother he had none' (Solís de Merás 1923: 229). Even Tequesta, a relative of Antonia's and ostensibly subservient to Carlos, had defied Carlos by protecting Spanish mutineers who had come on shore near present-day Miami.[8] Carlos was so disgraced by his failure that only the expulsion of the

8. Usually captives were brought to Carlos in tribute. In 1566 Tequesta withheld them from Carlos. When Carlos sent soldiers to kill Tequesta's Spanish refugees, Tequesta's warriors killed some of the Calusa. Tequesta justified this action by saying that the Spanish must be allies: had not Carlos himself pledged allegiance to Menéndez and offered Antonia, Tequesta's kinswoman, to be Menéndez's wife? Carlos was clearly in a double bind.

Spanish would suffice to erase his shame. But he went about this task clumsily, and seemed to lack coordinated support. One can only suspect collusion between the Spanish captain Reinoso and Felipe, Carlos's captain general and brother-in-law. When the Spanish assassinated Carlos, Felipe was away — beyond suspicion — and had to be called into town to assume the paramountcy, a transition that apparently went smoothly.

But this scenario also seems contradictory. *If Felipe was Carlos's brother-in-law rather than his son, how could he so easily succeed to power? If he was Carlos's captain general, how could he turn against Carlos, if indeed he did?* To answer these questions, it is necessary to examine the genealogy of the royal family (Figure 11.2), a task already accomplished by Goggin and Sturtevant (1964) and by Lewis (1978), based on the account of Juan Rogel (Zubillaga 1946: 309–11).

An uncle of Carlos named Senquene, who is also referred to as Carlos in some accounts, was once paramount chief. It was probably he who, as a young chief, allowed Cuban refugees to settle in south Florida, c.1514.[9] Because Senquene had no male heirs, he adopted as his son the child (Felipe) of his sister, and named him as his successor to the paramountcy. Felipe's father (Senquene's sister's husband) was named captain general. When Felipe was about eight years old (c.1532), Senquene put on him the gold pendant and leg beads that symbolize the paramountcy. Senquene had a daughter, Antonia, who, when she was four years old (1534), was married to Felipe, then about ten. When Felipe became old enough to govern, Senquene planned to enthrone Felipe and take for himself both the positions of captain general and chief priest, positions then held by his sister's husband and his brother respectively. Two towns gave women to the boy Felipe in recognition of his chieftainship. About the time of the marriage of Felipe and Antonia, Senquene died. Felipe's natural father (the captain general) and his uncle (the chief priest) decided they would rule together, the chief priest actually holding the seat of power until Felipe was old enough. While the chief priest was in power he had a son, Carlos (c.1536), and did not yield the paramountcy as he had promised. Instead, he pressured his sister-in-law (Senquene's widow) to divorce her son Felipe from Antonia so that Antonia, then about twelve years old, could marry the chief's own son, Carlos, then about six (c.1542). Felipe's natural father was angry, but to placate him Carlos's father gave one of his daughters to Felipe and named Felipe captain general. Thus, at about age eighteen Felipe became captain general, his brother-in-law Carlos, then only six, became heir to the seat of power,

9. The eradication of the Cuban natives is well documented (see summary by Weddle, 1985: 22–33), and it is the flight of the so-called 'Caribs' into Florida to which Fontaneda derisively refers (1945: 29). Probably their search for magic restorative waters was the result of a millenarian movement forged in the desperation of their plight (Dobyns 1983: 255–6).

Figure 11.1. Genealogy of the Calusa royal family, sixteenth century.

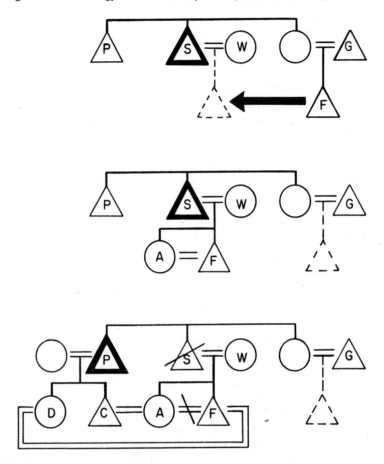

From top to bottom, stage 1 shows the adoption by Senquene (S) of his sister's child (F), later to be called Felipe. Senquene's brother (P) is chief priest and Senquene's sister's husband (G) is captain general. In stage 2 Felipe (F) marries his sister (A), daughter of Senquene; she will later be called Antonia. In stage 3 Senquene (S) has died, the chief priest (P) has assumed the paramountcy, and Senquene's widow (W) has been forced to divorce Felipe (F) from Antonia (A), so that the latter can be married to Carlos (C), young son of the paramount chief (P). To mollify Felipe's real father (G), the paramount chief provides his daughter (D) to be the wife of Felipe (F), and Felipe becomes captain general, succeeding his real father in the post.

Symbols: triangles signify males, circles females. The paramount chief is indicated by a bold triangle. Single horizontal lines represent sibling relations, double horizontal lines marriage relations, and vertical lines direct descent. In stage 3, the slashes indicate that Senquene (S) is deceased and that the marriage of Felipe (F) and Antonia (A) has been terminated.

and Antonia, then twelve, became Carlos's principal wife and future queen. Naturally, Felipe as captain general commanded more respect than did the child Carlos, especially in view of the fact that Felipe had been designated the heir by Senquene before his death.

The date of the assumption of chiefly power by Carlos is uncertain, but a good guess is 1556, when he would have been about twenty. It is not known whether his father died or abdicated. On the occasion of his succession to the seat of power, chiefs of subject polities customarily sent women to Carlos. I suggest that the daughter of chief Oathchaqua of Canaveral was being sent to Carlos in 1556 when Serrope intercepted the party (probably at Lake Okeechobee) and claimed the bride for himself.[10] Doing so would have been tantamount to denying the legitimacy of Carlos's reign.

Two other events probably occurred between 1556 and 1566: Carlos divorced Antonia, or at least took a new woman to be his principal wife (the latter was twenty years old in 1566 when Menéndez met Carlos) and Tocobaga seized or otherwise acquired twelve Calusa hostages, including one of Antonia's sisters. I speculate that both of these events occurred closer to 1566 than to 1556, and that probably Tocobaga's action was still fresh in the minds of the Calusa 'principal Indians' when word of the imminent arrival of the governor of Spanish Florida reached Carlos. Carlos would have been under pressure to make war on Tocobaga. His legitimacy always in doubt, his supply lines to the interior compromised, and being challenged on the north by Tocobaga and threatened by the superior military strength of the Spanish fleet moving into Charlotte Harbor, in 1566 Carlos chose to become Menéndez's client under the expectation that Menéndez would then join him in defeating Tocobaga. The expectation was ill-founded, however, as has been discussed above, and Carlos died at the hands of the Spanish in 1567.

Following the death of Carlos, Felipe also faced both external and internal challenges. First, upon Carlos's death, Tocobaga had won the allegiance of several Calusa town chiefs. Second, there was open distrust of the Spanish, and Felipe's association with them was suspect.[11] It seems ironic that, having served in the small shadow of Carlos for so many years, Felipe's rule as Senquene's intended heir lasted less than two years.

10. After Serrope claimed the bride, the Spaniard who in 1564 related the story to Laudonnière (1975: 111) had gone to dwell with Oathchaqua and had been there for eight years. Subtracting eight from 1564 gives 1556, when Carlos would have been about nineteen or twenty years old.

11. Felipe's alliance with the Spanish was probably opposed by many of his own advisers, but Felipe must have reasoned that Spanish assistance was necessary to his polity's preservation against the ambitious Tocobaga. Contradictorily, the favor of the Spanish was contingent upon Felipe's renouncing a spiritual relation that was an important determinant of his own authority to govern. Felipe's double bind was as serious as Carlos's had been (note 8, above).

Little is known about south Florida polities in the last three decades of the sixteenth century, but a report from 1612 says that a chief named Carlos has 'more than seventy towns of his own, without counting another very great number which . . . pay him tribute' (Olivera, quoted in Goggin and Sturtevant 1964: 187). Apparently some reconsolidation of the Calusa domain had occurred over a forty-two-year period. The details are not known, but one can surmise that the power of the Timucuan polities of northern Florida had slowly declined as a chain of Spanish missions was established across north Florida (Boyd *et al.* 1951; Geiger 1937; Milanich 1978a).

In both 1607 and 1628 the south Florida Indians were invited to come to St Augustine to be entertained; apparently their goodwill was still considered of strategic importance (Parks 1985: 43–4).

In 1696 Jonathan Dickinson and twenty-four other people were shipwrecked along the east coast of Florida. His detailed eyewitness account provides insights into the life of the Jeaga (Hobe), St Lucia and Ais (Jece) polities, whose modes of production seem hardly at variance with what is known for sixteenth-century south Florida (Dickinson 1985: 1–46).

By the early eighteenth century Lower Creek Indians, allied loosely with the British, had arrived in south Florida, and Yamassee Indians were attacking residents of the Florida Keys in attempts to enslave them. The Keys natives were actually the disrupted remnants of several south Florida polities. In 1711 a Spanish ship succeeded in rescuing 270 natives, including the hereditary chiefs of Jeaga, Miami, Concha, Muspa, Rioseco and Carlos. Some 1700 Florida natives had to be abandoned to their fate with the Yamassees, but of the 270 who went to Havana, over 200 died immediately from diseases, including four of the chiefs. Attempts to bring Florida refugees to Havana in the 1700s were largely unsuccessful (Parks 1985: 52–5).

The Spanish established a short-lived mission in the Keys in 1743, but the Indians — perhaps realizing the strategic importance of a south Florida presence for the Spanish — demanded tribute from them in rum, clothing and food (Parks 1985: 56–65; Sturtevant 1978: 141–9). At the conclusion of the Seven Years War in 1763 Florida was transferred to England in exchange for Havana. By the early 1760s only a few Florida natives still lived in the Florida Keys. An account published in 1775 says that the last remnants had left Florida for Havana in 1763 (Romans, cited from Sturtevant 1978: 141).

The narrative of south Florida's aboriginal peoples ends in 1763. Many details are only poorly known and there are gaps (for example, from 1570 to 1612) in knowledge of sociohistorical processes. Archival research is reaching a point of diminishing returns, and archaeology would seem to hold the only hope of adding significantly to our collective knowledge.

Unanswered questions: the development of Calusa complexity

In this chapter I have characterized the social formation of the Calusa domain in the sixteenth century and suggested explanations for some of the processes that took place in the 260-year protohistoric period, *c.*1503–1763; but nothing has been said about the more than 10,000 years of prehistory that leads up to the time of the European conquest. The tributary, class and ideological relations that characterized so much of Florida in the sixteenth century did not spring up overnight — but the developmental history of Florida social formations is virtually unknown.

Only one scholar has stepped forward with a comprehensive hypothesis about the development of the Calusa social formation (Widmer 1988), a highly orthodox cultural materialistic model in which internal sociohistorical processes play few or no causative roles (see Marquardt 1986 for a critique). Confirming or challenging this hypothetical model will require both extensive and intensive investigations, and in such a study paleoenvironmental and archaeological studies must proceed hand in hand. Those of us for whom anthropology is a social, not merely a natural, science face an exciting challenge to discover ways of recognizing in the archaeological record the emerging relations of inequality. The well-preserved middens and mounds of south-west Florida hold the keys to these important questions. Given enough resources, time, thought and care — and assuming that these remarkable sites continue to be preserved under the stewardship of south-west Florida's citizens and governmental authorities — the answers will eventually be known.

Conclusions

The sixteenth-century south Florida social formation was a ranked and tributary one. In the Calusa heartland a rich coastal environment provided the foundation of a multifaceted mode of production that depended on the acquisition of raw materials and food resources from noncoastal as well as coastal areas. A rigid estate structure denied commoners access to their own produce. Surpluses produced by commoners went to support the royal family, the nobility, the military and other specialists. A formidable military force under the direction of the paramount chief could be augmented at his command by warriors from subject towns. Each town was governed by a town chief, who extracted surplus and oversaw the movement of tribute to the paramount. A town chief's disloyalty was punishable by death.

On the broader scale of the Calusa domain, which at certain times comprised all of south Florida, chiefs of other polities were also subject to the Calusa paramount. Each provided tribute to the paramount and confirmed his authority by providing a noble woman to be one of his wives. The paramount provided military assistance to his subject chiefs when necessary and sometimes redistributed wealth to them.

The paramount chief's ultimate authority was supernatural. Although he was not a king-god on earth, his intervention with the supernatural world was necessary to obviate calamities, such as hurricanes, and to cause the environment to continue to provide its bounty. Succession to the paramountcy was effected by means of 'royal "sibling" marriage', a practice restricted to the paramount chief.

Contradictions are inherent in all social formations. At the scale of the royal family, an ostensibly orderly, supernaturally sanctioned succession to the seat of power was in fact beset by rivalry, jealousy and tension. The paramount, supposedly imbued with the power to rule alone, in fact was restricted in his decision-making by his 'principals' or close advisers, and sometimes, as in the case of Carlos, by unspoken but none the less enervating doubts about his legitimate right to govern.

On the intra-polity scale the paramount was supposedly master of all his town chiefs, yet sometimes these chiefs changed their allegiance to that of his rivals. At the scale of the inter-polity domain, he was supposed to be served and respected by chiefs of other polities, yet on at least two occasions (Serrope's interception of his bride and Tequesta's denial to him of Spanish captives) his authority was defied.

Contradictions are raw materials for sociocultural change, yet sometimes in the absence of external insult or perceived opportunity they can remain nearly dormant, as tensions, incompatibilities or minor struggles over access to privileges or information. The European presence did much to stimulate change in south Florida, and I have argued that this presence was felt in the very earliest years of the sixteenth century. At first the Floridians were amazed by the Spanish (Fontaneda 1945: 34), who must have appeared as startling to them as we imagine that interplanetary travelers might appear to us. But soon the Spanish and other marauding Europeans showed themselves to be flesh and blood, helpless and fearful when deprived of their cannons and swords. Spanish food, clothing, precious metals and other artefacts soon acquired high value among the chiefs and nobles. Gold and silver, previously unknown to the natives, became highly prized, especially when it was found that the Europeans seemed to worship it and seemed never to cease talking about it. As ships piled up on Florida's shores such items became more and more readily accessible, probably becoming available to certain people who had not previously enjoyed special status, and possibly entering exchange and trade networks that were outside the bounds of the hierarchical tributary establishment. I conjecture that the Calusa tributary mode, ostensibly more 'Asiatic' than 'feudal', would have had a tendency toward decentralization as wealth came into the hands of more and more people, possibly entering barter systems and intertown exchange networks such as the one hinted at by Laudonnière's (1975: 111) account of the arrogant root and palm fruit traders of Serrope.

At the scale of the greater arena of European–native interaction throughout Florida and the Caribbean, the contradiction of the Spanish as both conquerors and saviors is perhaps the most obvious. Believing (probably quite sincerely) in an ideology of honor and service to Christ, the Spanish sought to save the souls of the natives on the one hand even as they simultaneously killed and enslaved them on the other. Possibly the greatest stimulus to major structural change in eighteenth-century south Florida native society were the devastating diseases unintentionally introduced and spread by Europeans throughout North and South America (see Dobyns 1983: 250–90 for a survey of the Florida data; Wolf 1982: 133–5 and *passim* for the hemisphere as a whole). Escalating competition among the French, Dutch, Spanish and English, especially between the last two of these, drove refugees into peninsular Florida in the seventeenth and early eighteenth centuries, as European conflicts were played out through the agency of native American groups. The anticlimactic departure of south Florida natives in the early 1700s was ultimately the result of processes set in motion an ocean away in the banks and drawing rooms of Europe.

12.   Hunters and gatherers of the sea

Gísli Pálsson

Introduction

This chapter discusses the anomalous status of fishing in orthodox classifications of subsistence economies, and the similarities and contrasts between fishing and other modes of subsistence. I argue that in terms of social organization hunter-gatherers of aquatic resources are significantly different from hunter-gatherers of terrestrial resources. This conclusion is suggested by statistical analysis of data on gathering, hunting and fishing in *The Ethnographic Atlas*.[1]

Remarkably, anthropologists have largely ignored fishing adaptations in comparative studies. General books on the relationships between humans and animals (Leeds and Vayda 1965) and on hunter-gatherers (Lee and DeVore 1968b) hardly mention fishing. There is a tendency to see fishing activities either as a last resort, as a compensation for the deficiency of the terrestrial environment (Osborn 1977; 1980), or as mere fun (see Wright 1980: 87). It is true that some of the classic ethnographies describe fishing adaptations in great detail (for example, Firth 1946), and in recent years anthropologizing on fishermen has become quite an industry; but when it comes to theory and model-building the role of fishing seems to disappear. Apparently, the dominant attitude, with regard to hunter-gatherer studies, has been that fishing 'doesn't count'. Given the somewhat obsessive demand for typologies of adaptations in anthropological discussion, the relative absence from the scene of 'fishing' presents an interesting problem.

One of the reasons for such neglect has to do with the ambiguity of any definition of fishing (see Ellen 1982: 128–9; Ingold 1986b: chaps. 4 and 5). Should classifications of human subsistence activities be based on kinds of species, types of activity, or both? Are we to include in our

1. I wish to acknowledge the support of the Political Research Laboratory at the University of Iowa, which made a computer-readable version of *The Ethnographic Atlas* available to me under the exchange program between the University of Iowa and the University of Iceland. I thank Paul Durrenberger for his assistance concerning the analysis of statistical data and for his comments upon the argument presented. Also, I thank Tim Ingold, Thomas McGovern and Priscilla Renouf for their suggestions.

definition of fishing the hunting of aquatic mammals and the gathering of shellfish? As Faris remarks (1977: 235–6), lumping together every subsistence activity which has some relation to aquatic sources may be misleading: it makes 'about as much sense as . . . a biological classification which lumps together whales, fish and submarines and separates them from bats, birds and airplanes'.

Clearly, then, fishing is a marginal category in anthropological thought. Since fishing takes place in the context of radically different social structures ('primitive', peasant and industrialized), its common characteristics are bound to be limited to ecological and technical aspects — to the process of extraction. On the other hand, defining fishing as the hunting and gathering of aquatic resources may be useful for drawing contrasts between economic or social systems which are organized in *similar* ways.

An influential model of hunters, gatherers and fishermen emphasizes their unity as nomadic food collectors living in small groups (Lee and DeVore 1968b). This model has been attacked on various grounds in recent years by, for instance, Hunn and Williams (1982), Hamilton (1982: 236), G. Bailey (1983: 2) and Renouf (1984). One of the arguments against 'hunter-gatherer unity' is that hunter-gatherers of aquatic resources differ from the classic category of food collectors. The evidence presented is both ethnographic and archaeological: some commentators emphasize cognitive and technological characteristics; others stress sociological ones. Thus, the exploitation of resources located below the water-surface imposes heavy cognitive demands. Fishermen are not only forced to create cognitive maps to find the way and to locate fishing spots; they must also make descriptive models of an environment about which information can only be obtained from indirect observation (see Pálsson 1982). As to the contrast between hunting and fishing in terms of resource availability, time stress and technology, Torrence (1983) points out that tools used for the capture of aquatic animals tend to be particularly complex because the medium in which the animals move demands complicated retrieval strategies. Not only must the fish be speared, they must also be successfully brought ashore. And while such cognitive and technological aspects may not be very significant for social organization, there may yet be grounds for establishing a sociological contrast between maritime hunter-gatherers and the more familiar nonmaritime ones. It has long been known to both ethnography and archaeology that some fishing societies do not fit the classic image of the simple society of mobile hunter-gatherers. Societies of the north-west coast of North America are often mentioned as examples (see, for example, Richardson 1982; Hamilton 1982; Rowley-Conwy 1983: 112). Other cases of relatively large and complex communities of coastal hunter-gatherers have also been reported (M. Freeman 1969/70; McGovern 1985).

Deviations from the classic model of hunter-gatherers have, however, usually been taken as rare exceptions rather than as evidence suggesting new kinds of questions (see, for instance, Murdock 1968: 15); it has rarely been suggested that there is a *general* relationship among hunter-gatherers between dependence on aquatic resources and social complexity. But recently several authors have seriously considered such a possibility (Fitzhugh 1975; Yesner 1980; Perlman 1980). Thus Renouf (1984) develops a model of coastal hunter-fishers in northern (temperate, sub-arctic and arctic) environmental zones, in order to explain characteristics resembling food-producing societies, and differing from stereotypic hunter-gatherers. Compared with the latter societies, northern coastal hunter-fishers live in larger groups and in more permanent settlements; they have better defined territorial boundaries, more rigid restrictions of access to resources and more formalized leadership; they employ more specialized tools. Renouf challenges previous interpretations of archaeological data from Norway and argues for a model incorporating adjustment to the seasonal and spatial distribution of resources at northern latitudes (but see Engelstad 1984 and Helskog 1984). She suggests (1984: 22) that the periodicity of resources (fish, birds and caribou) passing by or near the same location encourages sedentary or semi-sedentary settlements at the point of overlap. Storing techniques make this possible and, in turn, the permanence of settlement affects many other social aspects. In the meantime, while Renouf argues that social complexity is characteristic of *northern* groups of hunter-fishers, Yesner (1980) suggests that there is a global pattern. On the basis of archaeological evidence, he distinguishes maritime adaptations as a subset of hunting and gathering capable of supporting complex social organization. But what exactly is the evidence from the 'ethnographic present'?

The relative importance of hunting, fishing and gathering

The Ethnographic Atlas (Murdock 1967) has inspired some previous comparative research on fishing, hunting and gathering, including research on the relative importance of these modes of subsistence and the extent to which they differ in terms of social organization (see, for instance, Lee 1968; Leap 1977). The use of information of this kind invites numerous problems relating to matters of ethnographic significance and reliability. Just as the archaeological record has to be considered in terms of both context and the processes which produced it, similar interpretation is ideally required if the numerical information of the *Atlas* is to be made meaningful. On the other hand, the *Atlas* provides an opportunity to examine a number of questions derived from isolated cases and statistically to test hypotheses which would otherwise remain sheer speculation. I do not discuss the ethnography in detail. The *Atlas* necessarily sacrifices detail for generality.

The evidence presented here is based on computations on the SPSSX package of the computer-readable version of the *Atlas*. The *Atlas* data on mode of subsistence are the result of scaling that is not very precise. Subsistence economy is scaled from 0 to 9, indicating relative dependence of the society (0–5 percent, 6–15 percent, etc.) on gathering, hunting, fishing, animal husbandry and agriculture. A 'mode of subsistence' is the particular combination of values for the subsistence variables. In the *Atlas* coding, 'fishing' includes 'shell fishing and the pursuit of large aquatic animals' (see Murdock 1967: 154–5).

The computations show that in the 220 societies recorded where agriculture and animal husbandry are minimal (less than 6 percent), hunting is usually not a primary subsistence activity. In most of these societies (76 percent) the relative dependence on hunting ranges from 16 percent to 45 percent (see Table 12.1). This does not come as a surprise. Lee argues (1968: 42), on the basis of just over a quarter of this sample (fifty-eight societies), that the hunting way of life is 'in the minority', in the sense that gathering and fishing usually provide the most important sources of food. Indeed, he indicates that gathering is the primary food source in 50 percent of his cases. He maintains (ibid.) that a population will emphasize the most reliable food source available, and gathering is precisely a low-risk, high-return subsistence activity. For Lee's Bushmen, gathering is 2.4 times more productive than hunting per unit of labor.

My computations in fact indicate that fishing is more important than gathering. As Table 12.1 shows, those societies which are primarily dependent on fishing represent 38.2 percent of the sample, and gathering 34.1 percent. This contradicts Lee's argument, but the difference between Lee's conclusion and the present one is probably due to differences in coding. Lee recoded shell fishing as 'gathering' and the pursuit of sea mammals as 'hunting'.

Furthermore, the computations indicate that the relative importance of resources provided by hunting is fairly consistent. The distribution is less skewed than in the case of fishing and gathering. The coefficient of variation (the standard deviation divided by the mean) is .46 for hunting, but .65 for fishing and .63 for gathering. The low coefficient of variation for hunting shows that the importance of this mode of subsistence is fairly similar from one case to another. Lee makes the same point (1968: 42).

If the importance of hunting is relatively stable, fishing and gathering should be negatively related to each other. The more the emphasis on fishing the less the importance of gathering, and the other way around. Such a conclusion is born out by the correlation coefficients between the subsistence variables (see Table 12.3). The negative correlation

Table 12.1: The relative importance of hunting, fishing and gathering

Relative	No. of cases		
dependence	Hunting	Fishing	Gathering
0–5	0	33	11
6–15	7	23	32
16–25	36	35	41
26–35	87	33	43
36–45	44	30	34
46–55	21	36	29
56–65	10	20	22
66–75	4	5	6
76–85	9	5	2
86–100	2	0	0
Total	220	220	220
Primary	61	84	75
Dependence	27.7%	38.2%	34.1%

between gathering and fishing is quite strong (–.67) while those between hunting and fishing and hunting and gathering are not as strong (–.51 and –.23, respectively). Thus, fishing and gathering flexibly parallel each other as alternative subsistence strategies. Note that Leap argues (1977: 256), to the contrary, that fishing and hunting 'may represent the same kind of subsistence effort' differing only with respect to the resources used.

As to the relationship between gathering and fishing, and hunting, Lee suggests (1968: 42) that the former are effectively alternatives to the latter and that environmental factors, 'latitude' or the variety of edible plants, largely affect the choice in each case. The statistics lend some support to this idea. The *Atlas* does not provide information on latitude, but it does have coded information on *temperature* for part of the sample — for sixty-three of the 220 hunting and gathering societies. (To indicate temperature, the *Atlas* variable on 'primary environment' has been recoded.) This measure may be taken as a gross measure of the variety of edible plants and latitude. Temperature is found to be unrelated to hunting (according to the chi-squared test, see Table 12.2), while there is a strong positive correlation with gathering (.50) and a strong negative correlation (–.46) with fishing (see Table 12.3). The warmer the climate the more important is gathering, and the colder the climate the greater the emphasis on fishing. By this evidence, then, fishing and gathering are alternatives to one another, depending on temperature.

The reasons for this pattern are not clear. Osborn (1980: 740), Schalk (1979) and Yesner (1980: 730) argue that there is a causal relationship between a reliance on fishing and latitude. Osborn and Yesner suggest that at low latitudes marine resources are poor in calories and vitamins, and vegetable foods must complete the diet. Reciprocally, as Osborn puts it (1980: 740), 'we can anticipate the manner in which marine animals will be used along a latitudinal gradient as a response to variations in terrestrial plant resources'. Thus Schalk argues (1979: 57) that the observed relationship between fishing and latitude is due 'more to the *deficiencies* of the terrestrial environment than the magnetism of the marine environment', and that marine exploitation is 'a means for compensating for the inadequacies of a terrestrial environment' (ibid.: 70).

Now, if these arguments are valid, there should be no relationship between a reliance on fishing and latitude when vegetation is held constant. Computations of the *Atlas* data do not confirm this ecological hypothesis. (To provide information on terrestrial ecology, the *Atlas* variable on 'primary environment' was recoded.) It was found that there *is* a relationship between a reliance on fishing and vegetation (see Table 12.2). But the relationship between a reliance on fishing and temperature is even stronger when controlled for vegetation ($r = -.54$; $s = .000$). In other words, if one assumes that vegetation remains the same there is still an inverse connection between the importance of fishing and temperature.

Reanalysis of Kelly's data (1983) on thirty-six hunter-gatherer-fisher societies confirms this point. His data have been carefully checked and they include quite precise information on ecology. The importance of fishing is negatively related to 'effective temperature' (ET), a gross measure of food abundance, or, of the total amount and yearly distribution of solar radiation ($r = -.46$; $s = .009$). The relationship remains more or less the same when one controls for terrestrial ecology. The partial correlation between fishing and ET is $-.53$ ($s = .002$); it is $-.35$ ($s = .033$) when controlled for primary production.

By this evidence one should reject the notion that terrestrial ecology is the cause of the latitudinal distribution of fishing. The reasons have probably more to do with social and political processes, state formation and colonialism. One must not forget that the 'present' of the *Atlas* represents post-colonial society and there is no guarantee that in the more distant past fishing, gathering and hunting showed the same geographical distribution.

Mode of subsistence and settlement pattern

Suggested by the archaeological argument outlined in the previous

Figure 12.1 Hypothetical model of dependence on aquatic and terrestrial resources

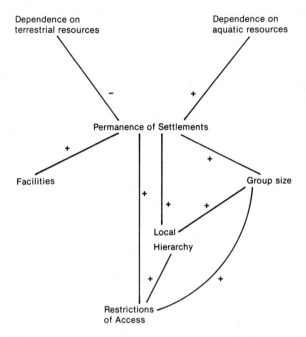

section is that there is a sociological contrast between societies dependent on aquatic resources and those which rely on terrestrial resources. Implicit in the argument is the hypothetical model of Figure 12.1. This modified model predicts that the more dependent a society is on terrestrial resources the less permanent the settlement, and the more dependent on aquatic resources the more permanent and compact the settlement. Also, it predicts that permanence of settlement is positively related to size of community and to restrictions on access to resources. Furthermore, there should be a positive relationship between group size, local hierarchy and restrictions of access. Finally, it predicts that sophisticated technology is associated with permanent settlements.

This model can be operationalized and tested by using the statistical data provided by the *Atlas*. A brief explanation of the scaling of the relevant variables in the *Atlas* is necessary: the variable on *settlement pattern* has eight values, ranging from 'fully migratory bands' to 'complex settlements'. *Group size* indicates the mean size of local communities — fewer than 50, 50 to 90, and so on. The variables on *restrictions of access* represent a recoding of variables on 'property rights' (the value of 1 was assigned to cases where property rights or inheritance rules are absent, the value of 2 to cases where they are present). *Hierarchy* of local community has five values indicating the number of levels of local hierarchy. There are two further measures of social complexity: social stratification, and form of domestic organization. *Stratification* has five values, indicating absence of stratification among freemen, wealth distinctions, the presence of an elite, hereditary aristocracy, and complex social classes. Form of *domestic organization* has ten values, ranging from independent nuclear families to large extended families.

Testing the hypothetical model involves three steps: examining (1) the relationships between modes of subsistence and settlement pattern; (2) the relationships between modes of subsistence and size of local community; and (3) relationships with further measures of complexity of social organization. The Pearson correlations are presented in Table 12.3, while Table 12.2 shows the chi-squared values. Strictly speaking, the Spearman test should be used to examine the statistical relationship between rank-ordered variables such as the ones used here. In general, there was no major difference between the Spearman and Pearson correlations.

Looking first at the relationship between modes of subsistence and *settlement pattern*, one finds that there is an association between degree of reliance on fishing and permanence of settlement, according to the chi-squared test. (All associations reported are significant at the .05 level or better unless otherwise stated.) The Pearson correlation (.46) shows that the relationship is positive and quite strong. The more important is fishing, the more compact and permanent the settlement. (The fishing societies with 'compact and relatively permanent settlements' are Aleut, Alsea, Bellacoola, Chinook, Chugach, Coos, Eyak, Haida, Hupa, Karok, Kwakiutl, Paraujano, Quileute, Siuslaw, Sivokakmei, Tanaina, Tillamook, and Wiyot.)

The opposite picture emerges in the case of hunting. The relationship between reliance on hunting and permanence of settlement is significant, negative, and fairly strong (-.38). Permanence of settlement is also negatively related to importance of gathering (-.20). Thus, the more reliant is a society on gathering or hunting, the more nomadic it is. Such a conclusion strikes a familiar note.

Settlement pattern is also related to a gross measure of ecological conditions, that is temperature (the chi-squared value is 26.448, or 15 degrees of freedom). The Pearson correlation is -.30 ($s = .008$), which suggests that the warmer is the climate the less permanent groups tend to be.

The observed relationships between mode of subsistence, temperature and permanence of settlement invite two mutually exclusive interpretations. First, extending Lee's argument that the importance of fishing and gathering varies with temperature, one might suggest that temperature or the variety of edible plants determines settlement pattern. Alternatively, one might argue that the relationship between

Table 12.2: Chi-squares, degrees of freedom (DF), significance (Sign.)

Var.	Gathering			Hunting			Fishing		
	Chi-sq.	DF	Sign.	Chi-sq.	DF	Sign.	Chi-sq.	DF	Sign.
1.	36.63	24	.048	90.43	24	.000	103.20	24	.000
2.	35.06	24	.067	8.55	18	.969	37.10	24	.043
3.	31.77	16	.012	25.22	16	.066	61.41	16	.000
4.	9.36	8	.310	6.55	7	.480	15.56	8	.049
5.	35.38	8	.000	13.06	7	.070	36.41	8	.049
6.	46.39	16	.000	49.29	18	.000	96.95	16	.000
7.	76.58	56	.035	126.87	63	.000	111.18	56	.000
8.	69.06	40	.003	46.01	45	.430	75.86	40	.000
9.	70.24	40	.002	43.31	45	.544	90.81	40	.000

Names of variables: 1. settlement pattern; 2. group size — see also n. 2, p. 199 below; 3. levels of hierarchy; 4. restrictions of access to land; 5. restrictions of access to movable property; 6. stratification; 7. form of domestic organization; 8. temperature; 9. vegetation

temperature and settlement pattern is a spurious one, and that settlement pattern is responsive rather to the nature of the resources exploited, that is, the extent to which they are terrestrial or aquatic.

Binford suggests (1980) that 'foragers', whom he defines as people living in areas where resources are more or less evenly distributed, have a high residential mobility, while 'collectors', who depend on seasonal and localized resources, are less nomadic and employ a 'logistical' strategy. He examines the relationship between settlement pattern and effective temperature and claims (ibid.: 14) that mobility among hunter-gatherers is responsive to conditions *other* than gross patterns of food abundance; but he fails to provide an adequate test for his argument. Also, while he maintains that mobility as a 'positioning' strategy may be most responsive to the 'particulars of food distributions that are not directly correlated with the more intuitively appreciated conditions of food abundance' (ibid.), he seems to assume that permanence of settlement is a response to the conditions of *terrestrial* ecology, the length of the growing season and the distribution of resources. Others have made use of Binford's argument that there is a latitudinal gradient in the occurrence of logistical strategies and permanence of settlement (see, for instance, Schalk 1977; 1979; and M. Cohen 1985). But Perlman (1980: 293) opts for the alternative hypothesis that permanence of settlement is related to a reliance on coastal resources.

Using the information of the *Atlas* one can further examine the relationship between settlement pattern, fishing and temperature as a gross measure of ecological conditions (see Figure 12.2). The partial correlation between temperature and settlement pattern, controlling

Figure 12.2 Fishing, settlement and temperature (partial correlations: Pearson correlations in parentheses)

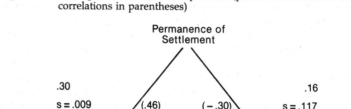

for degree of fishing, is .16 ($s = .117$); the statistical relationship earlier observed between settlement pattern and temperature disappears. In other words, if we assume that all hunter-gatherers rely equally on fishing, and remove the effects of fishing, there is no relationship between temperature and permanence of settlement. On the other hand, the relationship between degree of fishing and permanence of settlement remains fairly strong if one controls for temperature. The partial correlation is .30 ($s = .009$), which further suggests that settlement pattern is responsive to a reliance on aquatic resources and independent of temperature and latitude. Also, if one removes the effect of terrestrial ecology, by holding vegetation constant, the relationship between a reliance on fishing and permanence of settlement becomes even stronger ($r = .41$; $s = .001$). The pattern remains the same when one assumes that vegetation is everywhere the same. Clearly, permanence of settlement is unrelated to terrestrial ecology.

Reanalysis of Kelly's data (1983) largely confirms these calculations. For the thirty-six societies in his sample there is a positive correlation between the importance of hunting and number of residential moves per year (.50), and a negative correlation (–.40) between fishing and moves per year. In the case of gathering there is no correlation. Significantly, these relationships remain the same when controlled for effective temperature. The partial correlation between fishing and moves per year is –.52 ($s = .006$).

By this evidence one must reject Binford's interpretation that permanence of settlement is a function of distance from the Equator and accept the alternative argument that mode of subsistence is the critical variable. This confirms the hypothesis of Yesner (1980) and Perlman

(1980), and the observations of Renouf (1984) for archaeological data on northern hunter-fishers, that dependence on coastal resources encourages permanence of settlement.

Why does dependence on coastal resources correlate with permanence of settlements? Yesner argues (1980: 730) that the use of boats is important in that they allow dispersed resources to be exploited and brought back to a single location. The *Atlas* contains information on the presence or absence of boats ('boat building'). If the presence of boats is critical for permanence of settlements there should be no relationship between a reliance on fishing and permanence of settlements when one controls for the presence of boats. The contrary is the case. The partial correlation remains quite strong ($r = .31; s = .000$). If one looks only at the societies which have no boats (eighty-two societies) there is still a strong and positive correlation between dependence on fishing and permanence of settlements ($r = .26; s = .009$). Permanence of settlements seems therefore to be related to the nature of marine resources themselves, their spatial distribution and abundance.

Group size and social complexity

So far, the statistics confirm the predictions of the hypothetical model. To move on now to the question of group size and population densities, Yesner argues (1980) that these are relatively high for coastal populations, due to the productivity of marine ecosystems. It may be argued further that if the zone of resource exploitation is aquatic, people tend to live along a perimeter strip (a coast or a river bank) and that such a linear settlement pattern (Yesner 1980: 730) is itself likely to lead to higher density. Osborn (1980) and Schalk (1977; 1979) disagree with these proposals. Osborn suggests (1980: 74) that 'population density varies directly with terrestrial plant use and inversely with dependence on marine resources' and that high population density among some coastal populations is a function of the 'way in which marine resources are incorporated into terrestrial resource exploitative systems'.

The Pearson correlation for a modified sample from the *Atlas* shows that in the case of fishing there is a significant and positive relationship with group size, $r = .27; s = .002$.[2] (The fishing societies with the largest communities (100–399) are those of the Aleut, Haisla, Lummi, Makah,

2. The statistics reported for group size are calculated only for societies where horses are absent (185 cases). The total sample (220 cases) contains several societies where animal husbandry is either minimal or supplies less than 6 percent of subsistence input. In some of these horses are used for hunting large game. But the horse is a relatively new innovation and hardly typical of hunters and gatherers; it is therefore more revealing to examine the relationship between group size and modes of subsistence only for a modified sample. For the total sample there is no relationship between dependence on fishing and group size by

Shuswap, Tareumiut, Tenino, and Tlingit.) Hunting is negatively correlated with group size ($r = -.18$; $s = .027$), and in the case of gathering there is no correlation ($r = -.15$; $s = .058$). These calculations confirm the calculations of Yesner, and one must reject the alternative hypothesis of Osborn and Schalk. The more dependent on marine resources the larger the local group.

Osborn argues, as already noted, that population density is related to plant use, and it is possible that the observed pattern is in some way affected by vegetation. One way of testing this is to examine the relationship between the subsistence variables and group size by holding vegetation constant. (This requires two somewhat dubious assumptions — that group size reflects population density and that vegetation reflects plant use, or 'incorporation' in Osborn's terms. The *Atlas* coding precludes a more rigorous testing.) When the effect of vegetation is removed there is a weak negative correlation between hunting and group size ($r = -.23$; $s = .098$) and a weak positive correlation ($r = .26$; $s = .071$) in the case of fishing. Since the number of available cases is only thirty-one, this evidence is ambiguous. Nevertheless, this would support the position of Yesner rather than that of Osborn and Schalk. If Osborn and Schalk were right one would expect a negative correlation between group size and reliance on fishing.

The *Atlas* provides several variables which can be used as measures of the complexity of social organization. These measures are straightforward rank-ordered variables. Objections may be raised that none of the variables in the *Atlas* really measures the extent to which ownership of fishing territories is recognized, which is one of the elements of the hypothetical model. The closest approximation in the file is 'property rights' in relation to land, and there may not be a close relationship between restrictions on access on land and at sea. On the other hand, the ethnography indicates that access to fishing territories is restricted only where access to land is restricted (see, for example, Sudo 1984). The objection may also be raised that the issue of property and ownership presents a conceptual problem and that the respective variables in the *Atlas* do not reflect the real content of property relations. Certainly there exists a great deal of confusion in the ethnography over the issue of sea tenure, and 'ownership' of fishing territories (Pálsson and Durrenberger 1987), a confusion which parallels the debate on ownership of hunting territories (Ingold 1980).

The *P*earson correlation coefficients between modes of subsistence and variables measuring complexity of social organization confirm the basic predictions of the hypothetical model (Table 12.3). Dependence

---

the chi-squared test ($s = .239$); in the case of hunting there is a significant and positive relationship ($r = .24$); but in the case of gathering there is a significant negative relationship ($r = -.23$).

Table 12.3: Pearson correlations and significance

	Gathering	Hunting	Fishing
Settlement pattern	−.20 (.001)	−.38 (.000)	.46 (.000)
Group size[a]	−.15 (.058)	−.18 (.027)	.27 (.002)
Hierarchy	−.23 (.000)	−.14 (.019)	.31 (.000)
Restrictions of access to land	−.09 (.143)	−.14 (.049)	.19 (.010)
Restr. of access to mov. prop.	−.40 (.000)	−.08 (.173)	.40 (.000)
Stratification	−.25 (.000)	−.27 (.010)	.44 (.000)
Domestic organization	−.22 (.001)	−.03 (.336)	.25 (.000)
Temperature	.50 (.000)	−.27 (.289)	−.46 (.000)
Vegetation	−.17 (.106)	−.16 (.122)	.15 (.135)
Gathering		−.23 (.000)	−.67 (.000)
Hunting			−.51 (.000)

[a]See also n. 2, p. 199 above

on fishing is positively related to all the variables. The correlations are fairly strong, from .25 to .44, except in the case of restrictions on access to land where there is a weak relationship (.19). Reliance on hunting, on the other hand, is negatively related to levels of hierarchy (−.14), restrictions on access to land (−.14) and degree of stratification (−.27) but unrelated to other variables. Reliance on gathering is negatively related to all the variables (the correlations range from −.22 to −.40), except inheritance of land where there is no relationship.

The statistical results confirm the classic model as far as hunters and gatherers of terrestrial resources are concerned. An increased importance of these modes of subsistence is associated with less complex social organizations. But hunters and gatherers of aquatic resources provide a radical departure from the classic model. One has to conclude that fishing societies differ significantly from other hunting and gathering societies in that they exhibit a greater social complexity.

Conclusions

Archaeologists have provided increasing evidence suggesting that, in adapting to aquatic resources, prehistoric hunters developed communities which do not conform to the classic image of the hunter-gatherer in terms of size and stability of settlements and complexity of social organization. The evidence presented here, based on *The Ethnographic Atlas*, further indicates that the role of fishing among hunter-gatherers must be reevaluated.

The importance of fishing in the hunter-gatherer economy has been shown to be greater than usually implied. It has also been shown that if there is an equivalence between the various subsistence modes in this economy it is not between fishing and hunting, as Leap suggests (1977), but rather between fishing and gathering. Fishing and gathering are alternatives, whilst hunting is relatively consistent from one case to the next. Furthermore, there is statistically a stark contrast between fishing on the one hand and hunting and gathering on the other. The importance of fishing correlates positively with permanence of settlement, group size, levels of hierarchy, degree of stratification, restrictions on access to resources and form of domestic organization. In the case of hunting and of gathering there is either no correlation or a negative one.

Permanence of settlement is a key variable in this comparison, both because the classic model of hunter-gatherers emphasizes mobility and also because permanent settlement is a condition for social complexity, at least in the absence of animal husbandry. But the relationship between fishing and settlement pattern allows for more than one interpretation, since both variables are associated with temperature. By Murdock's measure, there is a negative correlation (−.46) between importance of fishing and temperature, and this indicates, assuming that temperature is a gross measure of latitude, that the importance of fishing increases with distance from the Equator. On this evidence one might argue that the permanence of settlement observed for fishing societies is due to latitude, temperature or the amount of solar radiation. But the statistics support the alternative interpretation, that permanence of settlement is due to a reliance on aquatic resources. The Pearson correlation between settlement pattern and temperature is −.30, indicating that the colder the climate the more permanent the settlement; but if one controls for the degree of fishing there is no relationship ($r = .16; s = .117$). In other words, if one removes the effect of fishing the relationship between temperature and permanence of settlement disappears. This suggests that it is not latitude itself that influences settlement pattern. Neither does terrestrial ecology seem to affect the relationship. When one controls for vegetation there is still a strong positive relationship between reliance on fishing and settlement pattern ($r = .41$; $s = .001$).

Such a conclusion supports the argument that settlement pattern is responsive to something else than distance from the Equator, the length of the growing season for plants or effective temperature, and confirms the hypothesis of Yesner (1980), and the observations of Renouf (1984) for archaeological data, that reliance on coastal resources is related to permanence of settlement. The periodic abundance of aquatic resources is the critical factor which allows for permanent settlements and complex social organizations.

One may speculate, on the basis of the relationship between a reliance on aquatic resources, permanence of settlement and group size, on the possible role of aquatic resources for prehistoric social development. Coastal zones may have provided an opportunity for the emergence of agriculture and the development of complex civilizations (see Marquardt, this volume). Quilter and Stocker (1983), for instance, argue for the 'maritime hypothesis' of development of civilization in Peru. Interesting as these speculations may be, they are beyond the scope of the present chapter.

Deterministic ecological models are often assumed to be particularly useful for the study of hunter-gatherers. Thus Lee suggests that 'it is essential that the incidence of hunting, gathering, and fishing be related to latitude' (1968: 42). Leap (1977: 254) reifies this reasoning as 'ecological logic'. An alternative interpretation gives priority to social factors or the interaction between social and ecological factors. Sometimes the issue of interpretation can be solved by empirical studies, and on occasions what was previously regarded as environmentally 'determined' behavior turns out to be a function of social factors (Ellen 1982: 4). Thus, the environment does not fully explain nomadic movements of food collecting communities (Woodburn 1972).

In this way, the importance of fishing may be responsive to both ecological and social factors. Computations from the *Atlas* data indicate that the importance of fishing is related to latitude, as measured by temperature, but it may still be argued that the incidence of fishing is dependent on social factors. The 'present' latitudinal distribution of fishing seems to be unrelated to terrestrial ecology, as there is a strong relationship between dependence on fishing and temperature when controlled for vegetation ($r = -.54$; $s = .000$). The geographical distribution of the subsistence modes observed for the *Atlas* data seems to be a result of social and political factors which have very little to do with ecology. The decision to fish may in fact depend on internal social dynamics. For example, a population of terrestrial hunter-gatherers may decide to exploit aquatic resources as an alternative to social fission, since aquatic resources allow for relatively permanent settlement, large groups and complex social organization. Rather than seeing marine resources as determinants of social complexity one should regard coastal niches as just one possible avenue for intensification (Lourandos, this volume).

Fishing is a marginal theoretical category, for fishing takes place in widely different social contexts and in combination with a range of subsistence activities. But while fishing is not a unitary phenomenon and little is gained by adding a new subset to anthropological taxonomy, a comparison of hunter-gatherers of aquatic resources with terrestrial hunter-gatherers reveals significant sociological contrasts. It is in the light of such evidence that the neglect of fishing in the literature becomes all the more surprising.

Part 4

Theoretical and comparative approaches

13. Hominids, humans and hunter-gatherers: an evolutionary perspective

Robert Foley

Introduction

Few conferences and subsequent publications have been as influential as *Man the hunter*. The book (Lee and DeVore 1968b) restored hunter-gatherers to their current position as Rousseau's 'noble savages' and Sol Tax's 'original affluent society'. Prior to this they were, in prehistory, tenuously clinging to survival until the invention of agriculture brought their tedious and hazardous life to an end and, in ethnography, the marginal peoples of anthropological research.

The influence of *Man the hunter* has been particularly marked in the field of human evolution. Hunting and gathering became central to human evolution, and the key perspectives of several chapters in the book have become axioms in our understanding of hominid evolution — that hunting-gathering was a stable way of life, existing in harmony with the environment; that while hunting was a central behavioural component, it was the totality of hunting *and* gathering that was critical; that the role of women was important, and so the division of labour and food-sharing were critical elements in the evolution of humans (Isaac 1978b). Overall, studies in human evolution shifted away from analysing bones and stones simply to construct a chronology and an evolutionary narrative, and towards behavioural and evolutionary ecology — to an approach in which the evolution of humans *was* the evolution of the hunter-gatherer adaptation.

One of the practical consequences for palaeoanthropology has been a model of human evolution that is essentially gradualistic and unilinear. In this model, it is argued that the essential elements of a hunter-gatherer way of life — food sharing, hunting, a division of labour, central place foraging, and so on — can be identified very early in the fossil and archaeological record; thus the differences between various chronologically separated hominid taxa have come to be seen as minor anatomical variations, not functionally and adaptively significant features. Early hominids *were* hunter-gatherers. Change through time was principally a question of the efficiency of that way of life, or its degree of advance towards a fully modern condition. All this had a significant effect on the interpretation of hominid fossils; even the Neanderthals, *bête noire* of previous generations of palaeoanthropologists, were placed within the mainstream of human evolution, and the critical changes in hominid evolution were placed far back in the Plio-Pleistocene among the australopithecines. The origins of anatomically modern humans became something of a scientific backwater. Until very recently, being a hominid, being a human and being a hunter-gatherer were very nearly the same thing.

Palaeoanthropologists, however, are beginning during the 1980s to question some of these conclusions. Rather than characterizing the various early hominid taxa in terms of their level of sophistication in hunting and gathering, more fundamental biological and behavioural differences are being recognized, leading to new insights into hominid evolution. Such biological distinctions may in turn have consequences for the way we view hunter-gatherers and their role in human evolution. In this chapter[1] I shall look at two particular problems from the point of view of evolutionary ecology: first, the extent to which anatomically modern humans may have differed from other hominids; and second, the extent to which hunter-gathering, as understood by studies of living hunter-gatherers, was the way of life of all non-agricultural peoples. In other words, I shall try to test Lee and DeVore's statement that 'Cultural man has been on earth for some 2,000,000 years; for over 99 per cent of this period he has lived as a hunter-gatherer. . . . Of the estimated 80 billion men who have ever lived out a life span on earth, over 90 per cent have lived as hunter-gatherers' (Lee and DeVore 1968a: 3).

Hominids before the evolution of anatomically modern humans

Clearly there are many important morphological and behavioural differences between modern humans and other recognized hominid taxa. These, after all, form the basis for understanding the pattern of hominid evolution. However, in this chapter I shall concentrate on a few functionally significant complexes that might highlight ways in which early hominids differed adaptively from anatomically modern forms.

The term 'hominid' will be used here to include all taxa that have evolved *since* the separation of the last common ancestor of modern

1. My interest in the problems considered here arose from discussions with Kristen Hawkes and Jim O'Connell and the questions that their work has posed for hunter-gatherer studies. Phyllis Lee has read an earlier draft and provided a large number of useful suggestions, particularly on the relationship between ecology and parental investment. Responsibility for any errors that remain, though, rests with the author.

Table 13.1: Temporal distribution of hominid taxa[1]

Hominidae[2]	Approximate age (millions of years)
Australopithecus afarensis	5.0 – <3.0
africanus	3.0 – 2.0
robustus	2.0 – 1.4
crassidens	2.0 – 1.4
boisei	2.0 – >1.0
Homo habilis	2.0 – 1.6
sp.nov.(?) (e.g. KNM–ER1813)	– 1.8
erectus (Africa)	1.6 – 0.2
erectus (Asia)	1.0 – 0.2
sapiens (Europe — archaic)	0.7 – 0.2
sapiens (Europe/W. Asia — Neanderthal)	0.07 – 0.03
sapiens (archaic — Africa)	0.2 – 0.1
sapiens (archaic — S.E. Asia)	>0.1
sapiens (archaic — E. Asia)	>0.1
sapiens (anatomically modern humans)	0.1 – 0

1. This table indicates the diversity of known hominid forms, although there is considerable debate about the precise nomenclature and taxonomy of these groups. An implication of the dicussion here is that *Homo sapiens* should be reserved for anatomically modern humans.
2. Recent interpretations suggest that the family Hominidae should include the living African apes.

humans and the African great apes. This usage is now problematical in terms of hominoid taxonomy as a whole (Szalay and Delson 1979; Ciochon 1983), but will be retained here for the sake of clarity. Within this family are at least two genera and several species (Table 13.1). The genus *Australopithecus* represents the oldest known hominids (*A. afarensis*, *A. africanus*), as well as later more specialized forms of African Pliocene and early Pleistocene hominid (*A. robustus*, *A. crassidens*, *A. boisei*). The genus *Homo* includes several taxa, possibly as many as four or five, and is more directly ancestral to anatomically modern humans. *Homo* forms the central focus for this discussion. These taxa will not be discussed separately, but in general terms under a series of headings.

Body size and robusticity

A general trend towards larger body size can be observed during the course of hominid evolution, from very small, possibly ancestral forms such as *A. afarensis* at between twenty-five and thirty kilograms, to later and modern hominids at approximately sixty kilograms. Increases in body size either lead to or are consequences of ecological changes (Peters 1983), an association which undoubtedly occurred in hominid evolution (Foley 1984; 1987). What is of interest here is the fact that the largest hominids do not appear to be modern humans, but the forms generally referred to as archaic members of *Homo sapiens*. For example, a particularly robust specimen from Bodo in Ethiopia dated to over 0.2 million years ago (Mya) may have been close to the weight of a male gorilla (Stringer 1984a). Furthermore, these earlier forms were not only large, but also had a more robust skeleton — both cranial and post-cranial bones were far thicker, with more marked surfaces for muscular attachments. It would seem that some earlier members of the genus *Homo* were extremely heavily built with a large muscle mass — animals built for power and strength. This contrasts with some features of anatomically modern humans who are more lightly built with, for example, characteristically thinner cranial bones. More specifically, the evolution of anatomically modern humans is marked by increased gracility.

Brain size

A general increase in brain size during the course of human evolution has been widely documented. This is true even if the increase in body size is taken into account. Currently it seems that there is little difference in brain size/body size ratios between some archaic *sapiens* forms, such as the Neanderthals, and anatomically modern humans, but quite a significant increase from *Homo erectus*. It must be remembered that brain enlargement is not just a simple unilineal process, as it involves various costs (R. Martin 1983). A larger brain imposes considerable energetic constraints on mothers, as most brain growth occurs during foetal and early post-natal development, and in the context of human bipedalism it may also conflict with the demand for efficient locomotor behaviour. Periods of brain growth, therefore, indicate the character of selective pressures operating on females and on the population as a whole. Humphrey (1976) has argued that rapid increases in brain size indicate selective pressure for social complexity and competition, but the energetic costs of brain growth suggest that this can only occur under certain ecological conditions (R. Martin 1983; Clutton-Brock and Harvey 1981).

Growth patterns

One of the most exciting developments in studies of human evolution in recent years is the use of tooth enamel prism development for ageing immature hominids. Since enamel is formed at a constant rate by the laying down of incremental layers, these may be counted and an age estimated. Bromage and Dean (1985) have analyzed these increments in some immature hominid fossil teeth, and have shown that they do not match the 'dental age' estimated by the pattern of tooth eruption. Estimated dental age for fossil hominids is greater than that counted by enamel increments. Bromage and Dean have suggested that this means that hominids were growing far faster than anatomically modern humans. For example, LH2, a specimen of *A. afarensis* from Laetoli in Tanzania, had a dental age of 4.45 years, but an age based on enamel formation of only 3.45. Sts24a (*A. africanus*) from Sterkfontein appears to be only 3.3 years old, not 6.05, as estimated on the basis of dental eruption stages. Even for early *Homo* (KNM–ER 820) there is a discrepancy of 1.8 years (5.3 rather than 7.1 years old). Similar although less extreme results have been reported for a Neanderthal specimen, the child from Devil's Tower, Gibraltar (Dean, Stringer and Bromage 1986). On the basis of the perikymata age estimates this specimen is thought to be about three years old, which suggests remarkably precocious growth rates. In other words, early, anatomically pre-modern humans grew rapidly, retaining to some extent the growth patterns of pongids, and lacking the characteristic slow and prolonged juvenile growth phase of modern humans.

Bipedalism

All known hominids appear to have been habitually bipedal. However, as Day (1985) has shown, there may have been some differences in bipedal performance between later and earlier hominids. Leaving aside the differences found in the very early australopithecines, *Homo erectus* has several important functional differences in femur and pelvic anatomy from anatomically modern forms. Although the functional significance of these differences is poorly understood, the energetics of locomotion of the earlier hominids may not have been the same as those of modern humans.

Subsistence

The subsistence behaviour of early hominids is one of the most contentious fields of study in the mid-1980s (see Bunn and Kroll 1986 for discussion). Many of the assumptions of the *Man the hunter* paradigm have been questioned. It has proved difficult to establish criteria that could unequivocally show either hominid hunting or the extent of meat-eating (Potts 1984). Although his work has been criticized (Potts 1984; Bunn and Kroll 1986), Binford (1981; 1984) has claimed that early hominids did not hunt and had only very small components of meat in their diet. While such a view is probably incorrect, it is equally untrue to say that early hominids were full hunters in the same way as modern hunter-gatherers. Also, although their foraging radius was larger than that of most non-human primates, early hominids do not appear to have had the very large home ranges associated with modern hunter-gatherers (Foley 1978; 1984; 1987). Furthermore, it has yet to be established whether earlier hominids engaged in what Isaac (1983) referred to as central place foraging, and so had a home base in the same way as do modern hunter-gatherers. Isaac's (1978b) inferences about early hominid food-sharing and division of labour are less certain if home bases did not exist. Overall, there is a declining willingness among palaeoanthropologists to accept the existence of modern forms of subsistence behaviour among anatomically pre-modern humans. It seems quite probable that the earlier hominids did eat meat, but that this was not integrated into a central place foraging and food-sharing system as found among modern hunter-gatherers.

Technology

One of the most striking differences between earlier and modern hominids lies in their technology. Although there are considerable problems in defining technological transitions, perhaps the most distinctive characteristic of early hominid technology is the fact that across large portions of space and time Lower and Middle Palaeolithic technology is remarkably stable and uniform. Although minor differences can be observed, pebble tool and hand-axe technology is essentially the same for a period of at least one million years across three continents. Even the Middle Stone Age and Middle Palaeolithic Mousterian industries display a stability of at least tens of thousands of years. This contrasts markedly with the rate of technological change once modern humans appear. As Isaac (1972) showed, technology changes rapidly and is much more spatially variable once anatomically modern humans are established. This suggests that with anatomically modern humans we see the appearance of more modern levels of technological variability and innovation, and that these do not occur with earlier forms of hominid. Earlier hominids were decidedly 'unmodern' in their technology, producing the same basic artefacts over enormous time spans.

Geographical distribution

The earliest hominids appear in sub-Saharan Africa. It is only with *Homo erectus* that we see any evidence for the expansion of hominids out of Africa, probably at approximately 1.0 Mya (Pope 1983). By the end of the Pleistocene hominids had colonized most parts of the world. However, for much of the early and middle Pleistocene hominids were much more limited in their distribution, suggesting a species less tolerant of certain environmental conditions, such as cold, than are anatomically modern humans. Earlier hominids seem to be essentially tropical, sub-tropical and warm temperate in their distribution, and confined to the central Old World continents. Gamble (1986) has argued that prior to anatomically modern humans the occupation of the colder parts of Europe was intermittent. Again this suggests a rather habitat-specific and more fixed and less flexible pattern of behaviour than that associated with recent hunter-gatherers. Furthermore, A. Turner (1984) has argued that there is a similarity between hominids and other, particularly carnivorous, large mammals in their pattern of dispersal through Europe. Hominids appear to have been colonizing new habitats and regions in ways that resemble other large mammals more than modern humans (Foley 1987).

Evolutionary diversity

One final aspect of early hominid evolutionary ecology that should be stressed is the actual pattern of evolutionary change. The simple unilinear view of a straightforward and world-wide evolution of the genus *Homo* — for example, Weiner and Campbell's (1964) 'spectrum hypothesis' — has been questioned on several grounds (Wood 1984; Stringer 1984b; Andrews 1984). First, there is the possibility of more than one species of very early *Homo* existing within East Africa — that is, the variability within what is referred to as *Homo habilis* is too great to be comfortably accommodated within a single species, and there are two species present. Second, what is normally incorporated within the taxon *Homo erectus* may in fact be far more regionally differentiated, with Asian, African and European populations not only relatively isolated and therefore perhaps adaptively different, but also having very different evolutionary fates. In particular, the European and Asian populations may well have undergone independent evolution — principally brain enlargement — into the Upper Pleistocene (for example, in Europe the evolution of the Neanderthals), only to be replaced 30,000 to 40,000 years ago by anatomically modern humans that evolved in Africa from about 0.1 Mya (Brauer 1984). This view (see Figure 13.1) has received considerable support from dates of both fossil hominids and archaeological sites in Africa (Stringer *et al.* 1984), and by studies of the diversity of human mitochondrial DNA (Cann *et al.* 1987). This new interpretation raises the possibility that very large portions of the earlier hominid population were not directly ancestral to modern humans. This lack of continuity between modern and earlier hominids in various parts of the world might imply great differences in adaptation, as competitive replacement of one population by another would seem to be involved.

In summary, this very brief review of some of the evidence and interpretations in the mid-1980s of the evolutionary and ecological

Figure 13.1: The adaptive radiation of the genus *Homo* and the evolution of anatomically modern humans

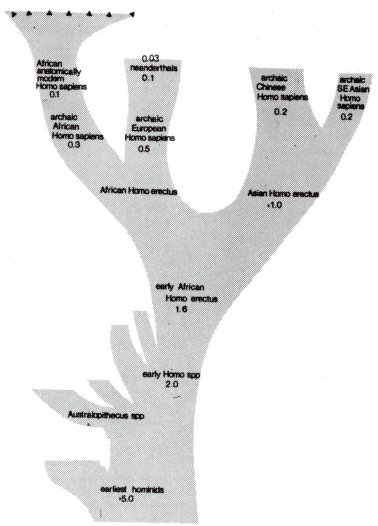

Note: When geographical and population factors are taken into account this is far from being a simple unilineal process. Anatomically modern humans most probably evolved from an archaic African population about 0.1 Mya and dispersed through the rest of the world with relatively little admixture. The numbers give the approximate dates for the various branchings, in millions of years. Traditional taxonomic nomenclature for the hominids are shown here for the sake of clarity. Acceptance of this model would require some taxonomic revision.

status of the earlier hominids presents a rather different picture from the consensus of the late 1960s. In the previous model, earlier hominids were not substantially different from modern humans, and possessed a subsistence ecology at least partially like that of modern hunter-gatherers. In the view presented here the evolutionary ecology of earlier hominids and modern *Homo sapiens* was markedly divergent. Anatomically pre-modern hominids were animals with large body and muscle mass, and so with considerable power and strength. While fully bipedal, their mode of locomotion may have involved different energetic/muscular principles associated with this robusticity. They grew and matured more rapidly than do modern humans. Their technology does not display the variability and flexibility associated with modern human technology. Regional populations may well have differed one from another genetically, morphologically and adaptively, at levels above those of modern human variability. They had no apparent dietary specializations. Despite being omnivorous there is no reason to assume that their foraging behaviour was of the same level of organization as modern hunter-gatherers in terms of planning depth, scheduling, subsistence activity and foraging flexibility. In the absence of clear-cut evidence for central place foraging similar to that of modern hunter-gatherers, inferences about the social and sharing behaviour of early hominids must be tentative only.

In other words, if the term 'hunter-gatherer' is to mean more than just wild resource omnivory (*contra* Teleki 1981) (in which case it would include baboons, chimpanzees and many other animals!), then early hominids were neither human nor hunter-gatherers. Trying to understand what they were is one of the most exciting challenges facing palaeoanthropology.

Evolutionary change in modern humans

Sharpening the distinction between modern humans and earlier hominids we can now revise the assertion of Lee and DeVore (1968a: 3, see above) that 99 per cent of the hominid time-span was occupied by hunter-gatherers. Assuming the appearance of modern humans in Africa and their spread throughout the world by 30,000 years ago, then perhaps a figure of around 5 per cent is closer to the mark. (It is impossible, and indeed not very meaningful, to be precise here because modern humans make their appearance in various parts of the world at dates ranging from possibly as early as 100,000 to as late as 30,000 years ago.)

A length of time of between 30,000 and 100,000 years ago is still, however, a substantial one. If hunting and gathering is of this antiquity, then its evolutionary importance for humans could still be considerable. However, this assumes that there has been little evolutionary change since the appearance of modern humans; that subsequent changes are cultural and economic — with biological consequences, perhaps, but not biological causes; and that all anatomically modern prehistoric hunter-gatherers were basically the same as those represented by contemporary hunter-gatherers.

Are these assumptions tenable? By considering evidence relating to evolutionary change in modern humans during the late Quaternary, and its implications for the development of modern hunter-gathering, we can perhaps address this question. Two trends are of particular interest: reduction in body size and changes in the degree of sexual dimorphism.

Body size in anatomically modern humans

The earliest anatomically modern humans are striking for their great stature. The Cro-Magnon populations of the Upper Palaeolithic of Europe are taller than most later populations. In a recent paper Frayer (1984) has documented the reduction of body size in European populations from these earliest anatomically modern human forms to those of the Holocene. Average male height during the Upper Palaeolithic was 1.74 metres, whereas in the Mesolithic it was 1.67 metres. For females the figures are 1.59 and 1.56 metres respectively. This evidence would seem to suggest that there is a marked reduction in human body size, particularly of males, at the end of the Pleistocene. This overall change in stature is mirrored in cranial and dental dimensions as well (Table 13.2). Furthermore, Henke (1981) has suggested that there is a reduction in robusticity as well as overall stature.

Table 13.2: Mandibular canine area (mm^2) and sexual dimorphism estimates for European Late Quaternary populations of anatomically modern humans

	Males $\bar{x}$	Females $\bar{x}$	Sexual dimorphism (%)
Upper Palaeolithic	63.7	54.4	117.1
Mesolithic	56.2	49.5	113.5

Source: Frayer 1984

Sexual dimorphism

As well as a reduction in overall body size from the Pleistocene to Holocene, there is a decrease in the degree of sexual dimorphism (Frayer 1984). In Europe the female/male ratio of stature during the

Upper Palaeolithic was 1:1.09, whereas during the Mesolithic it was 1:1.07. The earlier Upper Palaeolithic populations were among the most dimorphic of all anatomically modern humans, for example, male canine area in Upper Palaeolithic males was 117.1% of females', compared to 113.5% in Mesolithic populations (Table 13.2). These measures of dimorphism may not be fully comparable with estimates of sexual dimorphism in body mass in non-human primates, but they indicate changes in important aspects of biology that may throw light on the evolutionary ecology of the earliest anatomically modern humans.

Evolutionary ecology of Homo sapiens *during the late Quaternary*

What do these observations tell us about human evolutionary ecology, and in particular the role of the hunter-gatherer in the development of modern human society and cultural variability? The traditional view would be that among anatomically modern humans a basic hunter-gatherer way of life, comparable to that observed ethnographically, became established. This mode of life remained stable for some 20,000 years. From about 10,000 years ago some of these hunter-gatherer populations, for one reason or another, turned to food production. Others, though, survived where agriculture was not viable, either remaining much the same or adapting to the presence of agricultural populations. In this model, hunting and gathering is an adaptation 'ancestral' to agriculture, but one which also survived in a relatively unchanged form. From a biological perspective, what is most important about this model is that it assumes evolutionary stasis throughout this period.

As we have seen, this is not consistent with the fossil evidence of the late Quaternary. Upper Palaeolithic humans were larger and more sexually dimorphic than later hunter-gatherers. Perhaps, then, there are important evolutionary processes taking place at this time (Figure 13.2). To understand these it is necessary to adopt a broader approach derived from evolutionary ecology.

Body size and degree of sexual dimorphism have been related to various socio-ecological and environmental parameters in comparative studies of mammals (Clutton-Brock and Harvey 1978). Reductions in size and dimorphism within a species through time may therefore reflect some of these parameters.

High levels of sexual dimorphism and robust males are considered to reflect one or both of two principal selective pressures. Either there may be considerable male–male competition for females, and hence a selective advantage for larger males, or males and females may have different foraging strategies, in which males may be called upon either to cover larger distances or to employ considerable strength in forag-

Figure 13.2: Model of the evolutionary ecology of anatomically modern humans derived from the discussion presented here. Post-Pleistocene
hunter-gatherers are represented as a parallel evolutionary development to food production.

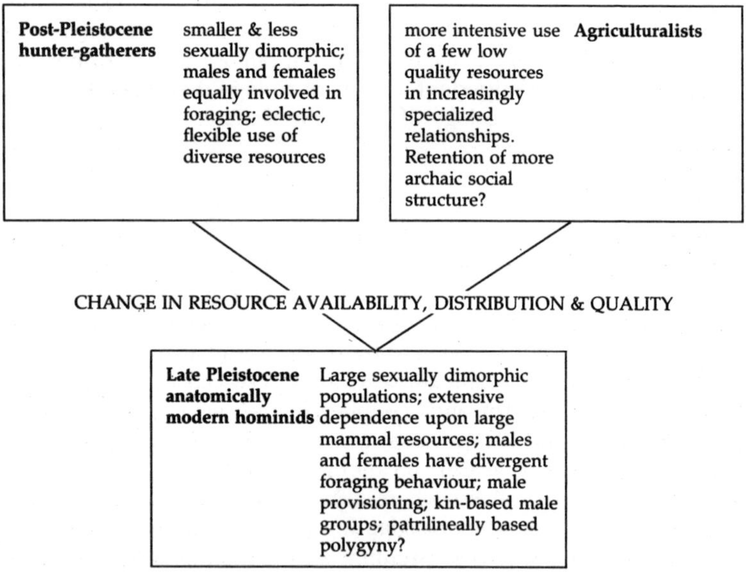

| **Post-Pleistocene hunter-gatherers** | smaller & less sexually dimorphic; males and females equally involved in foraging; eclectic, flexible use of diverse resources | more intensive use of a few low quality resources in increasingly specialized relationships. Retention of more archaic social structure? **Agriculturalists** |

CHANGE IN RESOURCE AVAILABILITY, DISTRIBUTION & QUALITY

| **Late Pleistocene anatomically modern hominids** | Large sexually dimorphic populations; extensive dependence upon large mammal resources; males and females have divergent foraging behaviour; male provisioning; kin-based male groups; patrilineally based polygyny? |

ing. In contrast, low levels of sexual dimorphism occur with monogam-
ous mating patterns and where males and females have similar
foraging strategies. Differences in size and level of sexual dimorphism
can thus reflect subsistence activities and reproductive strategies.
These two explanations, however, are not independent of each other.
When one sex is able to provision the other and thus reduce the
energetic demands of reproduction, differences between the sexes in
foraging strategies will evolve which may be reflected in levels of sexual
dimorphism. The presence of large, robust males can be linked either to
increased parental investment through provisioning and thus sex-
specific foraging behaviour, or to male–male competition for access to
females.

This comparative approach may have implications for understanding
the evolution of modern humans and hunter-gatherers. Essentially we
have a trend away from robusticity and sexual dimorphism, suggesting, first, that there was probably a reduction in the differences between male and female foraging behaviour, and second, possibly a
reduction in male–male competition. The first of these is perhaps the
most interesting. During the late Pleistocene the foraging strategies of

males and females may have been quite different from those of modern hunter-gatherers, reflecting a much greater level of hunting, and in particular the hunting of very large mammals. Significantly larger animals are found in Pleistocene faunas compared to those of today. Not only might the hunting of these animals require considerable strength and stamina but carcasses also provide food in very large 'package sizes'. Ecologically this has some interesting consequences. When food comes in large packages, then both cooperation between individuals and provisioning are much more likely to occur, either through kin selection, mutualism, or generalized reciprocal altruism. In this way uneven distribution (another likely consequence of large package size) can be minimized at no great cost to the individual.

The picture beginning to emerge is one where males are responsible for large proportions of the foraging, and are provisioning/sharing with females and young. This is likely to select for larger body-sized males, with considerable socio-ecological consequences—producing a pattern of behaviour quite different from that seen among modern hunter-gatherers. Male–male relationships may have been far more significant, placing emphasis, as is the case among chimpanzees (Wrangham 1979), on male relatedness within social groups. If males are provisioning females and young, then paternal certainty may have been important in the allocation of parental investment. A harem system of polygynous mating (monogamy being less likely in view of the sexual dimorphism involved), or more likely, perhaps, a system of patrilineal control and organization of females, would have ensured paternity certainty. What follows from these suggestions is that the foraging and reproductive strategies of Pleistocene anatomically modern humans differed markedly from those of most modern hunter-gatherers. This may have implications for understanding both the development of modern hunter-gatherer behaviour and also the preconditions of agricultural development.

Recent interpretations of Late Pleistocene hunter-gatherers indicate that they displayed greater social complexity than many recent hunter-gatherers. According to the model presented here, such social complexity would not be the product of evolutionary development, but rather reflects the different patterns of behavioural ecology and reproductive strategies found among early anatomically modern humans. Extensive male-kin-based alliances associated with a marked division of labour and intensive hunting activities would have produced a pattern of social organization very different from that found among more recent hunter-gatherers.

In this context, what we think of as modern hunter-gathering is a largely post-Pleistocene phenomenon. Rather than being an adaptation ancestral to food production, it is a parallel development. As the environment changed at the end of the Pleistocene, and in particular as game animals became scarcer and restricted to a smaller size range, human adaptation shifted, and with it came evolutionary changes in humans.

On the one hand there was the shift to modern hunter-gathering. With resource depletion and an increase in the importance of plant foods, females would have become more critical in the food quest, and selection for male body size and male–male relationships would have decreased. The combined result of these two factors would be both a decrease in body size and a reduction in the degree of sexual dimorphism. This may either have been a direct genetic change, or it may have been mediated through nutritional and environmental factors, as in modern populations where sexual dimorphism decreases with food quality. The small flexible band system, with general egalitarianism and both males and females contributing to the diet in approximately equal proportions, is an evolutionary response to changes in resource availability, quality and distribution.

The alternative response was the shift to agriculture. Most agricultural developments involve increased utilization of poorer-quality plant resources. Their exploitation would have depended upon greater levels of organization and of labour input and control. In the more structured social units of the Late Pleistocene a social pre-adaptation towards agricultural development exists; one in which male-kin-based groups and a pronounced sexual division of labour are maintained.

Overall, this tentative model of the evolutionary ecology of anatomically modern humans during the Later Quaternary has two principal components. The first is that there is an evolutionary basis to the adaptive, economic and social changes that occurred during this time. The second is that hunter-gathering in the form known to us today is a parallel development to agriculture, not an archaic, ancestral way of life. Both hunter-gatherer and agricultural systems developed as a response to resource depletion at the end of the Pleistocene from the rather different socio-ecology of Late Pleistocene anatomically modern humans. A conclusion to be drawn is that in socio-ecological terms modern hunter-gatherers do not necessarily represent the basal hominid way of life, as was suggested in the *Man the Hunter* conference. Rather, along with modern agriculturalists, they are an evolutionarily-derived form that appeared towards the end of the Pleistocene as a response to changing resource conditions.

Conclusions

The last twenty years has seen a major shift in palaeoanthropology, away from the narration of evolutionary sequences written in stone and bone, towards the analysis of function, both morphological and behavioural. The expanding knowledge of living hunter-gatherers has played an important part in this. There has, however, perhaps been too great a readiness to extrapolate their characteristics back into the remote past. As data have accumulated it is now clear that the variety of ecological and social behaviour in the past exceeds that visible in the archaeological and fossil record.

This chapter has attempted some reassessment of the evolutionary role of hunter-gatherers in the context of recent work in palaeoanthropology. Several conclusions may perhaps be tentatively drawn. The first is a terminological one. Categories such as human and hunter-gatherer have specific meanings. It is the purpose of palaeoanthropology to discover the extent to which they apply in the past, not to assume that they apply. Consequently it is suggested here that the term 'human' should be reserved for anatomically modern humans. It is now becoming clear that earlier hominids differed in adaptively significant ways from modern ones, and to refer to all hominids as human is to lose these important distinctions. Equally, we cannot assume that earlier hominids or early humans were sufficiently similar to modern hunter-gatherers for this latter label to be applied uncritically.

More specifically, it has been argued in this chapter that there may be substantial evolutionary changes taking place *after* the appearance of anatomically modern humans. Late Pleistocene humans were larger and more sexually dimorphic than early post-Pleistocene ones. This may reflect changes in adaptive strategy among humans — changes, it has been argued, that reflect responses to resource depletion at the end of the Pleistocene. In this view, *both* food production *and* modern hunter-gatherers are post-Pleistocene adaptive responses to a changing environment. While this model requires a great deal of further testing and development, it can at least serve to remind us that evolution did not 'stop' with the appearance of modern humans, but that adaptation and natural selection are mechanisms underlying all organic change.

14. Risk and uncertainty in the 'original affluent society': evolutionary ecology of resource-sharing and land tenure

Eric Alden Smith

Introduction

Ecological anthropology has as its primary goal the development of a body of theory capable of generating explanations for cross-cultural and historical variation in human social behavior — that is, explanations that have a more than local application. In pursuing this task, anthropologists have always leaned heavily on theoretical developments in biological ecology, with varying results (Vayda and Rappaport 1968: Orlove 1980; E.A. Smith 1984a). The ecological orientation has been particularly strong in anthropological analyses of societies whose economies are based on foraging or simple agriculture. The studies of foraging societies in the 1960s and 1970s were characterized by reliance on the very simple but initially useful concepts of 'cultural ecology' developed by Steward (1955) and those he influenced (for example, various contributors in Lee and DeVore 1968b; Bichierri 1972). While this approach is still in current use, more recent analyses of hunter-gatherer economies have emphasized the political and dynamic aspects of these systems, and place more reliance on paradigms from Marxism, economics, and evolutionary ecology (for example, Barnard 1983; Leacock and Lee 1982; Schrire 1984; Williams and Hunn 1982; Winterhalder and Smith 1981). This chapter draws its theoretical inspiration from the latter two paradigms, though, unlike many commentators, I do not see these as being so estranged from at least some varieties of Marxism (an argument that I do not have time to develop here).[1]

1. An earlier version of this chapter was presented at the Wenner-Gren Conference on 'Risk and Uncertainty' organized by Elizabeth Cashdan and myself. I thank the participants, especially Bruce Winterhalder, Cashdan, Hillard Kaplan, and Dave Stephens, for their helpful comments. Rob Boyd, Cashdan, Tim Ingold, and Nicolas Peterson offered detailed comments on the manuscript, for which I am grateful. Michael Taylor stimulated me to take a more systematic approach to strategic interaction, which I'm afraid is barely begun here.

While ecological analysis of the interaction between organisms and aspects of their environment is often limited to relatively short-term, homeostatic approaches, beginning with Charles Darwin's work it has been clear that the theory of natural selection can powerfully illuminate the ways in which living creatures adapt to their environments. Accordingly, in recent decades large segments of ecology and evolutionary theory have merged into a single discipline termed 'evolutionary ecology' (reviewed in Pianka 1983; May 1981; Roughgarden 1979). More recently, aspects of economic theory, particularly neoclassical decision models and game theory, have been borrowed or reinvented in attempts to deal with certain aspects of the evolutionary ecology of animal behavior (Krebs and Davies 1984 provides the best single review).

The early work in behavioral ecology involved deterministic models (in the mathematical sense of the term) that assumed — for simplifying purposes — that actors possess perfect information, and were concerned only with the *average* payoff of different choices; but more recent work has paid increasing attention to uncertainty and risk (concepts discussed below). In addition, evolutionary ecologists have come to realize that whenever fitness is frequency-dependent (for example, due to social interaction), the simple notion of optimality must be replaced with the strategic notion of game-theoretical equilibrium or evolutionary stability (Dawkins 1980; Maynard Smith 1982). Anthropological applications of evolutionary ecology have primarily drawn on the simpler 'classical' models of deterministic optimization (review in E.A. Smith 1983b), but there are good reasons for suggesting that the theory of risk and uncertainty developed by economists and evolutionary ecologists, as well as the theory of strategic games or evolutionarily stable strategies, be incorporated within ecological anthropology.

What are these reasons? First, as I argue in detail below, there are several phenomena, widespread among hunter-gatherers and of considerable anthropological interest, that cannot be fully understood without invoking risk, uncertainty, and strategic interaction: sharing of food, information and other resources, as well as certain patterns of land tenure and intergroup relations.[2] While the importance of these factors has long been recognized in an intuitive way, the position taken here is that anthropological emulation of the more rigorous and systematic treatment of risk and uncertainty developed in economic and ecological theory will significantly improve our explanation of why

2. There are a number of phenomena in non-market societies where consideration of the impact of risk and uncertainty would provide useful analytical elements. Among such topics that are *not* examined here are production strategies, demography and political organization. Furthermore, in keeping with the focus of this volume and the conference that spawned it, the substantive analysis is restricted to societies with foraging economies (though I see no compelling theoretical basis for restricting the general approach in this manner).

these social and ecological practices take the forms they do, and vary in the manner they do, from one time and place to another. Second, many anthropologists have criticized the use of ecological and economic models for ignoring the impact of imperfect information and subsistence risk, as well as the importance of social constraints on individual choice (see discussion in E.A. Smith 1983a). I hope to show that, to a large extent, these criticisms can be blunted without giving up the demonstrable virtues of simple, precise, and testable models anchored in general evolutionary and economic theory.

In fact, my argument is that by paying greater attention to the impact of risk and uncertainty on individual choice, one is compelled to pay explicit attention to social interaction and structural constraint. This means that two quite distinct attributes of that perennial whipping-boy, Economic Man — his omniscient focus on the Main Chance, and his Robinson Crusoe-like individualism — are dialectically linked, such that abandoning one undermines the other. Yet, as should be clear in what follows, I do not adopt the dominant stance of contemporary sociocultural anthropology in rejecting the analytical utility of general premises of economic choice and ecological adaptation, putting in their place historical indeterminacy and epistemological relativism. The model of the strategic actor that replaces Economic Man herein is humbler in information endowment and buffering abilities, and more constrained by those summed actions of others that we term 'society'; yet I contend she or he has attributes and takes actions that are illuminated in unique and powerful ways by the abstract models of evolutionary ecology and economics.

This chapter is organized as follows: the next section briefly states the central theoretical assumptions employed, and defines the main characteristics of risk and uncertainty as developed in economics and evolutionary ecology. The following section uses this theory to analyze variation in land tenure, interband visitation rights, and resource exchange as strategies of risk reduction. The final section examines the effect of uncertainty on such strategies, in particular the problems for evolutionary stability and collective provisioning of goods raised by sharing and visiting rights, and offers a reassessment of current views on these issues. Throughout the last two sections, I endeavor to bring out the commonalities and contrasts between the arguments derived from evolutionary and economic theory, and those developed for the most part independently by anthropologists; however, I caution that space and time constraints present me from offering a comprehensive or even extended review of the anthropological literature on these topics.[3]

3. Recent reviews focusing on these topics to one degree or another include Barnard (1983), Cashdan (1983; 1985), Hayden (1981), Ingold (1980), Kaplan and Hill (1985), Layton (1986), E.A. Smith (1981; 1985), Wiessner (1982), Winterhalder (1987 and in press), and Woodburn (1982a).

Evolutionary ecology, economics and risk: some general points

Central theoretical assumptions

In common with a growing body of investigations in anthropology, this chapter adopts the general theoretical orientation of evolutionary ecology in analyzing variation in human social behavior. The central (not necessarily unique) tenets of this approach can be stated rather baldly as follows:

(1) Methodological individualism. Social and ecological processes at the level of groups and populations can be analyzed most fruitfully as the result of the actions and motives of the component individuals making up these larger groupings.

(2) Optimization. Many properties (goals, attributes) of individuals can best be understood using the theory of natural selection; selection favors strategies of behavior that exhibit maximum *fitness* (replication rate) or *evolutionary stability* (cannot be outcompeted in a population of interacting strategies) relative to competing strategies.

(3) Deductive modeling. Simple, abstract models are useful tools for generating expectations with broad generality; general theory is often best constructed in a 'piecemeal' manner, by combining these simple models and empirical tests into larger sets of theories and findings.

(4) Phenotypic strategies. Most behavioral strategies, while influenced by inherited instructions (genes or culture), take the form of 'decision rules' or conditional strategies rather than being automatic, invariant actions.

Though this is not the proper place (and there is not room) to explicate and defend these principles in detail, some expansion and clarification is called for. The first tenet stated above, that of methodological individualism, may strike many readers as unproblematic, if unremarkable. It holds simply that

> all social phenomena (their structure and their change) are in principle explicable in terms of individuals — their properties, goals, and beliefs. This doctrine is not incompatible with any of the following true statements. (a) Individuals often have goals that involve the welfare of other individuals. (b) They often have beliefs about supra-individual entities that are not reducible to beliefs about individuals . . . . (c) Many properties of individuals, such as 'powerful', are irreducibly relational, so that accurate description of one individual may require reference to other individuals (Elster 1982: 453).

But even so, methodological individualism entails a set of procedures and an explanatory logic rarely followed by anthropologists, and is in fact actively resisted and disparaged.[4] The alternative view — that sociocultural variation is best explained in terms of functional consequences for supra-individual entities (communities, societies, cultures, even ecosystems) — has been the more common anthropological position, although atheoretical description or intuitive eclecticism (a bit of self-interest here, a batch of group functionalism there) is even more common.

There are two advantages to the stance of methodological individualism (in addition to the arguable advantage of being explicit and consistent about one's assumptions and procedures!). (1) Since (barring future revelations) supra-individual entities lack will or consciousness — that is, since there is no existing basis or mechanism for imbuing social change (or stasis) with its own motive power or rationality — the characteristics and dynamics of such entities must be explained in terms of the actions of conscious, individually motivated actors *or* in terms of some process of evolutionary change (which also normally requires attention to the properties of individuals). This means that explanations in terms of supra-individual function, while they may often be empirically supported, must necessarily be logically incomplete. In order to avoid spurious explanations, then, we must develop 'micro-foundations' that account for social structures and dynamics in terms of the properties and interactions of individuals (given their endowments and environmental context). (2) Adopting the stance of methodological individualism frees the anthropologist to adapt theories and models from economics and evolutionary biology (including game theory), or to invent new ones partaking of the same methodological individualist procedures. This is no panacea, but I submit that there is no comparably rich and methodologically sound source of explicit, testable theory.

To briefly anticipate some probable objections: against (1), it is often argued that methodological individualism supposes that actors always pursue their own material self-interest, but that this is belied by the

4. One currently popular rationale for rejecting methodological individualism (MI) is the charge that it reflects (and functions to support) conservative or bourgeois conceptions of the social order. Two brief comments on this: (1) While neoclassical economics is officially wedded to MI, and neoclassical economics is often used to support a conservative political agenda, bourgeois ideology *in general* does not generally involve (nor does it require) MI. Indeed, I submit that conservative political arguments more frequently hinge on a group-level functionalism, or at least on a poorly supported 'invisible hand' argument (see text, *infra*), than on MI *per se*; in any case, explicit adherence to MI can seriously undercut conservative arguments on the social value and progressive improvement resulting from unconstrained competition (for one such critique, see Hirshleifer 1982). (2) Those who assume that the class functionalism and anti-MI stance of classical Marxism is unproblematic should consult recent challenges to that stance emanating from within Marxism itself (especially Elster 1982; 1985; Roemer 1982a; 1982b). As this literature convincingly argues, the virtues of MI in providing solid explanatory 'micro-foundations' for larger patterns of historical and political process are available to all but the most dogmatic Marxists, and need not be monopolized by supporters of the bourgeois status quo.

cross-cultural evidence for altruism, ascetism, collective solidarity, and so on. To the contrary, methodological individualism by itself entails no specific assumptions about the *content* of individual goals and actions — that, indeed, is its signal lacuna, and the reason it is a methodological (rather than theoretical or empirical) element, which must be supplemented with theory that does predict something about the content of goals and actions. Both proponents and opponents of (1) frequently assume that one can move directly between individual preference and collective outcome, but this is often — perhaps usually — mistaken. Individual actions have many unintended consequences, some of which may be unperceived or (if the costs they impose fall either on someone for whom the source actor has no concern — 'externalities' — or fairly equally on the social group as a whole — 'collective bads') ignored by the source, even if harmful. Such consequences are not the goals of the actors who produce them, though they may have a considerable or even critical effect on the collectivity. More important, there are strong theoretical and empirical reasons for expecting that individual preference is often thwarted or constrained by the preferences and powers of others; as a consequence, one needs specific theoretical tools (such as game theory) to follow the often twisted path between individual intention and social outcome, though — as methodological individualism would predict — it is generally easier to follow the path from source (individual actors) to destination (social structure or process) than the reverse. Finally, against (2) it is often argued that anthropologists should not borrow theory from other fields (such as economics), and certainly not from natural sciences (such as biology); while admitting that in specific instances such borrowing can be inappropriate or even disastrous, I see no valid a priori grounds for adhering to such a prohibition.[5]

The use of optimality theory in analyzing ecological and behavioral phenomena is a complex and controversial topic, and there is a large body of literature covering theory, empirical results and critiques.[6]

5. There are two styles of argument against such interdisciplinary borrowing, one opposed in general, and the other opposed specifically to biology as a source of understanding human social behavior. The former often cautions that the donor discipline will set the agenda for the borrowing discipline (see Keene 1983). This claim, if true, is only a valid criticism if such an agenda is inferior to the existing one. In any case, it seems quite artificial to hold up a historically specific, transitory, and not necessarily rational division of contemporary Western academia as some sort of Platonic ideal or optimal arrangement; such an argument seems especially ironic when it comes (as it so often does) from Marxists or cultural determinists. The second stance, critical of biology, is in my experience usually based on a misinterpretation of what the application of evolutionary biology to humans entails. The notion that ecological models developed by biologists are necessarily 'mechanical' (Lee 1979: 434) in denying human consciousness a role, or that they focus on purely material processes and hence leave out intentionality or socially-informed motivations (Ingold, this volume), are examples of such misinterpretations, as I argue further in the text.

6. I refer the reader to the now classic papers collected in Sober (1984 — esp. Maynard Smith 1978; Gould and Lewontin 1979), the recent conference proceedings edited by Dupre

Evolutionary ecology and optimality theory have become so inter-twined in recent years (at least in analyses of behavior) that there is a danger of putting the cart before the horse, and forgetting that optimiz-ation and game theory are really just techniques — albeit powerful ones — for constructing and testing evolutionary explanations (Maynard Smith 1978). Since Darwin, natural selection has been recognized as the primary engine of evolutionary change, and hence as a critical element in any naturalistic attempt to explain the diversity of living things. Since natural selection favors variants with greatest relative fitness (replication rate), and since fitness is a correlated feature of phenotypes designed for effective survival and reproduction, it is quite understand-able that biologists should have turned to techniques such as optimality theory in order to formalize their predictions about evolutionarily successful design. But to repeat, in evolutionary explanations these techniques have no justification or theoretical status independent of this broader aim; they are means, not ends in themselves.

In evolutionary biology, an optimal strategy is the one of a set of feasible alternatives that yields the highest fitness (to its possessors) in comparison with other strategies, and is hence the one favored by natural selection acting on individual variants (though other evolution-ary forces, such as group selection or drift, can in principle override this selective advantage). An evolutionarily stable strategy (ESS) is 'unin-vadable' by alternative strategies, and is used in place of optimality whenever the fitness payoff to any strategy depends on its frequency (commonness or rarity) in the population. Put another way, optimality models are simpler, and thus preferred *if* (and only if) the payoff to any actor does not depend on what other actors in the population or social group are doing; otherwise, an ESS model is needed.

An ESS yields higher fitness relative to competing strategies when the population is at *equilibrium* (has ceased evolving with respect to the set of strategies in question); but, in contrast to simple optimality, an ESS may not be the strategy that started off with the highest fitness payoff, and the ESS equilibrium may even be a *mix* of strategies. ESS/game theory is an important tool for grasping the critical role of methodological individualism in framing explanations of social phenomena. Game theory shows us *why* we can expect that (1) some socially beneficial results will be by-products of the action of self-interested individuals (the 'invisible hand' theorem), but also why it is

(1987) and the several anthropological review articles on the topic (Foley 1985; Jochim 1983; Keene 1983; E.A. Smith 1983a; 1987; Winterhalder 1981 and in press; and J.F. Martin 1983 v. Smith and Winterhalder 1985). Almost all of the anthropological papers concern optimal foraging models, which accounts for the common misconception that all optimality theory in evolutionary ecology deals with feeding; however, I suspect that optimality and game-theoretical analyses of human mating systems, demography, and politics are destined to overtake foraging applications.

that (2) even when individuals all prefer some collective outcome, they may not be able to realize it through social interaction (the 'back of the invisible hand' theorem — Hardin 1982). (These game-theoretic insights are illustrated with ethnographic examples below.)

Optimality and ESS models provide formal techniques for analyzing the likely outcome of natural selection (or rational choice) in specific ecological and social contexts. I have discussed the rationale for employing simple, abstract models in studying complex social and ecological phenomena elsewhere (E.A. Smith 1983a), and will not repeat that discussion here. Let me simply state that while I agree that such models — and indeed any abstract representations of reality — are imperfect caricatures of actual processes, only the most radical form of empiricism would reject them on those grounds. Of course ecological models omit elements that are present in reality; a model by nature represents a hypothesis about which few of a vast array of factors are major determinants of the particular phenomena of interest. Any particular such hypothesis may be wrong, but the strategy itself is not thereby discredited. The important issue is whether the models assist us in our attempts to understand general patterns in the real world. That question cannot be answered in advance of the systematic application of such models (unless it can be shown that the models are either logically flawed, or make assumptions that lack even a rough correspondence to reality).

Finally, there is the question of the applicability of evolutionary theory to human social behavior. Out of the rather troubled sea resulting from all the ink spilled on this matter, I would pluck three points germane to this chapter. First, there is no need to see a narrow kind of genetic determinism either as being required to justify use of natural selection theory, or as following from it; both cultural inheritance and individual decisions can be given a place in the scheme (E.A. Smith 1983a; 1983b; Boyd and Richerson 1985; Durham 1988). Evolutionary ecologists do not expect that selection typically shapes the behavioral strategies of a population by acting on specific genes that link to specific behaviors; rather, the expectation is that genetic variation (and hence selection) influences behavior by modifying the expression of what are termed 'decision rules' (see Krebs 1978) or conditional strategies (Dawkins 1980). Such strategies involve (1) environmental assessment, (2) cognitive processing (which can in principle be as complex as a given creature's brain will allow) and (3) alternative courses of action chosen (either consciously or not) on the basis of the expected fitness payoffs. In effect, the models assume that selection has designed organisms to say 'If the environment or payoff matrix looks like X, then do Y'. This is a far cry from most anthropologists' notion of 'genetic determinism'. In the human case, not only is cognition extremely complex, involving what we intuitively perceive as consciousness and

intentionality, but selection and evolution act through a cultural channel that is independent in some senses from the genetic channel.[7]

Second, evolutionary arguments are necessary components of any
full account of variation in human behavior. There exists a long-
standing reluctance — understandable in the face of the distortions and
falsehoods of racism and 'social Darwinism' — to employ natural
selection explanations to account for our own behavior. In avoiding
Darwinism, social science has been able to point to two causal agents —
conscious choice and cultural inheritance — as alternative design
agents that are unique, or at least uniquely developed, in our species.
But ultimately, these both require an evolutionary underpinning:
choice must be based on preferences, and utilize cognitive machinery,
that were inherited (culturally or genetically) by the actor; and cultural
constructs are themselves subject to evolutionary change, including
natural selection (Boyd and Richerson 1985). The incompleteness of
rational choice or cultural inheritance as explanatory schemes thus
provides a justification for applying evolutionary theory, and particular
techniques such as optimization models, to human social behavior.

Third, most of the principles discussed in this chapter have clear
analogues in other fields of inquiry, including especially neoclassical
economics; what is specific to the evolutionary approach is the attention to *fitness consequences of strategic action*, rather than criteria such as
wealth or subjective utility. Much of the reaction against evolutionary
ecology within anthropology dwells on the uniqueness of human
action, but the critics frequently fail to realize that the propositions they
are arguing against are in many cases at least shared with certain
traditions in social science, and sometimes directly derived from them.
This does not make these propositions correct, of course, but it does
deflect the charge that they must be wrong because they are based on
an understanding of non-human species.

What are risk and uncertainty?

The concepts of risk and uncertainty are associated with stochastic
processes — that is, variation in outcomes that cannot be controlled by
the decision-maker. Following Knight (1921) and Hey (1979), Stephens
and Charnov (1982) have suggested the following analytical distinction

7. The question of when cultural evolution will parallel genetic evolution (but proceed at
a faster rate), and when it will follow trajectories that deviate widely from those predicted
by fitness maximization or ESS considerations, is as yet a difficult and unanswered one
(Boyd and Richerson 1985; Durham 1988; Flinn and Alexander 1982; Pulliam and Dunford
1980). Part of the procedure for answering this question should involve systematic testing of
predictions from evolutionary ecology, with no dogmatic bias for or against its applicability
to human behavior. That is the position I have taken in my own work, including this
chapter, although I personally feel that significant and lasting deviations from these
predictions probably do occur as a result of cultural evolution, and will prove important in
future analyses.

be made between risk and uncertainty: problems of risk concern the effects of stochastic variation in the outcome associated with some decision, while uncertainty refers to the lack of perfect information that afflicts decision-makers. As Stephens and Charnov recognize, in the real world many decision problems may include both risk and uncertainty; yet theory-building requires that we simplify the world in useful ways, and a separate consideration of risk and uncertainty is such a useful simplification.

Thus, whereas some decision theorists define the distinction between risk and uncertainty in terms of psychological states — does the actor have any probability estimates of the outcome, subjective or not? — the perspective adopted here (see also E.A. Smith 1983a) views this distinction in more instrumental terms. Risk then refers to the degree of stochastic variation in decision outcomes, while uncertainty refers to the stock of information that an actor has. Exactly how to define and measure risk is a matter of some controversy (see, for example, Roumasset *et al.* 1979; Hey 1981), but all technical definitions involve some measure of statistical dispersion.[8] Many decision problems may involve both risk *and* uncertainty, but problems of 'pure risk' do not necessarily indicate uncertainty on the part of the actor. Under conditions of risk, an actor may have a good notion of the probability distribution of outcomes for different choices, or may even know the outcomes with certainty, but must still deal with the fact that the value of the outcomes varies. Hence differential riskiness can affect the utility of different outcomes even when information is perfect, as long as the actor cannot use this information to eliminate risk altogether.

Economic and ecological theory leads us to expect actors to be risk-*seeking* under some conditions, but a comparable desire for increased uncertainty is not expected. Accordingly, actors may respond to risk by attempting to avoid it or to buffer it or (in certain cases) by seeking more of it; they respond to uncertainty by attempts to reduce it via collection of more information. In each case, the cost–benefit trade-off that defines the optimality problem differs: for problems of risk, the trade-off is between the mean value of an outcome and the variation in this value, and the optimum is determined by the shape of the actor's utility (or fitness) function; with uncertainty the trade-off is between the value of additional information (in raising, for example, the mean value of the outcome) and the cost of obtaining this information through search or social interaction. These basic distinctions between risk and uncertainty as I use the terms here are outlined in Table 14.1.

8. Note that an alternative definition of risk — the probability of coming home empty-handed, or more generally the probability of falling below some minimum threshold — differs from the technical meaning adopted here (cf. Winterhalder 1987: 383f.). As should become clear once the risk model has been presented, risk in the colloquial sense can be subsumed under the technical meaning, but technical risk can persist even when the payoff mean or range lies above some viability or expectation threshold.

Table 14.1: Contrasts between strategies dealing with risk and those dealing with uncertainty

	Risk	Uncertainty
Measured in units of:	'Income' variation	Information
Optimal strategies maximize expected value of outcome?	No	Often yes
Can actors ever benefit from increased levels?	Yes	No
Adaptive response:	Avoid, buffer, or seek out	Reduce via collection of information
Effect of complete information:	Possibly none (risk may persist)	Uncertainty eliminated or greatly reduced
Optimality trade-off:	Mean v. variation in income	Benefits of information v. cost of obtaining

In the following two sections I consider how economic and ecological theories that incorporate the concepts of risk and uncertainty and employ evolutionary game theory can be used to explain variation in hunter-gatherer social behavior involving land tenure and property rights, exchange of resources, and closely related aspects of social relations. While all these topics have concerned anthropologists for some time, they have rarely been considered within the unifying perspective of decision-making (or selection) under conditions of risk and uncertainty.[9]

Environmental risk and resource-sharing

Risk and sharing

Foraging is often an inherently risky and uncertain proposition: risky because for many resources (especially large game) capture often eludes the forager, and because when it is successful there may be a temporary glut; uncertain because the location, abundance, ripeness,

9. The work of Wiessner (1977; 1982) and Cas'.dan (1985) is notable in its systematic attention to the impact of risk on the social behavior of foragers. While inspired by their work, I have adopted my theoretical framework from evolutionary ecology and ESS/game theory, in contrast to Wiessner and Cashdan, who employ economic insurance theory. The resulting convergences as well as divergences are a matter not taken up directly here.

or behavior of the resource may be unpredictable over the short or long term. Dealing only with risk, we can ask how any actor might in fact reduce risk from variable foraging outcomes. There would appear to be five distinct (but not mutually exclusive) options: (1) alter foraging practices (for example, select less risky prey); (2) store resources on good days and consume these stores on bad days; (3) exchange some portion of resources for durable goods and exchange the goods for resources at some future time, in a manner similar to (2); (4) pool resource harvests with a sharing network prior to consumption; and (5) move to a locale with either lower variance in foraging returns, or a higher mean return. All of these options are ethnographically described for hunter-gatherers, often in simultaneous combinations, although (1) is harder to demonstrate and is less likely to be important on theoretical grounds (Winterhalder 1987); here, I am primarily interested in (4) and (5), but will touch on (3) at relevant points.[10]

Following standard practice, I refer to option (4) — engaging in reciprocal resource transfers through pooling and redistribution of individual harvests — as 'sharing'. The degree to which hunter-gatherers engage in sharing of food and other resources has long been noted (see, for example, Marshall 1961; Sahlins 1968), and the notion that hunter-gatherer economies are generous, sharing economies has become part of the conventional anthropological wisdom. Various explanations for this observation have been advanced. Some of these, such as the argument that foragers possess an ethic of 'generalized reciprocity', focus on the psychological or moral significance of sharing practices; these strike me as tautological, or at least highly limited in explanatory power. Others, such as the suggestion that sharing rules are a 'leveling device' impelled by an egalitarian ideology, draw attention to the political mechanisms by which sharing is maintained, but do not address the ultimate causes of sharing *per se* (nor of the egalitarian ideology that enforces it, for that matter).[11]

10. For discussion of the conditions favoring one option over another, see Wiessner (1977), Binford (1980), Cashdan (1985), Ingold (1983), Kaplan and Hill (1985) and Winterhalder (1987). To those who might think that storage is invariably an effective means of risk reduction, thus calling into question the basis for my argument concerning sharing as a means of risk reduction, let us remember that storage entails a number of costs that need to be subtracted from its benefits. These include the labor costs of effective preservation (which vary according to the type of resource, environment — for example, temperature and humidity — and technology, see Binford 1980), the costs of defending stores against thievery or forceful seizure, and the potential cost of reduced mobility which can tie foragers to their stores rather than releasing them for possibly more efficient foraging opportunities elsewhere. I do not doubt that these costs are often less than the benefits of storage, or even that the net benefits of storage often exceed those of alternatives, but the costs do need to be kept in mind, and may account for the existence of alternative, more social forms of risk reduction (such as sharing, exchange, and mobility) despite their enforcement costs.

11. I want to make myself perfectly clear here, as the original passage in the 'conference version' of this chapter was overstated, and occasioned some criticism. I do not deny that many foragers (but certainly not all — see Gould, 1982, for example) possess an ethic of widespread, if not quite 'generalized', reciprocity. But to point to such an ethic is not to

Even more common and long-standing in anthropology is the view that sharing among hunter-gatherers is an adaptation to periodic scarcity, a form of 'collective insurance against natural fluctuations' in both productive ability and available resources (Ingold 1980: 144; see also Dowling 1968; Lee 1968; Woodburn 1972; Yellen and Harpending 1972; and others). Ingold's (1980: 145) summary of the received view is exemplary: 'Were each hunter to produce only for his own domestic needs, everyone would eventually perish from hunger. . . . Thus, through its contribution to the survival and reproduction of potential producers, sharing ensures the perpetuation of society as a whole'. I will refer to this argument as 'the received view'. We are now ready to consider the contribution formal theory from evolutionary ecology can make to understanding hunter-gatherer sharing practices.

A simple model of risk

As noted above, the concept of risk is associated with stochastic variation in the outcome of some choice or action. But this variance can only have psychological or material significance — can only, in a sense, *become* risk — if there is a nonlinear relationship between the material outcome itself and the value of the outcome (measured psychologically in terms of subjective utility for economic analyses, or in terms of fitness consequences for evolutionary analyses). More specifically, when the nonlinear function relating outcome and value is accelerating (curves upwards), the actor should be risk-seeking (gaining greater utility or fitness from outcomes with greater variance, all else being equal); if the function is decelerating (curves downwards), we expect risk-averse preferences (see Figure 14.1).[12]

While most of the ecological work on risk has focused on production

---

explain its existence, nor the sharing behavior it may help motivate. In other words, such an ethic — like any culturally transmitted value or belief — is but one (intermediate) element in a longer causal chain. On the matter of 'leveling devices', as has been pointed out by others (notably Cashdan 1980), this view fails to explain variation in extent of sharing, or the rise and eventual dominance of nonegalitarian, nonreciprocal social formations. In some cases, it also tends to rely on a functionalist or social-teleological point of view. Again, I do not deny that such mechanisms exist — indeed, I give them a prominent role in my discussion of 'enforcement' (*infra*) — only that their identification provides a sufficient explanation for the existence of sharing practices.

12. The general theory of risk preference was first developed by Bernoulli, and then formalized by von Neumann and Morgenstern (1944). Application to ecological and evolutionary contexts can be found in Schaffer (1978), Caraco (1980), Real (1981), Rubinstein (1982) and Stephens and Charnov (1982). In adapting this concept to problems in evolutionary ecology, biologists have generally substituted the notion of 'fitness' for that of utility, with the proviso that natural selection designs organisms to respond to risky situations in a manner that maximizes their expected fitness. Since the actual psychological mechanisms that individuals use in making decisions may best be captured by some proximate goal equivalent to the economist's concept of utility, the necessary presumption in all of this is that there is a strong positive association between fitness and utility — something that is easy to assume, but hard to demonstrate as of yet.

Figure 14.1: A risk reduction model of resource-sharing

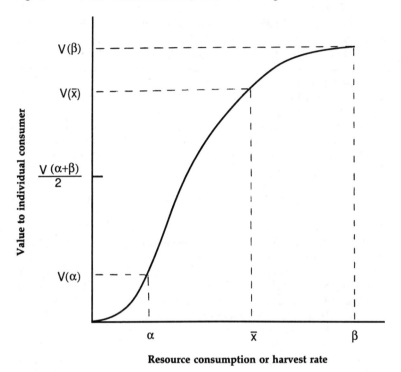

Resource consumption or harvest rate

Note: For any actor, the rate of resource harvest is assumed to be a random variable with a symmetric distribution whose mean is $\bar{x}$ and whose range (or standard deviation) is from α to β. With a diminishing marginal value curve (see text), those actors who pool their resources and then consume equal shares will realize a higher and more certain value, equal to $V(\bar{x})$, than those who consume their own resources at the stochastic rate determined by the harvest rate distribution, whose expected value equals $V(\alpha + \beta)/2$. For an accelerating value function (e.g., below the inflection point on the sigmoid curve shown here), the converse results hold (see text).

or consumption decisions of individual foragers — which prey types to harvest, which patches to utilize, and so on — some attention has been given to the effect of risk preference on social interaction. One case in point involves the role of risk in favoring systems of reciprocal exchange. The first formal treatment of this problem is that of Schaffer (1978). The essential features of the model are these (E.A. Smith 1987; see, for similar treatments, Rubenstein 1982; Kaplan and Hill 1985; Winterhalder 1987):

(1) A set of actors (two or more), who are at least sporadically in contact with each other, independently obtain resources (income)

which they can either consume individually or share to some degree.

(2) Each actor is subject to stochastic variation in rates of resource income, measured over some relevant period (such as a day).

(3) This variation is to some degree unsynchronized between actors (that is, the interactor correlation in resource income during each time period is less than unity).

(4) For any actor, the marginal value of resources consumed over the relevant period exhibits diminishing returns, at least over some frequently-realized portion of the fitness or utility function.[13]

(5) Actors seek to maximize the total expected value (utility or fitness) obtained from consumption, over the long run.

With these assumptions, the classical results of risk theory apply (Figure 14.1). Specifically, actors should be risk-averse (this maximizes expected value), and will even pay some premium (for example, in lower mean income) to obtain the benefits of reduced risk.[14]

Clearly, the risk model presented above can be viewed as a formalization of the received view that hunter-gatherers share food in order to even out fluctuations in their food supply and avoid the threat of starvation. But there are two primary ways in which theory from evolutionary ecology can be employed to modify or add to the received view. First, the formal risk model provides a general theoretical framework for predicting the advantages and disadvantages of sharing — in other words, a means of explaining the degree of variation in sharing from time to time and place to place, even from resource to resource; and it does so in a manner that is subject to quantitative (and hence more exacting and powerful) empirical test. Second, evolutionary game

13. This is perhaps the most difficult assumption in the list to verify. But I believe it plausibly applies to most hunter-gatherers, and indeed to people everywhere much of the time. Stated baldly, it assumes that the more one has of most things, the less pleasure or benefit one derives from additional amounts. In slightly more cautious language, the assumption states that the use-value of any material resource will decline at the margin, such that past some point each additional unit of resource will be 'worth' less and less to the consumer, where 'worth' is measured in terms of satisfaction (psychological utility) or effect on fitness (relative ability to survive and reproduce). This may not be true of certain non-material resources (such as religious knowledge or political prestige), and it may not apply to certain roles in a capitalist economy (for example, profit-maximizing firms), but I submit it is the most reasonable assumption we can make for the use-values of resources, such as food, raw materials and water, with which I am concerned in this chapter. At the same time, the general risk model allows for the opposite assumption — that marginal value accelerates, as in the lower-left segment of Figure 14.1 — and, as noted in the text and caption, predicts risk-seeking preferences in that case. Again, this is plausible for many use-values at the *lowest* consumption rates: the first few grams/hour of food consumed by a starving man, or liters/hour of water by a dehydrated woman, for example, will make much higher contributions to their utility and fitness than will higher and higher rates of consumption.

14. Specifically, actors should be willing to pay any amount less than $[V(x)]-[V(\propto+\beta)/2]$, which is equal to the difference in value (utility or fitness) between risk-free consumption rate and the mean risky consumption rate (E.A. Smith 1987: 238, n. 11).

theory specifies the additional conditions required for sharing to be perpetuated in a social group, and points to the possible evolutionary rationale for such phenomena as the egalitarian ethos, the conflict and bickering that sometimes surround resource distribution, the 'demand sharing' noted by N. Peterson (1986), and gift-exchange or other conventions structuring sharing alliances. In doing so, it rejects the social functionalism or teleology implicit in the second sentence of Ingold's summary, and in similar accounts that point to survival of the social group as the function of sharing practices.

On the first point, the ethnographic record reveals clearly that there is considerable variation in the degree of sharing and reciprocity from one hunter-gatherer society to another, and even from one type of resource to another within these societies (E.A. Smith 1981; Hayden 1981; Gould 1982). Some of this variation may be due to ecological causes (variation in characteristics of the resources or the way in which they are harvested), and some may be due to political factors (differences in the ways in which decisions and agreements are reached and enforced). This suggests that we should continue to search for the root causes of variation in reciprocity and sharing in the *interaction* between ecological context and political process. In any case, successful explanation of the why and when of sharing practices cannot ignore variation, but instead needs to account for it.

The risk model suggests the following ecological determinants of variation in the costs and benefits of sharing: (1) degree of variation in foraging success (some resources, such as game, are more likely to exhibit high degrees of stochasticity in yield); (2) package size and perishability (large values of either increase the marginal decline in the value of solitary consumption); (3) degree of interforager correlation in harvest success (Winterhalder 1987), which in turn is affected by such factors as environmental patchiness and foraging group size. In the simplest case, where each actor has the same expected income rate and returns to the same central location during each period (for example, to camp), and where the correlation in foraging success between foragers is low (zero or negative), direct pooling and equal sharing of the pooled catch may be very effective in reducing risk (Winterhalder 1987). It should be quite feasible to obtain sufficient data on these factors in order to test the explanatory force of the risk-reduction hypothesis of sharing in any given case. Kaplan and Hill (1985) provide the only rigorous test of what they call the 'variance reduction' hypothesis yet published (see also Hames n.d.). They show that among Ache foragers in Paraguay, riskier resources (those with greater package size and higher variance in availability across family units) are shared to a significantly greater extent, and that such sharing increases the nutritional well-being of most band members (though not equally).

It is also worth stressing that the risk model (Figure 14.1) also predicts that when resource income is very low, actors will be risk-seeking and avoid sharing (see note 8 above); this prediction is especially strong when expected resource income is below the minimum required to sustain life (Stephens and Charnov 1982). Hence, the model predicts the conditions under which sharing should diminish or cease even when resource income is variable and times are hard; this is not something the received view can accommodate, let alone explain, at all.[15]

The sharer's dilemma

The simple risk-reduction argument for sharing sketched above fails to consider any *cost* to sharing. But presumably sharing practices exact costs of various sorts, including both 'maintenance' costs (such as transporting resources to a central place, living in larger groups, and so on) and 'enforcement' costs (to prevent or reduce failure to reciprocate on the part of past recipients of one's aid). Leaving aside maintenance costs, which are comparatively straightforward (though not unimportant), let us consider enforcement costs, and take up the second component in our reevaluation of the received view of sharing. Assuming that ecological conditions are such that a system of sharing will reduce risk, what additional conditions are required to ensure that it will arise and persist? This takes us into the realm of politics; here, game theory is a most useful tool (see also Kaplan and Hill 1985; E.A. Smith 1985).

In simplest form, the payoff matrix for the sharing game might look as follows[16]:

15. Further discussion of the logic of risk-seeking preferences can be found in E.A. Smith (1983a), as well as in the references listed in note 12 (above). I am familiar with ethnographic evidence from the North American Arctic that supports the prediction of diminution or cessation of sharing during times of extreme scarcity (for example, Graburn 1969: 37f., 73f.; Riches 1982: 71f.), but have not made a systematic search of ethnographies from other areas. Ingold (1980: 149ff.) argues against such a claim, but I find his evidence quite incomplete or even irrelevant (for example, prevalence of domestic cannibalism over extra-domestic forms may simply reflect opportunity, especially if other households have dispersed, or it may reflect fear of revenge from non-kin; it certainly does not in itself indicate that extra-household sharing persists). Ingold's more general argument that sharing will peak in times of 'famine' and 'plenty' — given in a diagram (ibid.: 147) as well as the text — seems to conflate the benefits of information sharing and cooperative search when a mobile concentrated resource (such as caribou) is hard to locate (Wilmsen 1973; E.A. Smith 1981: 43f.; Heffley 1981) with those of food sharing *per se*. It also demonstrates the pitfalls that face analyses innocent of methodological individualism: for if 'famine' or 'plenty' apply indiscriminately to the condition of the social group, then there is no motivation for sharing, which requires interindividual *differences* (some individuals facing 'famine', others facing 'plenty' at a given point in time) in order for anyone to benefit from it.

16. By convention, payoffs are simply rank-ordered from highest (4) to lowest (1); those in the upper left of each cell apply to the row player (whose play is given on the left side of the matrix), while those in the lower right of each cell apply to the column player (at the top of the matrix). In the present matrix, the payoffs to row and column are symmetrical, but this is not a general requirement of the method.

	Share	Hoard
Share	3 / 3	1 / 4
Hoard	4 / 1	2 / 2

The rank ordering for the matrix is based on two assumptions: (1) the net benefits (in risk reduction) if both actors share are greater than the net benefits of hoarding; (2) unilateral hoarding (the 'free-rider' option) provides all benefits and no costs, while unilateral sharing (the 'altruist' option) provides all costs and no benefits.[17] The first assumption is derived directly from the risk model (Figure 14.1), while the second assumption can be restated colloquially as follows: most individuals would rather get something (their share of another's catch) for nothing (hoarding their share, at least within their household), all else being equal (specifically, if there are no costly sanctions — short- or long-term — that will be imposed for such selfish behavior). The second assumption is bound to disturb many anthropologists — I confess it bothers me. Yet notions of selfless hunter-gatherers who share even when they could get away with hoarding are in conflict with ethnographic data too numerous to cite here (some examples are given in N. Peterson 1986), as well as violating general expectations from evolutionary theory. If strict self-interest is unlikely to be universal and unyielding, generalized altruism is even less plausible.

Setting such arguments aside, we are faced with the finding that our exercise in game theory predicts it will never pay to share! If the other actor is altruistic or foolish enough to share, one wins the maximum payoff from hoarding, whereas if the other actor is equally selfish, hoarding pays worse, but still better than sharing. This result demonstrates the danger of functionalist thinking — just because it would be beneficial to society as a whole (less abstractly, to the sum total members of a society) to cooperate, this does not mean that self-interested actors will do so; and those that are optimistic enough to try it are vulnerable to victimization by the unscrupulous. Even if we posit an initial starting point of a society of sharers, the introduction of just one hoarder may eventually upset the applecart. If based on rational choice, the sharing strategy will see its gains eroded by hoarding, and its

17. NB: for both assumptions, 'benefits' and 'costs' refer to those received by the single actor adopting the strategy referred to, *not* to the joint or average benefits and costs.

practitioners will be tempted to switch; if based on cultural inheritance, the sharing strategy will dwindle (less resources to convert into offspring who follow the sharing ethic) and natural selection will eventually ensure that the hoarding strategy inherits the earth — unless checked by some other factor.

The sharing matrix given above is in fact an example of the classic game matrix known as the 'prisoner's dilemma' (PD). The PD payoff structure is widely viewed as the worm in the apple of social cooperation. But the pessimism generated by such a view may be unwarranted. The PD matrix is based on a game where the players interact only once, or if more than once then at random without memory; hence there is no opportunity for cooperation and reciprocity to pay. Once the sharing game is domesticated by allowing for (1) repeated interaction, (2) memory of past interactions, and (3) sanctions against unilateral selfishness by future selective refusal to share with such 'cheaters', the outcome can be quite different. Such an 'iterated PD' or 'PD supergame' may lead to a stable population of cooperators, with a few selfish cheaters thrown in but held in check by the force of frequent sanctions (Trivers 1971; Taylor 1976, 1987; Axelrod and Hamilton 1981; Kaplan and Hill 1985). In the present case, one obvious sanction involves suffering the effects of being denied a share of the collective pot.

This discussion of the sharing game, simplistic as it is, serves an important role in sharpening our thinking about the collective provisioning of a 'public good' such as generalized reciprocity. Two important conclusions suggest themselves: (1) truly generalized reciprocity (that is, altruistic or indiscriminate sharing) is unstable and will be undermined by free-riding, *even when it provides the greatest good for the greatest number*; (2) the existence of collective goods is therefore dependent on a system of monitoring, ongoing expectation of reciprocity, and costly sanctions against free-riders. The first point, if empirically verified, underlines the need for methodological individualism in explaining social phenomena (such as sharing), and further challenges the persistent group-level functionalism that views sharing (among other phenomena) as a means to ensure societal reproduction or to maximize or optimize population density.[18]

The second point stimulates the search for the socio-political mechanisms hunter-gatherers might employ to restrict sharing to those who are likely to reciprocate, and to detect and punish free-riders who would take unfair advantage of the ethic of generosity. While ethnogra-

18. Examples are numerous, but include Piddocke (1965) on North-west Coast Indians, Sahlins (1974) on the (reformed) domestic mode of production, and Spielman (1986) on exchange between egalitarian societies as a means to ensure survival and maximum population density. In each case, the functionalist error lies in assuming that a result — collective benefits widely or evenly shared — is a sufficient explanation for the individual actions that are the proximate cause of those benefits (for a general discussion of functionalism, see the superb treatment of Elster 1982; 1983, chap. 2).

phies are full of anecdotal examples of such mechanisms, only Wiessner (1977), to my knowledge, has given us a detailed and convincing set of data bearing on this matter. Briefly, her work shows that, among the !Kung — those supposed archetypes of generalized reciprocity — sharing of certain resources is hardly generalized or automatic, even among kin; instead, sharing partners are carefully selected, cultivated, and monitored, and failure to reciprocate when capable is cause for termination of the sharing bond.[19] However, Wiessner's data bear only on sharing of non-food items, and hence leave the question of the adequacy of the game-theoretical analysis of hunter-gatherer food sharing unanswered for now, even for the !Kung.

Sharing between bands

As noted above, two important variables determining the advantages of sharing (that is, of pooling risk) are the degree of risk experienced by each actor (expressed by the daily variance in food harvest) and the degree of asynchrony in resource income between actors. How might these variables relate to intra-band versus inter-band sharing? Whereas short-term asynchrony may be common among the members of a single local band, prolonged asynchrony, with more marked fitness effects, may often be much greater between members of *different* bands. That is, within a given region, the asynchrony of foraging success over a period of several days or weeks should often increase as the *distance* between any two individuals sampled increases. I expect this to be so because of such factors as patchy rainfall, movement of game, and stable habitat differences in seasonal production or resource availability. Increasing asynchrony as a function of distance implies that risk reduction through sharing should be greatest if conducted over longer distances. Yet the costs of such sharing, especially transport cost, should also increase with distance, particularly under the conditions of low population density and foot transport characteristic of many hunter-gatherers. This means that risk reduction through sharing of resources may often be most costly precisely where it would be most effective — between rather than within local hunter-gatherer bands.[20]

19. Four central findings emerge from Wiessner's work: (1) sharing networks are formed from dyadic components — the relationships between pairs of individuals are the fundamental units; this makes the two-person game, as opposed to a more complicated *n*-person game, a reasonably appropriate model; (2) individuals choose their partners in a way that will ensure ties to diverse natural and social resources; close kin with meagre or redundant resources may be passed over in favor of more usefully situated individuals; (3) *hxaro* — a form of conventionalized sharing — provides a continual check on partners' willingness to reciprocate, hence on the ongoing reliability of reciprocity bonds that may only occasionally be activated for major support, in times of critical need; (4) failure to reciprocate either at conventional (*hxaro*) or critical levels is cause for breaking of ties, and also leads to gossip and reluctance on the part of others to share resources with the unreciprocating individual.
20. Analytical (Winterhalder 1987) and empirical (Hill and Hawkes 1983) results indicate

Under these conditions, there would be a potential selective advantage to the development of some means of reducing risk other than interband resource transfers. Put another way, many hunter-gatherers — even those living in a region characterized by fluctuations in resource availability that decrease in synchrony as a function of distance — may find long-distance (interband) sharing too costly (in transport time and effort) in relation to its benefits (of risk reduction). The obvious alternatives are (1) local storage, and (2) movement of *people* (rather than goods) between local groups.[21] These each have their own costs and advantages, of course (for those of storage, see note 10 above). The second alternative — moving foragers between groups — is the one that concerns me here. Ethnographers have often remarked on the extensive visiting and frequent residential shifts noted among band societies, and a number have suggested that this characteristic of fluid local-group composition can be explained as an adaptation to equalize the consumer/resource ratio in situations where local resource availability fluctuates markedly and asynchronously (see Lee 1972; Yellen and Harpending 1972). In such a formulation, an extensive network of kin ties and other alliances combined with a communitarian attitude serves to ensure that all have equal and undivided access to the land and its fruits.

Again, the risk model can be used to formalize the received view, with the advantage of making it subject to greater logical and empirical examination. (It also allows one to formulate an explanation for the *absence* or underdevelopment of mobility between bands in situations where variance in resource harvest is low, and/or synchrony in harvest

---

that pooling of the harvest by a surprisingly small number of individuals will be effective in reducing risk at the level of the local band. This finding might appear to suggest that any further sharing between bands, such as discussed here, would be of little value. However, I do not think this necessarily follows, given the expanded temporal and spatial scale I envision with interband sharing. The diminishing returns to sharing *within* the band reflect the effects of sampling from a single population of foraging outcomes, on a daily basis. If, as assumed here, both the difference in mean foraging success and the asynchrony in outcome is greater for members of different bands than for those of the same band, especially when measured over periods longer than a day, interband sharing might still markedly reduce risk even after the benefits of sharing within each band had been exhausted.

21. A third alternative would be to amalgamate local groups at a large, centralized camp that could sample (forage over) an area extensive enough to include the necessary range of resource fluctuations, and then pool the catch (or at least information on resource locations) at the central place. This might be a viable hypothesis to explain the occurrence of large camps at certain seasons (such as the winter-sealing villages of Inuit [E.A. Smith 1984b: 78f]) or the settlement pattern of Caribou-eater Chipewyan (J.G.E. Smith 1978; Sharp 1977; Heffley 1981), but this strategy quickly runs into the same cost problems discussed for interband sharing. As band size and foraging radius expand to map onto more asynchronous resource patches, the mean cost of traveling to resource patches and bringing resources back to camp rises at an increasing rate (for example, because those foragers ranging farthest afield must stay overnight or longer, or can only carry back a portion of their catch). Hence this alternative should face approximately the same constraints as a strategy of interband sharing, and reach its adaptive limits almost as quickly under conditions of low population density and foot transport.

is high.) Specifically, the model predicts that systems of recipro al access to local foraging areas by members of different local bands would reduce risk under the following set of circumstances:

(1) diminishing marginal fitness to increased resource harvest over at least some portion of the fitness function;
(2) fluctuations in local resource availability substantial enough to make the benefits of risk aversion outweigh relocation costs;
(3) asynchrony (low temporal correlation) between local areas in such fluctuations, resulting in frequent reversals in their ranking by per capita resource availability;
(4) relatively high transport costs (for example, due to low population density and reliance on foot transport);
(5) relatively high storage costs (direct processing costs, indirect costs of defense, and/or opportunity costs for reduced seasonal mobility).

From the perspective adopted here (evolutionary ecology and methodological individualism), however, this kind of account appears rather naive. For while the preceding list may be sufficient to define the techno-environmental constraints favoring systems of reciprocal access between members of local bands, we need to consider social constraints as well. (Indeed, if individuals and groups always cooperated to achieve mutually beneficial goals, our task of explaining social behavior would be much simpler than it is![22])

My basic point is that, even if we can show that communal or reciprocal access would benefit individuals by reducing risk, it does not necessarily follow that such a system of land tenure will evolve or persist. As with resource-sharing within a band, reciprocal access between bands raises issues of monitoring and enforcing reciprocity, and of avoiding the material and evolutionary costs of indiscriminate altruism; it also raises some new issues involving the coordination of two sets of foragers. In particular, I suggest we need to pay attention to the costs to members of the host group of allowing visitors access to the local foraging area. The two main costs I want to consider are: (1) the potential cost that visitors who are allowed access to resources will not reciprocate, and hence of the necessity to maintain controls against possible cheating; and (2) the effects of visitor-foraging on host-foraging efficiency. In the following section, I argue that these problems can be illuminated by viewing them in terms of uncertainty and

22. A parallel form of naive functionalism has been prominent in explaining resource transfer between local groups among densely populated hunter-gatherers (see Piddocke 1965; M. Harris 1974). In this case as well, the analytical task is not just to show that such resource transfers would be beneficial, but that they would not be subject to the forms of cheating and evolutionary instability that often plague the provision of collective goods (see note 18).

information, and by employing the strategic logic of evolutionary game theory.

Uncertainty and reciprocal access

Land tenure diversity

The 'undivided access' view of hunter-gatherer land tenure presumes that there are no social barriers to resource utilization throughout a region — in effect, that the region is one vast commons. As discussed below, there are ethnographic examples approximating such a system. But there is also abundant ethnographic evidence that different systems of land tenure commonly occurred among hunter-gatherers, even among those meeting the usual requirements of 'egalitarian' or 'band society'. Yet the anthropological literature reveals a persistent tendency to deny the diversity of hunter-gatherer systems of land tenure, and a repeated insistence that communal ownership, or indeed absence of ownership, is not only widespread but of the essence for hunter-gatherers.[23] An excellent example is provided by Ingold's (1980: 161) unqualified statement — apparently arrived at through deduction rather than induction — that 'the hunting economy is based on the principle of undivided access to productive resources, including both the land and its fauna'.[24]

One alternative approach that allows for diversity in hunter-gatherer land tenure focuses on the ecological factors affecting the 'economic defendability' (J. Brown 1964) of different resources, and attempts to predict the presence or absence of territoriality in terms of the spatio-temporal *density* and *predictability* of key resources (Dyson-Hudson and Smith 1978; Richardson 1982). In this view, territorial exclusion is expected whenever resource density and predictability is sufficient to make the benefits of exclusive use outweigh the costs of defense.[25]

23. In the past, the opposing normative view — that hunter-gatherers were mostly or universally territorial — also had wide currency, and practised a similar denial of the ethnographic reality of alternative systems, such as communal tenure: see Dyson-Hudson and Smith (1978: 21) and M.K. Martin (1974) for summaries of and references to this literature. Perhaps because of repeated demonstrations that claims of territoriality or private land ownership were often based on faulty readings of the ethnographic data, many anthropologists came to believe that no such systems existed aboriginally, and that therefore all hunter-gatherers had fluid systems of land tenure *on the ground*, despite what they might appear to have as expressed in native ideology or ethnographic misinterpretation.

24. Exceptions to this portrait that are blatant enough, such as cases of explicit territorial boundaries and violent defense of same, have often been seen as pertaining only to societies with high population density, greater socioeconomic complexity, and low mobility — in a word, not band societies at all (see Fried 1967; Leacock 1982).

25. A conceptually similar idea is expressed in Blurton Jones's (1984) model of resource transfer as a form of 'tolerated theft' (see also Maynard Smith and Parker 1976; Moore 1984). Here, individuals may allow others to have some resources that are already harvested if the cost of defending them is higher than the benefit of exclusive use. According to Blurton Jones, one way this could arise is under conditions of diminishing marginal value of

Conversely, since relatively scarce and unpredictable resources do not 'pay' for territorial defense, foragers under these conditions are expected to treat land and unimproved resources more or less as a commons.

The economic defendability model has the virtue of testability (as shown in the animal ecology literature, reviewed in Davies and Houston 1984), and for hunter-gatherers it seems neatly to explain why territorial systems are found primarily in areas with high population density, since this indicates both lower defense costs for monitoring a territory and (under a Malthusian view of population equilibrium) a denser resource base. However, there are some problems with the model. First, in terms of the territorial cases, the model does not specify how local-group territories — a collective good — could result from the action of self-interested individuals. Second, hunter-gatherer societies lacking explicit territorial ownership rarely seem to treat local foraging areas as a commons. Rather, in such societies local groups frequently have ideologies of land ownership and attempt to control access to the resources surrounding them. These controls generally involve requirements that visitors gain permission to use the resources in a local area from the 'owners' of these resources. Because of these sorts of observations, it has been alleged that some degree of territoriality is ubiquitous among hunter-gatherers (N. Peterson 1975; 1979).

In retrospect, the economic defendability model is too restricted in scope to capture the diversity found in hunter-gatherer systems of land tenure. Part of the problem here lies in that model's failure to deal explicitly with the political mechanisms governing access to land. Although there is insufficient room to develop the conceptual scheme or review the ethnographic data fully here, let me outline a framework for describing variation in hunter-gatherer land tenure. Briefly, I suggest we view this as forming a continuum punctuated by the following ideal types:

(1)	(2)	(3)	(4)	(5)
COMMONS—	RECIPROCAL ACCESS —	TERRITORIALITY——	PRIVATE PROPERTY	
(common property)	(communal property)	(local-group ownership)	(kin-group owner-ship)	(individual ownership)

In system (1), land is treated as a commons and there is no enforce-

---

resource consumption (for example, as given in Figure 14.1). If intruders have less resources than residents (are lower on the fitness function), they should be willing to incur a higher marginal cost in contesting additional resources than the residents would be willing to incur in defending them. The equilibrium resource division equalizes the marginal net benefits to the contestants. As in the economic defendability model, no reciprocity is implied.

able control over access or over unharvested resources (though in fact there may be coordination of land use and resource harvests, reached by consensus — see below). Among others, some western Shoshone (Steward 1938), the Hadza (Woodburn 1972), and some Batek (K. Endicott 1988) approximate this ideal type. System (2), as noted above, is widespread, and is particularly well described for Australian societies and Kalahari San.[26] Two features of system (2) are of central interest here: reciprocal access between members of land-owning groups is highly developed; and transfer membership, which grants property rights, is relatively easily negotiated. In contrast, system (3), while exercising a form of communal property ownership quite similar to (2), is characterized by much stronger controls on local-group membership, and a corresponding reduction in reciprocal access as well. The north-west Alaskan Inupiat Eskimo case described by Burch (1980; 1988) approximates this ideal type. Systems (4) and (5) both involve private ownership by well-defined subsets of a local group; reciprocal access may be present to some degree, perhaps comparable to system (3). Examples of (4), involving kin-group ownership of land and un-harvested resources, are particularly well known for certain North-west Coast Indians (review in Richardson 1982), while individual ownership of unharvested resources is described for a number of Californian Indian groups (see Gould 1982).

Again, I want to emphasize that I view hunter-gatherer land-tenure systems as lying along a continuum, and the labeling of types and enumeration of their characteristics is heuristic rather than typological in intent. An additional caveat is that particular societies may well exhibit a *mix* of these systems, with different resources or sections of land falling at different points along the property–rights continuum.[27]

Let us return to system (2) — communal ownership with reciprocal access — and the failure of the economic defendability model to address it. Focusing on this latter problem, Cashdan (1983) has recently argued that social controls implied in this system bring the explanatory adequacy of the economic defendability model into question. Specifi-cally, she argues that evidence from four regional populations of San hunter-gatherers indicates that the greater the unpredictability of re-sources, the tighter are the social controls on visitor access to local

---

26. For Australians, see Myers (1982) on Pintupi, N. Williams (1982) on Yolngu, Altman and Peterson (1988) on Arnhem Landers, and N. Peterson (1975; 1979) on Western Desert Aborigines; for Kalahari San, see Lee (1972; 1979), Wiessner (1977; 1982), Barnard (1979), and Cashdan (1983).

27. The frequent occurrence in Australia of system (1) or (2) with respect to subsistence resources and harvesting sites, but system (3) or (4) with respect to sacred localities, may be a good example. A mixed system is equally possible for subsistence resources alone (Dyson-Hudson and Smith 1978: 33ff.). For example, among the Owens Valley Paiute, Steward (1938; 1955) reports a division of land into local-group territories, reflecting a system (3) for gathering purposes, but a rule allowing pursuit of game across boundaries reflecting a system (1) commons.

resources. Following Peterson (1975), Cashdan terms these controls 'social boundary defense', and contrasts this with what she terms 'perimeter defence' or what I would prefer to call 'spatial defense', the form of territoriality treated in the economic defendability model.[28] She concludes that whereas the economic defendability model may be a valid explanation for systems of perimeter defense, it fails to explain the occurrence of territorial systems that employ social boundary defense because it ignores the information-sharing capabilities of human beings, and the need to manage access to resources even when these are scarce and unpredictable.

It seems to me that there are two issues here, one semantic and the other analytic (E.A. Smith 1983c). The primarily semantic issue — that is, whether it is confusing or not to lump spatial defense and social boundary defense under the same category of 'territoriality' — can be set aside here (but see note 28 below). The more important claim that spatial defense and social boundary defense are functional equivalents, in the sense of realizing the same adaptive ends in controlling access to local resources, deserves further examination.

Uncertainty and reciprocal access

In a system of spatial defense, residents find the benefit of exclusive use sufficient to justify the costs of excluding competitors. There is no reciprocity between residents and outsiders (though with cooperative spatial defense — that is, group territoriality — there is reciprocity *within* the group, a problem not analyzed here). In denying others access to one's resources, one clearly reduces the incentive for those others to provide one with access to any resources they may control.[29] In contrast, hunter-gatherers who practice social boundary defense characteristically *do* allow outsiders access, but *only* after they have asked permission. Evidence from a number of groups, including that discussed by Cashdan for the San, indicates that this permission is

28. The term 'perimeter defense', employed by Cashdan but not by Dyson-Hudson and Smith, is somewhat misleading. The definition of 'territoriality' adopted by the latter is 'an area occupied more or less exclusively by an animal or group of animals by means of repulsion through overt defense or advertisement' (E.O. Wilson 1975: 256). The existence of well-defined boundaries is implied but not really required; but defense of the *perimeter* itself is certainly neither implied nor required. Thus, for example, the case described by Burch (1988) involving territorial defense but not perimeter defense, qualifies as territorial by the above definition, even though in Cashdan's terminology it would be called a perimeter defense system to distinguish it from a system of social boundary defense.

29. As noted earlier in the text, I am aware that system (3) territoriality may include some amount of reciprocal access involving members of other groups (often utilizing specific kinship ties). My claims are that such reciprocity is much less common than in societies with a system (2) form, and that the circumstances in which it occurs are much more restrictive, *because* — for the ecological reasons specified in the economic defendability model — most of the time residents stand to lose much more from allowing access, and can expect to gain much less from obtaining it themselves in the future.

rarely denied outright — indeed, to do so without very good justification (beyond the stated social fact of ownership) would be to invite
anger and perhaps even violence on the part of the visitors. In return
for granting permission, owners can expect to be granted rights of
access when they visit their former guests.

Thus, the spatial defense system is at base one of non-reciprocal
exclusion; the social boundary system one of non-exclusionary reciprocity. Both involve 'control over access to local resources', but by
very different means and to very different ends. How then can we
account for the development of systems of social boundary control on
access to local resources? I think the answer lies in the increased
uncertainty that uncontrolled access to foraging areas would entail.
This uncertainty has two aspects: (1) the threat that those allowed
access will fail to reciprocate in the future (the free-rider problem); and
(2) the threat to foraging efficiency posed by uncoordinated resource
depletion by 'residents' and 'visitors'.

On the first point, it is appropriate to recall the earlier analysis of the
'sharing game'. The sharing of land (and unharvested resources) differs
in a number of ways from the sharing of harvested resources, but the
basic payoff structure is plausibly still the same:

Again, the structure is that of a prisoner's dilemma, with the selfish
('exclude') strategy dominant over that of sharing.[30] And again, this

30. Although I am purposefully keeping the game-theoretical analysis exceedingly
simple here, two caveats are in order. First, there are good grounds for thinking that payoff
structures other than the prisoner's dilemma are often more germane to analysis of social
cooperation (Taylor and Ward 1982). For an example close to home, the 'labour contribution' game — should an individual contribute to the collective pot with his or her foraging
labor? — is more plausibly viewed in terms of the 'chicken' (also known as 'hawk/dove')
payoff matrix than the PD one. In chicken, free-riding is constrained by the very low payoff
for bilateral selfishness (in the present case, by no one going foraging because they do not
want to feed the lazy); hence, the predicted outcome is a *mix* of cooperation and selfishness.
Second, although I am limiting the present discussion to two alternatives (and a 2×2
matrix), game theory is capable of dealing with more complex games (for example, an
evolutionary game between three different land tenure systems, or games with more than
two actors — '*n*-person games').

outcome can be reversed if the interaction is repeated (with indefinite future expectation of same), but only if free-riders (guests who refuse to reciprocate as hosts) face suitable sanctions (such as future exclusion).

What is the evidence that systems of reciprocal access do involve the features suggested by the iterated prisoner's dilemma? First, I would argue that the very fact of requiring permission before allowing visitors to utilize the residents' resources is a way of keeping tabs on the balance of reciprocity, and hence on the ongoing stability (or lack thereof) of the particular partnerships involved. Failure to secure 'permission' from residents makes it harder for residents to update information on the balance of reciprocity between members of different bands. This additional information cost is unilateral (falling on the residents only), but it could motivate the residents to impose higher sanctions on intruders who are discovered, sanctions that might be greater than the intruders are willing to pay. The fact that permission is rarely denied to prospective visitors has been read by some as an indication that the requirement is purely symbolic, a mystification of the underlying system of undivided access. But another interpretation is that it is rarely denied because the existence of the requirement motivates people to behave in a way that will keep their good name as reciprocators, and prevent their future exclusion as 'poor credit risks'. (This is certainly an area that would benefit from more detailed modeling *and* ethnography.)

Second, there is some evidence that residents can develop sufficient experience to judge the reliability of potential guests as future hosts. Again, Wiessner's (1977; 1982) study is exemplary in its discussion of the ways in which individual !Kung San engage in long-term efforts to maintain ties of reciprocity with individuals in other bands, and to monitor the ability and willingness of these partners to reciprocate in times of need. She presents detailed evidence indicating that !Kung systematically cultivate exchange partners and affines over a broad region (partners are hyperdispersed) and then use these relationships to facilitate residence change when local resource fluctuations warrant it. Although as yet all too rare in the ethnographic literature, this approach provides an avenue for explaining fluid group composition as an individually-adaptive strategy for responding to risk under conditions where reciprocal access to (sharing of) unharvested resources is ongoing. It improves upon the received view by focusing attention on *individual* costs and benefits, rather than effects such as 'higher carrying capacity', and by providing an explanation for the existence of controls on access as well as frequent movement between areas.

As noted earlier, I think there is a second selective factor promoting a system of controlled reciprocal access, one involving the role of information in foraging efficiency. Hunter-gatherers, like other species of foragers, spend considerable time and effort in monitoring the changing availability of resources within their local area. This information requires updating, and is always less than perfect, but the complex communication made possible with language, coupled with the active information-sharing that occurs at the central place (camp), gives human foragers a density of information that undoubtedly surpasses that of any other species. Ecological theory predicts that foragers exploiting relatively ephemeral resources, or resources whose quantity greatly exceeds the requirements of a single forager, may be expected to develop active information-sharing at a central place (E.A. Smith 1981; Waltz 1982; Clark and Mangel 1986).[31]

If the local area is treated as a commons, however, this information will be degraded — that is, uncertainty will increase. Foragers from other camps who do not 'check in' with the residents will deplete local resources in a manner that cannot be predicted by those residents. This will lead to inefficient allocation of foraging effort by 'residents' and 'intruders' alike, as they unknowingly visit patches that have recently been exploited by others, or even to direct interference from simultaneous but unplanned use of the same patch.

In summary, these arguments suggest that social controls over access to local resources involving reciprocal access could be evolutionarily stable under the following conditions:

(1) Residents possess much more information about the location and abundance of local resources, and recent and current allocation of foraging effort, than do visitors (likely to be the case in situations characterized by moderate fluctuations in key resources and relatively slow resource renewal).

(2) Uncoordinated search exacts a penalty of interference and inefficiency through overcrowding of foraging effort above the equilibrium that would result with greater information.

(3) Today's visitors are likely to be tomorrow's hosts (for reasons discussed in the previous section).

(4) Residents can impose effective sanctions (such as failure to share information, denial of access, gossiping, and so on) against those who cheat (that is, either fail to ask permission or fail to reciprocate).

It is worth reiterating that under this formulation, social controls offer benefits to both residents and visitors (as Cashdan 1983 recognizes). Residents can reduce the uncertainty concerning foraging opportunities by monitoring their guests' foraging efforts, suggesting

---

31. This is one explanation for the very existence of local bands among hunter-gatherers, as well as such phenomena as camp 'leaders' who act as clearing-houses for information about the distribution of foraging effort by camp members — that is, as coordinators of such effort with advisory but not coercive powers (E.A. Smith 1981: 44f.).

foraging locations for these guests that minimize interference, and gathering information from them at the central place. Guests can benefit from obtaining the access at low cost (that is, avoiding hostile confrontations if caught 'poaching') and from the information-sharing available at their hosts' camp.

Of course, this is not likely to be a case of simple mutualism, and there is no doubt ample opportunity for misinformation and manipulation to occur. The game-theoretical conditions for cooperation, and the exact equilibrium defined by costs and benefits to each party, need to be worked out in much more detail than is done here. However, if one keeps in mind that such interactions are embedded in long-term reciprocal and repeated movements of individuals between locations in an asynchronously fluctuating environment, the costs of providing false information to guests, or denying them access altogether, are considerable.[32] This is not to deny that such exclusion may at times occur. At one extreme, if resource availability is no better in the residents' local area than back at the visitors', it may be in both parties' interests for the visitor to look for a better situation elsewhere. In addition, there may well be conflicts of interest — and of opinion — within the resident band regarding acceptance of a new member, depending on kinship and partnership ties to different residents.

My general point is that social boundary controls, while certainly affecting regional access to resources, are perhaps best viewed as ways of reducing the uncertainty that would arise if movement and resource utilization were anarchic. The lower the correlation in resource availability between adjacent regions, the more demand for reciprocal access, and hence the more likely elaborate devices will evolve to control this access and reduce the uncertainty it could bring. While clearly not a system of rigid territorial exclusion (which, following Dyson-Hudson and Smith 1978, I would still expect to encounter in areas with relatively dense and predictable resources), neither is it the simple system of undivided access envisioned in many portrayals of band society, which would turn the bush into a commons with uncertain yields for all.[33]

32. As discussed in note 25, an alternative explanation of reciprocal access as 'tolerated theft' would argue that residents allow visitors access if the *immediate* costs of excluding them are higher than the *immediate* benefit of exclusive use of local resources. Aside from the fact that this interpretation overlooks the competitive advantage that a large number of residents has over a (usually) smaller number of visitors, it obviously predicts rather different cost–benefit conditions for the occurrence of visitors' access, and cannot account for the role of personal ties or past reciprocity in establishing the right to such access.

33. One question not analyzed here is what conditions would select for a true commons (undivided access) system. Resource factors favoring such a system probably include extreme degrees of unpredictability in spatial location and abundance, which would select for high mobility and extremely opportunistic exploitation of ephemeral resource patches (Dyson-Hudson and Smith 1978).

15.   Reflections on primitive communism

Richard B. Lee

> . . . if a cabin of hungry [Iroquois] meets another whose
> provisions are not entirely exhausted, the latter share with the
> newcomers the little which remains to them without waiting to
> be asked, although they expose themselves thereby to the same
> danger of perishing as those whom they help at their own
> expense so humanely and with such greatness of soul
> (Lafitau 1974).

> It has been said that there are no [Ainu] who die of starvation
> but if any do the wealthy and poor perish together after the rich
> have exhausted their resources in supporting the poor
> (Watarashima notebook [1808], cited in Shinichiro 1960).

> In general it may be said that no one in a Nuer village starves
> unless all are starving (Evans-Pritchard 1951).

> The general point . . . is that primitive societies uniformly
> possess a communal economic base; economic exploitation of
> man by man, as we know it in archaic and modern civilizations,
> is absent. . . . Thus, we find that in primitive society in the
> ordinary course of events, no man need go hungry while
> another eats (Diamond 1974).

Primitive communism[1] — a simple concept, yet the very words evoke
uneasiness and embarrassment. It is a double whammy. Primitive is a
loaded term; but communism is even more loaded. Why should this be
the case? Communism is, of course, the Number One enemy in Ronald
Reagan's America, but that does not explain why the concept is such an
embarrassment to so many scholars, including many Marxists who
would rather ignore it. This is particularly curious because primitive
communism was a perfectly acceptable concept in the nineteenth

1. A version of this chapter will also appear in a book in preparation, *Kin, Class and State:
the Origins of Hegemony*. I wish to thank Richard Daly, George Dei, Christine Gailey, M.T.
Kelly, Harriet Rosenberg, Gavin Smith and the participants at the Fourth International
Conference on Hunting and Gathering Societies. This chapter is offered in recognition of
Eleanor Leacock whose work has been the source of enormous inspiration and influence.

century and well into the twentieth. It is easy to find anthropologists of the period from 1910 to 1930 talking about communism and communistic societies with no apologies, and no inverted commas around the word 'communism' at all.

And despite the emotional loading of the term, there is no great mystery about the phenomenon it describes. Before the rise of the state and the entrenchment of social inequality, people lived for millennia in small-scale kin-based social groups, in which the core institutions of economic life included collective or common ownership of land and resources, generalized reciprocity in the distribution of food, and relatively egalitarian political relations. This basic pattern, with variations, has been observed in literally hundreds of non-state societies, as indicated, for example, in Murdock's *Ethnographic Atlas* (1967). These societies, including bands, tribes, and some chiefdoms, have been known by a variety of names: savage, non-state, pre-state, non-literate, kin-based, primitive — in fact anything but communist. But the basic underlying principles are the same. Something is there that demands explanation.

Our task is twofold: first, to explore the phenomenon itself and to specify its content; and second, to examine *why* the concept of primitive communism arouses so much unease.

To touch on the second question: obviously, the concept is out of step with bourgeois ideology. Bourgeois ideology would have us believe that primitive communism does not exist. In popular consciousness it is lumped with romanticism, exoticism: the noble savage. 'Oh, surely you don't *really* believe that they're communists?' say opponents. There is a considerable industry in anthropology, and especially pop anthropology, to show the primitive as a Hobbesian being — with a life that is 'nasty, brutish and short'. In the current climate of opinion in the West, no one is going to go broke by appealing to the cynicism and sophistication of the intellectual in late capitalism. No one wants to be accused of romanticism, let alone of being soft on communism, even of the primitive variety. It is an aspect of capitalist hegemony that most intellectuals, and even Marxists, operate on a terrain set by bourgeois discourse. Many Marxists fail to acknowledge the significance or even the existence of primitive communism and the absence of private property as a central principle in precapitalist social formations.

In order to understand the history and evolution of property relations in hunter-gatherer and post-hunter-gatherer societies we must first unpack the concept of primitive communism and disengage it from the ideological matrix in which it is embedded. We must also acknowledge that the primitive communist past and the revolutionary communist future are two quite different creatures, and the reality of the former in no way depends on our acceptance or non-acceptance of the latter.

Does primitive communism exist?

'Primitive communism: This refers to the collective right to basic resources, the absence of hereditary status or authoritarian rule, and the egalitarian relationships that preceded exploitation and economic stratification in human history' (Leacock 1983: 394). One problem with such definitions — and Leacock could not avoid it — is that they are couched in terms of negatives: the *absence* of authoritarian rule, the *absence* of exploitation, and so on. Such usages are inevitable, because of the fundamental point that everyone who writes about the subject of primitive communism is a member of state society. We were all raised in states and are deeply embedded in state ideologies. Our very concept of the primitive is dichotomous: we and they; we are modern, they are traditional, or we are advanced and they are behind.

To its credit, one of the main advances of cultural anthropology has been to break out of this dichotomous thinking and deal with primitives in their own right and on their own terms. In anthropology, 'cultural relativism' is a worthy undertaking. But cultural relativism also has its problems, because it is a deeply ahistorical concept. It is not sufficient to say that all cultures are of equal value, or that all are unique, because such statements ignore history, ignore social evolution and, above all, ignore imperialism.

The real question, to my mind, is how we approach the definite social evolutionary sequence from simple to complex without pejorative value judgements. Between the kind of racism that sees the primitive as bad, and the cultural relativism that sees all cultures as of equal value, there has to be a third way: to see in the primitive an historically valid and workable social system.

Stanley Diamond has captured the degree of distortion civilization imposes on human reality in order to expunge the notion of the 'primitive' from consciousness:

> Primitive is, I believe, the critical term in anthropology, the word around which the field revolves, yet it remains elusive, connoting but never quite denoting a series of related social, political, economic, spiritual and psychiatric meanings. That is, *primitive* implies a certain level of history, and a certain mode of cultural being. . . . This mode of cultural being is continuously obliterated or attenuated by the processes of civilization and more radically so than we are usually able or willing to acknowledge; as a result, the image of the identifiable, cross-cultural, pre-civilized, and, yes, a priori human possibility has practically disappeared from our conceptual lexicon. Unyielding cultural relativism, cultural determinism and social scientism are, in part and each in its own way, rationalizations of a civilization that has forgotten what questions to ask of itself (1974: 132–3).

Pre-state societies had no overriding political authority. Political power of any kind was weak. Decisions were made in a diffuse way, usually democratically, by consensus, by elders, by family groups, and by a variety of other means. There was no private property in land; land was held in common, or collectively, for example by all or by kin groups; rarely was it held by individuals. Production was for use rather than for exchange. There were no markets, no currency. Where exchange existed, it was based on sharing and reciprocity. The law of hospitality was strong; more than that, it was inviolable. There were strong sanctions against wealth accumulation. Leaders existed, but where they existed they were redistributors, not accumulators. The main bases for what status distinctions did exist included age, gender, and locality. The whole population retained access to the means of production and reproduction. As Marx put it, 'it was a community of owners who also worked'. There was no division into economic classes.

Lest I portray too rosy a picture, I hasten to add that some pre-state societies did have the germs of inequality and did have chiefs, ranked lineages, wealth differences and slavery. The North-west Coast Indians are an example, and many other societies in North America, Africa and Polynesia followed this pattern. There are hundreds of other societies, however, including the bulk of the foraging societies, where these institutions were absent or only a present to a small degree. For my argument on the concept of primitive communism to be valid, I do not have to demonstrate that all pre-state societies were perfectly egalitarian, but only that a great many of them fit the definition on most of the criteria. And even these chiefly and ranked societies had by no means abandoned all the institutions of communalism. Many continued to hold land in common and to practice reciprocal economic relations. Therefore I would designate such societies as semi-communal. I shall return to such societies later.

Rather than accept the proposition that this remarkable clustering of traits is coincidental, historical materialism argues that there exists a core of culture in primitive society that is intimately linked to mode of production. It is much longer-lived, has a much deeper time-depth, than Western capitalist culture. Historical materialism further argues that this culture core is communist: it embraces the collective right to basic resources and an egalitarian political order. By any dictionary definition of communism, our ancestors were communists.

Morgan and the evidence

Neither Marx nor Engels, nor for that matter Fourier or Saint-Simon, can be regarded as the principal discoverer of primitive communism. That honour belongs to a Rochester ethnologist and staunch member of the bourgeoisie, Lewis Henry Morgan. In his last book, *Houses and house-life of the American Aborigines*, Morgan devoted over a hundred pages to the conceptualization and documentation of primitive communism, calling it 'communism in living' (1965: 63). He introduces the concept almost diffidently, as an extension of the law of hospitality, and in presenting his argument he notes in passing that this 'plan of life . . . has not been carefully studied or fully appreciated' (ibid.: 61). (We might add that the same is true today, a hundred years later.)

Noting the universal presence in Aboriginal America of the obligatory custom of offering hospitality to visitors, Morgan seeks to account for this phenomenon: 'The law of hospitality as administered by the American aborigines tended to the final equalization of subsistence. Hunger and destitution could not exist at one end of an Indian village or in one section of an encampment while plenty prevailed elsewhere in the same village or encampment' (ibid.: 61).

How does the system of communism in living arise? In a strikingly modern form of argument, Morgan derived the institution from the ecological and social constraints of the mode of life of savagery and barbarism — from what Marxists would call the low level of development of the productive forces:

> Communism in living had its origin in the necessities of the family, which, prior to the Later Period of barbarism, was too weak an organization to face alone the struggle of life. . . . Wherever the gentile organization prevailed, several families, related by kin, united as a rule in a common household and made a common stock of the provisions acquired by fishing and hunting, and by the cultivation of maize and plants. They erected joint tenement houses large enough to accommodate several families so that, instead of a single family in the exclusive occupation of a single house, large households as a rule existed in all parts of America in the aboriginal period. This community of provisions was limited to the household; but a final equalization of the means of subsistence was in some measure affected by the law of hospitality. To a very great extent communism in living was a necessary result of the condition of the Indian tribes. It entered into their plan of life and determined the character of their houses. In effect it was a union of effort to procure subsistence, which was the vital and commanding concern of life. The desire for individual accumulation had not been aroused in their minds to any sensible extent (ibid.: 63).

The notions of the law of hospitality and of communism in living were backed up by an overwhelming barrage of ethno-historic data. Morgan went as far back as the fifteenth-century journals of Columbus's voyages to document his thesis in relation to the earliest periods of European contact. Among his other sources were the journals of De Soto, Sir Walter Raleigh, Cortes, Pizzaro, Capt. John Smith, Marquette and Joliet, and Lewis and Clark.

Most anthropologists of the early part of the present century, while not necessarily accepting his use of the terms, did accept Morgan's thesis of communism in living, adding the proviso that while land and its resources were communally owned, movables — tools, weapons, cooking utensils, procured food, occasionally trees, and so on — could be owned individually. A few more or less random examples from the bookshelf of classic ethnographies will suffice. Radcliffe-Brown writes of the Andaman islanders:

> The economic life of the local group, though in effect it approaches to a sort of communism, is yet based on the notion of private property. Land is the only thing that is owned in common. The hunting grounds of a local group belong to the whole group, and all the members have an equal right to hunt over any part of it. There exists, however, a certain private ownership of trees. A man of one of the local groups of the coast may notice in the jungle a tree suitable for a canoe. He will tell the others that he has noticed such a tree, describing it and its whereabouts. Thenceforward that tree is regarded as his property, and even if some years should elapse, and he has made no use of it, yet another man would not cut it down without first asking the owner to give him the tree (1922: 41).

Clark Wissler was uncomfortable with the term 'communist', yet in his *Indians of the United States* he acknowledged, a half-century after Morgan, the major contours of Morgan's view:

> In the abstract, there are desirable practices in the Indian way of life. He was not really a communist, but he was liberal with food. So long as he had food, he was expected to share it. That he did not always do it we learn from legends, but since in these tales the one who concealed food always came to grief, there can be no doubt that to share it was the thing to do. This is sometimes called the law of hospitality, which is, in short, that the stranger is always welcome at your fireside. However, this did not extend to private property, such as bows and arrows, one's robe, shirt, medicine bag, etc. Every member of the band went to the dinner pot when he wished, so why not hand something to the stranger? The pipe, also, was the guest's due; and having smoked with his guest, the host was a friend and must so act. Even an enemy was safe if he reached a fireside and came without threats. Food and a smoke must be given him; both host and guest were then under obligations to each other (1966: 281)

In his *Indians of the Plains* Robert Lowie emphasized the democratic nature of Plains society and contrasted its egalitarianism with the hierarchies of the Polynesian kingdoms:

> A most important difference between the Plains Indians and the Tahitians concerns material property. Whereas in Tahiti a monarch could appropriate the possessions of a lesser man, on the Plains any comparable act was unthinkable. On the contrary, a great man could maintain his standards best

by lavish generosity to the poor. Such liberality, next to a fine war record, was the basis for high standing. The Oglala had a society of chiefs enjoying superior prestige, but when a novice was admitted, he was urged to look after the poor, especially the widows and orphans (1963: 124).

Clyde Kluckhohn and Dorothea Leighton carefully noted for the Navaho the various forms of collective and communal property that persisted even in the face of the attempts of white men to change them:

> Among the Navahos certain things are 'communal property', in which no individual or family has vested or exclusive rights. Water resources, timber areas, and patches of salt bush (which serve livestock in lieu of mineral salt) belong to all The People, and certain conventions are observed in regard to this type of property. It is not good form to cut wood within a mile or so of someone else's dwelling. One uses no other than his accustomed water hole except when that source fails or he goes on a journey. Attempts of some Navahos to emulate white practices with respect to wood and water rights are among the most bitterly resisted of all innovations (1962: 105–6).

A number of contemporary authors make wide use of the concept of primitive communism, while showing a certain reluctance to use the term. Sahlins (1974: 185–275) attempted to bring together the evidence for what I have called primitive communism under the rubric of 'generalized reciprocity'. This concept — the giving of something without the immediate expectation of return — expresses an aspect of primitive communism in 'social-science-ese' and therefore in a way less threatening to hegemonic ideology. The basic import of both terms is, I believe, the same. Other contemporary restatements of Morgan's position can be found in the writings of Stanley Diamond (1974), Morton Fried (1967), Eleanor Leacock (1981), and James Woodburn (1982a). Leacock and Diamond, in particular, have explored in their own work much of the ideological ground examined here, while Woodburn has given detailed attention to the substantive data.

The critiques

If the evidence for primitive communism is so obvious and so widespread, on what grounds do half the anthropologists in the world attempt to ignore it or explain it away? Let us look at several ways that scholars deal with and dispose of primitive communism.

First of all, they deny its existence. This critique is quite simple: all one does is take the highly problematic concept of human nature and say: 'Let's look at human beings: they're aggressive, they're acquisitive, and people naturally form themselves into hierarchies'. This popular and successful technique projects the values of bourgeois society, the values of possessive individualism, the will to power or other variants, on all cultures and on nature. Socio-biology is only the most conspicuous of the current crop — it is a serious intellectual enterprise with generous foundation support and a distinguished pedigree: recall, it was Spencer, not Darwin, who coined the term 'survival of the fittest' (Spencer 1866: 444). So, in this general way of thinking, primitive communism is disposed of by leaping over society to human nature itself. (The opposed position, of course, is that 'human nature' is socially constructed, and consequently bourgeois human nature is different from a slave society's human nature, and feudal society's human nature is different from human nature in Asiatic society. Human nature is a historically constituted subject, and not trans-historical.)

A second critique is to admit the existence of primitive communism but to belittle and dismiss it. The argument runs: 'Of course, the San in the Kalahari, the Inuit, the Pygmies are egalitarian; granted, they have no private property in land. But they are simple, they are childlike, and the sooner we can get them away from all this the better off they will be. They have to grow up to adulthood and learn the value of money, or hard work, or technology'. In the developed world, this view is a thin cover for racism and ethnocentrism. But such views are, unfortunately, also extremely popular in the Third World, in both left- and right-leaning countries, once more revealing an attitude of embarrassment: what Morgan and many others considered a virtue of primitive life, becomes something 'we' want to hide. The fact that 'they' are hospitable, share food, and take care of each other is something to be ashamed of rather than a source of pride.

A third critique of primitive communism has developed into a minor industry within cultural anthropology: to confront the evidence for primitive communism and try to explain it away. This is a very common enterprise, going back to the very roots of bourgeois social science. For example, some legal historians in the mid-nineteenth century looked at the roots of law in the Germanic tribal community and tried to argue that when the Germanic tribes first settled in what is now Germany they did so as individuals on private property. Marx's material on pre-capitalist economic formations, from the *Grundrisse* (1972), is precisely a debate with these legal historians. In fact, the majority opinion in the nineteenth century was that the German tribes began with collective ownership of land and in the course of their contact with the Roman Empire gradually adopted hierarchical forms and the privatization of property. More recently, this latter position has been argued convincingly by the British medievalist, E.A. Thompson (1965; see also Anderson 1974).

A parallel theme in twentieth-century anthropology is to discover private property and/or political hierarchies in primitive societies. The

American ethnologist Frank Speck 'discovered' the aboriginal 'family hunting territory' among the northern Algonquians (1915), a view which prevailed until Eleanor Leacock's rebuttal, and her demonstration that the family hunting territory was a late arrival; it was a product of the fur trade (1954). Whatever Speck's motives, his concept of the family hunting territory was an attempt to stretch private property back into previous history and make it appear as though at the very dawn of history the most 'primitive' Indians were hunting on their family plot of land. Speck's view, far from dead, is currently undergoing a revival.[2]

In contrast to these critiques of primitive communism, which clearly have their roots in bourgeois ideology and which can be confronted with empirical data, there are arguments by Marxists about the 'aboriginality' of primitive communism that are far more challenging. Let me gloss some of these views.

First, it is maintained that capitalism (read hierarchy, inequality, exploitation) is all-pervasive; therefore primitive communism, even if it exists, is irrelevant to the struggle for socialism. Second (more elaborately), since capitalism is all-pervasive, if primitive communism exists, it does so as an encapsulated structure, maintained by capital as a labour-/commodity-producing reserve. Third (and bluntly), primitive communism does not exist and never did.

These kinds of neo-Marxist thought are certainly out of step with the views of Marx and Engels themselves who, in a number of writings, expressed their own clear visions of primitive communism. Thus neo-Marxists, when they universalize capitalism, in effect deny to non-capitalist peoples their own history and autonomy. But, as Cabral argued in relation to African peoples, that history and autonomy did exist and must be recaptured. Cabral posed the ironic but critical question to his fellow Marxists: If the hitherto existing history of mankind is the history of class struggle, then where does that leave the social formations that lacked classes . . . outside of history? In Cabral's view the struggle for socialism must begin first with the recognition of the persistence of communal elements within African social formations, and second, with the recognition that these societies are no less historical for lacking classes and class contradictions (Cabral 1974).

The second argument presented by Marxists is the view that if primitive communal formations exist they do so on the sufferance, and indeed at the pleasure, of capital. The theory of articulation of modes of production holds that pre-capitalist social formations are maintained as

---

2. The same enterprise is going on today. Another generation of Canadian anthropologists is going back for a third time to the archives and picking up little clues that the family hunting territory and political hierarchies were present in the earliest explorers' accounts. See Morantz (1983) and also the symposium convened by Toby Morantz, 'Northern Algonquian Land Tenure Systems', Canadian Ethnology Society/American Ethnology Society Annual Congress, Toronto, 9–12 May 1985.

enclaves, to provide a reserve of labor power for the capitalist sector and to shift the burden of social reproduction from the factory owners to the 'traditional' sector. South Africa of course is cited as the classic example of this form of super-exploitation. But there is a world of difference between the artificially maintained and over-regimented structures of a South African Bantustan and what is found in hundreds of other Third World settings, for example in Ghana, Thailand, the Philippines, Botswana and Peru.[3] To argue otherwise is once again to deny to the societies of the Third World their history and autonomy.

One writer who seems to do precisely this is Eric Wolf in his *Europe and the People without History* (1982). While stressing the interconnectedness of all the world's societies, even before the rise of capitalism, Wolf's analysis tends to give all agency to the metropolitan powers. The peripheral peoples achieve historical animation, it appears, only in their resistence to or accommodation with the imperial powers. Historical visibility in Wolf's terms equates with the presence of long-distance trade, intersocietal warfare, or regional conquest. Societies that just go about their business hardly seem to exist. This is coupled with his explicit rejection of the existence of a baseline of equality in pre-class societies.

To argue against the thrust of Wolf's position would be foolhardy. The interconnectedness of the world's peoples cannot be denied. And it is true that anthropologists from the generation of Radcliffe-Brown, Mead, Kroeber and Lowie tended seriously to underestimate the effects of change on the people they studied. And yet I believe much will be lost by the general adoption of Wolf's view. There is a great deal of difference across a spectrum of intersocietal contacts, from occasional silent trade or regular economic exchange, to the domination and conquest of one society by another. The subtext of Wolf's argument is to see all forms of *contact* as forms of *domination*.

This topic was much debated at the conference from which this book is drawn: the question was posed as to whether modern foragers and their egalitarian ways should be best understood as products of encapsulation. For some analysts, forager social equality is a product of being born poor and powerless in a wealthy society and not from any qualities inherent in the small-scale society itself. For others, myself included, such a view seems to be a case of life imitating art. We would argue that, if such correspondences exist, it is favela dwellers who have reinvented primitive communism, not foragers driven to 'urban slum-dweller' types of survival strategy. The issue remained far from resolved, in no small part because no one at the conference could come up with a satisfactory definition of encapsulation, or for that matter of

3. For instance, the literature pertaining to the Andean peasants is particularly abundant on the question of persistence of communal forms. See, for example, Erasmus (1956).

autonomy or dependency.

It is clear that much remains to be done to clarify the issues. My own sense is that what we see here is a group of critical theorists who are so in awe of the power of expanding capital that they impute its hegemony even to areas outside its orbit. This view ultimately connotes a closed system. If the members of a given social formation exhibit the characteristics of dog-eat-dog, then it is proof of capitalist penetration. If, on the other hand, they share food, support one another and eschew accumulation and self-aggrandizement, then they do so as an encapsulated minority with a culture of poverty. Once again the historical autonomy of actors on the periphery of the world system is vitiated. If we are to have any hope of drawing upon ethnographic and ethnohistoric information for insights on the origins of social inequality and social evolution, then such an autonomy must be assumed, supposing that this can be sustained in the face of critical scrutiny. I am confident that primitive communism was not invented simply as a defence against capitalism.

Primitive communism and capitalism

Having established the historical existence of primitive communism, we must add that the past one hundred years have not been kind to communal social formations; the spread of capitalism has relentlessly destroyed the social base of thousands of local communities in tribal societies and agrarian states. And yet for all its economic and military power and its near monopoly of the ideological apparatus the capitalist state has not succeeded in eradicating innumerable pockets of communalism, in the Third and Fourth Worlds and some in the very belly of the beast itself.

This book testifies to the persistence of communal property concepts in hunting and gathering societies in the face of enormous pressure from the capitalist world system (see also Ingold, Riches and Woodburn 1988). A large number of pastoral and horticultural societies in the Third World share many of the same traits. In the numerous chiefdoms described by anthropologists in Africa, Oceania and lowland South America one notes, for example, that much of what tribute the chiefs receive is redistributed to subjects, and the chief's power is subject to checks and balances by the force of popular opinion and institutions.[4] And even in late capitalist society, the very antithesis to communalism and collectivism, we have evidence of the persistence of primitive communism.

First of all — in Canada, the USA, Australia and elsewhere — we

4. See, for example, Firth (1936), Gluckman (1965), Schapera (1938) and Service (1962).

have native people struggling for survival. They couch their struggle in terms of *cultural* survival; but what does that culture consist of, what are they trying to keep afloat? It is language, certainly; it is religious beliefs, too; but at a very deep level, it is communalism. It is the absence of private property. Some of the most creative work going on in Canada today is the dialogue between native peoples, lawyers, and anthropologists and other social scientists (Asch 1984; Watkins 1977). They are trying to find a formula for the preservation of communal organization that will hold up in a Canadian court. And of course this is very ironic, because if one goes back far enough in English law those same communal concepts are there, embedded in Anglo-Saxon or Anglo-Roman common law: there was communal landholding in England through the medieval period and beyond. So the native people are trying to come up with a land-claims position that has its roots deeply buried in our own legal system.

The point is that the notion of private property in land, which in the West is taken for granted, is a relatively recent notion. Starting from the Enclosure movements in fifteenth-century England, and spreading rapidly with the spread of capitalism, the whole land-tenure system of Europe and the Americas was transformed from communal to private within the space of a few hundred years (Dobb 1946; Tigar and Levy 1977).[5] And what transpires is that, in many states of the Third World, as well as in pre-state societies, *the common people have not yet been separated from the means of production, have not yet been divorced from their land*, as has occurred in Europe. The kin-ordered mode of production was and still is vital and indispensable. Marx was well aware of this in his formulation of the 'Asiatic mode of production' (though he paradoxically welcomed its destruction by British Imperialism in India).

Collectivism in the context of late capitalist society is also evident in such concepts as African socialism; there is an awareness on the part of African theoreticians that the historical experience of Africa was not only different from that of Europe but also this historical experience was in some large measure communal, as Amilcar Cabral (1974) pointed out. African socialism, as I understand it, is an attempt to enunciate, at the level of the state, a set of principles which worked in tribal and chiefly semi-communal societies. Foremost among these principles is the idea of the community safety net: nobody should be allowed to go to the bottom, nobody should be allowed to go destitute in a community if somebody has some food. Second is the law of hospitality, and third is the right to land and livelihood. In other parts of the world there are similar attempts to reinterpret and rearticulate the historical experience of communalism, although I should add that

---

5. The early-modern concepts of private property were in turn based on the rediscovery of long-buried texts on Roman jurisprudence.

much of this effort is now influenced by missionaries and has been filtered through Christian, Marxist and Moslem beliefs.

The secret of primitive communism

These are some of the debates, implicit and explicit, around the notion of primitive communism. Now we have to ask a further question: Is primitive communism something we can only define as a quintessential otherness, in negative terms, in the absence of leadership, absence of inequality, absence of property; or is there something else going on? A related question is this: Is the concept of primitive communism something that exists only in Utopian terms, an expression of the yearning of modern men and women for the oneness and unity of an imagined past? I will argue that, quite apart from the ideological load we place upon it, there is a great deal of concrete substance to the vision. For example, the !Kung did not know they were lacking all these things until the colonialists came along and pointed out to them their deficiencies!

What then *is* the particular character of the ideology in primitive communism? What constitutes the core of primitive communism, what is the appeal, and why have people the world over clung to its institutions so fiercely and given it up so reluctantly?

This is a large question and I can offer only a few suggestions as to where we might look for answers. A possible clue to the answer comes from an unlikely angle, the role of humour in communal societies. Simple foraging peoples around the world — the Inuit in the Arctic, the San in the Kalahari, the Australian Aborigines, the Pygmies (people widely separated by geography and history) — joke with each other in strikingly similar ways. There is a kind of rough good humour, put-downs, teasing, and sexual joking that one encounters throughout the foraging world. What conceivable reason could there be for the fact of such similar ways of joking?

People in these societies, and to a certain extent tribal peoples as well, have an absolute aversion to rank distinctions among them. You could say they are fiercely egalitarian. They get outraged if somebody tries to put on the dog or to put on airs; they have evolved — independently, it would seem — very effective means for putting a stop to it. These means anthropologists have called 'humility-enforcing' or 'levelling' devices: thus the use of a very rough joking is to bring people into line — a far rougher kind of joking than middle-class North Americans or Europeans would ever put up with. 'Please' and 'thank you' are almost completely unknown in these peoples' vocabulary. *Since sharing is a given, why say 'thank you'?*

Let me illustrate what seems to be the core of this phenomenon, using an example not from the !Kung but from the Innu (Naskapi) in Labrador. The Norwegian ethnologist Georg Henriksen, who spent two years with the Innu of Davis Inlet (Henriksen 1973), told me the following story. During a field trip he went off with two families of hunters into the forest for six weeks in the middle of winter. The men went hunting with rifles. After four weeks in the country the hunting had been good but one of the men started to run out of cigarettes. In the tent one evening Henriksen witnessed the following interaction. The fellow who was running out of cigarettes was sitting on one side, just at the edge of the tent, and casually reached into his jacket and pulled out a cigarette. He had only about four left and was trying to be unobtrusive. The second man, who had lots left, said: 'Give me a smoke'. The tent became silent. The first man was a little embarrassed, having been caught hoarding. 'Give me a smoke', repeated the second man. So the first man made a tentative gesture, offering him the pack with one cigarette sticking out; and the second man very deliberately took the whole pack and put it in his pocket. Then he gave the first man a cigarette back, and lit one up for himself. Henriksen could feel the palpable tension in the tent. Then someone made a joke and the tension evaporated. But for the rest of the trip the man who had lots of cigarettes left shared them with the man who had none.[6]

The story had a familiar ring; it was so like something that could have happened with the !Kung.

> The rough joking:
> 'So you'd take my last cigarette?'
> 'Yes, I would; in fact I *will* take your last cigarette.
> But by taking your last cigarette I'm signalling:
> we're going to pool your four and my two hundred, and
> we're going to smoke them, together.'

Another example of levelling. When a party of !Kung are out hunting, and one of them has killed an animal and is feeling good about himself, his comrades engage in a ritual insulting of the kill, belittling it and the hunter's prowess, and loudly proclaiming they would rather be somewhere else. Dialogue along the following lines takes place when they come upon the kill. One man says: 'Oh. It's pretty thin. It's not much at all. It's much smaller than I thought it was. It looked big in the bush, but it really is small'. A second man says: 'You know, it's so small, it's hardly worth our while; why don't we just leave it? It's still early; we could actually go and hunt something good'. The hunter must reply in kind. 'You know, you're right', he says. 'It really is

---

6. See Myers (1988) for a remarkably similar account of the hoarding of cigarettes among Pintupi Aborigines.

nothing. Why don't we just leave it, and go off and hunt something else. Even a porcupine, a rabbit — anything would be better than this.' And then after everyone has a good laugh they get to work and butcher the meat and bring it home. These exchanges occurred again and again. I was at a loss to figure out what was behind them until someone explained to me: 'This is the way we talk to each other, because we don't want anybody to get a big head. If you praise a hunter, then he will think, "Oh, I'm really pretty good, I'm really hot stuff"'. One man told me: 'If somebody gets a big head and thinks a lot of himself, he'll get arrogant; and an arrogant person might hurt someone, he might even kill someone. So we belittle his meat to cool his heart and make him gentle'.

Here the code of behaviour that people in the West are accustomed to is reversed. Modesty is bragging, and insults are praise. The more somebody insults your meat, the better you know it is. One sees this in Western culture with teenage boys, where you tease somebody you know can take it. The kind of rough good humour is an indication of your affection. (Of course, it can also be simple cruelty.) One can use the insult as a way of creating fellowship. This is a kind of machismo, but a very constructive machismo. The !Kung hate fighting, and think anybody who fought would be stupid; but anyone who can go out and hunt and kill something and then not expect to be showered with praise — *that* is high art. These patterns of modesty and deference appear in many parts of the world of foragers.

Levelling devices are widely used among women, but not around hunting, since they usually do not hunt. A lot of the rough joking that the !Kung do is sexual in nature; in fact there is more joking over sex than there is about hunting, and a veritable cornucopia of jokes about sex *and* hunting: the penis is the hunting bow and the woman is the game animal. !Kung women are no slouches at sexual imagery, they are very bawdy, too, especially the older ones (Lee 1979; 1984); they don't feel that they are being objectified, and they give at least as good as they get. If a man does not hunt, his wife will make pointed comments about his sexual prowess. And vice versa: if he is no good in bed, he cannot hunt. The !Kung and the great majority of primitive communist societies are very open about sexual joking. This, I think, is clearly another form of levelling.

We are now getting close to the heart of the way a system of primitive communism is reproduced. It is reproduced by positive injunctions against accumulation or against inequality. People like the !Kung and other hunter-gatherers would be very unwilling to have one of their own people become headman or a chief (but they are surprisingly agreeable to subordinating themselves to an outside authority — a colonial representative or Hudson's Bay factor). With the growth of inequality people gradually become accustomed to the fact that there's going to be wealth differences; but initially there's a lot of resistance to the idea. If somebody among the !Kung, by a stroke of fortune, gets two blankets, almost invariably somebody else will come and ask for one blanket; and it is hard to refuse it. You just simply cannot build up a little 'nest egg' because inevitably you have to give it away. You could say 'no', but then people will start grumbling, and gossiping about you. The !Kung use the word *a !xka ≠xan*, 'far-hearted', the equivalent of mean or stingy. The levelling device operates on the plane of ideology to reinforce the central values; but it also operates on the very concrete plane of redistributing all the goods that are available.

Communism, past and future

A useful way of looking at primitive communism is to visualize a ceiling of accumulation of goods above which nobody can rise, with the corollary that there is also a floor below which one cannot sink. The ceiling and the floor are dialectically connected; you cannot have one without the other. If there is any food in the camp, everybody in the camp is going to get some of it. The fact is that the obligation to share food and the taboo against hoarding is no less strong and no less ubiquitous in the primitive world than the far more famous taboo against incest. But unlike the incest taboo which persists to the present, the hoarding taboo became a casualty of social evolution.

One of the key developments of social evolution is the lifting of the ceiling of accumulation. Animal domestication represents such a shift. Instead of shooting the animal and eating the meat, one brings the cow into the camp and it sits there as property.

Once the ceiling is raised the possibility of wealth differences emerges. Somebody could have no goats and somebody else have one; and if you can have none and one, you can have none and ten, or ten and 100.

At a crucial point in the evolution of societies the floor is lowered. I do not know exactly how that happens. In primitive communism, if you saw somebody becoming a little uppity, you leveled them out; and by the same token, if you saw somebody falling through the cracks, you made sure that they did not. One of the really interesting things about social evolution is how the cracks get wider. Do people fall through those cracks by neglect, or are they preyed upon; does society devour itself by the rich preying upon the poor? In ancient Greece, as some people got wealthier they first took the land of their neighbours, then they enslaved them (discussed in Lee 1985). As I said, the ceiling and the floor are dialectically connected.

In the future, ideally, we will raise the floor *and* raise the ceiling. In a future communist society everybody will have goods — but no one will have much more than anyone else. Everyone will have a car but nobody will have a Bentley or a Rolls-Royce. It is a basic tenet of Marxist thought that the successful attainment of communism is dependent not on the return to primitive poverty, but rather on the development of the level of productive forces to the point where all share in the wealth of a wealthy society. This is what it might be like (if we survive).

Primitive communism, then, exists within a narrow range at the bottom of a scale; future communism would operate in a narrow range at the top. But whatever the future may hold, it is the long experience of egalitarian sharing that has moulded our past. Despite our seeming adaptation to life in hierarchical societies, and despite the rather dismal track record of human rights in many parts of the world, there are signs that humankind retains a deep-rooted egalitarianism, a deep-rooted commitment to the norm of reciprocity, a deep-rooted desire for what Victor Turner has called *communitas* — the sense of community (1969). All theories of justice revolve around these principles, and our sense of outrage at the violation of these norms indicates the depth of its gut-level appeal. That, in my view, is the secret of primitive communism.

16. Notes on the foraging mode of production

Tim Ingold

Introducing a recent volume of papers on hunting and gathering societies, Leacock and Lee (1982: 7–9) ask whether there exists a 'foraging mode of production'. They are inclined to answer in the affirmative, on the grounds of the striking uniformities among so-called 'band-living' foragers throughout the world, both in the manner of their subsistence and in their social organization. In this chapter I should like to take a critical look at the 'foraging mode', by examining three of the premises on which it rests: that foraging is an adequate description of what hunters and gatherers do; that there is more to their mode of production than the mode of subsistence; and that this additional component consists in the social relations that go along with 'band-living'. I shall argue that whereas the second premise is valid the first is not, and that in the field of interspecific relations, one can say that hunting and gathering is to foraging as mode of production is to mode of subsistence. I shall show, moreover, that the same contrast obtains between sharing and cooperation, as distinct aspects of the intraspecific relations of hunter-gatherer bands. This leads me to conclude that the opposition between the social and the material (or ecological) components of the mode of production does not simply coincide with that between the relations of human beings with one another and with environmental resources. Rather, both sets of relations have their social and ecological aspects.

Foraging, or hunting and gathering?

As a simple descriptive label, the notion of foraging has much to commend it. It is less cumbersome than 'hunting and gathering', and avoids arguments about the relative worth of each activity, or of the food yielded, as well as about whether such activities as fishing and trapping are included or excluded. But there are also objections. Some are merely expressions of anthropocentric prejudice, for example the

269

extraordinary claim of Hunn and Williams that, in speaking of foragers, one 'calls to mind dull-witted ungulates grazing their way through a field of daisies' (1982: 8). Behind such absurdity lies the more serious observation that foraging is a concept widely used and understood in behavioural ecology to denote the physical movements executed by animals of all kinds (with or without hoofs, quick-witted or dull) in extracting a subsistence from their environments. Thus a bee forages for nectar, a ladybird for aphids. Can we fully comprehend the activities of human hunters and gatherers in the same terms?

Certainly not, if the dictum of Marx and Engels is anything to go by, that humans 'begin to distinguish themselves from animals as soon as they begin to *produce* their means of subsistence' (1977: 42). Short of denying the humanity of hunters and gatherers, we must surely accept that to hunt or gather is to produce, and that there is more to such production than the overt patterns of extractive behaviour manifested alike by human and nonhuman animals. Our problem, then, is to discover in what respect the production of subsistence exceeds its extraction, for, by the same token, hunting and gathering must exceed foraging.

One possible approach to the problem is to follow Engels in linking production to the manufacture and use of tools. 'The tool', Engels wrote, 'implies specific human activity, the transforming reaction of man on nature, production' (1934: 34). With projectile implements, human hunters are routinely able to bring down prey substantially larger than themselves, a feat which few non-human predators can match (Teleki 1975: 139; Tanner 1981: 80–1). Other implements, such as those affording digging or smashing, open up a whole new range of foodstuffs, primarily vegetable, that are naturally 'embedded in a solid matrix such as the earth' (Parker and Gibson 1979: 371). Finally, carrying devices make it possible for garnered produce to be transported to a home base, for later consumption in the company of others, including juvenile, sick or elderly dependents who are inactive in the food quest. It could be argued, then, that just as hunting surpasses predation in the use of projectiles to kill animals larger than the hunter, so also gathering surpasses foraging in the aggregation of food for postponed consumption (Isaac and Crader 1981: 88), and represents no less than 'a new way of exploiting plant foods with tools' (Tanner 1981: 139).

Contrary to popular belief, however, the construction and manipulation of tools are not limited to human beings, nor even to our closest primate cousins, the chimpanzees. Examples may be found in every branch of the animal kingdom, with the curious exception of amphibians (Beck 1980). If there is something special about the way humans make and use tools, which is symptomatic of production, it cannot lie merely in constructive or manipulative behaviour. The missing element, I believe, is that of self-conscious planning, the harnessing of the range of possible behaviour patterns to the realization of an intentional project, hence 'the objectification of work' (Faris 1975: 236). The labour process in production, as Marx famously observed, 'ends in the creation of something which, when the process began, already existed in the worker's imagination, already existed in an ideal form' (1930: 170). However much the operations performed by the spider resemble those performed by the weaver, the spider has no idea at all of what it is constructing, whereas the weaver continually monitors her performance in order to adjust the outcome to conform with an internal representation of the expected product. Similarly, the behaviour of non-human foragers, of which the spider could again serve as our example, might be compared to that of human hunter-gatherers who — like spiders — sometimes weave traps to catch their prey. But the human trap was made and laid with a purpose in mind, and it is by this *subjection of procurement behaviour to intentional control* that hunting and gathering exceeds foraging.

This conclusion leads to a way of distinguishing hunting from gathering — a way which rests neither on the kinds of operations performed (whether or not involving pursuit), nor on the nature of the yield (animal or plant). I suggest that hunting and gathering denote alternating phases in a continuous process of production punctuated by events of extraction (foraging) and consumption (cooking and eating). They have in common that they involve a temporal extension beyond the immediate situation of extraction; but whereas with hunting this extension precedes the extractive situation, with gathering it follows on (Ingold 1986b: 92). To hunt is to set out with the *intention* of obtaining food, an intention that governs the behavioural operations of search, pursuit (in the case of a mobile quarry) and capture which, successfully accomplished, bring about its realisation. Gathering, whose consequence is the aggregation and transport of foodstuffs to a central place, begins at this point. The operations entailed in gathering are classed as such because they are, likewise, governed by an intention concerning the foodstuff's future distribution and consumption. If the goal of hunting is the procurement of raw materials, the goal of gathering is their utilization for subsistence. One might almost say that hunting is to gathering as production is to reproduction (Figure 16.1).

From our observation that hunters and gatherers are self-conscious, intentional agents, capable of setting up targets in advance of their realization and monitoring their behaviour accordingly, certain important consequences follow concerning the perception of the environment. Consider once more the spider: what does the environment look like to it? Confined to the execution of a given, more or less instinctive project, it perceives the constituents of its environment only in terms of what they may or may not afford for that project's realization. There are things that afford eating and things that do not, things that afford

Figure 16.1 The alternation of hunting and gathering in the process of
production (from Ingold 1986b: 92)

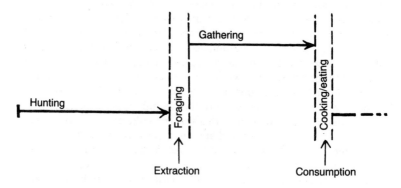

shelter and things that do not, and — most importantly for the spider
— things that afford retention (for threads) and things that do not.
Taken together, all these 'affordances', to use Gibson's term (1979: 127),
constitute the spider's niche. The human hunter-gatherer, however,
does not encounter a world already organized for the execution of a
received project, but rather confronts one that has still to be organized
according to a project of his own design. He sees, and classifies, objects
in the environment according to their essential attributes rather than
their functions: thus in the first place the environment exists for him as
a landscape or habitat rather than a niche (Ingold 1986b: 2–3). It
includes such categories of objects as plants and animals, from which
some are selected that will furnish suitable raw materials for consumption. The non-human forager, by contrast, merely responds to the
presence of environmental objects that are perceived to afford eating.
Whilst discriminating 'food' from 'non-food' objects, it does not recognize 'the animal' or 'the plant'. Only with the dawn of this recognition
does the forager become a hunter-gatherer.

Mode of production, mode of subsistence

'A mode of subsistence *per se* is not a "mode of production". The latter
includes not only the means for making a living but also the relationships involved' (Leacock and Lee 1982: 7). Hunting and gathering,
according to Lee, are but techniques, and as such belong quite definitely with the system of productive forces, rather than with the
relations of production (1980: 61). Ellen likewise includes both gathering and hunting, along with collecting, fishing and trapping, in his list
of the 'basic types' of subsistence technique for the procurement of

non-domesticated resources. Each technique is specified by 'a combination of material artifacts (tools and machines) and the knowledge required to make and use them'; the range of techniques employed by a single population then constitutes its mode of subsistence. Ellen insists that the concept of the mode of subsistence 'operates at the level of technical relations of production [and] indicates little about the *social* relations of production'. The latter, he argues, rest on a quite different foundation (Ellen 1982: 128; cf. idem, this volume).

Now if hunting and gathering were but techniques, in the sense of the definition just cited, they would comprise what hunters and gatherers use (their equipment) and what they know (their technology), but not what they actually *do*. Would anyone likewise suggest that cookery consists only in recipe books and kitchen utensils? The issue here again revolves around the question of whether, in hunting and gathering, human beings actually *produce* their subsistence. Consider one widely accepted definition of production, proposed by Godelier, and deliberately framed in such a way as to include the operations of hunting and gathering, in which objects are merely 'found' rather than physically transformed as in agriculture, craft and industry. 'Production', Godelier states, 'is the totality of the operations aimed at procuring for a society the material means of existence' (1972: 263). A structure of production is composed of three essential factors, which Godelier abbreviates as R (resources), I (instruments of labour) and M (men). Examining the third of these a little more closely, we find that M stands for the labour-power which may be delivered by the human body when put to work, and the skill and knowledge which underwrite the manufacture and use of the material instruments (I). In combination, I and M make up a working system of productive forces: thus in hunting I might include weapons, and M a set of operating instructions carried in men's heads, as well as the armature of their bodies.

In listing the elementary factors of the labour process in production, Marx likewise reduces them to three: 'First, purposive activity, or the labour itself; secondly, its subject matter; and thirdly, its instruments' (1930: 170). When it comes to 'the gathering of ready-made means of subsistence, such as fruits', Marx continues, 'man's own bodily organs suffice him as the instruments of labour' (ibid.: 171). Thus within the class of instruments we must include not only extrasomatic tools but also the apparatus and techniques of the body which are likewise integral to the system of forces operated by human beings in their productive activity. In short, the category I expands to include everything that for Godelier comes under M. So what remains? The answer lies in the conclusion of the last section, that the essence of hunting and gathering as *production* lies in the intentional control of procurement behaviour by the self-conscious human subject. We may retain the formula for production, as a combination of R, I and M, so

long as we take M to stand for the hunter-gatherer in his or her capacity
as an intentional agent rather than as a repository of bodily powers and
skills, that is as a person rather than an individual. Remove the person,
and hunting and gathering cease to be kinds of purposive activity, and
reduce to the mechanical execution of technique. This is equivalent, as
we have seen, to the reduction of production to extractive behaviour,
and of hunting and gathering to foraging.

Recall Ellen's definition of the mode of subsistence: a range of
techniques in use, each a combination of tools and operating skills. In
Marx's analysis of the labour process this clearly corresponds to the
instrumental component, consisting of the sum of somatic and extrasomatic forces. When set in motion, we characterize the resultant of
these forces as foraging, insofar as the outcome is resource extraction:

$$\text{foraging}$$
$$I \longrightarrow R$$

More generally, foraging can be written as a material interaction between one biological organism (the forager) and one or more others of
different species, resulting in the death of the latter and usually their
conversion into food for ingestion by the former (Ingold 1986b: 103–4).
As such it is a mode of subsistence, common to both human and
non-human animals. Hunting and gathering, however, correspond to
what Marx called 'the labour itself', *conducted* by the instrumental
apparatus, and directed on those constituents of the natural environment valorized as resources. It is the control, by the wilful subject, of
foraging interactions in which the subject's own body is engaged with
environmental objects:

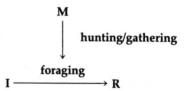

Thus conceived, hunting and gathering, *pace* Leacock and Lee, Ellen,
and many others, is no less than a mode of production. By that we
mean that it is not merely a pattern of subsistence behaviour but a way
in which people go about *producing* their subsistence, and indeed their
lives, through purposive social action.

Now by common consent, a mode of production is constituted by the
conjunction of a given set of technical forces of production and a
system of social relations of production; that is, it includes not only
what a person uses to produce, but also how he relates to other
persons, whether producers or non-producers. If it were true that the

practice of hunting and gathering could be wholly encompassed within the mechanical operation of the forces — if it were but a mode of subsistence — it must follow that the social relations are *external* to productive practice. And indeed we find that these relations are usually understood as a system of quasi-jural *rules*, in contradistinction to the technical rules governing the conduct of the labour process. These rules stipulate rights of access and control over means of production, specify how the available labour is to be allocated among diverse tasks, and lay down the form of redistribution of the product (Godelier 1978: 763). Among hunters and gatherers, the relations of production are said typically to include generalized or open access to resources, individual possession of tools and equipment, sexual division of labour, and sharing of produce (Lee 1980: 61–5).

What are the consequences of this separation of social relations from practical procurement activity, from 'the labour itself'? Curiously, they are to partition off the work of the human being from his or her life in society. In an idiom more reminiscent of Durkheim than Marx, it is supposed that whereas the technical rules (being contraposed to the social) are located in the consciousness of the *individual*, the jural rules (essentially social) are founded in a consciousness of the *collectivity*. Accordingly, when a man goes out hunting, whether alone or in company, he expresses his own individuality as an organic being, equipped with certain mental and physical powers constitutive of human nature. But on return with his kill, his individual identity is promptly submerged into that of the social group; and in submitting to the rules governing the distribution of the meat he expresses the collective will of society. Recalling Durkheim's celebrated dictum that there are 'two beings' in man, 'an individual being which has its foundations in the organism . . . and a social being which represents . . . society' (1976[1915]: 16), it appears that it is the individual who hunts and the social being who shares.

Sahlins expresses the same idea when, in attempting to define the economy, he opposes 'the process of (materially) provisioning society' to 'the human act of satisfying wants' (1974: 187 n.2). Procurement processes such as hunting and gathering, whose object is to provide food to provision *people*, are relegated to the (non-economic) sphere of need-fulfilling individual behaviour. But the transaction of food as in sharing, although it does not add to the stock of consumables, represents for Sahlins nothing less than 'the material life process of society' (ibid.: 186 n.1). Thus at the instant when transaction takes over from production, or sharing from hunting and gathering, the life of the individual gives way to the life of society.

This kind of polarization of individual and society, as distinct living entities, fundamentally distorts the reality of social life, which is a process going on between *persons*, each of whom is a responsible agent whose identity is constituted by his or her involvement with others in a wider field of relations. Hunting or gathering is not a moment in the life of the individual, any more than sharing is a moment in the life of society; rather both are moments in the social life of persons. Thus it is the hunter-gatherer *in person* who both labours to procure food and shares it out; and both production and distribution have equal claim for inclusion within the sphere of social action. It follows that the social relations of production, in hunting and gathering, are those constitutive of the hunter-gatherer as an intentional agent, as the *single* centre of consciousness from which productive and distributive activity issues.

No more can these relations be withdrawn from the labour process than can the purpose that presents and directs it. Even should a man or woman hunt and gather alone, the activity would still be social and not merely technical, since it discharges a purpose founded in the hunter-gatherer's responsibility towards other participants in his or her social ambience. But of course in speaking of social relations in this sense, we no longer understand them to be the building blocks of an *idéel* order, or a cognized system of rules; rather they have to be understood as relations of intersubjective involvement, or mutuality, binding persons directly as selves and not as the incumbents of positions in an objective structure.

I want to insist, then, that only by virtue of their involvement in relations of a particular kind can the practical activity of human beings be regarded as hunting and gathering; considered apart from these relations it is merely foraging. The notion that it might be possible to isolate a form of social relations specific to hunting and gathering has recently come in for a good deal of criticism, on the grounds that one cannot derive social relations from technical processes, or that to do so is to confuse the mode of production with the mode of subsistence (see, for example, Ellen 1982: 175). I fully concur with such objections to technological determinism; what I *reject*, however, is the assumption that hunting and gathering are but techniques. For this assumption entails the withdrawal of social consciousness from productive work, so that the labour process ceases to be regarded as a flow of intentional activity, and is fragmented into a string of discrete behavioural emissions generated as the mechanical output of a system of forces. And by the same token, appropriation — detached from production — becomes the expression of a structure of abstract, *idéel* rules. My view, to the contrary, is that hunting and gathering are socially directed, appropriative acts in which human beings purposively 'take hold' of the resources of their environments. Far from predicating social relations on technical criteria, I maintain that the social relations themselves both constitute and characterize the practical activities of hunting and gathering.

Band-living

The objection will surely be raised at this point that, whilst grounding hunting and gathering in relations of a particular kind, I have so far failed to specify anything about the form of these relations. For Leacock and Lee, they are bound up with 'band-living', yet just what a band is, and what life in a band entails, remain far from clear. In the two parts of this section, I intend to show first that the band is essentially a unit of cooperation, and that cooperative interaction — like foraging — represents one aspect of a mode of subsistence. In the second part I shall show that the social relations of hunting and gathering are those of sharing, or mutual 'face-to-face' involvement, and that these relations consequently stand to those of cooperation as hunting and gathering stands to foraging.

On cooperation

The production of life, wrote Marx and Engels, is social in that it involves 'the cooperation of several individuals, no matter under what conditions, in what manner, and to what end' (1977: 50). They were referring, of course, to *human* individuals; indeed Marx claimed to discern the earliest and simplest form of cooperation among hunter-gatherers, or 'tribes living by the chase'. In such tribes, he went on, 'the individual member is part of the community in the same sense in which the individual worker bee is part of the hive'. But the cooperation both of bees in the hive and in the human hunter-gatherer band was, for Marx, of a 'primitive' kind, and should be 'sharply distinguished from capitalist cooperation' (Marx 1930: 350–1). In reality, however, there is more in common between cooperation in the insect colony and in the manufacturer's workshop than meets the eye, and both may be similarly distinguished from the cooperation of the band. This common element lies in the observation that neither bees nor factory workers cooperate *in person* (Ingold 1986a: 250–1).

The criterion of cooperation is commonly emphasized in modern biological definitions of sociality, which are designed to be generally applicable right across the animal kingdom, and hence to be as appropriate to insects as to human beings. Dobzhansky, for example, defines society as 'a complex of individuals bound by co-operative interactions that serve to maintain a common life' (1962: 58). E.O. Wilson proposes an almost identical definition: '*Society*: A group of individuals belonging to the same species and organized in a co-operative manner' (1978: 222). There is no suggestion, in these definitions, that the cooperating individuals should be in the slightest degree self-aware; indeed among the so-called 'social' insects, cooperative behaviour is widely (though not universally) supposed to be guided automatically by a set of genetically encoded instructions. Clearly, therefore, cooperation is to be understood as the functioning of a complex mechanical system composed of an aggregate of relatively autonomous working parts (individuals). In such a system, the relations between the parts are of things and not persons, objects and not subjects.

Now consider capitalist manufacture. The definitive characteristic of this form of production is that for the duration of the labour process, the individual's capacity to work — including his knowledge and skill, and the apparatus of the body — is placed at the disposal of an alien will, that of the employer. Hence, when a number of individuals labour side by side, it is not they who co-operate, rather it is their labour-power that is co-*operated* by the employer. As Marx explains: 'Their co-operation does not begin till the labour process begins, but in the labour process they have already ceased to belong to themselves' (1930: 349). Whatever relations may exist between them as *selves*, that is as persons, must therefore be extrinsic to the labour process. In assembling numerous workers in the factory, each one detailed to execute but one specific operation in a production sequence, the employer creates what Marx (1930: 356) calls 'the living mechanism of manufacture' whose components consist of efficient human bodies. Cooperation, then, must lie in the physical workings of this mechanism, in the functioning of a super-individual system of productive forces.

In line with this conclusion, cooperation may be redefined as 'the conjoint engagement of working bodies whose result, in terms of the extraction or transformation of environmental materials, exceeds the sum of the effects of each body working independently' (Ingold 1986b: 120). It will immediately be apparent that this definition applies equally to the cooperation of bees in the hive and workers on the factory floor. Indeed, it seems no accident that only under capitalism does the scale and complexity of cooperation begin to approach that of the insect colony. For the more that consciousness develops, the less the individual is constrained by the conditions of the conspecific environment, and the greater are its powers of autonomous action. The advent of large-scale cooperation in human society had to await the systematic *repression* of these powers through historical forms of class exploitation, culminating in the alienation of labour-power under capitalist relations of production.

Though the scale of cooperation among hunters and gatherers is small by comparison, it is by no means negligible. Unlike insect foragers, hunter-gatherers act as self-conscious agents endowed with subjective intentionality; unlike factory workers, they remain in command of their own labour-power. The blueprint for cooperation, in this case, lies neither in the plan of a despotic authority (the capitalist), nor in genetically encoded predispositions, but in an acquired, *cultural* tradition. In his classic application of the method of cultural ecology to hunting and gathering societies, Steward demonstrated that the extent and nature of cooperation can be derived from a consideration of environmental conditions, including the habits of the species being exploited, together with the instrumental devices available for exploiting them. Thus cooperative arrangements are an important aspect of the 'behaviour patterns involved in the exploitation of a particular area by means of a particular technology' (Steward 1955: 40). Or as Murphy (1970: 155) has shown, they are part of the organization of work, establishing a programme to be followed in the course of normal procurement activity. In different environments, or in the exploitation of different species with different techniques, alternative patterns of cooperation will be required, each with its own characteristics of size and internal organization.

Now it is this organizational framework that constitutes the 'band' as an effective subsistence unit; that is, as a temporary aggregation of individuals or families that come together for the purpose of procuring food from a common range of country surrounding one or more residential centres. As Meillassoux has noted, the members of a band are generally differentiated, if at all, by their respective roles in the tasks of extraction (1981: 17). Most hunter-gatherers, of course, exploit quite a diversity of resources, and the same local group can switch with ease and spontaneity from one pattern of work to another as the situation demands. This organizational flexibility has repeatedly been shown to be of the essence of the foraging adaptation. Therefore, just as the mode of subsistence is defined as the range of subsistence techniques in use, we should perhaps also define the band as a unit organized to execute the entire mode rather than its particular, constituent operations. In other words, the band is not constituted to implement this or that technical form of labour, but to allow the concurrent implementation of a range of forms. Those recruited from the band for a specific procurement operation, of limited duration, form what Helm has called the 'task group' (Helm 1965: 378).

Let me now return to the definition of cooperation that emerged from our comparison of the insect colony and the manufacturer's workshop. It is clear that this definition may be extended to cover the patterns of cooperative behaviour entailed in 'band-living' which, just like patterns of foraging behaviour, are generated through the setting in motion of an instrumental apparatus, in this case comprising the bodily powers and skills of not only one but a plurality of individuals, harnessed to a common task. So long as the effect of cooperation is to make food procurement more efficient or reliable than if each individual were to forage alone, it is not difficult to see how it can arise as part of a population's adaptive response to the environmental conditions of extraction, just as it does among non-human foragers (Schaller and Lowther 1969: 330–3; Teleki 1975: 161–2). But if band-living implies cooperative foraging, it must represent the functioning of a mode of subsistence, not a mode of production. Recalling our formula for production as a combination of resources (R), instruments (I) and labour (M), and bearing in mind that I includes the apparatus and techniques of the body whereas M stands for human agency or the purpose that sets the body to work, cooperative relations — according to our definition — must be of the form I–I, and not M–M. Though they may exist between human beings, they do so only in so far as those human beings themselves exist as the bearers of bodily powers, as organisms. Thus we can write cooperative foraging in the following form:

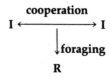

But the social relations of production, as I argued in the last section, exist between persons as subjects *in respect of* the instrumental apparatus: they are the relations M–M. Among hunters and gatherers such relations bind the very persons who act together in the labour process, and impart to it the purpose that puts their combined powers to work. Thus we can speak of their cooperation in two distinct senses: in terms of the *co*-operation of persons (M–M) and in terms of the co-*operation* of individual natures (I–I). It is by adopting the former, social sense of cooperation, referring to the intersubjective aspect of 'acting together', that Peter Wilson can assert that 'human hunters and gatherers are distinguished by the fact of their *co-operation and sharing*' (1975: 12). Yet as I shall show in the next part of this section, such cooperation is itself really a kind of sharing: namely, the sharing of activity. In drawing a distinction between sharing and cooperation, I therefore restrict the meaning of the latter term to its technical sense, pertaining to the organization of work. For only in this sense can the cooperative arrangements of human hunter-gatherers be compared with the organizations of non-human foragers on the one hand, and with the division of tasks in manufacture on the other.

Putting all our terms together — sharing, cooperation, hunting/gathering and foraging — we arrive at the picture shown in Figure 16.2. Here the relations of cooperation I–I compose a system of mechanical forces, operated in such a way as to generate foraging interactions with environmental objects (R). The operators are persons (M), bound by relations of sharing, and their joint, intentionally motivated action amounts to hunting and gathering. It remains for us to point out that in setting up a systematic contrast between relations of the form M–M and I–I, denoting the mutual involvement of persons and the interaction of

Figure 16.2 The relation between sharing and cooperation, and between hunting and gathering and foraging

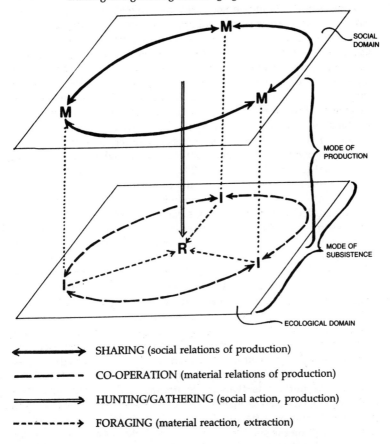

⟷ SHARING (social relations of production)

▬ ▬ ▬ ▬ ▬ CO-OPERATION (material relations of production)

⟹ HUNTING/GATHERING (social action, production)

- - - - - - - → FORAGING (material reaction, extraction)

individuals respectively, we are also distinguishing the specifically anthropological conception of sociality from that invoked in biological definitions, such as those already cited, which rest on the criterion of cooperation. For what the biological view equates with the social are here opposed to it, as forces to relations of production (Ingold 1986b: 23).

On sharing

The centrality of sharing to the way of life of human hunter-gatherers is a matter of general agreement. There is much less agreement, however, about what is actually *meant* by sharing. Broadly speaking we find, in the anthropological literature, three views of the ontological status of sharing: the first assumes it to be a type of behaviour; the second treats it as a cultural rule; whereas the third equates it with the experience of companionship in intimate social groups (Ingold 1986b: 113–17). Of these views, the first is most commonly encountered in discussions of the evolution of human subsistence patterns, which invariably draw on the possible comparisons and contrasts between the presumed practices of prehistoric hunter-gatherers and those of contemporary non-human primates (Teleki 1975: 151–5, Isaac 1978a). Underlying these discussions is the common assumption that what is at issue is the presence or absence of a particular behavioural trait or attribute. Sharing, thus, is reduced to a thing that humans (and possibly other primates) 'have', taking its place among such other contested criteria of human uniqueness as language, tool-making, sexual division of labour and bipedal locomotion (Ingold 1982: 163). As a kind of behaviour, sharing appears in the form of events of distribution whose consequence is the consumption of food by individuals other than the procurer, and is regarded as the spontaneous expression of innate dispositions fixed at some point in the phylogenetic history of the human species.

Pitted against this view of sharing is the second, which regards it as an expression not so much of desires inherent in the nature of individuals as of an imposed code of regulations emanating from an external source in society. As Peter Wilson puts it, 'the individual does not share "naturally" — it is the obligation to share that counts' (1975: 12). Fortes takes a similar view, treating sharing as an instance of what he calls 'prescriptive altruism'. The cohesion of hunter-gatherer communities, he writes, 'is based on the dominance of the rule of prescriptive altruism reflected in their ethic of sharing in all aspects of their social and economic life' (1983: 26). By 'prescriptive altruism', Fortes specifically has in mind acts that are 'culturally defined, rule-governed, intentionally exercised, perceived as moral obligations' (ibid.: 29). This sense of sharing will be recalled from our earlier discussion of the effects of writing the social relations of production as a set of jural rules governing distribution, such that sharing is set apart from hunting and gathering as the expression of the collective rather than the individual will. Our view, to the contrary, is that responsibility for both production and distribution lies neither with the individual (outside society) nor with society (outside the individual), but with the person constituted as a wilful agent within a matrix of intersubjective relations. This conclusion serves to introduce the third sense of sharing, as an experience of intersubjective involvement.

The idiom that best captures what we mean by this experience is one of *companionship*, or 'shared activity in itself' (Gibson 1985: 393). This idiom, as Gibson shows, 'implies that social actors come together as autonomous agents to pursue a common goal', and may be contrasted with the idiom of kinship which implies the placing of people under obligation, creating mutual dependency rather than preserving the personal autonomy of those involved. Now for Fortes the very essence of kinship is the rule of prescriptive altruism, whose expression among hunters and gatherers he equates with sharing. Thus sharing as experience differs from sharing as rule precisely as companionship differs from kinship. In my view, the former comes closer to the reality of sharing in hunter-gatherer communities which, by and large, are *not* significantly structured by formal kinship relations. To lend weight to this view, I would stress the regular conjunction of the idiom of sharing with an equally strong emphasis on the preservation of personal autonomy. Far from being an index of the submission of the particular man or woman to the authority of the social collectivity, sharing *underwrites* the autonomy of the person, who thus remains wholly accountable for his or her actions. In short, it is not in spite of their mutual involvement, but because of it, that people in hunting and gathering societies enjoy a fundamental autonomy of intention and action (Ingold 1986b: 239–40).

I believe that this sense of sharing, as companionship, is what is conveyed by the many ethnographic accounts that attribute the cohesion of hunter-gatherer communities to 'face-to-face relationships'. Such relationships, as the phrase implies, bind persons directly, as selves rather than as the occupants of positions in a rule-governed 'social structure'. Projected over an extended period of time, they compose in Price's terms an 'intimate social group . . . small in scale and personal in quality' (1975: 4). Moreover, as he points out, in an intimate economy the experience of mutual 'face-to-face' involvement is intrinsic to productive activity as well as to distribution. Thus sharing does not come into play at the *end* of production, but rather constitutes the common purpose that people *bring into* the productive process itself. This purpose both originates with, and seeks fulfilment through, the community as a whole. Of course, in arguing that sharing is equivalent to integration through face-to-face relationships, we are not limiting the objects of sharing to food, since food-sharing may itself be only one aspect of the sharing of activities and company. In a word, people in hunting and gathering communities share *one another*: these are the social relations of the hunter-gatherer mode of production, determining both the responsibilities taken into procurement activity and the manner of distribution of the products.

Conclusion

I should like to end with some remarks on the way in which we draw the boundary between social and ecological systems. By definition, ecology deals with the interrelations between organisms and their environments (Odum 1975: 1–4). For an individual organism, the environment normally comprises three components: inanimate objects, individuals of other species, and conspecifics. Thus both the extractive relations of foraging and the cooperative relations of the band may equally be comprehended within an ecological framework, covering respectively the fields of interspecific and intraspecific organism–environment interactions. Referring back to Figure 16.2, these correspond to the relations I–R and I–I, all of which are located in the ecological domain. But these are quite distinct from the relations between human beings of the kind we call social (M–M), which among hunters and gatherers take the form of sharing, and link them in their capacity as persons rather than as individuals. Hence, sharing and cooperation represent two facets, the one social and the other ecological, of the totality of intraspecific relations.

This duality was long ago anticipated by Marx and Engels in their remark that 'the production of life . . . appears as a double relationship: on the one hand as a natural, on the other as a social relationship' (1977: 50). As Cohen has pointed out, this is an initial statement of a pervasive dichotomy in the Marxian paradigm, 'between *material and social relations of production*' (G. Cohen 1978: 92). The distinction being made here is not simply one between inter- and intraspecific relations, placing, for example, relations linking human hunter-gatherers and their prey on one side, and relations among the hunter-gatherers themselves on the other. For to the extent that human beings (in addition to individuals of the species they exploit) exist as components of the natural world, as organisms, *so also must the relations between them* (Ingold 1986b: 124). Hence, both foraging interactions (I–R) and cooperative interactions (I–I) belong to the field of what Marx called 'natural' or 'material' relations, and what we — following more modern usage — regard as the relations that make up an ecological system.

Having distinguished the social and ecological aspects of the intraspecific relations of human beings, it is evident that a precisely equivalent dichotomy can be drawn, in regard to interspecific relations, between social action and ecological reaction: the one issuing from the person who is the subject of social relations, the other from the individual organism within an environment of other organisms. I have argued that the first is hunting and gathering, the second foraging. Thus interspecific relations, just as intraspecific ones, have their social and ecological aspects. Sharing is a social relation, but then so is hunting and gathering a social action. Foraging is an ecological reaction, but then so is cooperation an ecological interaction.

We cannot therefore place the boundary between the social and the ecological at the boundary of the human species, putting all intraspecific relations into the domain of the former and all interspecific relations into the domain of the latter. Nor (*pace* Lee 1969: 73) does it make sense to set up a division of anthropological labour between economists who study intraspecific, distributive exchange and ecologists who study interspecific, trophic exchange (Cook 1973: 42–3). It is precisely this sort of division that has both perpetuated the reduction of human productive practice to patterns of extractive behaviour strictly comparable to those of non-human foragers, and promoted the belief that humans are distinguished from non-human animals not by the production but by the distribution of the means of subsistence. In fact, patterns of food distribution may be observed in many animal species; but only when distributive behaviour is brought under the control of a socially constituted purpose does it amount to sharing. And only when extractive behaviour is likewise controlled does it amount to production. Our conclusion, then, is that the boundary between the social and the ecological corresponds to that between the intentional and the behavioural components of action, marking the point — in human life — where purpose takes over from, and proceeds to direct, the mechanism of nature.

References

Allen, H. 1974. 'The Bagundji of the Darling Basin: cereal gatherers in an uncertain environment', *World Archaeology, 5*, 309–22.

Althabe, G. 1965. 'Changements sociaux chez les Pygmées Baka de l'Est-Cameroun', *Cahiers d'Etudes Africaines, 5*, 561–92.

Altman, J. and N. Peterson 1988. 'Rights to game and rights to cash among contemporary Australian hunter-gatherers', in T. Ingold, D. Riches and J. Woodburn (eds.), *Hunters and gatherers II: Property, power and ideology*, Oxford: Berg.

Ames, K.M. 1985. 'Hierarchies, stress and logistical strategies among hunter-gatherers in Northwest America', in T. Price and J. Brown (eds.), *Prehistoric hunter-gatherers: the emergence of cultural complexity*, Orlando, FL: Academic.

Anderson, P. 1974. *Passages from antiquity to feudalism*, London: New Left Books.

—— 1983. *In the tracks of historical materialism*, London: Verso.

Andrews, P. 1984. 'An alternative explanation of the characters used to define Homo erectus', *Cour. Forsch. Inst. Senckenberg, 69*, 167–75.

Arbruzzi, W. 1980. 'Flux among the Mbuti Pygmies of the Ituri forest', in E. Ross (ed.), *Beyond the myths of culture: essays in cultural materialism*, New York: Academic.

Ardrey, R. 1961. *African genesis*, New York: Dell.

Asch, M. 1982. 'Dene self-determination and the study of hunter-gatherers in the modern world', in E. Leacock and R. Lee (eds.), *Politics and history in band societies*, Cambridge: Cambridge University Press.

—— 1984. *Home and native land: Aboriginal rights and the Canadian constitution*, Toronto: Methuen.

Axelrod, R. and W. Hamilton 1981. 'The evolution of cooperation', *Science, 211*, 1390–6.

Bagshawe, F. 1925. 'The people of the Happy Valley (East Africa): the aboriginal races of Kondoa Irangi', *Journal of the African Society, 24*, 117–30.

Bahuchet, S. and H. Guillaume 1982. 'Aka–farmer relations in the north-west Congo basin', in E. Leacock and R. Lee (eds.), *Politics and history in band societies*, Cambridge: Cambridge University Press.

Bailey, G. 1981a. 'Concepts of resource exploitation: continuity and discontinuity in palaeoeconomy', *World Archaeology, 13*, 1–15.

—— 1981b. 'Concepts, time-scales and explanations in economic prehistory', in A. Sheridan and G. Bailey (eds.), *Economic archaeology*, Oxford: BAR International Series 96.

—— 1983. 'Hunter-gatherer behaviour in prehistory', in G. Bailey (ed.), *Hunter-gatherer economy in prehistory: a European perspective*, Cambridge: Cambridge University Press.

Bailey, R. 1985. *The socioecology of the Efe Pygmy men in the Ituri forest, Zaire*, Ann Arbor, MI: University Microfilms.

Bailey, R. and N. Peacock. 1988. 'Efe Pygmies of northeast Zaire: subsistence strategies in the Ituri forest', in I. de Garine and G.A. Harrison (eds.), *Coping with uncertainty in food supply*, Oxford: Clarendon Press.

Barnard, A. 1979. 'Kalahari Bushman settlement patterns', in P. Burnham and R. Ellen (eds.), *Social and ecological systems*, London: Academic.

—— 1983. 'Contemporary hunter-gatherers: current theoretical issues in ecology and social organization', *Annual Review of Anthropology*, 12, 193–214.

Barrau, J. 1959. 'The sago palms and other food plants of marsh dwellers in the South Pacific Islands', *Economic Botany*, 13, 151–62.

Beaton, J. 1982. 'Fire and water: aspects of Australian Aboriginal management of cycads', *Archaeology in Oceania*, 17, 51–8.

Beck, B. 1980. *Animal tool behaviour: the use and manufacture of tools by animals*, New York: Garland STPM Press.

Bellwood, P. 1976. 'Prehistoric plant and animal domestication in Austronesia', in G. Sieveking, I. Longworth and K. Wilson (eds.), *Problems in economic and social archaeology*, London: Duckworth.

Bender, B. 1978. 'Gatherer-hunter to farmer: a social perspective', *World Archaeology*, 10, 204–23.

—— 1981. 'Gatherer-hunter intensification', in A. Sheridan and G. Bailey (eds.), *Economic archaeology*, Oxford: BAR International Series 96.

—— 1985. 'Emergent tribal formations in the American midcontinent', *American Antiquity*, 50, 52–62.

—— 1988. 'The roots of inequality', in M. Rowlands, D. Miller and C. Tilley (eds.), *Domination and resistance*, London: Allen & Unwin.

Bern, J. 1979. 'Ideology and domination: towards a reconstruction of Australian Aboriginal social formation', *Oceania*, 50, 118–32.

Bicchieri, M. (ed.) 1972. *Hunters and gatherers today*, New York: Holt, Rinehart and Winston.

Binford, L. 1962. 'Archaeology as anthropology', *American Antiquity*, 28, 217–25.

—— 1980. 'Willow smoke and dog's tails: hunter-gatherer settlement systems and archaeological site formation', *American Antiquity*, 45, 4–20.

—— 1981. *Bones: ancient men and modern myths*, New York: Academic.

—— 1983. *In pursuit of the past: decoding the archaeological record*, London: Thames and Hudson.

—— 1984. *Faunal remains from Klasies River mouth*, New York: Academic.

Binford, L. and J. Sabloff 1982. 'Paradigms, systematics and archaeology', *Journal of Anthropological Research*, 38, 137–53.

Bird, N. (afterwards Bird-David) 1982. '"Inside" and "outside" in kinship usage: the hunter-gatherer Naiken of South India', *Cambridge Anthropology*, 7, 47–57.

—— 1983a. 'Conjugal units and single persons: analysis of the social system of the Naiken of South India', PhD dissertation, Cambridge University.

—— 1983b. 'Wage-gathering: socio-economic change and the case of the Naiken of South India', in P. Robb (ed.), *Rural South Asia: linkages, changes and development*, London: Curzon Press.

Bird-David, N. (formerly Bird) 1987 'Single person and social cohesion in a hunter-gatherer society', in P. Hockings (ed.), *Dimensions of social life: essays in honour of David G. Mandelbaum*, Berlin: Mouton.

Blackburn, R. 1970. 'A preliminary report of research on the Ogiek tribe of Kenya', Discussion Paper 1, Institute for Development Studies, University College, Nairobi.

—— 1971. 'Honey in Okiek personality, culture and society', PhD dissertation, Michigan State University.

—— 1974. 'The Okiek and their history', *Azania*, 9, 139–57.

—— 1982. 'In the land of milk and honey: Okiek adaptations to their forests and neighbours', in E. Leacock and R. Lee (eds.), *Politics and history in band societies*, Cambridge: Cambridge University Press.

Blurton Jones, N. 1984. 'A selfish origin for human food sharing: tolerated theft', *Ethology and Sociobiology*, 5, 1–3.

Bonner, P. 1981. 'The dynamics of late eighteenth century northern Nguni society: some hypotheses', in J. Peires (ed.), *Before and after Shaka. Papers in Nguni history*, Grahamstown: Rhodes University Institute for Social and Economic Research.

Bose, N. 1956. 'Some observations on nomadic castes of India', *Man in India*, 36, 1–6.

Boyd, M., H. Smith and J. Griffith 1951. *Here they once stood: the tragic end of the Apalachee missions*, Gainesville: University of Florida Press.

Boyd, R. and P. Richerson 1985. *Culture and the evolutionary process*, Chicago: University of Chicago Press.

Braudel, F. 1980. *On history*, London: Weidenfeld and Nicolson.

Brauer, G. 1984. 'A craniological approach to the origins of anatomically modern *Homo sapiens* in Africa and implications for the appearance of modern Europeans', in F. Smith and F. Spencer (eds.), *The origins of modern humans*, New York: A.R. Liss.

Breeks, J. 1873. *An account of the primitive tribes and monuments of the Nilgiris*, London: India Museum.

Bromage, T. and M. Dean 1985. 'Re-evaluation of the age at death of immature fossil hominids', *Nature*, 317, 525–7.

Bronson, B. 1977. 'The earliest farming: demography as cause and consequences', in C. Reed (ed.), *Origins of agriculture*, The Hague: Mouton.

Brown, J. 1964. 'The evolution of diversity in avian territorial systems', *Wilson Bulletin*, 76, 160–9.

Brown, P. 1978. *Highland peoples of New Guinea*, New York: Cambridge University Press.

Bunn, H. and E. Kroll 1986. 'Systematic butchery by Plio-Pleistocene hominids at Olduvai Gorge, Tanzania', *Current Anthropology*, 27, 431–52.

Burch, E. 1980. 'Traditional Eskimo societies in Northwest Alaska', in Y. Kotani and W. Workman (eds.), *Alaska native culture and history*, Osaka: National Museum of Ethnology (Senri Ethnology Series 4).

—— 1988. 'Modes of exchange in Northwest Alaska', in T. Ingold, D. Riches and J. Woodburn (eds.), *Hunters and gatherers II: Property, power and ideology*, Oxford: Berg.

Burnham, P. 1980. *Opportunity and constraint in a Savanna society*, London: Academic.

Butlin, N. 1983. *Our original aggression: Aboriginal populations of southeastern*

Australia 1788–1850, Sydney: Allen & Unwin.

Cabral, A. 1974. 'The weapon of theory', in *Return to the source: selected speeches*. New York: Monthly Review Press.

Cann, R., M. Stoneking and A. Wilson 1987. 'Mitochondrial DNA and human evolution', *Nature*, 325, 31–6.

Caraco, T. 1980. 'On foraging time allocation in a stochastic environment', *Ecology*, 61, 119–28.

Carlos II, King of Spain. 1698. Manuscript, Archivo General de Indias, Seville. Photostat copy, Gainesville: P. K. Yonge Library of Florida History, Stetson Collection.

Carolis, A. de 1977. 'Changements socio-économiques et dégradation culturelle chez les Pygmoïdes Ba-Twa du Burundi', *Africa* (Rome) 32, 201–32.

Cashdan, E. 1980. 'Egalitarianism among hunters and gatherers', *American Anthropologist*, 82, 116–20.

—— 1983. 'Territoriality among human foragers: ecological models and an application to four Bushman groups', *Current Anthropology*, 24, 47–66.

—— 1985. 'Coping with risk: reciprocity among the Basarwa of Northern Botswana', *Man*, 20, 454–74.

Chang, C. 1982. 'Nomads without cattle: East African foragers in historical perspective', in E. Leacock and R. Lee (eds.), *Politics and history in band societies*, Cambridge: Cambridge University Press.

Ciochon, R. 1983. 'Hominid cladistics and the ancestry of modern apes and humans'. in R. Ciochon and R. Corruccini (eds.), *New interpretations of ape and human ancestry*, New York: Plenum.

Clark, C. and M. Mangel 1986. 'The evolutionary advantages of group foraging', *Theoretical Population Biology*, 11, 19–34.

Clutton-Brock, T. and P. Harvey 1978. 'Mammals, resources and reproductive strategies', *Nature*, 273, 191–5.

—— 1981. 'Primate home range size and metabolic needs', *Behavioural Ecology and Sociobiology*, 8, 151–5.

Cohen, G. 1978. *Karl Marx's theory of history: a defence*, Oxford: Clarendon Press.

Cohen, M. 1985. 'Prehistoric hunter-gatherers: the meaning of social complexity', in T. Price and J. Brown (eds.), *Prehistoric hunter-gatherers: the emergence of cultural complexity*, Orlando, FL: Academic.

Cohn, B. 1961. 'Chamar family in a North Indian village', *Economic Weekly*, 13, 1051–5.

Colson, E. 1962. 'Residence and village stability among the Plateau Tonga', in E. Colson (ed.), *The Plateau Tonga of Northern Rhodesia*, Manchester: Manchester University Press.

Conkey, M. 1984. 'To find ourselves: art and social geography of prehistoric hunter-gatherers', in C. Schrire (ed.), *Past and present in hunter-gatherer studies*, London: Academic.

Conner, J. (trans. and ed.) 1925. *Colonial records of Spanish Florida: letters and reports of governors and secular persons, vol. 1, 1570–1577*, Deland: Florida State Historical Society, Publications 5.

Cook, S. 1973. 'Production, ecology and economic anthropology: notes towards an integrated frame of reference', *Social Science Information*, 12, 25–52.

Cowgill, G. 1975. 'On causes and consequences of ancient and modern population changes', *American Anthropologist*, 77, 505–25.

Cumbaa, S. 1971. 'A comparison of animal bone from six Indian sites on Marco Island, Florida', manuscript on file, Gainesville: Florida State Museum.

Cushing, F. 1897. 'Exploration of ancient key dweller remains on the gulf coast of Florida', *American Philosophical Society Proceedings*, 35, 329–448.

Cutler, H. 1975. 'Appendix D: Two kinds of gourds from Key Marco', in M. Gilliland, *The material culture of Key Marco, Florida*, Gainesville: University Presses of Florida.

Davies, N. and A. Houston 1984. 'Territory economics', in J. Krebs and N. Davies (eds.), *Behavioural ecology: an evolutionary approach*, Oxford: Blackwell.

Davies, O. 1975. 'Excavations at Shongweni South Cave: the oldest evidence to date for cultigens in southern Africa', *Annals of the Natal Museum*, 22, 627–62.

Dawkins, R. 1980. 'Good strategy or evolutionarily stable strategy?', in G. Barlow and J. Silverberg (eds.), *Sociobiology: beyond nature/nurture?*, Boulder, CO: Westview.

Day, M. 1985. 'Bipedalism: pressures, origins and modes', in B. Wood, L. Martin and P. Andrews (eds.), *Major topics in primate and human evolution*, Cambridge: Cambridge University Press.

de Carolis, A. See Carolis, A. de

Deacon, H. 1976. *Where hunters gathered*, Cape Town: South African Archaeological Society.

Dean, M., C. Stringer and T. Bromage 1986. 'Age at death of the Neanderthal child from Devil's Tower, Gibraltar and the implications for studies of general growth and development of Neanderthals', *American Journal of Physical Anthropology*, 70, 301–9.

Deetz, J. 1968. 'Hunters in archaeological perspective', in R. Lee and I. DeVore (eds.), *Man the hunter*, Chicago: Aldine.

Denbow, J. 1984. 'Prehistoric hunters and foragers of the Kalahari: the evidence for 1500 years of interaction', in C. Schrire (eds.), *Past and present in hunter-gatherer studies*, London: Academic.

Denbow, J. and E. Wilmsen 1983. 'Iron age pastoralist settlements in Botswana', *South African Journal of Science*, 79, 405–7.

Diamond, S. 1974. *In search of the primitive: a critique of civilization*, New Brunswick, NJ: Transaction Books.

Dickinson, J. 1985. *Jonathan Dickinson's journal or God's protecting providence, being the narrative of a journey from Port Royal in Jamaica to Philadelphia, August 23, 1696 to April 1st, 1697*, Port Salerno, FL: Florida Classics Library.

Dobb, M. 1946. *Studies in the development of capitalism*, London: Routledge and Kegan Paul.

Dobyns, H. 1983. *Their number become thinned*, Knoxville: University of Tennessee Press.

Dobzhansky, T. 1962. *Mankind evolving*, New Haven, CT: Yale University Press.

Dongen, G.J. van 1906. 'Bijdrage tot de kennis van de Ridan-Koeboes', *Tijdschrift voor het Binnenlandsch Bestuur*, 30, 225–63.

—— 1910. 'De Koeboes in de Onderafdeeling Koeboestreken der Residentie Palembang', *Bijdragen tot de Taal-, Land-, en Volkenkunde*, 63, 73–110.

Dowling, J. 1968. 'Individual ownership and the sharing of game in hunting societies', *American Anthropologist*, 70, 502–7.

Drucker, P. 1963. *Indians of the Northwest Coast*, Garden City, NY: The Natural History Press.
—— 1965. *Cultures of the north Pacific coast*, San Francisco: Chandler.
Dumont, L. 1953. 'The Dravidian kinship terminology as an expression of marriage', *Man* (old series), 54, 34–9.
Dunn, F. 1975. *Rainforest collectors and traders: a study of resource utilization in modern and ancient Malaya*, Monograph of the Malaysian Branch of the Royal Asiatic Society.
Dupre, J. (ed.), 1987. *The latest on the best: essays on evolution and optimality*, Cambridge, MA: Bradford Books/MIT Press.
Durham, W. 1988. *Coevolution: genes, culture and human diversity*, Stanford, CA: Stanford University Press.
Durkheim, E. 1976. *The elementary forms of religious life* (trans. J. Swain), 2nd ed, London: Allen & Unwin, first published in 1915.
Dwyer, P. 1974. 'The price of protein: five hundred hours of hunting in the New Guinea highlands', *Oceania*, 44, 278–93.
Dyson-Hudson, R. and E. Alden Smith 1978. 'Human territoriality: an ecological reassessment', *American Anthropologist*, 80, 21–41.
Eisner Putnam, A. 1954. *Madami: my eight years of adventure with the Congo Pygmies*, New York: Prentice Hall.
Elder, J. 1978. 'Caloric returns to food collecting: disruption and change among the Batak of the Philippine tropical forest', *Human Ecology*, 6, 55–69.
Ellen, R. 1973. 'Nuaulu settlement and ecology: an approach to the environmental relations of an eastern Indonesian community', PhD dissertation, London University.
—— 1975. 'Non-domesticated resources in Nuaulu ecological relations', *Social Science Information,* 14, 51–61.
—— 1977a. 'The place of sago in the subsistence economies of Seram', in K. Tan (ed.), *The equatorial swamp as a natural resource*, Kuala Lumpur: Kemajuan Kanji.
—— 1977b. 'Resource and commodity. Problems in the analysis of the social relations of Nuaulu land use', *Journal of Anthropological Research*, 33, 50–72.
—— 1978a. *Nuaulu settlement and ecology: an approach to the environmental relations of an eastern Indonesian community*, The Hague: Martinus Nijhoff.
—— 1978b. 'Problems and progress in the ethnographic analysis of small-scale human ecosystems', *Man*, 13, 290–303.
—— 1979. 'Sago subsistence and the trade in spices. A provisional model of ecological succession and imbalance in Moluccan history', in P. Burnham and R. Ellen (eds.), *Social and ecological systems*, London: Academic.
—— 1982. *Environment, subsistence and system. The ecology of small-scale social formations*, Cambridge: Cambridge University Press.
—— 1984. 'Trade, environment and the reproduction of local systems in the Moluccas', in E. Moran (ed.), *The ecosystem concept in anthropology*, Boulder, CO: American Association for the Advancement of Science.
—— 1985. 'Patterns of indigenous timber extraction from Moluccan rain forest fringes', *Journal of Biogeography*, 12, 559–87.
—— 1987. 'Environmental perturbation, inter-island trade and the re-location of production along the Banda arc; or, why central places remain central', in T. Suzuki and R. Ohtsuka (eds.), *Human ecology of health and survival in Asia and*

the South Pacific, Tokyo: University of Tokyo Press.

—— 1988. 'Ritual, identity and the management of inter-ethnic relations on Seram', in H. Claessen and D. Moyer (eds.), *Essays in honor of P.E. de Josselin de Jong*.

Elster, J. 1982. 'Marxism, functionalism and game theory', *Theory and Society 11*, 453–82.

—— 1983. *Explaining technical change: a case study in the philosophy of science*, Cambridge: Cambridge University Press.

—— 1985. *Making sense of Marx*, Cambridge: Cambridge University Press.

Endicott, K. 1979. *Batek Negrito religion*, Oxford: Clarendon Press.

—— 1983. 'The effects of slave raiding on the Aborigines of the Malay Peninsula', in A. Reid and J. Brewster (eds.), *Slavery, bondage and dependency in Southeast Asia*, St Lucia: University of Queensland Press.

—— 1984. 'The economy of the Batek of Malaysia: annual and historical perspective', *Research in Economic Anthropology*, 6, 29–52.

—— 1988. 'Property, power and conflict among the Batek of Malaysia', in T. Ingold, D. Riches and J. Woodburn (eds.), *Hunters and gatherers II: Property, power and ideology*, Oxford: Berg.

Endicott, K.L. 1981. 'The conditions of egalitarian male–female relationships in foraging societies', *Canberra Anthropology*, 4, 1–10.

Engels, F. 1934. *Dialectics of nature*, Moscow: Progress.

Engelstad, E. 1984. 'Diversity in arctic maritime adaptations: an example from the Late Stone Age of arctic Norway', *Acta Borealia*, 2, 3–23.

Erasmus, C. 1956. 'Culture, structure and process: the occurrence and disappearance of reciprocal farm labor', *Southwestern Journal of Anthropology*, 12, 444–69.

Estevan, J. 1698. 'Declaration' (transl. V. Johnson). AGI: Santo Domingo, 154, Archivo General de Indias, Seville. Translation on file, Gainesville: Florida State Museum.

Evans-Pritchard, E. 1951. *Kinship and marriage among the Nuer*, London: Oxford University Press.

Falk-Rønne, A. 1972. *I Stanleys fotspor gjennom Afrika*, Oslo: Lutherstiftelsen.

Faris, J. 1975. 'Social evolution, population and production', in S. Polgar (ed.), *Population, ecology and social evolution*, The Hague: Mouton.

—— 1977. 'Primitive accumulation in small-scale fishing communities', in M.E. Smith (ed.), *Those who live from the sea*, St Paul, MN: West Publishing Company.

Feit, H. 1986. 'Anthropologists and the state: the relationship between social policy advocacy and academic practice in the history of the Algonquian hunting territory debate, 1910–50', paper presented at the Fourth International Conference on Hunting and Gathering Societies, London.

Fernandez, C. and F. Lynch 1972. 'The Tasaday: cave-dwelling food gatherers of South Cotabato, Mindanao', *Philippine Sociological Review*, 20, 279–313.

Firth, R. 1936. *We the Tikopia*, London: George Allen & Unwin.

—— 1946. *Malay fishermen: their peasant economy*, London: Routledge and Kegan Paul.

Fitzhugh, W. (ed.), 1975. *Prehistoric maritime adaptations in the circumpolar zone*, The Hague: Mouton.

Flinn, M. and R. Alexander 1982. 'Culture theory: the developing synthesis from biology', *Human Ecology*, 10, 383–400.

Flood, J. 1980. *The moth hunters*, Canberra: Australian Institute of Aboriginal Studies.

Foley, R. 1978. 'Incorporating sampling into initial research design: some aspects of spatial archaeology', in J. Cherry, C. Gamble and S. Shennan (eds.), *Sampling in contemporary British archaeology*, Oxford: BAR (British Series) 50.

—— 1984. 'Early man and the Red Queen: tropical African community ecology and hominid adaptation', in R. Foley (ed.), *Hominid evolution and community ecology: prehistoric human adaptation in biological perspective*, London: Academic.

—— 1985. 'Optimality theory in anthropology', *Man*, 20, 222–42.

—— 1987. *Another unique species: patterns in human evolutionary ecology*, London: Longman.

Fontaneda, Do. d'Escalante 1945. *Memoir of Do. d'Escalante Fontaneda respecting Florida, written in Spain, about the year 1575* (transl. B. Smith and with editorial comments by D. True), Coral Gables, FL: Glade House.

Forrest, T. 1969. *A voyage to New Guinea and the Moluccas, 1774–1776*, Kuala Lumpur: Oxford University Press, first published 1779.

Fortes, M. 1983. *Rules and the emergence of society*, London: Royal Anthropological Institute.

Fox, J. 1977. *Harvest of the palm: ecological change in eastern Indonesia*, Cambridge: Cambridge University Press.

Fox, R. 1969. '"Professional primitives": hunters and gatherers of nuclear south Asia', *Man in India 49*, 139–60.

Fradkin, A. 1976. 'The Wightman site: a study of prehistoric culture and environment on Sanibel Island, Lee county, Florida', MA thesis, University of Florida.

Frayer, D. 1984. 'Biological and cultural change in the European late Pleistocene and early Holocene', in F. Smith and F. Spencer (eds.), *The origins of modern humans: a world survey of the fossil evidence*, New York: Alan Liss.

Freeman, L. 1968. 'A theoretical framework for interpreting archaeological materials, in R. Lee and I. De Vore (eds.), *Man the hunter*, Chicago: Aldine.

Freeman, M. 1969–70. 'Studies in maritime hunting I: ecologic and technologic constraints on walrus hunting, Southampton Island, N.W.T.', *Folk, 11–12*, 155–71.

Fried, M. 1967. *The evolution of political society*, New York: Random House.

Friedman, J. 1979. *System, structure and contradiction in the evolution of 'Asiatic' social formations*, Copenhagen: The National Museum of Denmark.

Friedman, J. and M. Rowlands 1978. 'Notes towards an epigenetic model of the evolution of "civilization"', in J. Friedman and M. Rowlands (eds.), *The evolution of social systems*, London: Duckworth.

Gamble, C. 1986. *The Palaeolithic settlement of Europe*, Cambridge: Cambridge University Press.

García, G. (ed.), 1902. *Dos antiguas relaciones de la Florida*, Mexico City: J. Aguilar Vera.

Gardner, P. 1965. 'Ecology and social structure in refugee populations: the Paliyans of South India', PhD dissertation, University of Pennsylvania.

—— 1966. 'Symmetric respect and memorate knowledge: the structure and ecology of individualistic culture', *Southwestern Journal of Anthropology, 22*, 389–415.

—— 1969. 'Paliyan social structure', in D. Damas (ed.), *Contributions to anthropology: band societies*, Ottawa: National Museums of Canada.

—— 1972. 'The Paliyans', in M. Bicchieri (ed.), *Hunters and gatherers today*, New York: Holt, Rinehart and Winston.

—— 1978. 'India's changing tribes: identity and interaction in crises', in G.R. Gupta (ed.), *Main currents in Indian sociology. Volume 3: Cohesion and conflict in modern India*, Durham, NC: Carolina Academic Press.

—— 1982. 'Ascribed austerity: a tribal path to purity', *Man*, 17, 462–9.

—— 1983. 'Cyclical adaptations on variable cultural frontiers', *Nomadic Peoples*, 12, 14–19.

—— 1985. 'Bicultural oscillation as a long-term adaptation to cultural frontiers: cases and questions', *Human Ecology*, 13, 411–32.

Geiger, M. 1937. *The Franciscan conquest of Florida, 1573–1618* (Studies in Hispanic-American History, volume 1), Washington, DC: Catholic University of America Press.

Gibson, J.J. 1979. *The ecological approach to visual perception*, Boston: Houghton-Mifflin.

Gibson, T. 1985. 'The sharing of substance versus the sharing of activity among the Buid', *Man*, 20, 391–411.

Giddens, A. 1981. *A contemporary critique of historical materialism*, London: Macmillan.

—— 1984. *The constitution of society. Outline of the theory of structuration* Cambridge: Polity Press.

Gilliland, M. 1975. *The material culture of Key Marco, Florida*, Gainesville: University Presses of Florida.

Gilman, A. 1984. 'Explaining the Upper Palaeolithic revolution', in M. Spriggs (ed.), *Marxist perspectives in archaeology*, Cambridge: Cambridge University Press.

Glover, I. 1977. 'The Hoabinhian: hunter-gatherers or early agriculturalists in South-east Asia?', in J. Megaw (ed.), *Hunters, gatherers and first farmers beyond Europe*, Leicester: Leicester University Press.

Gluckman, M. 1965. *Politics, law and ritual in tribal societies*, Chicago: Aldine.

Godelier, M. 1972. *Rationality and irrationality in economics*, London: New Left Books.

—— 1975. 'Modes of production, kinship and demographic structures', in M. Bloch (ed.), *Marxist analyses and social anthropology*, London: Malaby Press.

—— 1977. *Perspectives in Marxist anthropology*, Cambridge: Cambridge University Press.

—— 1978. 'Infrastructures, societies and history', *Current Anthropology*, 19, 763–71.

Goggin, J. 1940. 'The Tekesta Indians of southern Florida', *Florida Historical Quarterly*, 18, 274–84.

Goggin, J. and W. Sturtevant 1964. 'The Calusa: a stratified non-agricultural society (with notes on sibling marriage)', in W. Goodenough (ed.), *Explorations in cultural anthropology: essays in honor of G.P. Murdock*, New York: McGraw-Hill.

Golson, J. 1985. 'Agricultural origins in Southeast Asia: a view from the east', in V. Bellwood (ed.), *Recent advances in Indo-Pacific prehistory*, Leiden: Brill.

Gordon, R. 1984. 'The !Kung in the Kalahari exchange: an ethnohistorical perspective', in C. Schrire (ed.), *Past and present in hunter-gatherer studies*, London: Academic.

Gough, E.K. 1956. 'Brahman kinship in a Tamil village', *American Anthropologist*, 58, 826–53.

Gough Aberle, E.K. 1978. *Dravidian kinship and modes of production*, New Delhi: Indian Council of Social Science Research.

Gould, R. 1980. *Living archaeology*, Cambridge: Cambridge University Press.

—— 1982. 'To have and have not: the ecology of sharing among hunter-gatherers', in N. Williams and E. Hunn (eds.), *Resource managers: North American and Australian hunter-gatherers*, Boulder, CO: Westview.

Gould, S.J. and R. Lewontin 1979. 'The spandrels of San Marcos and the Panglossian paradigm: a critique of the adaptationist programme', *Proceedings of the Royal Society of London* (Series B), 205, 581–98.

Graburn, N. 1969. *Eskimos without igloos*, Boston: Little, Brown.

Grebenart, D. 1983. 'Les métallurgies du cuivre et du fer autour d'Agadez (Niger); des origines au debut de la période médiévale', *Memoires de la Société des Africanistes*, 9, 109–35.

Griffin, J. 1946. 'Historic artifacts and the buzzard cult in Florida', *Florida Historical Quarterly*, 24, 295–301.

Griffin, P. 1984. 'Forager resource and land use in the humid tropics: the Agta of northeastern Luzon, Philippines', in C. Schrire (ed.), *Past and present in hunter-gatherer studies*, London: Academic.

Hagen, B. 1908. *Die Orang Kubu auf Sumatra* (Veröffentlichungen aus dem Städtischen Völker-Museum II), Frankfurt am Main: Joseph Baer and Co.

Hall, M. 1981. *Settlement patterns in the Iron Age of Zululand*, Oxford: BAR.

—— 1983. 'Tribes, traditions and numbers: the American model in southern African Iron Age studies', *South African Archaeological Bulletin*, 38, 51–61.

—— 1984. 'The burden of tribalism: the social context of southern African Iron Age studies', *American Antiquity*, 49, 455–67.

—— 1985. 'Beyond the mode of production: power and signification in southern African precolonial archaeology', paper presented at the conference of the Southern African Association of Archaeologists, Grahamstown.

—— 1986. 'The role of cattle in southern African agropastoral societies: more than bones alone can tell', *South African Archaeological Society Goodwin Series*, 5, 83–7.

—— 1987. *The changing past: farmers, kings and traders in southern Africa, 200–1860*, London: James Curry.

Hall, M. and J. Vogel 1980. 'Some recent radiocarbon dates from southern Africa', *Journal of African History*, 21, 431–55.

Hames, R. n.d. 'Risk reduction and sharing among the Yanomamo', Manuscript, Department of Anthropology, University of Nebraska, Lincoln.

Hamilton, A. 1980. 'Dual social systems: technology, labour and women's secret rites in the eastern Western Desert of Australia', *Oceania*, 51, 4–19.

—— 1982. 'The unity of hunting-gathering societies: reflections on economic forms and resource management', in N. Williams and E. Hunn (eds.), *Resource managers: North American and Australian hunter-gatherers*, Boulder, CO: Westview.

Hammond-Tooke, W. 1984. 'In search of the lineage: the Cape Nguni case', *Man*, 19, 77–93.

Handsman, R. 1986. 'How histories were made by hunter-gatherers, then disciplined, and finally made to disappear by us', paper presented to the Fourth International Conference on Hunting and Gathering Societies, London.

Harako, R. 1976. 'The Mbuti as hunters: a study of ecological anthropology of the Mbuti Pygmies', *Kyoto University African Studies*, 10, 37–99.

Hardin, R. 1982. *Collective action*, Baltimore, MD: Johns Hopkins University Press.

Harms, R. 1981. *River of wealth, river of sorrow. The Central Zaire basin in the era of the slave and ivory trade, 1500–1891*, New Haven, CT: Yale University Press.

Harris, D. 1973. 'The prehistory of tropical agriculture: an ethnoecological model', in C. Renfrew (ed.), *The explanation of culture*, London: Duckworth.

—— 1977a. 'Subsistence strategies across Torres Strait', in J. Allen, J. Golson and R. Jones (eds.), *Sunda and Sahul: prehistoric studies in Southeast Asia, Melanesia and Australia*, London: Academic.

—— 1977b. 'Alternative pathways towards agriculture', in C. Reed (ed.), *Origins of agriculture*, The Hague: Mouton.

Harris, M. 1974. *Cows, pigs, wars and witches*, New York: Random House.

Hart, C. and A. Pilling 1960. *The Tiwi of North Australia*, New York: Holt, Rinehart and Winston.

Hart, T. and J. Hart 1986. 'The ecological basis of hunter-gatherer subsistence in African rain forests: the Mbuti of Eastern Zaire', *Human Ecology*, 14, 29–55.

Hayden, B. 1981. 'Subsistence and ecological adaptations of modern hunter/gatherers', in R. Harding and G. Teleki (eds.), *Omnivorous primates*, New York: Columbia University Press.

Hedges, D. 1978. 'Trade and politics in southern Mozambique and Zululand in the eighteenth and early nineteenth centuries', PhD dissertation, London University.

Heffley, S. 1981. 'Northern Athapaskan settlement patterns and resource distributions: an application of Horn's model', in B. Winterhalder and E.A. Smith (eds.), *Hunter-gatherer foraging strategies*, Chicago: University of Chicago Press.

Helm, J. 1965. 'Bilaterality in the socio-territorial organization of the arctic drainage Dene', *Ethnology*, 4, 361–85.

—— 1969. 'A method of statistical analysis of primary relative bonds in community composition', in D. Damas (ed.), *Contributions to anthropology: band societies*, Ottawa: National Museums of Canada.

Helskog, K. 1984. 'The Younger Stone Age settlements in Varanger, North Norway: settlement and population size', *Acta Borealia*, 1, 39–69.

Henke, W. 1981. 'Entwincklungstrends und Variabilität bei Jungpaläolithikern und Mesolithikern Europas', *Homo*, 32, 177–96.

Henriksen, G. 1973. *Hunters in the barrens: the Naskapi on the edge of the White Man's world*, St John's, Newfoundland: Institute of Social and Economic Research, Memorial University.

Hey, J. 1979. *Uncertainty in microeconomics*, New York: New York University Press.

—— 1981. *Economics in disequilibrium*, Oxford: Martin Robertson.

Hill, K. and K. Hawkes 1983. 'Neotropical hunting among the Ache of eastern Paraguay', in R. Hames and W. Vickers (eds.), *Adaptive responses of native Amazonians*, New York: Academic.

Hindess, B. and P. Hirst 1975. *Precapitalist modes of production*, London: Routledge and Kegan Paul.

Hirshleifer, J. 1982. 'Evolutionary models in economics and law: cooperation versus conflict strategies', *Research in Law and Economics*, 4, 1–60.

Hodder, I. 1982. *Symbols in action*, Cambridge: Cambridge University Press.

Hoffman, C. 1984. 'Punan foragers in the trading networks of Southeast Asia', in C. Schrire (ed.), *Past and present in hunter-gatherer studies*, London: Academic.

Huffman, T. 1978. 'The origins of Leopard's Kopje: an eleventh century difaquane', *Arnoldia*, 7, 1–12.

—— 1982. 'Archaeology and ethnohistory of the African Iron Age', *Annual Review of Anthropology*, 11, 133–50.

—— 1983. 'The trance hypothesis and the rock art of Zimbabwe', *South African Archaeological Society Goodwin Series*, 4, 49–53.

Hugh-Jones, C. 1979. *From the milk river: spatial and temporal processes in Northwest Amazonia*, Cambridge: Cambridge University Press.

Humphrey, N. 1976. 'The social function of intellect', in P. Bateson and R. Hinde (eds.), *Growing points in ethology*. Cambridge: Cambridge University Press.

Hunn, E. and N. Williams 1982. 'Introduction', in N. Williams and E. Hunn (eds.), *Resource managers: North American and Australian hunter-gatherers*, Boulder CO: Westview.

Huntingford, G. 1955. *The Galla of Ethiopia*, London: International African Institute.

Hutterer, K. 1977. 'Prehistoric trade and the evolution of Philippine societies: a reconsideration', in K. Hutterer (ed.), *Economic exchange and social interaction in Southeast Asia: perspectives from prehistory, history and ethnography*, Ann Arbor: University of Michigan Press.

Hynes, R. and A. Chase 1982. 'Plants, sites and domiculture: Aboriginal influence upon plant communities in Cape York Peninsula', *Archaeology in Oceania*, 17, 38–50.

Ichikawa, M. 1978. 'The residential groups of the Mbuti Pygmies', *Senri Ethnological Studies*, 1, 131–88.

—— 1981. 'Ecological and sociological importance of honey to the Mbuti net-hunters, eastern Zaire', *African Study Monographs*, 4, 55–68.

Ingold, T. 1980. *Hunters, pastoralists and ranchers*, Cambridge: Cambridge University Press.

—— 1982. 'Review of *Omnivorous primates* (eds. R. Harding and G. Teleki)', *Man*, 17, 162–4.

—— 1983. 'The significance of storage in hunting societies', *Man*, 18, 553–71.

—— 1986a. *Evolution and social life*, Cambridge: Cambridge University Press.

—— 1986b. *The appropriation of nature: essays in human ecology and social relations*, Manchester: Manchester University Press.

Ingold, T., D. Riches and J. Woodburn (eds.), 1988. *Hunters and gatherers II: Property, power and ideology*, Oxford: Berg.

Isaac, G. 1972. 'Chronology and tempo of cultural change during the Pleistocene', in W. Bishop and J. Miller (eds.), *Calibration of hominoid evolution*, Edinburgh: Scottish Academic Press.

—— 1978a. 'The food-sharing behaviour of protohuman hominids', *Scientific*

American, 238, 90–108.

—— 1978b. 'Food sharing and human evolution: archaeological evidence from the Plio-Pleistocene of East Africa', *Journal of Anthropological Research, 34,* 311–25.

—— 1983. 'Bones in contention: competing explanations for the juxtaposition of artefacts and faunal remains', in J. Clutton-Brock and C. Grigson (eds.), *Animals and archaeology, I: Hunters and their prey,* Oxford: BAR International Series.

Isaac, G. and D. Crader 1981. 'To what extent were early hominids carnivorous?', in R. Harding and G. Teleki (eds.), *Omnivorous primates: gathering and hunting in human evolution,* New York: Columbia University Press.

James, B. 1961. 'Social-psychological dimensions of Ojibwa acculturation', *American Anthropologist, 63,* 721–46.

Jellife, D. *et al.* 1962. 'The children of the Hadza hunters', *Journal of Pediatrics, 60,* 907–13.

Jochim, M. 1983. 'Optimization models in context', in A. Keene and J. Moore (eds.), *Archaeological hammers and theories,* New York: Academic.

Johnson, G. 1982. 'Organizational structure and scalar stress', in C. Renfrew, M. Rowlands and B. Seagraves (eds.), *Theory and explanation in archaeology,* New York: Academic.

Jones, R. 1975. 'The Neolithic Palaeolithic and the hunting gardeners: man and land in the Antipodes', in R. Sudgate and M. Cresswell (eds.), *Quaternary Studies,* Wellington: Royal Society of New Zealand.

Jones, W. 1979. 'Up the creek: hunter-gatherers in the Cooper Basin', MA dissertation, University of New England.

Kaplan, H. and K. Hill 1985. 'Food sharing among Ache foragers: tests of explanatory hypotheses', *Current Anthropology, 26,* 223–46.

Keen, I. 1982. 'How some Murngin men marry ten wives: the marital implications of matrilateral cross-cousin structures', *Man, 17,* 620–42.

Keene, A. 1983. 'Biology, behavior and borrowing: a critical examination of optimal foraging theory in archaeology', in A. Keene and J. Moore (eds.), *Archaeological hammers and theories,* New York: Academic.

—— 1986. 'Stories we tell: gatherer-hunters as ideology', paper presented at the Fourth International Conference on Hunting and Gathering Societies, London.

Kelly, R. 1983. 'Hunter-gatherer mobility strategies', *Journal of Anthropological Research, 39,* 277–306.

Khazanov, A. 1982. *Nomads and the outside world,* Cambridge: Cambridge University Press.

Kimber, R. 1984. 'Resource use and management in central Australia', *Australian Aboriginal Studies, 2,* 12–23.

Klapwijk, M. 1973. 'An early Iron Age site near Tzaneen, north-east Transvaal', *South African Journal of Science, 69,* 324.

Kluckhohn, C. and D. Leighton 1962. *The Navaho,* Garden City, NY: Natural History Library.

Knaap, G. 1985. 'Kruidnagelen en Christenen: de Verenigde Oost-Indische Compagnie en de bevolking van Ambon, 1656–1696', PhD dissertation, Rijksuniversiteit te Utrecht.

Knight, F. 1921. *Risk, uncertainty and profit,* New York: Harper and Row.

Kolenda, P. 1967. 'Regional differences in Indian family structure', in R. Crane (ed.), *Regions and regionalism in South Asian studies: an exploratory study*, Durham, NC: Duke University Program in Comparative Studies on Southern Asia.

Kratz, C. 1981. 'Are the Okiek really Maasai? Or Kipsigis? Or Kikuyu?', *Cahiers d'Etudes Africaines*, 79, 355–68.

Krebs, J. 1978. 'Optimal foraging: decision rules for predators', in J. Krebs and N. Davies (eds.), *Behavioural ecology: an evolutionary approach*, Oxford: Blackwell.

Krebs, J. and N. Davies (eds.) 1984. *Behavioural ecology: an evolutionary approach* (2nd ed.), Oxford: Blackwell.

Kroeber, A. 1919. *Peoples of the Philippines*, New York: American Museum of Natural History.

—— 1945. 'The ancient Oikoumenê as an historic culture aggregate', *Journal of the Royal Anthropological Institute*, 45, 9–20.

Kuper, A. 1982. 'Lineage theory: a critical retrospect', *Annual Review of Anthropology*, 11, 71–95.

Kuper, A. and P. Van Leynseele 1978. 'Social anthropology and the "Bantu expansion"', *Africa*, 48, 335–52.

Lafitau, J.-F. 1974. *Custom of the American Indian*, Vol. 1 (trans. and ed. W. Fenton and E. Moore), Toronto: The Champlain Society, first published in 1724.

—— 1977. *Custom of the American Indian*, Vol. 2 (trans. and ed. W. Fenton and E. Moore), Toronto: The Champlain Society, first published in 1724.

Laudonnière, R. de 1975. *Three voyages* (trans. C. Bennett), Gainesville: University Presses of Florida.

Laughlin, W. 1968. 'Hunting: an integrating biobehaviour system and its evolutionary importance', in R. Lee and I. DeVore (eds.), *Man the hunter*, Chicago: Aldine.

Layton, R. 1986. 'Political and territorial structures among hunter-gatherers', *Man*, 21, 18–33.

Leacock, E. 1954. *The Montagnais 'hunting territory' and the fur trade*, Washington, DC: American Anthropological Association.

—— 1981. *Myths of male dominance*, New York: Monthly Review Press.

—— 1982. 'Relations of production in band society', in E. Leacock and R. Lee (eds.), *Politics and history in band societies*, Cambridge: Cambridge University Press.

—— 1983. 'Primitive communism', in T. Bottomore *et al.* (eds.), *A dictionary of Marxist thought*, Cambridge, MA: Harvard University Press.

Leacock, E. and R. Lee (eds.) 1982. *Politics and history in band societies*, Cambridge: Cambridge University Press.

Leap, W. 1977. 'Maritime subsistence in anthropological perspective: a statement of priorities', in M.E. Smith (ed.), *Those who live from the sea*, St Paul, MN: West.

Lee, R. 1968. 'What hunters do for a living, or, how to make out on scarce resources', in R. Lee and I. DeVore (eds.), *Man the hunter*, Chicago: Aldine.

—— 1969. '!Kung Bushman subsistence: an input–output analysis', in D. Damas (ed.), *Contributions to anthropology: band societies*, Ottawa: Museums of Canada.

—— 1972. '!Kung spatial organization: an ecological and historical perspective', *Human ecology*, 1, 125–47.

—— 1979. *The !Kung San: men, women and work in a foraging society*, Cambridge:

Cambridge University Press.
—— 1980. 'Existe-t-il un mode de production "fourrageur"?', *Anthropologie et Sociétés*, 4, 59–74.
—— 1984. 'Work, sexuality and aging among !Kung women', in J. Brown and V. Kens (eds.), *In her prime*, New York: J. Bergin.
—— 1985. 'Greeks and Victorians: a reexamination of Engels's theory of the Athenian polis', *Culture*, 5, 63–74.
Lee, R. and I. DeVore 1968a. 'Problems in the study of hunters and gatherers', in R. Lee and I. DeVore (eds.), *Man the hunter*, Chicago: Aldine.
—— (eds.) 1968b. *Man the hunter*, Chicago: Aldine.
Lee, R. and S. Hurlich 1982. 'From forager to fighter: South Africa's militarization of the Namibian San', in E. Leacock and R. Lee (eds.), *Politics and history in band societies*, Cambridge: Cambridge University Press.
Leeds, A. and A. Vayda (eds.) 1965. *Man, culture and animals*, Washington, DC: American Association for the Advancement of Science.
Lewis, C. 1978. 'The Calusa', in J. Milanich and S. Proctor (eds.), *Tacachale: essays on the Indians of Florida and southeastern Georgia during the Historic period*, Gainesville: University Presses of Florida.
Lewis-Williams, J.D. 1977. 'Ezaljagdspoort revisited: new light on an enigmatic rock painting', *South African Archaeological Bulletin*, 32, 165.
—— 1980. 'Ethnography and iconography: aspects of southern San thought and art', *Man*, 15, 467–82.
—— 1981. *Believing and seeing: symbolic meanings in southern San rock paintings*, London: Academic.
—— 1982. 'The social and economic context of southern San rock art', *Current Anthropology*, 23, 429–49.
—— 1984. 'Ideological continuities in prehistoric southern Africa: the evidence of rock art', in C. Schrire (ed.), *Past and present in hunter-gatherer studies*, London: Academic.
Linares, O. 1976. '"Garden Hunting" in the American tropics', *Human Ecology*, 4, 331–49.
López, F. 1698. 'Letter written by Fray Feliciano López after his return from Carlos to Havana in the spring of 1698' (trans. V. Johnson). AGI Santo Domingo 154, Archivo General de Indias, Seville. Translation on file, Gainesville: Florida State Museum.
López de Velasco, J. 1894. *Geografía y descripción universal de las Indias, recopilada por el cosmógrafo-cronista Juan López de Velasco desde el año de 1571 al de 1574 . . . con adiciones é ilustraciones, por don Justo Zaragosa*, Madrid: Establecimiento Tipográfico de Fortanet.
Lourandos, H. 1977. 'Aboriginal spatial organization and population: south-western Victoria reconsidered', *Archaeology and Physical Anthropology in Oceania*, 12, 202–25.
—— 1980a. 'Change or stability?: hydraulics, hunter-gatherers and population in temperate Australia', *World Archaeology*, 11, 245–64.
—— 1980b. 'Forces of change: Aboriginal technology and population in south-western Victoria', PhD dissertation, University of Sydney.
—— 1983. 'Intensification: a late Pleistocene-Holocene archaeological sequence from south-western Victoria', *Archaeology in Oceania*, 18, 81–94.
—— 1985. 'Intensification and Australian prehistory', in T. Price and J. Brown

(eds.), *Prehistoric hunter-gatherers: the emergence of cultural complexity*, Orlando, FL: Academic.

—— 1987. 'Pleistocene Australia: peopling a continent', in O. Soffer (ed.), *The Pleistocene Old World*, New York: Plenum.

Lowery, W. 1901. *The Spanish settlements within the present limits of the United States, 1513–1561*, New York: G.P. Putnam's Sons.

Lowie, R. 1963. *Indians of the Plains*, Garden City, NY: Natural History Library, first published in 1954.

Luer, G., D. Allerton, D. Hazeltine, R. Hatfield and D. Hood 1986. 'Whelk shell tool blanks from Big Mound Key (8CH10), Charlotte county, Florida: with notes on certain whelk shell tools', in G. Luer (ed.), *Shells and archaeology in southern Florida*, Tallahassee: Florida Anthropological Society.

Lyon, E. 1976. *The enterprise of Florida*, Gainesville: University Presses of Florida.

McBryde, I. 1978. 'Wil-im-ee Moor-ing: or, where do axes come from?', *Mankind*, 3, 354–82.

McDowell, W. 1981a. 'Hadza traditional economy and its prospects for development', paper written for the Rift Valley Project, Ministry of Information and Culture, Division of Research, P.O. Box 4284, Dar es Salaam.

—— 1981b. 'A brief history of Mangola Hadza', paper written for the Rift Valley Project, Ministry of Information and Culture, Division of Research, P.O. Box 4284, Dar es Salaam.

McGovern, T. 1985. 'The arctic frontier of Norse Greenland', in S. Green and S. Perlman (eds.), *The Archaeology of Frontiers and Boundaries*, New York: Academic.

Mackenzie, J. 1871. *Ten years north of the Orange River*, Edinburgh: Edmonston and Douglas.

McKnight, D. n.d. 'Hunting for money: gambling in an Australian Aboriginal community', unpublished.

Maddock, K. 1972. *The Australian Aborigines*, London: Allen Lane.

Maggs, T. 1973. 'The NC3 Iron Age tradition', *South African Journal of Science*, 69, 326.

—— 1976a. 'Some recent radiocarbon dates from eastern and southern Africa', *Journal of African History*, 17, 161–95.

—— 1976b. *Iron Age communities of the southern Highveld*, Pietermaritzburg: Natal Museum.

—— 1980. 'Msuluzi Confluence: a seventh century Early Iron Age site on the Tugela River', *Annals of the Natal Museum*, 24, 111–45.

—— 1984. 'The Iron Age south of the Zambezi', in R. Klein (ed.), *Southern African prehistory and palaeoenvironments*, Rotterdam: Balkema.

Mandelbaum, D. 1970. *Society in India, volume 1*, Berkeley: University of California Press.

Maquet, J. 1961. *The premise of inequality in Ruanda. A study of political relations in a Central African kingdom*, Oxford: Oxford University Press.

Marquardt, W. 1984. *The Josslyn Island mound and its role in the investigation of southwest Florida's past* (Department of Anthropology, Miscellaneous Project Report Series 22), Gainesville: Florida State Museum.

—— 1986. 'The development of cultural complexity in southwest Florida: elements of a critique', *Southeastern Archaeology*, 5, 63–70.

—— 1987. *Calusa news*, number 1, Gainesville: Florida State Museum.

—— n.d. Field notes, laboratory notes, computer printouts, Southwest Florida Project, on file, Gainesville: Florida State Museum.

Marshall, J. and C. Ritchie 1984. *Where are the Ju/Wasi of Nyae Nyae? Changes in a Bushman society, 1958–1981*, Communications No. 9, Centre for African Studies, University of Cape Town.

Marshall, L. 1961. 'Sharing, talking, and giving: relief of social tensions among !Kung Bushmen', *Africa*, 31, 231–49.

—— 1976. *The !Kung of Nyae Nyae*, Cambridge, MA: Harvard University Press.

Martin, J. 1983. 'Optimal foraging theory: a review of some models and their applications', *American Anthropologist*, 85, 612–29.

Martin, M.K. 1974. 'The foraging adaptation — uniformity or diversity?', *Modules in Anthropology*, 56.

Martin, R. 1983. *Human brain evolution in an ecological context*, New York: American Museum of Natural History.

Marx, K. 1930. *Capital*, London: Dent.

—— 1972. *The Grundrisse*, New York: Harper and Row.

Marx, K. and F. Engels 1977. *The German ideology*, London: Lawrence and Wishart.

Mason, R. 1981. 'Early Iron Age settlement at Broederstroom 24/73, Transvaal, South Africa', *South African Journal of Science*, 77, 401–16.

Mathews, R. 1903. 'The Aboriginal fisheries at Brewarrina', *Journal of the Royal Society of New South Wales*, 37, 146–56.

May, R. (ed.), 1981. *Theoretical ecology: principles and applications*, Oxford: Blackwell.

Maynard Smith, J. 1978. 'Optimization theory in evolution', *Annual Review of Ecology and Systematics*, 9, 31–56.

—— 1982. *Evolution and the theory of games*, Cambridge: Cambridge University Press.

Maynard Smith, J. and G. Parker 1976. 'The logic of asymmetric contests', *Animal Behaviour*, 24, 159–75.

Mazel, A. 1984. 'Through the keyhole: a preliminary peep at the lithic composition of Later Stone Age sites in the central and upper Tugela River basin, Natal', in M. Hall, G. Avery, D. Avery, M. Wilson and A. Humphreys (eds.), *Frontiers: southern African archaeology today*, Oxford: BAR International Series.

Meggitt, M. 1964. 'Aboriginal food-gatherers of tropical Australia', in *The ecology of man in the tropical environment*, Morges: International Union for the Conservation of Natural Resources.

—— 1966. 'Indigenous forms of government among Australian Aborigines', in H. Hogbin and L. Hiatt (eds.), *Readings in Australian and Pacific anthropology*, Melbourne: Melbourne University Press.

Meillassoux, C. 1972. 'From production to reproduction', *Economy and Society*, 1, 93–105.

—— 1973. 'On the mode of production of the hunting band', in P. Alexandre (ed.), *French perspectives in African Studies*, London: Oxford University Press.

—— 1981. *Maidens, meal and money*, Cambridge: Cambridge University Press.

Milanich, J. 1978a. 'The western Timucua: patterns of acculturation and change', in J. Milanich and S. Proctor (eds.), *Tacachale: essays on the Indians of Florida and southeastern Georgia during the Historic period*, Gainesville: University Presses of Florida.

—— 1978b. 'The temporal placement of Cushing's Key Marco site, Florida', *American Anthropologist*, 80, 682.

—— 1987. 'Corn and Calusa, DeSoto and demography', *Anthropological Research Papers*, 38, 173–84. Tempe: Arizona State University.

Milanich, J., J. Chapman, A. Cordell, S. Hale and R. Marrinan 1984. 'Prehistoric development of Calusa society in southwest Florida: excavations on Useppa Island', in D. Davis (ed.), *Perspectives on Gulf Coast prehistory*, Gainesville: University Presses of Florida.

Miller, D. 1988. 'The limits of dominance', in M. Rowlands, D. Miller and C. Tilley (eds.), *Domination and resistance*, London: Allen & Unwin.

Miller, D. and C. Tilley 1984. 'Ideology, power and prehistory: an introduction', in D. Miller and C. Tilley (eds.), *Ideology, power and prehistory*, Cambridge: Cambridge University Press.

Miller, S. 1969. 'Contacts between the Later Stone Age and the Early Iron Age in southern Central Africa', *Azania*, 4, 12–29.

Modjeska, C. 1982. 'Production and inequality: perspectives from central New Guinea', in A. Strathern (ed.), *Inequality in New Guinea Highlands Societies*, Cambridge: Cambridge University Press.

Mohn, A. 1960. *Kongo kaller*, Oslo: Gyldendal.

Moore, J. 1984. 'The evolution of reciprocal sharing', *Ethology and Sociobiology*, 5, 5–14.

Morantz, T. 1983. *An ethnohistoric study of eastern James Bay Cree social organization, 1800–1850*, Ottawa: National Museums of Canada.

Morgan, L.H. 1965. *Houses and house-life of the American aborigines*, Chicago: University of Chicago Press, first published in 1881.

Morren, G. 1977. 'From hunting to herding: pigs and the control of energy in montane New Guinea', in T. Bayliss-Smith and R. Feachem (eds.), *Subsistence and survival: rural ecology in the Pacific*, London: Academic.

Morris, B. 1975. 'An analysis of the economy and social organization of the Malapantaram', PhD dissertation, London University.

—— 1977. 'Tappers, trappers and the Hill Pandaram (South India)', *Anthropos*, 72, 225–41.

—— 1982a. *Forest traders: a socio-economic study of the Hill Pandaram*, London: Athlone Press.

—— 1982b. 'The family, group structuring and trade among South Indian hunter-gatherers', in E. Leacock and R. Lee (eds.), *Politics and history in band societies*, Cambridge: Cambridge University Press.

Murdock, G.P. 1949. *Social structure*, New York: Macmillan.

—— 1967. *The Ethnographic Atlas*, Pittsburgh: University of Pittsburgh Press.

—— 1968. 'The current state of the world's hunting and gathering people', in R. Lee and I. DeVore (eds.), *Man the hunter*, Chicago: Aldine.

Murphy, R. 1970. 'Basin ethnography and ethnological theory', in E. Swanson (ed.), *Languages and cultures of western North America*, Pocatello: Idaho State University Press.

Murphy, R. and J. Steward 1956. 'Tappers and trappers: parallel processes in acculturation', *Economic Development and Cultural Change*, 4, 335–55.

Myers, F. 1982. 'Always ask: resource use and land ownership among Pintupi Aborigines of the Australian Western Desert', in N. Williams and E. Hunn (eds.), *Resource managers: North American and Australian hunter-gatherers*, Boulder, CO: Westview.

Nadel, S. 1953. *The foundations of social anthropology*, London: Cohen and West.

—— 1957. *The theory of social structure*, London: Cohen and West.

Ndagala, D. 1982. 'Kuna Uwezekano wa Jamii ya Wawindaji kuishi Vijijini? Maelezo Mafupi Juu ya Wahadzabe: Hali ya Yaeda Chini Wilayani Mbulu', in *Kumbukumbu za Warsha Juu ya Wahadzabe*, Wizara ya Habari na Utamaduni, S.L.P. 4284, Dar es Salaam: Government Printer.

—— 1985a. 'Local participation and development decisions: an introduction', *Nomadic Peoples*, *18*, 3–6.

—— 1985b. 'Attempts to develop the Hadzabe of Tanzania', *Nomadic Peoples*, *18*, 17–26.

Ndagala, D. and S. Waane 1982. 'The effects of research on the Hadzabe, a hunting and gathering group of Tanzania', *Review of Ethnology*, *8*, 94–105.

Nisbet, R. 1968. 'Cooperation', *International Encyclopaedia of Social Science 3*, 384–90.

NSID 1918. *A manual of Netherlands India*, London: Naval Staff Intelligence Department.

Nyerere, J. 1967. *Socialism and rural development*, Dar es Salaam: Government Printer.

Obst, E. 1912. 'Von Mkalama ins Land der Wakindiga', *Mitteilungen der Geographischen Gesellschaft in Hamburg*, *26*, 2–27.

Odum, E. 1975. *Ecology*, New York: Holt, Rinehart and Winston.

Odum, W., C. McIvor and T. Smith 1982. *The ecology of the mangroves of south Florida: a community profile*, FWS/OBS–81/24, Washington, DC: US Fish and Wildlife Service, Office of Biological Services.

Ohtsuka, R. 1978. 'The Oriomo Papuans: gathering versus horticulture in an ecological context', in V. Misra and P. Bellwood (eds.), *Recent advances in Indo-Pacific history*, New Delhi: Oxford University Press.

Oliver, R. and B. Fagan 1975. *Africa in the Iron Age*, London: Cambridge University Press.

Olivera, J.F. de 1612. Letter to the King of Spain, 13 October 1612, transcript, Conner Collection, in W. Lowery (ed.), *The Spanish settlements in the United States*, *Mss. Florida VI, 1608–1620*, Washington, DC: Library of Congress, manuscripts division.

Orans, M. 1965. *The Santal: a tribe in search of a great tradition*, Detroit, MI: Wayne State University Press.

Orlove, B. 1980. 'Ecological anthropology', *Annual Review of Anthropology*, *9*, 235–73.

Osborn, A. 1977, 'Strandloopers, mermaids, and other fairy tales: ecological determinants of marine resource utilization', in L. Binford (ed.), *For theory building in archaeology*, New York: Academic.

—— 1980. 'Comments on Yesner ("Maritime hunter-gatherers")', *Current Anthropology*, *21*, 740–1.

Pálsson, G. 1982. 'Representations and reality: cognitive models and social relations among the fishermen of Sandgerdi, Iceland', PhD dissertation, Manchester University.

Pálsson, G. and E.P. Durrenberger 1987. 'Ownership at sea: fishing territories and access to sea resources', *American Ethnologist 14*, 508–22.

Parker, S. and K. Gibson 1979. 'A developmental model for the evolution of language and intelligence in early hominids', *The Behavioural and Brain Sciences*, 2, 367–408.

Parkington, J. and M. Hall 1987. 'Patterning in recent radiocarbon dates from southern Africa as a reflection of prehistoric settlement and interaction', *Journal of African History*, 28, 1–25.

Parks, A. 1985. *Where the river found the bay: historical study of the Granada site, Miami, Florida* (Archaeology and History of the Granada Site, Volume 2) Tallahassee: Florida Division of Archives, History and Records Management.

Peebles, C. and M. Schoeninger 1981. 'Notes on the relationship between social status and diet at Moundville', *Southeastern Archaeological Conference Bulletin*, 24, 96–7.

Pehrson, R. 1964. *The bilateral network of social relations in Könkämä Lapp District*, Oslo: Universitetsforlaget.

Perlman, S. 1980. 'An optimum diet model, coastal variability, and hunter-gatherer behavior', in M. Schiffer (ed.), *Advances in archaeological method and theory, vol. 3*, New York: Academic.

Peters, R. 1983. *The ecological implications of body size*, Cambridge: Cambridge University Press.

Peterson, J.T. 1978. *The ecology of social boundaries: Agta foragers of the Philippines*, Urbana: University of Illinois Press.

Peterson, J.T. and W. Peterson 1977. 'Implications of contemporary and prehistoric exchange systems', in J. Allen, J. Golson and R. Jones (eds.), *Sunda and Sahul: prehistoric studies in Southeast Asia, Melanesia and Australia*, London: Academic.

Peterson, N. 1975. 'Hunter-gatherer territoriality: the perspective from Australia', *American Anthropologist*, 77, 53–68.

—— 1979. 'Territorial adaptations among desert hunter-gatherers: the !Kung and Australians compared', in P. Burnham and R. Ellen (eds.), *Social and ecological systems*, London: Academic.

—— 1982. 'Aboriginal land rights in the Northern Territory of Australia', in E. Leacock and R. Lee (eds.), *Politics and history in band societies*, Cambridge: Cambridge University Press.

—— 1986. 'Reciprocity and the demand for generosity', paper presented at the Fourth International Conference on Hunting and Gathering Societies, London.

Petrie, C. 1902. 'Tom Petrie's reminiscences of the Aborigines of Queensland', *Science of Man*, 5, 15–16, 29–30, 47–48.

Phillipson, D. 1976. *The Iron Age in Zambia*, Lusaka: Historical Association of Zambia.

—— 1977. *The later prehistory of eastern and southern Africa*, London: Heinemann.

—— 1985. *African archaeology*, Cambridge: Cambridge University Press.

Pianka, E. 1978. *Evolutionary ecology*, New York: Harper and Row.

Piddocke, S. 1965. 'The potlatch system of the Southern Kwakiutl: a new perspective', *Southwestern Journal of Anthropology*, 21, 244–64.

Pope, G. 1983. 'Evidence for the age of the Asian hominidae', *Proceedings of the National Academy of Sciences, USA*, 80, 4988–92.

Potts, R. 1984. 'Hominid hunters? Problems of identifying the earliest hunter-gatherers', in R. Foley (ed.), *Hominid evolution and community ecology: prehistoric human adaptation in biological perspective*, London: Academic.

Price, J. 1975. 'Sharing: the integration of intimate economies', *Anthropologica*, 17, 3–27.

Price, T. and J. Brown (eds.) 1985. *Prehistoric hunter-gatherers: the emergence of cultural complexity*, Orlando, FL: Academic.

Pulliam, H. and C. Dunford 1980. *Programmed to learn: an essay on the evolution of culture*, New York: Columbia University Press.

Putnam, P. 1950. 'The Pygmies of the Ituri Forest', in C.S. Coon (ed.), *Reader in general anthropology*, London: Cape.

Quilter, J. and T. Stocker 1983. 'Subsistence economies and the origins of Andean complex societies', *American Anthropologist*, 85, 545–62.

Radcliffe-Brown, A. 1922. *The Andaman Islanders*, London: Cambridge University Press.

—— 1940. 'On social structure', *Journal of the Royal Anthropological Institute*, 70, 1–12.

Rappaport, R. 1967. *Pigs for the ancestors*, New Haven, CT: Yale University Press.

Real, L. 1980. 'Fitness, uncertainty and the role of diversification in evolution and behaviour', *American Naturalist*, 115, 623–33.

Renouf, M.A.P. 1984. 'Northern coastal hunter-fishers: an archaeological model', *World Archaeology*, 16, 18–27.

Richardson, A. 1982. 'The control of productive resources on the Northwest Coast of North America', in N. Williams and E. Hunn (eds.), *Resource managers: North American and Australian hunter-gatherers*, Boulder, CO: Westview.

Riches, D. 1975. 'Credit, cash and gambling in a modern Eskimo economy: speculations on origins of spheres of economic exchange', *Man*, 10, 21–33.

—— 1982. *Northern nomadic hunter-gatherers: a humanistic approach*, London: Academic.

Rivers, W. 1906. *The Todas*, London: Macmillan.

Roemer, J. 1982a. 'Methodological individualism and deductive Marxism', *Theory and Society*, 11, 513–20.

—— 1982b. *A general theory of exploitation and class*, Cambridge, MA: Harvard University Press.

Romanucci-Ross, L. 1985. *Mead's other Manus: phenomenology of the encounter*, South Hadley, MA: Bergin and Garvey.

Rosaldo, R. 1982. 'Utter savages of scientific value', in E. Leacock and R. Lee (eds.), *Politics and history in band societies*, Cambridge: Cambridge University Press.

Ross, A. 1981. 'Holocene environments and prehistoric site patterning in the Victorian Mallee', *Archaeology in Oceania*, 16, 145–54.

Roughgarden, J. 1979. *Theory of population genetics and evolutionary ecology: an introduction*, New York: Macmillan.

Roumasset, J., J.-M. Boussard and I. Singh (eds.) 1979. *Risk, uncertainty and agricultural development*, New York: Agricultural Development Council.

Rowley-Conwy, P. 1983. 'Sedentary hunters: the Ertebølle example', in G. Bailey (ed.), *Hunter-gatherer economy in prehistory*, Cambridge: Cambridge University Press.

Rubenstein, D. 1982. 'Risk, uncertainty and evolutionary strategies', in King's College Sociobiology Group (eds.), *Current problems in sociobiology*, Cambridge: Cambridge University Press.

Ruddle, K., D. Johnson, P. Townsend and J. Rees 1978. *Palm sago: a tropical starch from marginal lands*, Honolulu: University Press of Hawaii.

Sachse, F. 1907. *Het eiland Seran en zijne bewoners*, Leiden: Brill.

Sahlins, M. 1968. 'Notes on the original affluent society', in R. Lee and I. DeVore (eds.), *Man the hunter*, Chicago: Aldine.

—— 1974. *Stone age economics*, London: Tavistock.

Salmon, M. 1978. 'What can systems theory do for archaeology?', *American Antiquity*, 43, 174–83.

Salzman, P. 1985. 'Preface', *Nomadic Peoples*, 18.

Sandbukt, Ø. 1984. 'Kubu conceptions of reality', *Asian Folklore Studies*, 42, 85–98.

—— 1986. 'The historical ecology of Sumatran tribes and trading states', paper presented at the 85th Annual Meeting of the American Anthropological Association, Philadelphia.

—— 1988. 'Resource constraints and relations of appropriation among tropical forest foragers: the case of the Sumatran Kubu', *Research in Economic Anthropology*, forthcoming.

—— n.d. 'The Orang Kuala of Johor: from intertidal foraging to commercial fishing', in R. Gianno and B. Nowak (eds.), *Diversity in proximity: Orang Asli social systems of Peninsular Malaysia*, forthcoming.

Sansom, B. 1974. 'Traditional economic systems', in W.D. Hammond-Tooke (ed.), *The Bantu-speaking peoples of southern Africa*, London: Routledge and Kegan Paul.

Sarma, J. 1964. 'The nuclearization of joint family households in West Bengal', *Man in India*, 44, 193–206.

Scarry, C. 1985. 'Paleoethnobotany of the Granada site', in J. Griffin (ed.), *Excavations at the Granada site* (Archaeology and History of the Granada Site, volume 1), Tallahassee: Florida Division of Archives, History, and Records Management.

Schaffer, W. 1978. 'A note on the theory of reciprocal altruism', *American Naturalist*, 112, 250–3.

Schalk, R. 1977. 'The structure of an andromous fish resource', in L. Binford (ed.), *For theory building in archaeology*, New York: Academic.

—— 1979. 'Land use and organizational complexity among foragers of North-western North America', in S. Koyama and D. Thomas (eds.), *Affluent foragers: Pacific Coast east and west*, Osaka: National Museum of Ethnology.

Schaller, G. and G. Lowther 1969. 'The relevance of carnivore behaviour to the study of early hominids', *Southwestern Journal of Anthropology*, 25, 307–41.

Schapera, I. 1938. *A handbook of Tswana law and custom*, London: Oxford University Press.

—— 1956. *Government and politics in tribal societies*, London: Watts.

Schebesta, P. 1926. 'Kubu and Jakudn (Jakun) als Protomalayen', *Mitteilungen der Antropologischen Gesellschaft in Wein*, 56, 192–201.

—— 1936. *My Pygmy and Negro hosts*, London: Hutchinson.

Schrire, C. (ed.) 1984. *Past and present in hunter-gatherer studies*, Orlando, FL: Academic.

Schultz, M. 1986. 'Economic relations between Batua and Baoto of Bibelo village', *Sprache und Geschichte in Afrika*, 7.

Sears, W. 1982. *Fort Center*, Gainesville: University Presses of Florida.

Service, E. 1962. *Primitive social organization*, New York: Random House.

Sharp, H.S. 1977. 'The Caribou-Eater Chipewyan: bilaterality, strategies in caribou hunting and the fur trade', *Arctic Anthropology*, 14, 35–40.

Shinichiro, T. 1960. 'The Ainu of northern Japan', *Transactions of the American Philosophical Society*, 50(4), 1–74.

Slater, H. 1976. 'Transitions in the political economy of south-east Africa before 1840', PhD dissertation, University of Sussex.

Smith, E. Alden 1981. 'The application of optimal foraging theory to the analysis of hunter-gatherer group size', in B. Winterhalder and E. Alden Smith (eds.), *Hunter-gatherer foraging strategies*, Chicago: University of Chicago Press.

—— 1983a. 'Anthropological applications of optimal foraging theory: a critical review', *Current Anthropology*, 24, 625–51.

—— 1983b. 'Evolutionary ecology and the analysis of human social behaviour', in R. Dyson-Hudson and M. Little (eds.), *Rethinking human adaptation*, Boulder, CO: Westview.

—— 1983c. 'Comment on Cashdan', *Current Anthropology*, 24, 61.

—— 1984a. 'Anthropology, evolutionary ecology, and the explanatory limitations of the ecosystem concept', in E. Moran (ed.), *The ecosystem concept in anthropology*, Boulder, CO: Westview.

—— 1984b. 'Approaches to Inuit socioecology', *Inuit Studies*, 8, 65–87.

—— 1985. 'Inuit foraging groups: some simple models incorporating conflicts of interest, relatedness, and central-place sharing', *Ethology and Sociobiology*, 6, 37–57.

—— 1987. 'Optimization theory in anthropology: applications and critiques', in J. Dupre (ed.), *The latest on the best: essays on evolution and optimality*, Cambridge, MA: Bradford Books/MIT Press.

Smith, E. Alden and B. Winterhalder 1985. 'On the logic and application of optimal foraging theory: a reply to John Martin', *American Anthropologist*, 87, 645–8.

Smith, J.G.E. 1978. 'Economic uncertainty in the "original affluent society": Caribou and Caribou-Eater Chipewyan adaptive strategies', *Arctic Anthropology*, 15, 68–88.

Smith, M.A. 1986. 'The antiquity of seedgrinding in Central Australia', *Archaeology in Oceania*, 21, 29–39.

Sober, E. (ed.), 1984. *Conceptual issues in evolutionary biology*, Cambridge, MA: MIT Press.

Solís de Merás, G. 1923. *Pedro Menéndez de Avilés, Adelantado, Governor and Captain-General of Florida: memorial* (transl. with notes by J. Conner), Deland: Florida State Historical Society.

Speck, F. 1915. 'The family hunting band as a basis of Algonkian social organization', *American Anthropologist*, 17, 289–305.

Spencer, B. and F. Gillen 1912. *Across Australia*, London: Macmillan.

Spencer, H. 1866. *The principles of biology*, New York: D. Appleton.

Spencer, P. 1973. *Nomads in alliance. Symbiosis and growth among the Rendille and Samburu of Kenya*, London: Oxford University Press.

Spielman, K.A. 1986. 'Interdependence among egalitarian societies', *Journal of Anthropological Archaeology*, 5, 279–312.

Stemler, A. 1984. 'The transition from food collecting to food production in northern Africa', in J. Clark and S. Brandt (eds.), *From hunter to farmer: the causes and consequences of food production in Africa*, Berkeley: University of

California Press.

Stephens, D. and E. Charnov 1982. 'Optimal foraging: some simple stochastic models', *Behavioural Ecology and Sociobiology*, 10, 251–63.

Steward, J. 1936. 'The economic and social basis of primitive bands', in R. Lowie (ed.), *Essays in anthropology in honor of Alfred Louis Kroeber*, Berkeley: University of California Press.

—— 1938. *Basin-plateau Aboriginal sociopolitical groups*, Washington, DC: Bureau of American Ethnology.

—— 1955. *Theory of culture change*, Urbana: University of Illinois Press.

—— 1961. 'Carrier acculturation: the direct historical approach', in S. Diamond (ed.), *Culture in history: essays in honor of Paul Radin*, New York: Columbia University Press.

Stringer, C. 1984a. 'Human evolution and biological adaptation in the Pleistocene', in R. Foley (ed.), *Hominid evolution and community ecology: prehistoric human adaptation in biological perspective*, New York: Academic.

—— 1984b. 'The definition of *Homo erectus* and the existence of the species in Europe and Africa', *Cour. Foursch. Inst. Senckenberg*, 69, 131–43.

Stringer, C., J. Hublin and B. Vendermeersch 1984. 'The origins of anatomically modern humans in Western Europe', in F. Smith and F. Spencer (eds.), *The origins of modern humans*, New York: A.R. Liss.

Sturtevant, W. 1978. 'The last of the south Florida aborigines', in J. Milanich and S. Proctor (eds.), *Tacachale: essays on the Indians of Florida and southeastern Georgia during the Historic period*, Gainesville: University Presses of Florida.

Sudo, K. 1934. 'Social organization and types of sea tenure in Micronesia', in K. Ruddle and T. Akimichi (eds.), *Maritime institutions of the western Pacific*, Osaka: National Museum of Ethnology.

Sullivan, H. 1977. 'Aboriginal gatherings in south-east Queensland', BA thesis, Australian National University.

Suttles, W. 1960, 'Affinal ties, subsistence, and prestige among the Coast Salish', *American Anthropologist*, 62, 296–305.

—— 1968. 'Coping with abundance: subsistence on the Northwest Coast', in R. Lee and I. DeVore (eds.), *Man the hunter*, Chicago: Aldine.

Sutton, P. and B. Rigsby 1982. 'People with "politicks": management of land and personnel on Australia's Cape York peninsula', in N. Williams and E. Hunn (eds.), *Resource managers: North American and Australian hunter-gatherers*, Boulder, CO: Westview.

Szalay, F. and E. Delson 1979. *Evolutionary history of the primates*, London: Academic.

Tanner, N. 1981. *On becoming human*, Cambridge: Cambridge University Press.

Tanno, T. 1976. 'The Mbuti net-hunters in the Ituri forest, eastern Zaire: their hunting activities and band composition', *Kyoto University African Studies*, 10, 101–35.

Taylor, M. 1976. *Anarchy and cooperation*, Chichester: Wiley.

—— 1987. *The possibility of cooperation*, Cambridge: Cambridge University Press.

Taylor, M. and H. Ward 1982. 'Chickens, whales, and lumpy goods: alternative models of public-goods provision', *Political Studies*, 30, 350–70.

Teleki, G. 1975. 'Primate subsistence patterns: collector-predators and gatherer-hunters', *Journal of Human Evolution*, 4, 125–84.

—— 1981. 'The omnivorous diet and eclectic feeding habits of chimpanzees in

Gombe National Park, Tanzania', in R. Harding and G. Teleki (eds.), *Omini-vorous primates*, New York: Columbia University Press.

Terashima, H. 1983. 'Mota and other hunting activities of the Mbuti archers: a socio-ecological study of subsistence technology', *African Study Monographs, 3*, 71–85.

—— 1985. 'Variation and composition principles of the residence group (band) of the Mbuti Pygmies — beyond a typical/atypical dichotomy', *African Study Monographs, 4*, 103–20.

Testart, A. 1981. 'Pour une typologie des chasseurs-cueilleurs', *Anthropologie et Sociétés, 5*, 177–221.

—— 1982. 'The significance of food storage among hunter-gatherers: residence patterns, population densities, and social inequalities', *Current Anthropology, 23*, 523–37.

—— 1985. *Le communisme primitif*, Paris: Maison des Sciences de L'Homme.

Thompson, E.A. 1965. *The early Germans*, Oxford: Clarendon Press.

Thomson, D. 1939. 'The seasonal factor in human culture', *Proceedings of the Prehistoric Society, 5*, 209–21.

—— 1949. *Economic structure and the ceremonial exchange cycle in Arnhem Land*, Melbourne: Macmillan.

Tideman, J. 1938. *Djambi*, Amsterdam: Koninklijke Vereeniging 'Kolonial Instituut'.

Tigar, M. and M. Levy 1977. *Law and the rise of capitalism*, New York: Monthly Review Press.

Tindale, N. 1977. 'Adaptive significance of the Panara grass seed culture of Australia', in R. Wright (ed.), *Stone tools as cultural markers*, Canberra: Australian Institute of Aboriginal Studies.

Torrence, R. 1983. 'Time budgeting and hunting-gatherer technology', in G. Bailey (ed.), *Hunter-gatherer economy in prehistory: a European perspective*, Cambridge: Cambridge University Press.

Trigger, B. 1968. 'Major concepts of archaeology in historical perspective', *Man, 3*, 527–41.

Trivers, R. 1971. 'The evolution of reciprocal altruism', *Quarterly Review of Biology, 46*, 35–57.

Turnbull, C. 1965a. *Wayward servants: the two worlds of the African Pygmies*, London: Eyre and Spottiswoode.

—— 1965b. *The Mbuti Pygmies: an ethnographic survey*, New York: Anthropological Papers of the American Museum of Natural History.

—— 1965c. 'The Mbuti Pygmies of the Congo', in J. Gibbs (ed.), *Peoples of Africa*, New York: Holt, Rinehart and Winston.

—— 1968. 'The importance of flux in two hunting societies', in R. Lee and I. DeVore (eds.), *Man the hunter*, Chicago: Aldine.

—— 1972a. 'Demography of small-scale societies', in G.A. Harrison and A. Boyce (eds.), *The structure of human populations*, Oxford: Clarendon Press.

—— 1972b. *The mountain people*, New York: Simon and Schuster.

—— 1983. *The Mbuti Pygmies. Change and adaptation*, New York: Holt, Rinehart and Winston.

Turner, A. 1984. 'Hominids and fellow travellers: human migration into high altitudes as part of a large mammal community', in R. Foley (ed.), *Hominid evolution and community ecology: prehistoric adaptation in biological perspective*,

London: Academic.

Turner, V. 1969. *The ritual process: structure and anti-structure*, Chicago: Aldine.

Valeri, V. 1976. 'Alliances et exchanges matrimoniaux à Seram Central (Moluques)', IV-V, *L'Homme*, 16, 125–49.

Vallois, H. and P. Marquer 1976. *Les Pygmées Baká du Cameroun: anthropologie et ethnographie avec une annexe démographique*, Paris: Mémoires du Museum National d'Histoire Naturelle.

Van Beck, J. and L. Van Beck 1965. 'The Marco midden, Marco Island, Florida', *The Florida Anthropologist*, 18, 1–20.

Vansina, J. 1986. 'Do Pygmies have a history?', *Sprache und Geschichte in Afrika*, 7, 431–45.

Vargas Ugarte, R. 1935. 'The first Jesuit mission in Florida', *The United States Catholic Historical Society, Historical Records and Studies*, 25, 59–148.

Vayda, A. and R. Rappaport 1968. 'Ecology, cultural and non-cultural', in J. Clifton (ed.), *Introduction to cultural anthropology*, Boston: Houghton-Mifflin.

Vierich, H. 1982. 'Adaptive flexibility in a multi-ethnic setting: the Basarwa of the southern Kalahari', in E. Leacock and R. Lee (eds.), *Politics and history in band societies*, Cambridge: Cambridge University Press.

Von Neumann, J. and O. Morgenstern 1944. *Theory of games and economic behavior*, Princeton, NJ: Princeton University Press.

Von Sturmer, J. 1978. 'The Wik region: economy, territoriality and totemism', PhD dissertation, University of Queensland.

Vorbichler, A. 1966. *Die Phonologie und Morphologie des Balese (Ituri-Urwald; Kongo)*. Gluckstadt: J.J. Austin.

Wæhle, E. 1986. 'Efe (Mbuti Pygmy) relations to Lese Dese villagers in the Ituri forest, Zaire: historical changes during the last 150 years', *Sprache und Geschichte in Afrika*, 7, 375–411.

Walker, N. 1983. 'The significance of an early date for pottery and sheep in Zimbabwe', *South African Archaeological Bulletin*, 38, 88–92.

Wallace, A. 1962. *The Malay archipelago*, New York: Dover, first published 1869.

Walters, I. 1985. 'The Toorbul Point Aboriginal fish trap', *Queensland Arch. Res.*, 2, 38–45.

Waltz, E. 1982. 'Resource characteristics and the evolution of information centers', *American Naturalist*, 119, 73–90.

Waselkov, G. 1987. 'Shellfish gathering and shell midden archaeology', in M. Schiffer (ed.), *Advances in archaeological method and theory, vol. 10*, Orlando, FL: Academic.

Washburn, S. and C. Lancaster 1968. 'The evolution of hunting', in R. Lee and I. DeVore (eds.), *Man the hunter*, Chicago: Aldine.

Waterschoot van der Gracht, W. van 1915. 'Eenige bijzonderheden omtrent de oorspronkelijke Orang Koeboe in de omgeving van het Doewabelas-Gebergte van Djambi', *Tijdschrift van het Koninklijk Nederlandsch Aardrijkskundig Genootschap*, 32, 219–25.

Watkins, M. (ed.) 1977. *The Dene nation: the colony within*, Toronto: University of Toronto Press.

Watson, J. 1977. 'Pigs, fodder and the Jones effect in post-ipomoean New Guinea', *Ethnology*, 16, 57–70.

Watters, R. 1960. 'Some forms of shifting cultivation in the southwest Pacific', *Journal of Tropical Geography*, 14, 35–50.

Weddle, R. 1985. *Spanish sea: the Gulf of Mexico in North American discovery*, College Station, TX: Texas A. & M. University Press.

Weiner, J. and B. Campbell 1964. 'The economic status of the Swanscombe skull', in, C. Ovey (ed.), *The Swanscombe skull: a survey of research on a Pleistocene site*, London: Royal Anthropological Institute.

Wenhold, L. (trans.) 1936. 'A 17th century letter of Gabriel Diaz Vara Calderon, Bishop of Cuba, describing the Indians and Indian missions of Florida', *Smithsonian Miscellaneous collections*, 95, 16.

Were, G. and D. Wilson 1972. *East Africa through a thousand years*, London: Evans Brothers.

White, J. and J.O'Connell 1982. *A prehistory of Australia, New Guinea and Sahul*, Sydney: Academic Press.

Widmer, R. 1986a. *Prehistoric estuarine adaptation at the Solana site, Charlotte County, Florida*, Tallahassee: Florida Division of Archives, History and Records Management.

—— 1986b. 'Sociopolitical implications of off-shore fishing in aboriginal southeast Florida', *The Florida Anthropologist*, 39, 244–52.

—— 1988. *The evolution of the Calusa, a non-agricultural chiefdom on the southwest Florida coast*, Tuscaloosa: University of Alabama Press.

Wiessner, P. 1977. 'Hxaro: a regional system of reciprocity for reducing risk among the !Kung San', PhD dissertation, University of Michigan.

—— 1982. 'Risk, reciprocity, and social influence on !Kung San economics', in E. Leacock and R. Lee (eds.), *Politics and history in band societies*, Cambridge: Cambridge University Press.

Williams, B.J. 1974. *A model of band society*, Washington, DC: Society for American Archaeology.

Williams, E. 1987. 'The rise of complex hunter-gatherers: the view from Australia', *Antiquity*, 61, 310–21.

Williams, N. 1982. 'A boundary is to cross: observations on Yolngu boundaries and permission', in N. Williams and E. Hunn (eds.), *Resource managers: North American and Australian hunter-gatherers*, Boulder, CO: Westview.

Williams, N. and E. Hunn (eds.) 1982. *Resource managers: North American and Australian hunter-gatherers*, Boulder, CO: Westview.

Wilmsen, E. 1973. 'Interaction, spacing behaviour and the organization of hunting bands', *Journal of Anthropological Research*, 29, 1–31.

Wilson, E.O. 1975. *Sociobiology: the new synthesis*, Cambridge, MA: Harvard University Press.

—— 1978. *On human nature*, Cambridge, MA: Harvard University Press.

Wilson, P.J. 1975. 'The promising primate', *Man*, 10, 5–20.

Wing, E. 1965. 'Animal bones associated with two Indian sites on Marco Island, Florida', *The Florida Anthropologist*, 18, 21–8.

Wing, E. and L. Loucks 1985. 'Granada site faunal analysis', in J. Griffin (ed.), *Excavations at the Granada site* (Archaeology and History of the Granada site, volume 1), Tallahassee: Florida Division of Archives.

Winter (H.R. Rookmaker) 1901. 'Ook onderdanen onzer Konigin (Een bezoek aan de tamme Koeboes)', *De Indische Gids*, 23, 208–48.

Winterhalder, B. 1987. 'Diet choice, risk, and food sharing in a stochastic environment', *Journal of Anthropological Archaeology*, 5, 369–92.

—— in press. 'The analysis of hunter-gatherer diet: stalking an optimal foraging model', in M. Harris and E. Ross (eds.), *Food preferences and aversions*, Philadelphia: Temple University Press.

Winterhalder, B. and E.A. Smith (eds.) 1981. *Hunter-gatherer foraging strategies: ethnographic and archaeological analyses*, Chicago: Chicago University Press.

Wissler, C. 1966. *Indians of the United States*, Garden City, NY: Doubleday, first published in 1940.

Wizara ya Habari na Utamaduni 1982. *Kumbukumbu za Warsha Juu ya Wahadzabe*. Dar es Salaam: Research Department, Ministry of Information and Culture, P.O. Box 4284.

Wobst, M. 1978. 'The archaeo-ethnology of hunter-gatherers, or, the tyranny of the ethnographic record in archaeology', *American Antiquity*, 43, 303–9.

Wolf, E. 1982. *Europe and the people without history*, Berkeley: University of California Press.

Wolters, O. 1967. *Early Indonesian commerce. A study of the origins of Srivijaya*, Ithaca, NY: Cornell University Press.

Wood, B. 1984. 'The origin of *Homo erectus*', *Cour. Forsch. Inst. Senckenberg*, 69, 99–111.

Woodburn, J. 1962. 'The future of the Tindiga', *Tanganyika Notes and Records*, 58–9, 268–74.

—— 1968a. 'An introduction to Hadza ecology', in R. Lee and I. DeVore (eds.), *Man the hunter*, Chicago: Aldine.

—— 1968b. 'Stability and flexibility in Hadza residential groupings', in R. Lee and I. DeVore (eds.), *Man the hunter*, Chicago: Aldine.

—— 1970. *Hunters and gatherers. The material culture of the nomadic Hadza*, London: The British Museum.

—— 1972. 'Ecology, nomadic movement and the composition of the local group among hunters and gatherers: an East African example and its implications', in P.J. Ucko, R. Tringham and G. Dimbleby (eds.), *Man, settlement and urbanism*, London: Duckworth.

—— 1978. 'Sex roles and the division of labour in hunting and gathering societies', paper presented at the First International Conference on Hunting and Gathering Societies, Paris.

—— 1979. 'Minimal politics: the political organization of the Hadza of North Tanzania', in P. Cohen and W. Shack (eds.), *Politics in leadership: a comparative perspective*, Oxford: Clarendon Press.

—— 1980. 'Hunters and gatherers today and reconstruction of the past', in E. Gellner (ed.), *Soviet and Western anthropology*, London: Duckworth.

—— 1982a. 'Egalitarian societies', *Man*, 17, 431–51.

—— 1982b. 'Social dimensions of death in four African hunting and gathering societies', in M. Bloch and J. Parry (eds.), *Death and the regeneration of life*, Cambridge: Cambridge University Press.

Wrangham, R. 1979. 'On the evolution of ape social systems', *Social Science Information*, 18, 335–68.

Wright, A. 1985. 'Marine resource use in Papua New Guinea: can traditional concepts and contemporary development be integrated?', in K. Ruddle and R. Johannes (eds.), *The traditional knowledge and management of coastal systems in Asia and the Pacific*, Jakarta Pusat: UNESCO.

Yates, R., J. Golson and M. Hall 1985. 'Trance performance: the rock art of Bootjieskloof and Sevilla', *South African Archaeological Bulletin*, 40, 70–80.

Yellen, J. and H. Harpending 1972. 'Hunter-gatherer population and archaeo-
    logical inference', *World Archaeology*, 4, 244–53.

Yen, D. 1974. 'Arboriculture in the subsistence of Santa Cruz, Solomon Islands',
    Economic Botany, 28, 247–84.

—— 1976. 'The ethnobotany of the Tasaday, III. Notes on the subsistence
    system', in D. Yen and J. Nance (eds.), *Further studies on the Tasaday*, Makati,
    Rizal, Philippines: Panamin Foundation.

—— 1985. 'Wild plants and domestication in Pacific Islands', in V. Bellwood
    (ed.), *Recent advances in Indo-Pacific prehistory*, Leiden: Brill.

Yesner, D. 1980. 'Maritime hunter-gatherers: ecology and prehistory', *Current
    Anthropology*, 21, 727–50.

Zubillaga, F. 1946. *Monumenta antiquae floridae (1566–1572)*, Rome: Monumenta
    Historica Societatis Iesu 69; Monumenta Missionum Societatis Iesu 3.

Zwanenberg, R. van 1976. 'Dorobo hunting and gathering: a way of life or a
    mode of production?', *African Economic History*, 2, 12–21.

Index

Names

Subjects

labour (*see also* wage labour) 32, 56, 58–9,
    153, 271, 274–5, 278, 285
land, *see* ownership, property relations,
    territoriality
land alienation 34, 44–5, 48–9, 60, 69–72
land claims 11
language (*see also* neighbouring
    societies) 38
  borrowing of 49
latitude 35, 191, 193–4, 197, 202–3
leadership (*see also* nobility) 46, 132, 151,
    191, 250, 255
  outsider appointment 93
  weakness of leadership institutions 7,
    24, 26, 66, 69, 254, 267
leisure 63, 66
levelling mechanisms 57, 62, 233, 264–7
lineage, *see* clan systems, descent groups
lineage mode of production 146–7
livestock, *see* pastoralism
local group organization (*see also*
    residence, settlement patterns) 27–8,
    78–81, 90, 246
Maasai 36, 41–2, 46, 54
Malays 108–10, 112
Malaysia 35, 107
malnutrition 39
Manjo 45
Manus 176
Mapungubwe 146
marine mammals 164–5
maritime adaptations (*see also*
    fishing) 191, 194, 199–200, 203–4
market economy, *see* production for
    exchange
marriage (*see also* conjugal relationship,
    matrimonial alliance) 82, 96, 114–15
  age relating to 100–1, 104
  ceremonial 104
  exchange marriage 82, 98
  payments 114–15
  preferences/rules 99–101, 106
  remarriage 101–4, 106
  secondary marriage 43
Marxism 5–6, 10–11, 252–3, 260–2
material culture (*see also* tools,
    weaponry) 142–3, 154, 158, 169–70,
    172, 175
  as symbols 138, 141–3, 146
materialism (*see also* accumulation) 259
matrilateral relations 82, 89
matrimonial alliance (*see also* affinal
    relations) 7–8, 15, 34, 130–2
Mauritania 36

Mbuti 17–18, 26, 28, 33, 35–7, 42–3, 45,
    47–8, 51, 55–9, 61, 64, 75–90
meat 16, 34, 41, 43, 51, 62
medicines 40, 51, 56
mediums of exchange 110
men (*see also* gender relations)
  contribution to foraging 118
  as hunters 5
metal (*see also* tools, weaponry) 46, 85–6,
    140, 144
military class 171, 174, 186
minority relations (*see also* colonialism,
    neighbouring societies) 65–72
mobility 33, 37, 64, 66, 88–9, 102, 105,
    111–12, 124–5, 128, 198, 202–3, 233,
    242, 251
mode of production 133–4, 139, 142, 147,
    149–50, 269, 272, 274
'modern' humans (*see also* hominids)
  biological differences among (including
    sexual dimorphism) 216–17, 219–20
  social relations among 219–20
moth hunting 156, 158
Mousterian industries 212
myth 41

Naiken 12, 17–30, 35
names 25
Namibia 35–6
Naskapi 265
nation-state 6, 65–72, 111–12, 138, 263
  resistance to 223
natural selection, *see* evolutionary ecology
Neanderthals 208, 210–11, 213
neighbouring societies (*see also*
    nation-state) 47, 65, 69, 107
  alienation of land/property by 34, 44–5,
    48–9, 60, 69–72
  avoidance of 7, 12, 33, 38, 41, 44, 48–9,
    51, 111–12
  ceremonial exchange/ritual relations
    with 58, 85
  commensality with 23, 45, 53
  common culture with 40–2, 91–2
  co-settlement with 21–5, 38, 69–72, 85,
    93, 97
  cultural accommodation to 29, 54–5,
    92, 98
  degree of contact with 36–7, 55
  economic exchange with (*see also*
    production for exchange) 19, 22, 24,
    26, 31, 33, 46, 50–1, 60–1, 77–8, 85–7,
    112, 177, 261
  enclavement by 5, 7–8, 12, 21, 26–7,

Notes on the Contributors

Barbara Bender Barbara Bender's published books are *Farming in prehistory: from hunter-gatherer to food producer* (John Baker) and *The archaeology of Normandy, Brittany and the Channel Islands* (Faber & Faber). She has also published papers in *World Archaeology*, *American Antiquity* and other leading journals and collections.

Nurit H. Bird-David Since completing her PhD at Cambridge University Nurit Bird-David has published several papers on the Naikens of south India in *Cambridge Anthropology* and in various other collections.

Roy Ellen Roy Ellen's books include *Nuaulu Settlement and Ecology* (Martinus Nijhoff) and *Environment, Subsistence and System* (Cambridge University Press). He has published both on his fieldwork in the Moluccas and on general problems in ecological anthropology and systems of classification.

Robert Foley Robert Foley has written *Another Unique Species: patterns in human evolutionary ecology* (Longman) and edited *Hominid Evolution and Community Ecology* (Academic Press). His papers have been published in *Man* and other leading journals and collections.

Peter M. Gardner Peter Gardner has published many papers in leading journals and collections on the Paliyans of south India. He has co-authored (with Jane Christian) a monograph on *The Individual in Northern Dene Thought and Communication* (National Museums of Canada).

Martin Hall In addition to his many papers on the archaeology of southern Africa Martin Hall has recently published, *The Changing Past: farmers, kings and traders in southern Africa, 200–1860* (James Curry).

Tim Ingold Tim Ingold's books include *Hunters, Pastoralists and Ranchers* and *Evolution and Social Life* (both Cambridge University Press) and *The Appropriation of Nature* (Manchester University Press). He is the editor of *What is an Animal?*, recently published by Unwin Hyman. He was Malinowski Memorial Lecturer in 1982, and will be the Curl Lecturer in 1989.

Richard B. Lee   Among a number of milestones in hunter-gatherer studies, Richard Lee co-edited *Man the Hunter* (Aldine) and *Kalahari Hunter-Gatherers* (Harvard University Press) with Irven DeVore, and *Politics and History in Band Societies* (Cambridge University Press) with Eleanor Leacock. His other main books are *The !Kung San* (Cambridge University Press) and *The Dobe !Kung* (Holt, Rinehart & Winston).

Harry Lourandos   Harry Lourandos has published extensively on Australian Aboriginal archaeology, in *World Archaeology* and other journals and collections.

William H. Marquardt   William Marquardt is the author of papers and reports on the prehistory and history of the Calusa of Florida. He has recently co-edited *Regional Dynamics: Burgundian landscapes in historical perspective* (Academic Press).

Brian Morris   Brian Morris's *Forest Traders: a socio-economic study of the Hill Pandaram of south India* was published in the London School of Economics monographs series, and Cambridge University Press recently brought out his *Anthropological Studies of Religion*. He has published numerous papers, in *Man* and other leading journals and collections.

D.K. Ndagala   Daniel Ndagala's many papers are based on his research into problems of development among the Hadza and other Tanzanian peoples.

Gísli Pálsson   Gísli Pálsson has carried out fieldwork in Iceland and Cape Verde Islands. He has published numerous papers on maritime adaptations, in the *American Ethnologist* and elsewhere, and is currently preparing a book on the anthropology of fishing.

Jon Pedersen   In addition to his research on Central African Pygmies, Jon Pedersen has published a monograph based on fieldwork in the Seychelles.

David Riches   David Riches's comparative study, *Northern Nomadic Hunter-Gatherers*, is published by Academic Press. He is editor of *The Anthropology of Violence* (Blackwell), and his papers on the Inuit Eskimo and on other topics have been published in *Man* and other journals and collections.

Øyvind Sandbukt Øyvind Sandbukt has carried out extensive field-work among the Kubu of Sumatra and other Indonesian peoples, and has published several papers.

Eric Alden Smith Eric Smith co-edited *Hunter-Gatherer Foraging Strategies* (University of Chicago Press) with Bruce Winterhalder, and has published widely on optimal foraging theory and Inuit socio-ecology, in *Current Anthropology* and other leading journals and collections.

Espen Wæhle Espen Wæhle's research and published papers are on the Mbuti Pygmies of central Zaire.

James Woodburn James Woodburn's extensive publications on the Hadza of Tanzania, and on the comparative study of hunting and gathering societies, include his Malinowski Memorial Lecture, 'Egalitarian societies' (*Man* 1982), and 'Hunters and Gatherers: the material culture of the nomadic Hadza' (British Museum).